Foreword

Recreation vehicle (RV) service and maintenance is what I've termed, one of the many "RV Facts of Life." We have all had exposure to these necessities at one time or another. In the vast realm of RV options such as floorplans, color schemes, chassis types, interior furnishings and other assorted appointments, there can be no denying the eventuality of maintenance and repairs. This is especially evident today in this new era of higher fuel costs. We tend to keep and utilize our RVs longer and perhaps take shorter trips, albeit more often. Each new model that is designed becomes more challenging, from a technical standpoint. Virtually all RV manufacturers agree that in order to receive the most out of our recreational investment, adequate maintenance must be performed regularly.

As an example, a typical motorhome with a generator and two roof top air conditioners requires a minimum of 16 to 18 retail hours of mandated maintenance that should be performed each and every year. That's correct, about 18 hours worth! With an average hourly retail labor rate of say $100 per hour, that's close to $1800 per year just trying to avoid a major problem. And this does not include any troubleshooting and repair costs. Individual product makers usually recommend periodic maintenance on their products at least once each season as a precautionary step in order to obtain the optimum use of that product. It is noted, however, that all RVs will not automatically self-destruct if the maintenance is not performed, but one will certainly gain additional service life from these units if they are maintained and checked regularly. Some areas requiring seasonal attention that you may choose to do yourself include:

- Checking and sealing the roof, windows, storage compartments and doors.
- Cleaning and servicing the LP appliances.
- Changing the oil in the generator and chassis engine, and checking all fluid levels.
- Cleaning the filters in the air conditioning system.
- Cleaning and treating the holding tanks.
- Flushing and sanitizing the fresh water system.
- Performing battery maintenance.
- Washing and protecting the roof and exterior portions of the RV.

If you've ever attended one of my RV Doctor Seminars, you've probably heard me speak of two types of RV service: crisis repair and preventive maintenance. The aforementioned 16 to 18 hours would be classified as time devoted to preventive maintenance—the steps performed before there is an actual need for repair. Think preventive medicine—something you do now to prevent something worse from taking place later. A little insurance, if you will. Crisis repairs, on the other hand, are not optional. The problem is already at hand and needs immediate attention!

A few examples of crisis repairs would be an abnormally worn tire or blowout, a blocked cooling unit in the refrigerator, a blown engine, an electrical short, a leaky termination valve, or a burned out roof top air conditioner compressor. The important thing to remember is: Preventive maintenance will minimize the frequency and the intensity of the crisis-type repairs. Routine tire inspection and careful study of inflation pressures, checking and cleaning the refrigerator components and checking the LP gas pressure, making sure all electrical connections are clean, dry and tight, sound waste management practices, regular oil changes and periodic cleaning of the air conditioner filters can prevent the above crisis repairs from happening. Realize it is a choice each owner must face— preventive maintenance or crisis repair. There is no third option.

Do It Yourself?

Alas, this discussion is not about the types of RV service but about whether or not you should attempt some of the maintenance items yourself. As owners, can we control our own RV repair destiny? Is that possible or feasible, or should we simply leave all types of service up to the professionals? I, for one, have always been in favor of owner involvement in the technical arena concerning RVs. I have devoted a large chunk of my time over the last three decades educating the RV enthusiast specifically in some of these areas. Additionally, Woodall Publications has, for many years, provided the very best in consumer repair manuals for the RVer.

However, unless properly prepared and equipped, I do not believe most owners should attempt to make repairs or perform service on any RV, product or component. This is especially true during any factory warranty period of a new RV. All repairs should be performed by authorized persons during this time. In extreme cases, warranties may even be voided or manufacturer liability lessened if unauthorized repairs are performed. (In the context of the RV Owner's Handbook, it is assumed your vehicle is not under a new warranty situation.) Professional RV service technicians (those certified by RVIA/RVDA) stand at the ready to perform any or all maintenance requirements.

But here is a vital concern. Most maintenance items, though mandated by the product manufacturer and/or coach maker, are not covered by new or extended warranties. Some items are simply destined to be the sole responsibility of the RV owner. Rarely are maintenance items ever covered under any warranty, yet they too scream for attention. In such cases, and in instances of out-of-warranty RVs, many owners actually enjoy delving into the various technical aspects of their coaches. The key is knowing when to actively participate and when to simply

make an appointment at a professional facility.

So who among us should consider performing maintenance tasks on our rigs? Here are some demographics. An informal survey taken at one of my RV Doctor Seminars revealed that the RV owner who actively performs routine service typically:

- Is mechanically inclined or has past experiences in labor trades
- Has an impressive assortment of hand tools and test devices
- Has a keen interest in the technology of RVs
- Travels and camps often in remote areas, far from any RV service center, and has no choice but to learn to become an RV technician
- Has as much or more of a technical aptitude than the average professional
- Is now, has been, or will soon become a full-time RVer or what I call a "serious RVer"

If you recognize yourself in the list above or are wondering whether or not you should attempt a maintenance task, here are a few considerations for you to ponder. Keep in mind, however, this list is not all-inclusive and all items may not apply evenly across the board. These are just a few thoughts to explore.

Review your own mechanical/technical aptitude. The important thing here is to realize your limitations. As you ponder a task, ask yourself, "Can I physically perform the steps necessary to do this?" Many items in, under, on and around an RV require a certain physical dexterity. Physical limitations may prohibit some of us from performing certain maintenance items. Sort of like when the brain says "yes" but the body says "no way!" Also, realize and admit it when the subject at hand is truly over your head. There is no need to be a hero. You definitely do not want to risk converting a simple maintenance task into a costly crisis repair! It may cost substantially more to undo an error than to simply make an appointment with a service center if the subject is beyond your scope. You are not expected to know absolutely everything about your RV, but you should be able to honestly recognize the point at which you do not understand something. This maxim is true even with professional service technicians as well. Foolish is the RVer who trusts his or her coach to a service shop that proclaims its technicians know all there is to know about RVs.

Have a willingness to learn. If you truly want to be able to perform routine maintenance and repair functions, be willing to do a little homework. Servicing liquid propane-related appliances and components, for instance, virtually mandates a basic understanding of the sequence of operation of that appliance. Each appliance is different, but your advantage is that you only need to learn those that pertain to your rig. And it is not that difficult to learn. Oh, it requires reading and studying the literature that came with your coach, perusing this manual time and again, and perhaps researching a product maker's website, but for the most part, it can be enjoyable. Especially when you consider that any knowledge gained, nurtured and then applied will ultimately save real dollars in repair costs. You wouldn't consider jumping in the coach and taking off down a road you've never been on before without a road map or at least a general knowledge of where it leads. So it is with most technical matters on your RV. You are holding that road map in your hands right now. You might even invest in the RV Doctor's Do-It-Yourself RV Care series of DVDs as an addendum to this manual.

Be properly equipped. Be aware that many maintenance tasks require a well-balanced selection of tools, and some require specialty tools that you may not have in your tool kit. If you commit to performing this procedure yourself, purchasing that needed specialty tool would be a wise investment. Read Chapter 3, Recommended Tools, for the detailed list of tools you should always carry with you as you travel.

Pay close attention also as to when replacement parts are required for a certain task. As an example, when performing a cleaning procedure on the RV furnace, it is recommended that all gaskets be replaced. Be sure to have the correct gaskets on hand prior to beginning the cleaning. You will want to avoid being partially through a task and having to stop, thereby running the risk of not finding the parts immediately. One goal should be to keep your down time to a mini-

mum. Always keep a small assortment of frequently replaced parts on hand. Gather all the necessary tools and parts before beginning your maintenance task.

Consider the time factor. Always plan your approach to any maintenance task appropriately. Realize that all maintenance requires time. Be sure to allot yourself plenty of time to complete the task you are undertaking. Do not rush. You are more likely to omit a step or make a mistake if you are under pressure to complete a task under the duress of a time constraint. Remember, the next time you perform that same task, that time element will be reduced. Familiarity and repetition will breed speed.

How to "Do It Yourself"

Okay, so you feel like you just may qualify as a true RV do-it-yourselfer, so now what? Well, it's time for some strategic planning and implementation. The following suggestions will get you started.

Prepare a proper and clean work area. Having a clean work area for the task is vital in order to avoid confusion and also help keep the RV clean if you must traipse in and out of it several times. When servicing the appliances, for example, it is best to perform the maintenance tasks with the appliances left in their installed positions. An exception would be the RV furnace. In some instances concerning the furnace, better results are attained if the furnace is removed and the work performed on a bench. Also, in some cases, the absorption refrigerator may need to be partially removed to gain access to certain components for cleaning. Therefore, be sure to cover and protect carpeting or finished floors. When changing the oil in the generator or on the chassis engine, have an area cleared so complete access is easily accomplished. If you will be needing electricity, have your extension cord uncoiled and strategically placed prior to starting. Likewise, if using a drill motor, have the correct size drill bit, or screwdriver tip at hand. Proper preparation will make any maintenance task easier.

Have all replacement parts ready to go. Have all replacement parts prepared and laid out for easy access. If your maintenance task involves threaded fittings, a handy tip is to pre-apply the correct thread sealant before actually starting the work. It's much neater and easier when your hands are relatively clean. Lay the fittings aside and cover them with a shop towel or cloth until needed. If the new parts need pre-assembly, do it now, before you get engrossed in the task. If some parts in a repair kit will not be needed, separate and discard them prior to beginning. This will simplify your task and avoid any confusion you may encounter when you realize you have a few parts remaining.

Obtain the necessary support materials.
As mentioned earlier, have the *RV Owner's Handbook* and all wiring diagrams, service notes, installation instructions or any other type of related resource open and within easy reach before starting the job. If you feel you may need additional help or support information, postpone the maintenance until all the necessary information is in your hand.

Backup vehicle. It's always advisable to have access to another available vehicle "just in case." Whether it is a neighbor's second vehicle or perhaps it's the small car you usually tow behind your rig. In any event, always plan to have a mode of transportation available just in case you forgot something or for emergencies.

Establish a relationship with a local service facility. This step is vital, if geographically possible. Even though you may want to perform the maintenance and repairs yourself, always get to know a local dealer or service center in your area. Aside from being there to order parts for you, the service technicians can also be a good source of information. They should work in concert with you and not feel threatened that you elect to perform some of your own maintenance tasks. Obviously, you will need to rely on them for those technical areas you decide not to pursue, and there will be plenty left for them to do. All major repairs and many items that will require costly specialty equipment is best left to the professional shop as we have discussed. Of course, you will want to check in your local area to find the appropriate service department that best fits your needs. All service facilities are not created equal. As mentioned

earlier, seek out service shops staffed by RVDA/RVIA Certified Technicians. That certification means they have gone through the necessary training, so look for that patch on the sleeve!

By carefully evaluating your technical expertise, learning and gathering a resource library for those items on your coach, acquiring the proper tools and parts and most importantly, having the right attitude, you may be just the candidate to experience the fun of maintaining your investment for your leisure enjoyment. In any case, it is hoped that major repair costs are avoided and total contentment is realized from the experiences of working on your own RV. Keep this handbook close by and refer to it often. You will not be disappointed. And remember, RVing is more than a hobby, it's a lifestyle!

Gary Bunzer
Author

Introduction

If you've spent any time in this century on any major roadway, you've no doubt viewed all types of motorhomes, travel trailers, pickup campers, tent trailers and possibly some vehicle types you've not seen before flying down the highway in search of adventure, escape or simply relaxation. You may have noticed how families, intent on doing things together, seem to be doing it in a recreational vehicle. RVing is enjoying a popularity of astounding proportion even with higher gas prices. And you have now wandered into that realm. You've been bitten by the RVing bug and can now be identified as an RVer—one who travels in a recreation vehicle. But it is truly much more than a simple labeling of one method of transportation/recreation.

If you are a seasoned RVer, you already know of the joys associated with RV travel. If you happen to be fairly new to the RVing lifestyle, then you will soon become aware of its multitude of benefits. RVing knows no state or provincial boundaries and has contributed more to family togetherness, environmental awareness and the simple appreciation of natural beauty than any other hobby or pastime. Though all forms of travel have some intrinsic value, none can compare to traveling in an RV. Simply talk for a few minutes with an active RVer and you will soon be exposed to the many advantages of traveling in your own "home on wheels." Spend a weekend in one at a regional campground and you will be hooked for life.

Whether you favor a luxurious, ultramodern RV resort as a destination, with every amenity imaginable including wireless Internet access, cable TV and satellite radio, or you prefer to be totally isolated, far from any ribbon of concrete whatsoever, beside a quiet stream, simply dry-camping (camping with no hookups), the RVing lifestyle offers an option for you. You may prefer to travel and camp while wrapped in the lap of luxury on your own custom bus, complete with washer, dryer, high-definition satellite television and every digital whatchamacallit available. Or perhaps you would be happier simply camped along a secluded beach in a used pop-up tent camper passed on to you by a distant relative. The fact is, literally hundreds of options are available for those who adopt the RVing lifestyle.

It has often been mentioned that an RV is considered a recreational investment. True enough, and like other types of investments, its security and viability must rely upon a valid understanding of its intricacies and nuances. As an RV owner, having a technical understanding of the various systems associated with your rig is a must. Being able to maintain, troubleshoot and repair those systems and components independently is a bonus—a bonus that will indeed reap additional rewards.

You are currently holding Woodall's RV Owner's Handbook, the complete RV repair and information manual that can literally save you real dollars. This popular owner's manual will guide you through all the technical aspects of RVs with a system-by-system analysis of each major RV component.

Many of the maintenance procedures detailed in this manual will, in some cases, virtually eliminate the need for future repairs. Written generically, this handbook is applicable to any RV. Continuing in the finest Woodall's tradition, this edition of the RV Owner's Handbook will become the book for those used or obsolete

RVs and a must have complement for all
new RVs.

In addition, videotapes and DVDs offering
supplemental information on various topics
mentioned throughout the book can be ordered
by contacting the author at www.rvdoctor.com.

I encourage you to truly embrace this RVing
lifestyle and go for it! May you have many
happy and safe RVing miles in your future.
Enjoy!

Table of Contents

RV Types and Categories

Overview

To the novice, the vast diversity of RV styles may seem complicated and frustrating as well as confusing. To simplify your familiarization with the various types of recreation vehicles (RVs), I will follow the descriptions of each category as set forth by the Recreation Vehicle Industry Association (RVIA)[1], the industry's self-regulating agency. These descriptions and categories have been placed at this point in the book to help you better understand the complete spectrum of RVs early in your study. When appropriate, additional clarifying text will supplement the official definitions.

What is an RV? The most basic definition, according to RVIA, is that it is a vehicle that combines transportation and temporary living quarters for travel, recreation and camping. RVs can be either motorized (motorhomes), towed behind a vehicle (travel trailers, fifth-wheel trailers, folding camping trailers) or carried in a pickup truck (truck camper). RVs do not include mobile homes, park trailers or off-road vehicles. Also excluded from the definition of an RV are conversion vehicles. Conversion vehicles are typically manufactured by an automaker and then "converted" for recreational use. Such examples would include van conversions, pickup truck conversions, sport-utility conversions and custom vans.

A new RV may cost as little as $4,000 for a folding camping trailer to well over $1 million for a high-end motorhome. Some custom coaches can approach $2 million dollars or more if decorating tastes run rampant. The most recent numbers published indicate there were about 353,400 new units shipped to dealers in 2007. There are currently over 30 million RV enthusiasts, including renters in the United States alone driving around or hauling about 8.2 million new and used RVs! Nearly one out of every twelve households now owns at least one RV. Indeed, somewhere there is an RV for you!

Types of Recreation Vehicles

Fig. 1-1; Folding Camping Trailer

Folding Camping Trailer

This is a recreational camping unit designed for temporary living quarters, which is mounted on wheels and constructed with collapsible sidewalls intended to fold compactly so the entire trailer can be towed by a motorized vehicle. New units are typically priced between $4,000 and $13,000.

Also called folding tent trailers or pop-ups, these vehicles have come a long way in the past several years with respect to ease of setup and interior comfort. Most are equipped with hard laminated walls instead of the older, traditional canvas or fiberglass panel. It is not unusual to find complete kitchen and bathroom amenities, along with other self-contained features normally associated with larger RVs, even slide-outs! Most tent trailers are relatively lightweight and can be towed by many cars and all trucks. Many can be made fully livable within 10 to 20 minutes, often by only one person—full setup is easy.

As the name implies, these RVs fold into a low-profile package, which, because of the smaller frontal area, helps improve towing vehicle gas mileage. Other benefits of the low silhouette include improved handling in high winds and the ability to store the unit in a standard-size garage.

1– Recreation Vehicle Industry Association. The national trade association representing 500 manufacturers and component suppliers producing approximately 98% of all RVs and conversion vehicles manufactured in the United States.

Fig. 1-2; Truck Camper

Truck Camper

The truck camper is a recreational camping unit designed to be loaded onto, or affixed to, the bed or chassis of a pickup truck. It is designed to provide temporary living quarters for recreational, camping or travel use. Truck campers cost anywhere from $4,000 to $26,000 for a fancy one.

Often referred to as a "slide-in camper," this type of RV is one of the most popular. Since a truck camper can be loaded on and off of a pickup truck with relative ease, this type of RV is favored by those who enjoy the RV lifestyle on weekends, yet still want a truck for work or transportation during the week. Additionally, families that already own a suitable pickup truck have an advantage over those who do not since they can become involved in the RV lifestyle with a smaller initial investment.

Modern truck campers are extremely comfortable and sometimes luxurious thanks to continuous upgrading by the manufacturers in order to meet the demands of the buying public. Often these campers come equipped with a full bathroom and shower, roof-mounted air conditioning, a complete kitchen including a microwave oven, sewage holding tanks, slideouts, awnings and sometimes an on-board generator.

When considering buying a truck camper, one must also give thought to the cost of a properly equipped truck prior to the purchase. If you have a pickup already, you still need to evaluate its capability to safely carry the camper, your gear and you. We'll delve into this a little deeper later.

Travel Trailer (General)

A travel trailer is designed to be towed by a motorized vehicle (auto, van or truck) whose size and weight does not require a special highway moving permit. It is designed to provide temporary living quarters for recreation, camping or travel use, and does not require permanent on-site hookup. A travel trailer can be one of the following types:

Fig. 1-3; Conventional Travel Trailer

Conventional Travel Trailer

A conventional travel trailer typically ranges from 12 to about 35 feet in length and is towed by means of a bumper or frame-mounted hitch attached to a towing vehicle. New units cost as low as $8,000 and as much as $65,000.

In addition to all the normal conveniences expected of any modern RV, travel trailers have an advantage: You can disconnect them and leave them at the campsite while the tow vehicle is used for running errands, taking side trips or sightseeing.

In any towing situation, including towing travel trailers, specific requirements exist to ensure that tow vehicles are properly equipped to safely handle the additional weight and stress. Whether discussing autos or trucks, the key words are properly equipped. Nearly every pick-up can tow or haul something, but a common mistake is to assume that just because you have a pickup or large vehicle, you can tow any travel trailer. That is not necessarily the case. Properly equipping a tow vehicle requires specialized evaluation and professional advice. Many vehicles can be damaged when attempting to tow a trailer. Later chapters will address these specific concerns.

Though not a mandate, it is ideal when the tow vehicle and the travel trailer purchase are considered at the same time. An analogy would be buying a suit, shirt and tie combination at the same time as opposed to purchasing the suit one day, the shirt another day and finally trying to find the right tie to match both. It can be done, but it takes proper planning and a little homework.

Conventional travel trailers are constructed with an A-frame hitch design. Typically, the hitch is also where the liquid propane (LP) cylinders are mounted. The lifting jack is also attached to the frame to facilitate raising and lowering the tongue of the trailer. Obviously, travel trailers are often hitched and unhitched regularly and occasionally backed into RV spaces when pull-through spots are unavailable. These tasks should not be approached with fear or reservation. Trailer handling can be fun and is quite easy once you get the hang of it. As with any learned task, practice makes perfect! And professional driving courses are available in many locales.

Technical chassis maintenance is minimal with all types of trailers, because they lack the steering system and mechanical drive-line of a motorhome. There is no engine, transmission, differential, etc. to maintain on a travel trailer. However, these high maintenance items do exist on the tow vehicle so you still have to plan for periodic checkups. The less expensive chassis of the travel trailer contributes to the lower purchase price of this type of RV, plus, insurance and license fees, in most cases, are significantly lower.

Fig. 1-4; 5th Wheel Travel Trailer

Fifth-Wheel Travel Trailer

This unit can be equipped the same as the conventional travel trailer but is constructed with a raised forward section that allows a bi-level floorplan. This style of RV is designed to be towed by a pickup truck equipped with a device known as a fifth-wheel hitch. Fifth-wheel travel trailers run the gamut as far as accoutrements and price. Some can be purchased for as little as $13,000, while others top out at or near $100,000.

Despite being sold in smaller numbers than conventional travel trailers, fifth-wheel models are popular because of their unique split-level floorplans and their propensity for slide-out rooms. 2004 saw the introduction of a five slide-out fifth-wheel trailer produced by Carriage, Inc.

Another popular benefit is the reduced length of the overall truck-and-trailer combination when towing. The connecting point, the hitch, is in the bed of the pickup as opposed to at the rear of the truck. This, in effect, shortens the overall length of the towing configuration.

The term fifth-wheel is derived from the round plate found on the hitch mechanism used to connect the trailer to the tow vehicle. Though smaller in design, it is similar to those found on commercial tractor trailer rigs. Also, since the majority of fifth-wheel travel trailers are built with tandem axles, this type of travel trailer actually becomes the "fifth wheel" when the combination is in motion. Some longer, more elaborate units come equipped with triple axles. Technically, these units would be considered a "seventh-wheel" travel trailer if we follow the same logic. However, the predominant features that define this unit are the split-level design and the method of attachment to the tow vehicle.

In use, the fifth-wheel travel trailer's attachment point or "gooseneck" overlaps the tow vehicle by six feet or more. As mentioned previously, this reduces the overall combined length of the two vehicles, which results in improved traction and easier, safer handling.

Many RV veterans consider fifth-wheel hitching to be easier than a conventional hookup because the driver can visually guide the connection without the assistance of the co-pilot or spotter or specialized equipment. One perceived negative feature associated with fifth-wheel trailers is the manner in which they "cheat" on turns. Because the pivot point is located several feet forward than that of a conventional hitch, the trailer tires do not follow directly in the path of the tow vehicle. Instead they significantly cut to the inside of the tow vehicle's track. This condition can lead to curb jumping, especially on right-hand turns. Additionally, increased tire wear may result. Handling at highway speeds is not a problem. Many enthusiasts contend fifth-wheel towing is superior to that of conventional travel trailers. As before a little practice makes fifth-wheel handling second nature.

Motorhome (General)

This is a recreational camping and travel vehicle on, or is an integral part of, a self-propelled motor vehicle chassis. It provides at least four of the following permanently installed living systems (most contain all of them):

- Cooking appliances
- Refrigeration
- Heating and air conditioning
- Self-contained waste plumbing
- Portable water system including water tank, faucet and sink
- Separate 120-volt electrical system
- LP gas supply
- Sleeping accommodations

Fig. 1-5; ; Class A Motorhome

Conventional Motorhome (Type A)

In this type of motorhome the living unit has been entirely constructed on a bare, specially designed motor vehicle chassis. Conventional motorhomes sell anywhere between $58,000 and $400,000 or more when equipped with custom options.

This motorhome is also known as a Class A, or full-size motorhome. It remains very popular among RVers. As noted in the official definition, the living quarters are built on a heavy-duty motorized chassis designed specifically as an RV. Mainstream automotive chassis manufacturers, as well as many specialized makers, produce a selection of chassis and frames for the RV industry. Many utilize gasoline engines; some come equipped with diesel engines. Some are "pushers" with the power plant in the rear of the coach, while some have the engine up front.

Advanced chassis technology today has increased the buyer's options when considering Class A motorhomes. Bus-style basement models have become the most popular Class A motorhome design. Constructed with a subfloor, the main living area is completely on one level and the lower "basement" is dedicated for storage and installation of the various system components. The proliferation of double, triple and even quadruple slide-out rooms have increased living space immensely as well as floorplan options. Many Class A interiors come equipped with trash compactors, garbage disposals, washer and dryer combinations, ice makers, dishwashers, satellite antenna, global positioning systems (GPS), sophisticated media and entertainment centers and more. There are plenty of options from which to choose. Understandably, these units usually occupy the higher end of the price spectrum.

Many consider motorhomes in this category to be the most comfortable RVs because of the typically larger interior that allows occupants to move about freely. Another big plus comes when it is time to move to the next destination. All that is necessary is to unhook from the campground utilities, start the engine and drive away.

Maneuvering and backing is generally considered to be easier in a motorhome than with a towable because a motorhome responds to steering adjustments similar to an automobile. Excepting the larger physical dimensions and extended stopping distance requirements, learning to drive a Class A motorhome comes extremely easy to most drivers.

The majority of Class A's range in length from 28 to 45 feet. Once they are parked and set up, most owners hesitate to disconnect the coach for a quick sightseeing trip or to run an errand. This has led to the common practice of towing a small vehicle behind the motorhome for those quick yet necessary side trips. The subject of "dinghy towing" will also be addressed later in this book.

Van Camper (Type B)
This is a panel-type truck to which the RV manufacturer adds two of the following conveniences:

- Sleeping accommodation
- Kitchen facility
- Toilet facility
- 120-volt hookup
- Fresh water storage
- City water hookup
- Extended top for more head room

Fig. 1-6; Class B Van Camper

Van campers are popular for weekend trips and short outings. The average price is about $57,500 with some models running upwards of $74,000. The primary advantage of these units is that they retain the versatility of a large family car or van as well as provide the amenities mentioned above for recreational camping. Van campers are capable of the same duty a minivan might offer during the week, but can also be used for enjoying the RV lifestyle. Another advantage of this type of RV is its relative ease of driving in traffic.

Fig. 1-7; Class C Motorhome

Chopped Van (Mini-Motorhome or Type C)
This unit is built on an automotive van frame with an attached, stock cab section. The RV manufacturer completes the body section containing the living area and attaches it to the cab section.

Sometimes called mini-motorhomes or Class C motorhomes, this variety is also very popular with RVers. Ease of handling is one of the strong selling points to this type of coach. Less intimidating than the larger Class A's, Class C units are built on a standard van chassis. The driver's section is identical to that of a production model van. The chassis is often lengthened or "stretched" to accommodate the RV portion. Lengths typically run from 18 to 29 feet, with the average length being about 24 or 25 feet. A new Class C will set you back between $48,000 and $140,000 for the top of the line with multiple slideouts.

Most C's sport some form of enclosed cabover structure above the driver's compartment. Quite often this space is used for sleeping, though on occasion, it is dedicated solely to storage or for mounting a multimedia entertainment center. Many models come equipped with bunk beds or a convertible dinette that pulls double duty as a sleeping area when not in use as a table. The amenities found in Class C's rival those found in the larger Class A motorhomes. Many are downright luxurious.

Primarily because they are shorter, other major advantages accredited to Class C's include the aforementioned ease of handling and livability. Many floorplan options are available to satisfy just about every kind of RVer—even those who prefer the very popular slide-out room. The most often heard disadvantage is the necessity on most units to crawl up and into the cabover section to go to bed. Also, there exists a false sense of size since the unit is built on a standard van chassis and looks just like a van from the driver's view. Gas stations, ATMs and fast food outlets take on a whole new perspective when traveling in a Class C. It takes a little concentration to realize you are much taller, longer and wider than a typical van.

Sport Utility Vehicle

A relatively new type of recreation vehicle has been developed over the past few years – the Sport Utility Vehicle (SURV). The SURV can either be towable (conventional or fifth-wheel travel trailer) or motorized (motorhome). The single most defining

Fig. 1-8; Sport Utility Vehicle

characteristic of all SURVs is the huge, cavernous, built-in "garage" section that houses off-road vehicles, motorcycles or other sports-related gear. It has proven to be very popular for individuals and families with other outdoor hobbies. Rather than the RVing lifestyle being the focus, the SURV provides the means to an alternative recreation end.

As well as the bountiful garage section, the remainder of the SURV houses the typical trimmings found in any recreation vehicle, including multiple slideout rooms. SURVs can cost anywhere between $21,000 and $58,000 or more while sleeping up to eight people.

Expandable Travel Trailer

Fig. 1-9; Expandable, Hybrid Travel Trailer

Another relatively new type of RV is the Hybrid. Also called an Expandable Travel Trailer, the hybrid is built with hard sidewalls, but comes equipped with expandable sleeping accommodations similar to that of the Folding Camping Trailer. It is basically a cross between the conventional travel trailer and the folding tent trailer.

Its design permits a lighter towing requirement and a roomy interior since the bedroom sections expand outward for sleeping. They are also popular with young families just starting out in the RV lifestyle. Their entry level price is around $9,000 and some units can run upwards to about $18,000 new.

RV Ownership by Category

The following numbers, courtesy of RVIA, display the categories of RVs and their total deliveries for 2007[2]. The totals are not the actual retail sales of RVs, but the number of new units delivered to the RV dealers. Many more additional RVs were sold that are not reflected in the total. Pre-owned coaches and units sold between private parties translate into many, many more families now engaged in one of America's favorite pastimes.

Category	Number of RVs
Travel Trailers (Conventional & Hybrid)	180,200
Fifth-Wheel Trailers	81,500
Truck Campers	7,500
Folding Camping Trailers	28,800
Class A Motorhomes	32,900
Class B Motorhomes	3,100
Class C Motorhomes	19,400
Sport Utility Vehicle (All)	21,600

All in all, about 55,400 motorhomes and 353,400 towable RVs were delivered to dealers in 2007. One interesting side note: the largest gain in ownership over the past four years involved those under the age of 35! If you are still not an active RVer, now is the time for you to become a participant!

2 – Totals for 2008 were not yet available at the time of this printing. To learn more about RVIA and the demographics of RVing in general, be sure to visit www.rvia.org. Many resources are available for your education and enjoyment from RVIA.

Photos of RVs provided by RVIA.

Basic Interior and Exterior Care

Overview

Though most RVers are quite cognizant of the aesthetics in and about their RV, oftentimes silent processes are at work seeking to put a damper on enjoying this lifestyle. Consider the following scenarios.

Scenario 1: Undetected rainwater seeps through an inadvertent tear in the rubber roofing membrane caused by a low-hanging tree branch allowing water to permeate the substrate decking below. It continues to seek its own level, as leaking water will, propelled by gravity, until it soaks the ceiling and is absorbed into the wall panels. What could be the result if left unabated? Probably a loosened rubber membrane, stained ceilings, damaged side walls and possible loss of structural integrity in the RV. The translation—big bucks repair bill!

Scenario 2: A finely made window dressing is removed from its position above the dinette and tossed into the washing machine after a slight spill created a small stain. It comes out clean, but now it only hangs half-way down the window. These accidental damages rarely happen in conventional homes, but in RVs, they can be commonplace if owners are unaware or inattentive.

The best prevention for these scenarios is to be thoroughly acquainted with the various interior materials and their proper care, and to actively and assertively inspect every square inch of the exterior of your RV periodically. Although it is virtually impossible to list all of the different materials and fabrics used by manufacturers today, this chapter is designed as a general guide to basic interior and exterior care.

Interior RV Care

Interior RV walls, floors, ceilings, countertops, cabinets, appliances, fixtures and furnishings are all made from a variety of materials. A short list would include: linoleum, tile, vinyl, stainless steel, chrome, glass, plastic, Formica, Avonite, Corian, SSV, Surrel, painted or stained wood and various laminates and synthetics. "Soft goods" such as upholstery, drapes, curtains, dividers, leather chairs, couches and bed

coverings may demand particular cleaning techniques common only to that product. Though many come close, unfortunately, there is no across-the-board aftermarket product that will effectively clean and treat every type material or composite found on a typical RV. There are some stain removers that are quite versatile such as InstaGone Multi-Purpose Stain Remover (www.instagoneproducts.com). But before trying any cleaner or preservative, check out the following general tips.

Fig. 2-1; Multipurpose stain remover

General Tips for Interior RV Care

- Read all labels and literature available for that particular component. Look for cleaning or washing precautions. Keep this information handy. File it with your other RV literature. If you have Internet access, try a search for that type of material or composite.

- Use cleaning products that you've had success with in other applications, such as at home. Try them out in areas that will have minimum impact in case they do not prove effective. For instance, try out a carpet cleaner under a bed or in a cabinet before attempting to clean the entire carpet. Or give that new spray-on wall brightener a test inside a wardrobe closet first.

- Look for a manufacturer name or brand on tags or labels. If cleaning or care instructions are not readily available on the product, contact the maker directly. Most will be more than willing to provide written instructions for the upkeep of their products.

- Remember, what may work well with one certain fabric or component may not work so well with another. Realize that all finishes, fabrics and materials differ. Ask other RVers what works for them. Be willing to share and pass on care secrets you uncover.

In this and in other chapters to follow, I will mention specific products I have tested over the years. However, only you can determine if a product works on your RV. My strongest advice is to test many of the leading brands and stick with the ones that work best for you. Those products mentioned by name by no means eliminate similar products from other suppliers. It only means I have personally tested these and they pass my standard for effectiveness. All of the products displayed or mentioned are readily available at any well-stocked RV supply store or online.

Walls

Many interior walls are plywood or wood-grained hardboard panels with a thin veneer or wood finish on the exposed side. Wall coverings such as wallpaper or a vinyl layer are common as well as various types of fabric or carpeting. Scratches are the most common problem with keeping your walls in good condition. Wood scratches can be stained to match, or a colored putty stick can be used to fill in the deeper grooves.

For stained-wood paneling, apply a home-type furniture polish or treatment at least once a year or more often if necessary. If the wood is painted, wash it down periodically with a mild detergent and water.

Bathroom walls may be made of enamel or vinyl-coated hardboard. Some may be covered with a durable wallpaper. These should be wiped dry after use to prevent mildew. It is possible to strip and apply new wallpaper to this type of panel if you choose to do so.

Floors

RV floors are usually either covered with linoleum, tile, carpeting or wood finishes. Dirt not cleaned from linoleum can become ground in and ruin the finish. Use a name brand

Fig. 2-2; Vacuum the RV regularly

household cleaner and treat the floor to lengthen the time between cleanings.

Frequent vacuuming before dirt has a chance to migrate further is the best method of keeping your carpeted floors looking their best. Central vacuum systems make this a simple task. If you don't have a central vacuum, there are a number of reliable 12-volt auto vacuums that are inexpensive and take up little storage space. Of course, the carpet can simply be vacuumed at home before and after a trip, but an on-board vacuum is a good idea if carpeting is in high-traffic areas. Also, once a year clean the carpet with a multipurpose cleaner such as Quick 10 (www.instagoneproducts.com).

Ceilings

Ceilings are usually wood fiber panels, fabric over plywood or acoustical paneling. There is little need to clean this area often since it is seldom touched, but fingerprints and other soiling can be removed with a damp cloth. In some instances, the ceiling may be covered with a fabric. Consult your owner's manual or contact the manufacturer if you are unsure what type of ceiling is in your RV.

Fig. 2-3; Carpet and upholstery stain remover

Fabrics

The list of different types of fabrics used in RVs is growing every day. Most upholstery fabrics used in RVs are not washable, and many are not dry-cleanable. Soiling is controlled by spot cleaning performed with one of the many upholstery cleaners marketed for home furniture. The aforementioned Quick 10 works well on a variety of carpet and upholstery materials. Use a commercial vinyl cleaner for vinyl upholstery. Curtains and drapes are usually dry-cleanable, but check the tag to be sure.

Windows

The usual home window cleaners will work fine on glass. On plastics though, avoid abrasives. A small amount of ammonia and a mild detergent with water, however, is safe for both.

Kitchen and Galley Area

Appliance manufacturers routinely provide literature on care and maintenance. (If you have long since lost the literature or if you are the second owner of an RV, contact each appliance manufacturer individually or the author for specific instructions.)

Refrigerator

Cleaning of the interior of the RV refrigerator is similar to its home counterpart with one difference: RV refrigerators are more vulnerable to high heat. This means that attempting to speed up a defrost cycle with the aid of a hair dryer will result in damage that could necessitate a new refrigerator.

Make sure the controls are turned off and clean the interior with two tablespoons of baking soda dissolved in a quart of warm water. Rinse and dry. Wash the crisper pan and other removable parts with warm, sudsy water. Wipe the exterior with a cloth dampened in a mild detergent water, rinse and wipe dry with a soft cloth.

In older refrigerators, metal racks that seem nonremovable because of plastic stops can often be jockeyed out by using a screwdriver to lift up the clip. Be careful that you do not damage the inner liner.

Oven

Most RV oven interiors have a porcelain enamel finish. This is easily identifiable by its smooth shiny surface. Use a mild detergent with water to remove soil before it has a chance to cook on. Wipe burned-on spots with ammonia to soften them and then clean with detergent and water. Remove plated oven racks and use a soap-filled scouring pad to clean. Rinse and dry. A solution of mild detergent and water is also good for cleaning microwave oven interiors.

A few RV ovens have a "continuous cleaning" finish on the oven's interior. It is recognized by its rough, dull surface. These ovens have a porous ceramic coating that allows soil to disperse over a large surface area and the coating, with the help of baking temperatures, acts as a catalyst to evaporate the residue.

Cooktop

Clean the stove or cooktop often to prevent spills from becoming baked on and to keep the burner ports unclogged. Before cleaning, be sure the stove is cool and all burners are turned off. The outside metal should be cleaned with a sudsy cloth using mild liquid dishwashing detergent and water. Rinse with a cloth dampened with clean water and dry the surface with a soft cloth.

Make sure the burner ports are open by poking each with a wooden toothpick. Do not use a metal object or probe since it could damage and distort the port. Avoid using steel wool, abrasive cleaners and cleaners containing ammonia, acids or commercial oven cleaners on any exterior portions of the range.

The underside of the cooktop in many RV ranges is prone to rust. Keep this area dry and treat it monthly with chrome cleaner to prevent corrosion.

Range Hood and Vent
Clean the stainless steel portions as you would the sink (see Metallic Surfaces below). At least twice a year, clean the filter element with warm water and detergent, or simply replace it.

Stainless Steel Sinks
Ordinary detergent is good for this type of receptacle. Rinse and wipe dry with a clean cloth. If there is a problem with fingerprints, apply a cleaner that leaves a thin film of wax, then fingerprints wipe up easily. Stainless steel polishing solutions are also available at any well-stocked, home improvement store.

Counters and Tabletops
These are usually covered with a durable plastic, acrylic laminate, granite or Formica or a derivative. Use a plastics or glass cleaner. A word of caution about those seemingly indestructible surfaces: hot objects may injure the laminate, causing it to pull away from the bonded wood base.

Metallic Surfaces
Metal decorative trims are easily cleaned with a glass or appliance cleaner. There are many chrome and metal cleaners, so choose a name brand product for best results.

Bathroom Fixtures
The lavatory, shower stall, tub and toilet are typically formed of acrylonitrile-butadiene-styrene (ABS) plastic or a plastic derivative. These fixtures can be damaged by the use of abrasive cleaners. Use only products recommended by the manufacturer or a mild, low-acid household detergent. Named brand plastic cleaners are acceptable.

There are a few products available that can have a tremendous cleaning effect on numerous surfaces and interior components. One such product is Protect All Shine Plus (www.protectall.com). It's used quite sparingly and seems to work on many of the above mentioned surfaces found in and around the typical RV.

Fig. 2-4; Wash the RV prior to inspecting

Exterior RV Care
The most basic exterior task is simply to keep the rig clean. The cleaner the RV, the easier it is to recognize problem areas that may be masked or hidden behind a layer of dirt or caked-on mud. Realize, also, that the exterior includes the undercarriage of your RV. Do not overlook the importance of keeping the entire coach as clean as feasibly possible.

Invest in quality cleaning equipment. Avoid pressure washers since they will open loose seams and force water past seals and gaskets. The cleaning brush must be suitable for the type of exterior materials on your rig. Mr. LongArm produces some fine brush attachments for its flow-through extension poles that are perfect for reaching the uppermost areas of the exterior of the RV. The brushes, too, are flow-through and are available in four different bristle types. Use incorrect brushes and you may scratch or

Fig. 2-5; Use brushes appropriate for RV surfaces

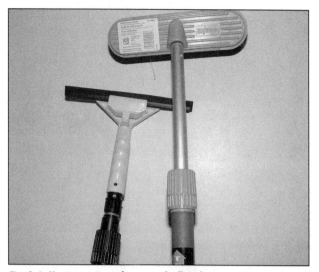

Fig. 2-6; Use extension poles to reach all surfaces

damage the finish on the siding or worse yet tear the rubber membrane on the roof.

The wise RVer knows the types of construction materials used on his or her rig. Only by knowing for sure the types of composites used on your RV will you be able to effectively clean, treat and maintain them. As previously mentioned, not all cleaning products will work on all types of finishes. In some cases, in fact, irreversible damage can occur if the wrong product is used.

Before beginning exterior RV care, ask yourself: Is the roof material constructed of a rubber membrane, aluminum, polyvinyl chloride (PVC), thermoplastic polyolefin (TPO), fiberglass reinforced plastic (FRP) or fiberglass? Are the exterior sidewalls made of aluminum, fiberglass, ABS plastic or FRP? In order to develop an exterior maintenance plan, it is vital to know the answers to these questions. That having been said, let's look at these portions of the RV.

Roof Area
Careful inspection and cleaning go hand in hand with your RV roof area. Check the roof in the spring and in the fall or just before storing the rig and once again when de-winterizing. If, during your travels, you drive through an area with low hanging branches, check it again as a precaution. Also stop and inspect the roof area if you experience high winds, sandstorms, hail or extreme rainstorms. The last thing you'll want

is undetected damage to be exposed to the elements over a prolonged excursion.

Two very popular roofing materials used today are ethylene propylene diene monomer (EPDM) rubber membrane and TPO. A later chapter covers the complete spectrum of EPDM and TPO care and repair, which differs significantly from RV roofs covered with aluminum, plastic or fiberglass.

For roofing types other than EPDM or TPO, check the seams, vents and roof edges carefully. In some climates, it may be necessary to reseal the roof on an annual basis. There are a number of reliable RV roof sealants available for both aluminum and FRP surfaces. A common sealant is an asphalt-based mix with aluminum powder that reflects sunlight. More reflective white plastic sealants are also available. In hot, dry areas, a reflective aluminum surface is the better choice. In hot regions where the insulation factor is valued, choose the white sealant.

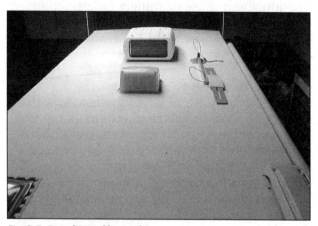

Fig. 2-7; Typical RV rubber roof

Stay with the well-known brands such as Elixir Industries' Plas-T-Cote brand, Geocel or the products from Eternabond (www.eternabond.com) or Liquid Roof (www.proguardcoatings.com). Be sure the sealing products you choose are indeed applicable for the material on the roof. This is especially crucial when choosing products such as putty tape, butyl caulk, lap sealants and roof coatings. Note that not all products will adhere to all roofing materials.

One of the better and easier-to-use products for roof repair is Eternabond. Eternabond is effective on any roofing material and is quite easy to install. Available in different widths, this versatile repair product will adhere to virtually all roofing materials. Eternabond Roof Seal comes in a three- or four-inch roll. Double Stick is a one- or two-inch sealing tape with a release liner on both sides. Double Stick is applied between two surfaces or can be molded to fill gaps around plumbing drain lines or other entry points under the RV. Web Seal is a two-inch wide sealing tape laminated to a cloth webbing which can be painted to match the color of the front or real caps.

Sidewalls

RVs with aluminum siding thankfully are not prey to the body rust that plagues automobiles, but the baked enamel finish can become streaked from roof and window sealant residue or from oxidizing EPDM rubber membrane. Exposed aluminum also oxidizes and can develop a mottled, pitted appearance. Care includes a thorough cleaning to remove grime, bugs and stains and a wax or protective coating to prolong the scrubbed state and restore luster to faded colors.

Though there are many excellent brand name washes, cleaners, waxes and black streak removers available today, studies have indicated that three main factors determine how effective any given product will be:

- The type of surface material on the RV
- The degree of oxidation or corrosion at that time
- The surrounding climate

I've recommended certain products before only to receive a plethora of emails indicating how wrong I actually was. In other words, how could I have possibly recommended X as a good product? So it takes a bit of experimenting for your RV, with its specific level of oxidation, in your location, to see which product works the best. As I mentioned earlier, try a few of the brand names and stick with those that best satisfy you. Once you determine those certain products, stick with them. Do not keep switching products. It either works or it doesn't.

Protect All (www.protectall.com) has been a provider of exterior care products for years and comes highly recommended. Its product line includes Protect All—All Surface Care with carnauba wax, a rubber roof cleaner and treatment, and Quick & Easy Wash, and a fine Fiberglass Oxidation Remover & Color Restorer among others. Camco also makes a fine line of exterior care products as do a host of other suppliers.

Fig. 2-8; Exterior oxidation remover

Fiberglass and an FRP called Filon are the predominant materials used for RV siding today. Other forms of PVC and ABS plastics are also common. Fiberglass is quite prone to oxidation, and when ignored for long periods, substantial oxidation can permanently damage the finish beyond a simple cleaning and polishing job. However, with severe oxidation, the only true remedy is a new paint job. Most damaging to fiberglass are the ultraviolet (UV) rays from the sun. For long storage periods, especially in hot, dry climates, a total coach cover will prolong the luster of gelcoat and fiberglass components. Let's delve deeper.

To give fiberglass that smooth, shiny surface you've seen on the front and rear caps of new units, clear or colored gel resin material is applied to the outer surface during one of the first phases of fiberglass lay-up during production. What you are really eyeing is the hardened gel resin on the top surface of the fiberglass underlayment, called gelcoat.

Today, the term gelcoat and fiberglass are used interchangeably. The gelcoat resin is available in many colors, but its surface will become dull or begin to fade due to the constant bombardment of UV rays and exposure to ozone. Realize that this constant attack begins on day one when the coach rolls off the production line. Left unprotected, the fading turns to a "chalking." We've all seen this chalking effect of some fiberglass front and rear caps. Eventually, the gelcoat surface becomes prone to oxidation by its exposure to sunlight, heat and moisture. Fading is the first phase of severe oxidation. Chalking is actually a form of advanced oxidation and an indication that damage to the surface has taken place.

To combat this degradation effect, astute RVers learn that it's crucial to protect the surface of the gelcoat with a layer of wax or polish. Fiberglass polish is similar to wax, but some polishes do contain an abrasive of sorts; read the label carefully. Compound polishes almost always contain heavier abrasives. Always use a cleaner, then polish, then finally a protective layer of wax to keep your fiberglass surfaces looking new. How often? Every three to six months; every six months if the rig is kept out of direct sunlight and the elements. It does take effort, but the results are quite rewarding.

Caulk/Sealants

Examine the sealant around windows, storage compartments and vents for aging. The oil-based caulk used to seal joints and windows will repel other caulking compounds so scrape it off before applying fresh caulk of a different type.

Fig. 2-9; Caulking the window

Black Streaks

What causes those unsightly black streaks on RV sides? We've all seen it; we've all probably expe-

rienced it! There is a cause and a solution, however. Here's a simplified overview:

It starts with an accumulation of dust and dirt on the flat RV roof. All flat surfaces will collect dirt and dust. Add moisture and neglect (or forgetfulness) to the mix and you've got the impetus of those unsightly black streaks on the sides of the RV.

Fig. 2-10; Exterior cleaner

As you camp overnight, moisture in the form of dew settles over the dust and dirt on your rig. As it collects, it gains mass and flows over the edges of the roof and down the sides. The next day, the moisture evaporates, but the residue of dirt remains stuck to the sides, microscopic though it may be. The next evening, dust settles again, moisture covers the dirt that evening and again, the following morning, the moisture evaporates and yet another layer of dirt residue attaches itself to the preceding layer. And so on…

It is a gradual progression, until you notice the dirt as visible stains down the sides of the coach. The longer it goes unattended, the harder it is to remove. The cure for removal? Thorough and regular washings and the application of a wax to protect the surface. Occasionally, remnants of the black streaks will remain even after a thorough washing. The black streaks, left unattended, will actually oxidize onto the surface. This requires additional treatment aimed specifically at the layer of oxidation. The typical black streak remover product is simply the last resort to removing the streaking.

Keep in mind any oxidation remover will remove the protective wax, so it is paramount that a rewaxing takes place in those areas where the black streak remover was applied. Oftentimes RVers feebly try the black streak remover and then do not re-apply a protective wax. This simply makes it easier for the dirt molecules to grab hold the next day after the dust settles and the moisture evaporates.

When you use a black streak remover or cleaner, do not spray it directly onto the sides of the RV. Spray the remover into a soft, clean cloth and use plenty of pressure on the RV to directly attack the streaks. A second clean cloth will brighten the surface to a clean luster.

To minimize future black streaks, wash the coach about every three months. Apply a protective wax every six months. A slick, antistatic finish resists that initial attack of dirt residue. Also, invest in a total coach cover for those periods of nonuse.

Undercarriage

I call the undercarriage the forgotten exterior surface. Be sure to regularly inspect under your rig, looking specifically for road debris you may have picked up along the roadway. Look for loose or damaged wiring, plumbing components, etc. Also check closely around any holes drilled through the bottom of the exposed undercarriage where plumbing pipes or wires may have been routed. Be sure of the integrity of the sealants around these areas. Any small opening or crack in the sealant is an invitation for mice and other critters to come onboard.

Look regularly for damage caused by road trash. Check all tire and chassis-related components. Basically look for anything "out of the norm." The time to address these issues is now!

Proper care concerning the interior and exterior will add many miles to your RVing enjoyment level. Plus you will reap some payback when it's time to trade or sell that RV. A nicer looking vehicle will always be worth more than an abused, neglected coach.

Chapter 3

Recommended Tools and Safety

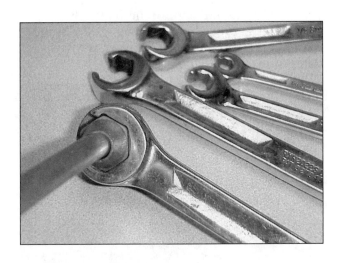

Overview

Since the dawn of time, humans have designed, used and improved upon a myriad of tools. Today thousands of different kinds and types of tools exist—the book you are now holding is, in itself, a type of tool. Throughout the ages it has been decidedly proven that people simply cannot survive without tools. Likewise, today's RV advocate cannot get by without tools. Here's another RV Fact of Life: You cannot have too many tools!

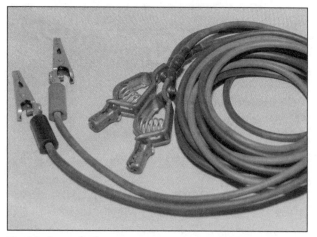

Fig. 3-1; Jumper leads

Whether you are a tinkerer, a backyard mechanic or a seasoned technician, if you own an RV there will be times when an adjustment may be necessary—a screw may need tightening or a component may need replacing; particularly if you find yourself traveling in the boondocks, miles from the nearest service facility. Full-timers especially should be "well tooled" while living aboard an RV. Additionally, there is a justified feeling of satisfaction knowing that you repaired that water pump or found that short. Having the right tool makes that task a lot easier.

Throughout this handbook, many detailed instructions will be provided that may or may not depict all of the possible scenarios you'll encounter. It is important when you follow these instructions and procedures that you satisfy yourself thoroughly that neither personal nor product safety will be compromised or jeopardized. If you are in doubt about a procedure and do not feel comfortable, do not continue.

Simply call your local service facility and make an appointment with them. Safety is the number one priority, always!

Tools and Their Uses

It is assumed that you posses a basic knowledge of hand tools and at least some mechanical aptitude. If you are not sure about making a somewhat simple repair, try anyway. Experience is the best teacher. Even the most non-technical RVers are usually successful at tracking down squeaks, rattles and leaks. You need not feel helpless if you own an RV and are not mechanically inclined. The procedures here will give you the road map to follow. Just remember never to compromise the safety factor.

Fig. 3-2; Mini tubing cutter

The balance of this chapter will display lists of tools that are recommended for general and specific tasks associated with an RV. Three categories of tools follow:

- Basic tool kit
- Advanced tool kit
- RV specialty tool kit

Basic Tool Kit
The basic tool kit is comprised of those tools that should be found in your RV even if you do not plan to get heavily involved in troubleshooting and repair. These are the common hand tools that will simply come in handy in many scenarios.

- Socket set (3/8-inch drive): Typically you will only use a few different size sockets. It is advisable to have an assortment of extensions of different lengths and a universal joint. You will also need a spark plug-sized socket for the spark plugs in the generator, if so equipped.

- Combination wrench set (1/4–1-inch): This is the type that has a box-end wrench on one end and an open-end wrench on the other.

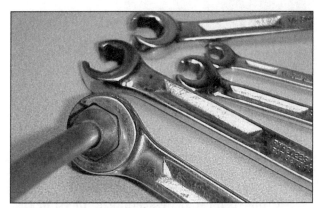

Fig. 3-3; Flare nut wrenches

- Crescent wrenches (6-inch, 12-inch): These adjustable wrenches are handy for many chores.

- Pliers assortment: Needle-nose, 8-inch groove joint (water pump), standard slip joint pliers.

- Locking pliers: One small and one large.

- Tire gauge: Be sure the pounds per square inch (psi) range is applicable for your tires.

- 12-volt test light: Will quickly become one of your very best friends on the road.

- Flashlight

- Hacksaw

- Ball Peen hammer

- Screwdrivers: Flat blade, Philips, clutch-head (figure eight-shaped), Robertson (square-head) and Torx (star-shaped). Different sizes of vary-ing lengths, including flat blade and Phillips "stubby" drivers, thin pocket screwdriver and one magnetic multitip screwdriver. You can never have too many screwdrivers.

- Nut drivers: Most hex-head screws used on RVs

require a 1/4-inch socket. Some, however, may be 5/16-inch.

- AC polarity tester: Some even come with a built in voltmeter as well.

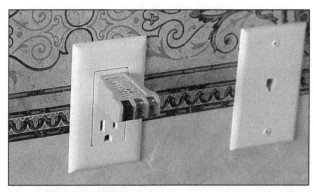

Fig. 3-4; AC polarity tester

- Wire brush

- Eye goggles

- Rubber gloves

- Pry bar/nail puller

- Battery terminal post cleaner

- Owner's manuals/user's guides: That's right. All service literature should be considered a very reliable tool. Try to assemble data sheets, parts listings and service information for all of the LP appliances and any other major component or device found on the RV.

Advanced Tool Kit

The advanced tool kit adds a few more tools to the basic kit. The inclusion of these tools will enable you to perform some troubleshooting and minor repairs on most major systems on the RV. In addition to the basic kit:

- Caulking gun

- Diagonal wire cutters

- Spark plug gap tool

- Portable battery charger (6 amps minimum): To be used as a small battery charger and as a

12-volt source of power when troubleshooting or "bench testing."

- Battery tools:
  - Terminal puller
  - Terminal spreader
  - Terminal pliers
  - Terminal post cleaning tool
  - Battery strap

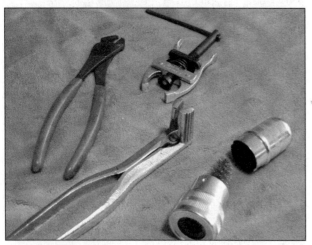

Fig. 3-5; Miscellaneous Battery Tools

- Volt-ohm meter (VOM): Preferably digital. It need not be the most expensive model, yet it should be somewhat rugged in design and accurate to within +/– 5% of full scale.

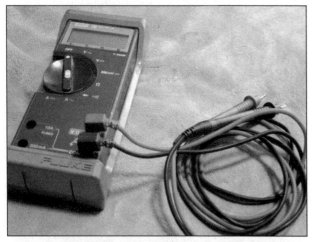

Fig. 3-6; Digital Volt, Ohm meter (VOM)

- Cordless, reversible drill: Invaluable if you need to remove more than a couple screws, drill a bunch of holes or install accessories.

A 3/8-inch chuck is recommended in order to accommodate a twist drill of that size. A fast charging, heavy duty drill is well worth the extra dollars.

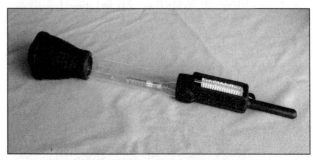

Fig. 3-7; Temperature compensated Battery Hydrometer

- Battery hydrometer (temperature compensated): An absolute must when troubleshooting battery systems.

- Crimpers for solderless terminals: Invest in a good quality pair. The cheaper, inexpensive combination stripper/crimper/cutter is not fully reliable for solderless terminals. A good crimper will deeply penetrate the terminal resulting in a lasting connection that will not pull loose.

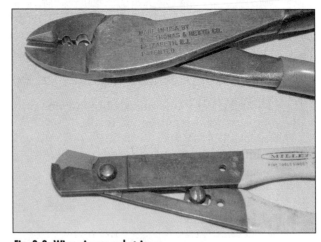

Fig. 3-8; Wire crimper and stripper

- Crescent wrenches (4-inch, 8-inch): These two sizes are complementary to the 6-inch and the 10-inch in the basic set. When working with LP fittings, always use a backup wrench to tighten and loosen fittings. The small 4-inch size will come in handy when working on appliances.

RV Specialty Tool Kit

The RV specialty tool kit includes those items that are specific to the world of RVs. The addition of these tools, coupled with the knowledge in this handbook, will enable you to attack almost every troubleshooting task and maintenance procedure encountered. However, the specialty kit does not include large pieces of equipment normally found only in service shops. With one possible exception, each of the tools listed in all of the sets can be purchased for below $300. In addition to the advanced set:

- Manometer (preferably water-column type): Available in spring-gauge type or the more cumbersome, yet preferable water column type. Why the water-column type? It's 100% accurate every single time. This device will allow you to set the liquid propane (LP) regulator and test the entire coach for LP leaks.

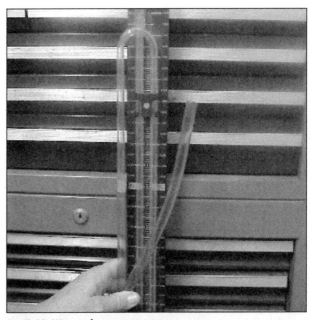

Fig. 3-10; Water-column type manometer

Fig. 3-9; Gauge-type manometer

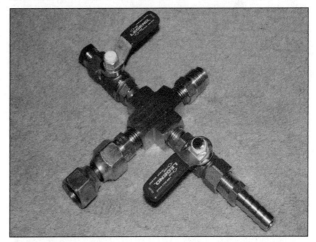

Fig. 3-11; LP test device

- LP Test Device: Used in conjunction with the manometer to set the LP pressure and test the system.

- Mercury oven thermometer

- Refrigerator thermometers: Two are needed: one for the freezer compartment and one for the main food section.

- Brake adjusting tool: For travel trailer/fifth-wheel electric brakes.

- Inductive-type ammeter: This device can be slipped over a brake magnet wire to measure the current draw of each magnet without

Fig. 3-12; DC inductive ammeter

having to cut the wire or otherwise tap into the circuit. A must for testing travel trailer brake magnets the easy way.

• Circuit breaker test leads: For checking electrical shorts. Easily made by attaching alligator test leads to each post of a standard 12-volt, 20-amp circuit breaker. It is placed in a circuit while troubleshooting a fuse that keeps blowing.

• Alligator test leads (attached to a 470-ohm resistor): For testing the light emitting diode (LED) circuits of monitor panels and tank probes.

• Inspection mirror: Allows inspection of components in those hard-to-see places.

• Refrigerator flue brush: A soft bristle brush the same diameter as the flue. For cleaning out the flue once or twice a year.

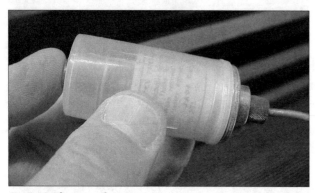

Fig. 3-13; Thermocouple tester

• Thermocouple tester: Available through your RV service facility or at heating, ventilation and air conditioning (HVAC) supply houses. This device can bench test any thermocouple while it is out of the appliance. (This tester is not needed if all the appliances are direct-spark ignited.)

• Frequency meter: Used to measure the output frequency of the generator or the frequency of the incoming shore power. Knowing the frequency is most crucial when running the on-board generator. A generator with the frequency out of calibration can damage sensitive equipment. This test device monitors

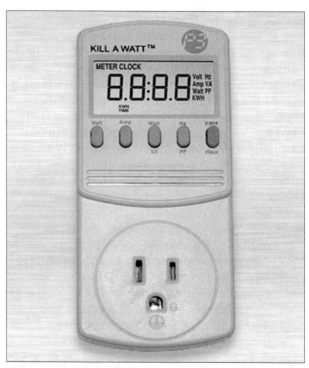

Fig. 3-14; Kill-A-Watt Test Device

not only the frequency but also the voltage and current use. A good device to have onboard.

Tool Safety

Now that you know the different sets of tools needed, it is imperative that you understand the issue of safety when it comes to tools. The number one rule is to use the right tool for the right job. Never pry with a long screwdriver, never hammer with an end wrench, etc. Tool safety is directly proportional to your safety and the safety of your RV components. For example, when working around lead/acid batteries, always wear eye protection and rubber gloves. Inexpensive goggles can save your eyesight while working with battery electrolyte.

Quality of Tools

It is nice to have that shiny new Cadillac, but that 40-year-old Volkswagen bug can still get you down the road. Use common sense when purchasing tools. If a cheaper tool will perform the same as a similar top-dollar tool, fine. If a cheaper tool appears fallible or prone to breaking, thereby compromising the safety factor, buy the more expensive version. Obviously, the quality-made tools will last longer, yet may cost you more initially.

Look for a good warranty. Any tool that has free replacement value or an extended warranty is much better than one that is limited. Let your budget be your guide. You can always upgrade later. If a certain tool or brand of tool will make your task easier, faster or safer, then it could be considered a justified purchase. Take care of your tools. Do not allow them to rust, corrode or become lost.

When purchasing tools to carry with you as you travel, it is important to keep in mind space limitations. The tools listed in this chapter are simply suggestions. You may choose to add some tools of your own or delete some tools from these lists. Choose tools that you know are applicable to you and your RV. If you perform your own engine tune-ups for instance, there are additional automotive tools that you probably need as well. Tools should be purchased for a specific purpose, and it is doubtful you could ever have too many.

12-Volt DC Electrical Systems

Overview

By far one of the most confusing yet least under-stood entities within the RV realm is electricity. The electrical systems found in RVs today have become far-reaching and technically advanced. Unlike years past when one could, for instance, simply bypass certain functions and manually light the refrigerator, today it is virtually impossible to operate most appliances without a healthy 12-volt battery system. Electricity is vital to an RV, especially when it comes to dry camping and being totally "self-contained." It is certainly one of the commodities RVers must learn to conserve.

This chapter will present a brief overview of the different systems found in the typical RV as well as more detailed looks into the 12-volt direct current systems. The following chapter will delve into the 120-volt alternating current components and devices.

Types of Electrical Systems

As mentioned in the overview, there are two basic types of electrical systems found in an RV: alternating current (AC) and direct current (DC). The AC system is considered the high voltage system while the DC circuits are considered low voltage. Both systems should be treated with respect. It is not the voltage in a system that is harmful; it is the current that can be lethal.

Shared Attributes of AC and DC Systems

Before we look at each system separately, there are a few shared attributes that apply to both. In the RV, the AC system and DC system have these items in common:

- Conductors (AC uses solid wires, DC uses stranded wires)
- Protective devices (fuses and circuit breakers)
- Resistive units (components and items that use the electricity)
- Means of making and breaking a circuit (switches or relays)

Combined and appropriately situated, these four items form an electrical circuit. The AC and DC circuits must be kept separate. High and low voltages are not compatible.

Helpful Electrical Definitions

Though not intended to be a complete tome on electricity, in order to better understand the electrical happenings in your RV, here are some definitions to help bring things into perspective.

- Voltage: The force that causes free electrons to move on a conductor as an electric current. It can also be called electromotive force (EMF), or the difference in potential. In the world today, there are six basic methods of producing voltage. Interestingly, five out of the six are viable to RVs in one form or another. The methods of producing voltage are:

    Friction: An example would be static electricity.

    Pressure: The principle found in piezo ignitors on some pilot model appliances.

    Heat: Also called thermoelectricity, exemplified in thermocouples used in flame failure safety systems for RV appliances.

    Light: Photoelectricity is used with today's solar panels.

    Chemical action: The common flooded, lead acid RV storage battery.

    Magnetism: Used in auxiliary RV generators and automotive alternators.

- Current: The amount of electron flow in any given circuit. It is a quantity of energy commonly called a "draw" or "drain". For instance, one might hear, "How much of a current draw does that fan motor use?" Or, "The battery has a 650-milliamp drain on it."

- Resistance: A form of friction to the current that impedes the flow of electrons. All resistive loads, those items that use the electricity, have a set value of resistance that is measured in units of measurement called Ohms.

• Power: The amount of electrical work used by any of the resistive loads, or the time rate of doing electrical work. Within the RV realm, this term is used quite liberally and mostly in error, for example, "There is not enough power in the battery to start the engine." This statement actually refers to current. Power in an electrical circuit is measured in watts. Watts, as a unit of measurement, equals the voltage of a circuit multiplied by the current of that same circuit.

Understanding Electrical Relationships

As inches are to feet and feet to yards, so also are volts to voltage, amps to current and ohms to resistance. The following chart may be helpful to separate and understand the differences between the physical property, unit of measurement and form of the electrical terms discussed so far.

The symbol in parentheses that follows each unit of measurement is simply a universal, single-letter designator used to represent each of the electrical forms, an abbreviation, if you will.

Ohm's Law
Ohm's Law is defined as the way to express the relationship between voltage, current and resistance in any given circuit. They are mathematically relative to one another in the same unique way in each type of circuit. If any two of the three values are known in a circuit, the third can be determined by applying Ohm's Law.

Ohm's Law can be expressed in three ways. In text format, Ohm's Law states that the current equals the voltage divided by the resistance. Also, the voltage equals the current multiplied by the resistance. Or, the resistance equals the voltage divided by the current. The following diagram further illustrates the law. By simply covering the value that is unknown (but that you wish to determine) with your finger on the above diagram, the remaining properties will be presented in mathematical formation.

For instance, you want to find the current in a

Fig. 4-1; Ohm's Law

certain circuit. Using the chart, cover the I (current) with your finger. What remains is the E over the R. As you would with a fraction, divide the known value of the resistance into the known voltage. The result will be the previously unknown current value.

The magnitude of the electrical current, or amperage, depends on the resistance of the circuit and the voltage applied to the circuit. Ohm's Law indicates how much current flows. The resistance, however, does not depend on either current or voltage. The characteristic and physical properties of the conductors and the load itself determine the resistance. Resistance cannot be changed by simply changing the current or the voltage. Ohm's Law determines how much resistance is contained in any given circuit.

Similarly, the voltage in a circuit does not depend on either current or resistance. The voltage in the circuit is determined entirely by the health and condition of the battery in that circuit, or how much is being delivered by the generator or shoreline power source. Ohm's Law will, however, indicate how much voltage is required for a given current through a given resistive unit.

It is evident that all three of these properties relate to each other in a unique way and that each pertain to simple electricity within the circuits found in any RV.

Power Law (Watts Law)
Power, as mentioned earlier, is a property usually associated with alternating current circuits and components. A derivative of Ohm's Law, the Power Law, also called Watts Law, is easy to calculate as long as you know any two of the three properties. Fig. 4-2 shows the diagram for the Power Law.

Power, or the amount of watts within the RV arena, is exemplified when determining, for instance, the size of a generator that is needed for a particular application. On-board power plants are rated in watts or a variation of watts called kilowatts (watts divided by 1000). As an example, after calculating each alternating current load in an RV (most appliances and components list the amperage or current rating on the nameplate or in the owner's manual), it is determined that a generator is needed that can produce 50 amps. Since power equals the current times the voltage, it can now be determined that 50 amps multiplied by the standard 120 volts necessitates a generator that can produce at least 6,000 watts, or 6.0 kilowatts.

Fig. 4-2; Watt's Law

Understanding the unique relationship among the above-mentioned electrical properties will greatly enhance your ability to troubleshoot electrical systems with minimal effort and downtime. But before we can successfully troubleshoot, let's explore the major systems involved.

RV Battery Systems

The DC systems associated with the RVs are sometimes referred to as simply the battery systems. Every RV contains at least two distinct battery systems. One is the automotive system that typically starts the engine (in the motorhome or tow vehicle) and powers the dash, horn, all running lights and electric brakes (on the travel trailer), among other things. The other is the house, or RV system, sometimes referred to as the auxiliary battery system. This system provides the current for everything in the house portion of the RV: the water pump, furnace blower, exhaust vents, low voltage lighting and a myriad of different

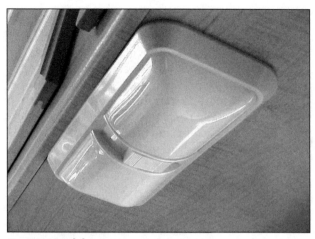

Fig. 4-3; 12-volt lamp

12-volt products available today. Current for the 12-volt DC systems is produced by:

- Battery banks
- Power converter
- Automotive alternator
- Solar panels

Though we will take an in-depth look at each of the above, the battery is always at the center of the 12-volt DC system. Everything in a 12-volt system revolves around this chemical wonder, so a well-rooted understanding of batteries should be the goal of the conscientious RVer. And even trumping this understanding is the importance of battery safety!

Battery Safety

All wet cell RV batteries contain sulfuric acid as a component of the liquid electrolyte. Additionally, rapid charging of a battery results in the production of hydrogen gas a by-product. Couple that with the hazards of charging and discharging and it should be obvious that safety measures must be taken seriously whenever working on or near batteries. Here are some safety guidelines for working on RV batteries.

- Always wear safety goggles. Be sure they are splash proof.
- Wear protective clothing such as rubber gloves that extend well up the forearms.
- Avoid any contact between the electrolyte and the skin, eyes or clothing.
- If electrolyte contacts the eyes, flush

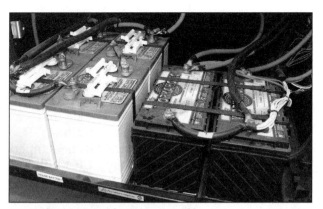

Fig. 4-4; Carry as many batteries as possible

Fig. 4-5; Spiral cell deep cycle battery

immediately with fresh water for a minimum of 15 minutes.

• If electrolyte is ingested, drink large quantities of milk or water, followed by milk of magnesia, vegetable oil or a beaten egg. Call a physician immediately.

• Keep sparks and open flames away from the battery.

• Provide for proper ventilation while working on the battery.

• Use a plastic funnel or battery filler container when adding water to the electrolyte.

• Do not allow metallic tools to fall across the battery terminals at any time.

• Never disconnect a live circuit at the battery terminals. Arcing could ignite hydrogen vapors near each cell.

• Always disconnect the negative cable first at the battery and attach it last when the job is finished.

• Always reinstall the cell caps prior to charging or rapid discharging.

• Use proper battery tools such as terminal puller, terminal spreader, terminal/post cleaning tool, battery carrying strap and battery terminal pliers.

• Protect the RV. Do not allow battery electrolyte to splash on any exterior surface.

Considering the components of even the simplest of circuits, it has been determined that the single-most confusing entity that lies within the very heart of virtually all RVs is the 12-volt battery. Not only do we have to contend with just one battery, it is not uncommon to see a minimum of three, and sometimes four or more

of these current-storing wonders aboard an RV. Check out the accompanying photo: six batteries (four 6-volt batteries and two 12-volt batteries). And what is more, there are different types of batteries we must understand.

The lead acid battery utilized today is defined as a power source, or an electrical power accumulator—an energy bank, if you will. The current or amperage is the energy stored. The key is to be able to store more (have more on hand at any given time), than you, the system or any circumstance can utilize, waste or let slip away. In many situations, this is usually a break-even scenario at best.

Two overworked and seemingly nebulous terms talked about today with regard to batteries are efficiency and capacity. A novice RVer might ask, "How much power does that thing have?" (a question of capacity) or "How come it's dead already, I only used the furnace overnight?" (a question of efficiency).

An important factor concerning the capacity of batteries is to remember that they will deliver the maximum amount of their available capacity if they are discharged within 20 hours or more. If the normal use or discharge on any given battery is spread out over a 20-hour period or more, that available current will be delivered at 100%. Notice that it was termed "available capacity," as there will be a vast difference concerning exactly how much capacity any given battery might have at any given time.

To be a little more specific, the capacity of any battery is dependent upon:

- The area of the plates that is in direct contact with the electrolyte
- The actual specific gravity of the electrolyte
- The type and thickness of the internal separators and plates
- The general condition of the plates (how much sulfation has taken place)
- The limiting voltage (the limit beyond which there is very little useful amperage or energy available)

Battery capacity is directly proportional to the efficiency of a battery. How efficient a battery may be is determined primarily by the following three factors:

- The mechanical and physical condition (concerning the internal and external components)
- The state of charge of the battery
- How temperature affects it

Battery Ratings

Traditionally, batteries are rated in ampere-hours (AH). This is the most common method for rating RV batteries. The AH rating is based on a 20-hour time span, an industry figure accepted for all batteries. An example of an AH rating would be if a battery could deliver a constant 5 amps for the accepted time frame (20 hours), then it would be considered a 100AH battery. Theoretically, as well as mathematically, a battery could deliver 10 amps for 10 hours and still be a 100AH battery, but remember, the accepted rule is based on the 20-hour figure. If a battery manufacturer does not list the AH rating, it can be approximated if the reserve capacity (RC) is known. By multiplying the RC by a factor of 0.65, the result would be the nominal AH rating.

The RC rating represents the actual number of minutes during which a charged battery can supply 25 amps while maintaining a voltage of not less than 1.75 volts per cell. This is the amount of time (in minutes) the battery will last if the alternator belt flies off and the current use is 25 amps at the time, or your charging converter quits functioning while you are using

25 amps worth of current. RC can be approximated by dividing the ampere-hour by 0.65.

Another method of rating batteries is by cold cranking amperage, or CCA. CCA can be technically defined as the amount of current (amps) that a battery can supply for engine cranking under low-temperature conditions. Usually the current rated is listed for the temperature of $0°F$. If a start battery has a CCA rating of 380, for instance, that indicates the amount of amps that can be delivered for 30 seconds at $0°F$, while maintaining a voltage of 1.2 volts per cell. This method of rating is pertinent for automotive start batteries.

A relatively new method of comparing batteries is by looking at life cycles. This is especially common with sealed, lead acid batteries. This method of rating takes into account the depth of discharge (how low a battery is drained) in relationship to how many times that battery can be discharged to that degree. When considering an upgrade to the more costly, advanced batteries currently available, use life cycles as a factor of comparison.

Collectively these methods of rating batteries are set forth by the battery industry and are simply a way to distinguish the differences between all batteries. Using these methods, any battery can be sized accordingly to the task it is being asked to perform.

Types of Batteries

There can be no discussion of batteries within the world of RVs without differentiating between what is commonly called a deep cycle battery and the standard automotive start battery. Currently we can add battery design terms absorbed glass mat (AGM), gel-filled, oil-filled and spiral cell design to the lingo. Initially limiting the discussion to simply a standard automotive start battery and a deep cycle RV battery, the substantial differences must be understood.

Automotive Start Battery

At the root level the differences between the two types of batteries are basic. Simply stated, the standard automotive start battery is constructed in such a manner that will allow for a very high rate of discharge or amp draw, with the stipulation that the duration of such current usage will be for a short time span - high amps delivered over a very short period of time. This occurs, for instance, when the engine is started. The starter motor draws, or uses, a considerable amount of current, but only for the time it takes to start the engine. This point is proven when some unforeseen situation prohibits the vehicle from starting and a seemingly good-start battery becomes very dead in a short period of time. In reality it was designed to deliver a high amount of current for no more than a few seconds.

The capacity of a standard auto start battery is lessened considerably each time it becomes discharged and recharged after the abuse endured in the above situation. The positive plates actually become weakened and sulfation occurs faster. Sulfation and other internal battery happenings will be discussed in detail a little later.

Deep Cycle Battery

On the other side of the ledger, a deep cycle battery is constructed with thicker, denser plates alloyed with antimony or calcium to make them harder. These types of batteries have specially developed glass mat separators. Additionally, the plates and separators are bonded using a special "hot metal" process. This design allows for the consumption of current to be relatively low in amps, nominally speaking but to be delivered over a longer period of time. Typically, this is the type of usage found during dry camping while still utilizing the low voltage equipment. This also results in the battery capacity lasting almost four times longer than that of a similar size automotive type battery - even though it will be discharged and recharged many times over. If utilizing flooded batteries, two 6-volt golf cart batteries wired in series is yet a better

Typical Life Cycles (Deep Cycle Battery)	
Depth of Discharge Percentage	**Number of Cycles When Depleted to 50% Depth**
75%	2200
50%	1000
25%	550
0%	325

configuration, since 6-volt golf cart batteries are true deep cycle batteries. It has always been my preference to use 6-volt batteries wired in series, or even a series/parallel configuration whenever feasible (more on the various battery configurations later).

For today's RVer, many options for battery types exist. One thought is important though; have on hand the best 12-volt battery configuration the coach can carry and the wallet can endure. Contact some of the prominent battery manufacturers and seek additional information from fellow RVers and other battery experts in order to make an informed decision as to which type deep cycle battery is best suited for your needs. Many types of deep cycle batteries exist today.

Sealed Lead Acid Battery

In recent years, a new element of battery design has become commonplace within the realm of RVs, the SLA, or sealed lead acid battery, sometimes referred to as VRSLA (valve regulated, sealed lead acid) batteries. These include the flooded cell battery, the gelled acid battery and the AGM battery. These batteries all have models available for starting applications and for deep cycle RV applications.

SLAs typically have a higher specific gravity but come with an increased initial cost. The initial cost, however, should not deter an RVer from upgrading to an SLA battery. Higher efficiency, extremely low internal resistance and the ability to be charged more quickly are just a few of the benefits of this newer technology. In addition, they typically have greater life cycles.

Gel-Filled Battery

One type of SLA battery available today is the gel-filled battery. In contrast to the flooded lead acid battery which uses a liquid electrolyte, the gel battery has its electrolyte suspended permanently in a thixotropic gel that contains a phosphoric acid additive. The end result; the gel battery provides many benefits not currently found in flooded, lead acid batteries.

The predominant feature of gel batteries is their fairly low self-discharge rate. Developed by the German company Sonnenschein about four decades ago, these batteries can realistically

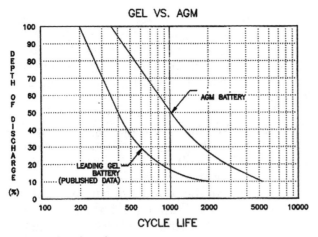

Fig. 4-6; Life cycle performance comparison

perform for five to seven years. Since they contain no liquids, they can be installed in virtually any position, even sideways or upside down! Like all SLAs, they internally recombine the hydrogen and oxygen gases produced by charging and rapid discharging. They are, however, highly susceptible to heat and have a history of being sensitive to high current charging.

One nice thing about gel batteries though, is that they have equal voltages across each cell. Therefore, the battery is less likely to short internally. Because gel batteries use a mixture of silica gel and acid, voids or gaps in the gelled material inherently develop to allow the gases to pass to the vents. These voids can dry out and eventually reduce the capacity of each cell. Also, because of the high current sensitivity for RV deep cycling applications, it is often times recommended that an automatic voltage regulator and a sophisticated three- or four-step charger be employed as well.

Absorbed Glass Mat Battery

Another good performer within the RV world of deep cycle batteries is the AGM battery. AGM batteries are not to be confused with gel batteries even though AGM batteries are considered SLAs. AGM batteries were developed in 1985 primarily for military projects, such as the stealth bomber and the military version of the Hummer. In such applications, safety, efficiency and reliability played a key role. An eventual adaptation to RVs was only logical. Additionally, AGM batteries are highly resistant to vibration and shock, another plus for RV applications

when you consider the jostling and bouncing the RV does on the road.

Highly touted, the AGM battery has many intriguing features. Its recombinant gases are effective to about 99%. The hydrogen and oxygen are recombined inside the battery within each separator, unlike the gel type where the recombining occurs between the plates and the battery top. This keeps dangerous hydrogen gas levels to a minimum. Most AGM batteries vent hydrogen vapors at less than 2%, where 4.1% is needed to support flammability in air.

The inherently low internal resistance of AGM batteries is another welcomed benefit to RVers who store their RVs much of the year. According to one maker, during storage, the self-discharge rate of an AGM battery is 3 to 10 times better than a gel battery, and 5 to 50 times better than a typical flooded lead acid battery.

This occurs because the electrolyte is not liquefied, but rather absorbed into a fiber floss glass matting with an exceptional wicking ability allowing faster migration of the acid in the electrolyte. AGM delivers current and can be recharged much faster and at the higher charge rates available today. AGM batteries can be charged ten times faster than a same rated gel battery and five times as fast as a like-sized flooded lead acid battery.

As mentioned earlier, a viable method of comparing SLA batteries can be accomplished by looking at their respective life cycles. Here is where the AGM battery really excels. Notice in the following chart that an AGM battery reduced to 50% depth of discharge is rated for about 1,000 cycles, compared to about 400 life cycles for a gel battery.

Because AGM battery technology permits more positive plate material to be saturated by the absorbed mats in each cell, there is an automatic increase in the battery's capacity in virtually every area. More life cycles, reduced internal resistances, higher amp hour rating, more reserve capacity and deeper depth of discharge cycles are some of the improvements over other types of SLAs.

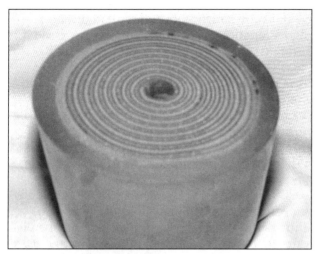

Fig. 4-7; Spiral cell battery cutaway

Fig. 4-8; L16 HC battery

Spiral-Celled Battery

Another interesting, albeit radical, design for an AGM RV battery has been developed by Optima Batteries (www.optimabatteries.com). This company's unconventional "spiral design" uses only two plates per cell: one positive and one negative. The plates are wound into a tight spiral, separated by absorbed glass matting. The close proximity of the thin lead plates in each cell enhances the flow of current and lowers the internal resistance yet further. The spiral cells are pressure-inserted into individual cylinders in the battery case. After being inserted into their own cylinder, the cells are then injected with an electrolyte that absorbs into the mat, effectively sealing each cell. According to the manufacturer, this design prevents the active material on each plate from drying out. The accompanying photo shows one of the spiral cells isolated from the battery and sliced in half.

Battery Sizes

There are several sizes of deep cycle batteries available for RV use. Most are still rated in amp-hours. Physical size will vary with manufacturer, yet when upgrading, overall dimensions may well be a factor when considering space limitations. The following chart lists the most common sizes of deep cycle batteries rated in amp hours. The golf cart battery listed is a 6-volt battery; therefore, two batteries must be wired in series in order to produce the 12-volt DC needed for the system and they will take up twice the space. The L16 and L16 HC (high capacity) industrial 6-volt batteries maintain the same

footprint as a golf cart battery but are about twice the height. These are recommended for high storage capabilities if you have the clearances to mount them.

Inside the Battery

Still the most popular as deduced by the sheer numbers of them, the flooded, wet cell battery is assertively being challenged by the AGM technology for the top spot. The accompanying diagram will illustrate, however, the physical layout of a typical flooded, lead acid battery. Keep in mind that it is not necessary to label this battery a start battery or a deep cycle battery, but only that the differences between the two are understood.

Battery	Amp-Hour Rating
Group 24	85
Group 27	105
4D	180
8D	250
Golf Cart	225
Industrial L16	350
L16 HC	420

A typical battery has a case made of polypropylene or similar plastic and more often than not is of a one-piece construction that also includes a one-piece cover. Indentations and ribs impart strength to the case, however, care must always be taken never to drop a battery. Always use a proper battery strap or clamp for carrying. It is further recommended that eye protection and rubber gloves be worn whenever handling lead acid batteries. Remember the safety reminders above?

The typical 12-volt storage battery has six individual compartments known as cells. These compartments house the positive and negative plates. The positive plates and the negative plates make up the bulk of the battery's interior. The plates must be insulated and separated from each other while immersed in the electrolyte.

A plate separator is positioned between each plate. This separator is usually constructed of a mat-type glass material, as it must be resistant to the acid in the electrolyte as well as heat, since charging and discharging a battery always produces a temperature rise. Each cell's plates are connected by the use of a welded strap or cell connector. They are interconnected in series. With each cell producing approximately 2 volts each, being connected in series results in the six cells being able to produce the nominal 12 volts required. When a battery is said to have a bad cell, this usually means that a cell has one or more of the plates that could

be partially shorting out, or sulfated. The characteristics of sulfation will be discussed a little later.

One positive plate and one negative plate ultimately end up on either end of the battery protruding through the top of the battery—the terminal posts. Some construction modifications have allowed for the emergence of side-post batteries for certain situations based on design intent.

A portion of each plate called the plate foot, allows for each plate within each cell to be elevated above the very bottom of the battery case so that internal contamination can be kept to a minimum. This plate foot rests on the ribbed bottom of the case. Any contaminates in the sulfuric acid-water mixture that sink to the bottom along with the shedding of the active materials from each plate lie within the ribbed portion on the very bottom. The sediment can internally short circuit the cells if the level of contaminates rises above the height of the ribbed bottom and the plate foot. Battery manufacturers recommend only purified or distilled water be added to the battery because purified and distilled waters contain less contaminates than normal tap water. Do not use mineral water.

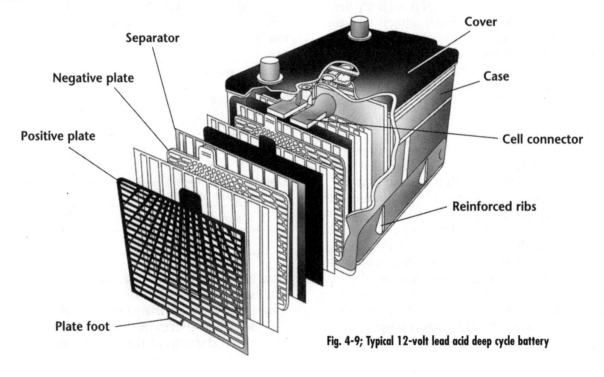

Fig. 4-9; Typical 12-volt lead acid deep cycle battery

Certain chemicals are found in all flooded lead acid batteries that play a big role in understanding what happens during the discharging and recharging of a typical wet cell battery. The electrolyte liquid in the battery is made up of sulfuric acid and water. The sulfuric acid portion of the electrolyte is a combination of hydrogen and sulfate. Water, as you may remember, is made up of a combination of hydrogen and oxygen. Although these elements can be combined during the charging cycle, they can be separated, as well, during discharge.

All positive plates in the battery contain an active material called lead oxide. This is a combination of lead and oxygen. Again, keep in mind that although they form a single compound, they can be separated. The negative plates contain sponge lead as its active material.

Fig. 4-10; Battery cutaway

Battery Discharge
During periods of battery discharge, different reactions happen to the positive plates, negative plates and the electrolyte simultaneously.

The lead portion of the lead oxide on the positive plates starts to mix with the sulfate found in the sulfuric acid. This forms lead sulfate on the positive plates. At the same time, lead of the negative plates combines with the sulfate from the sulfuric acid to form lead sulfate on the negative plates. The oxygen portion of the active

material on the positive plates combines with the hydrogen of the sulfuric acid to form water. This water drastically reduces the strength of the electrolyte. The battery is said to be in a sulfated condition. Both the negative plates and the positive plates now contain heavy concentrations of lead sulfate and which are immersed in a solution of mostly water. The battery is basically dead at this time.

Battery Charge Cycle
During recharging of the battery, the above chemical reactions are reversed. The individual chemicals split from their new compounds and reform to their original state. The lead sulfate splits into elements of lead and sulfate. The water splits into hydrogen and oxygen. The sulfate combines again with the hydrogen to form sulfuric acid. The oxygen forms chemically with the lead to form the lead oxide on the positive plate, while the excess lead forms on the negative plate. The sulfuric acid that is formed replaces the water, which will increase the specific gravity and the battery becomes charged. This constitutes one life cycle.

Battery Banks
Not unlike any traditional financial banking institution, the conscientious RVer must make substantial deposits (of current) into the RV battery system in order to avoid becoming electrically bankrupt! If you take out more than you put in, well, you can do the math and easily determine the result; for both the financial bank as well as what we refer to as the RV "battery bank."

Every battery has a limit to just how much electrical current it can store at full charge. With the electrical demands of today's recreation vehicle, oftentimes it's necessary to add more batteries to the same system in order to store enough current to be able to satisfy the DC power requirements for that RV. Anytime more than one battery is electrically connected to the same DC system, those batteries constitute the commonly used phrase, bank of batteries.

In fact, the vast majority of recreation vehicles will come equipped from the factory with at least two, 12-volt batteries wired in parallel to double the capacity to store current rather than

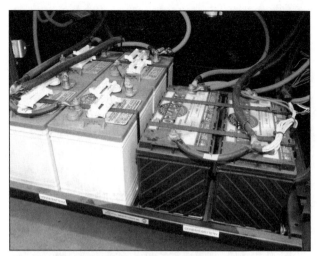

Fig. 4-11; Typical battery storage compartment

a single battery in the same system. In some cases, two 6-volt batteries are wired in series to provide double the capacity.

The photo above shows the two distinct battery systems in a large Class A motorhome. Two 12-volt batteries wired in parallel (on the right), used to start the engine and (on the left), four 6-volt batteries, wired in a series/parallel configuration, used for the RV supply. Okay, I know I lost a few of you when I mentioned series, parallel and series/parallel arrangements, but let's take a look at the various configurations that will be found on many RVs today.

Before we get into a deeper study, however, realize that at the basic level, all DC components found in today's RVs are powered by 12-volts. If 6-volt batteries are employed, a minimum of two must be connected together in order to provide the 12-volt output needed.

Batteries Wired in Series

With a few rare exceptions, only 6-volt batteries will be connected in series within the world of recreation vehicles. A series configuration is obtained by connecting two 6-volt batteries as in Fig. 4-12.

Notice the output voltage is still 12-volts. If the same positive-to-negative interconnection was made using 12-volt batteries, the output would be 24-volts. But since everything DC in the RV uses a nominal 12-volts, the interconnected batteries must total 12-volts output.

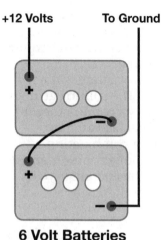

6 Volt Batteries

Fig. 4-12; Two 6-volt batteries wired in series

When multiple 12-volt batteries are installed in the battery bank, parallel connections must be made.

Parallel Battery Bank

A parallel battery bank is nothing more than a minimum of two 12-volt batteries wired positive-to-positive and negative-to-negative.

Here's how two 12-volt batteries should be wired in parallel:

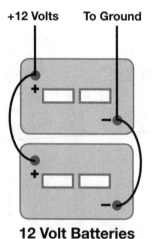

12 Volt Batteries

Fig. 4-13; Two 12-volt batteries wired in parallel

In this illustration, the batteries are connected positive-to-positive and negative-to-negative with the resulting voltage still at 12-volts DC. This type of configuration literally doubles the capacity to store current. If yet more current is required for the RV, simply adding more 12-volt batteries in parallel will result in added storage while maintaining the necessary 12-volt output

Next is an example of multiple 12-volt batteries wired in parallel.

In the illustration in Fig. 4-14, the storage capacity quadrupled the amount a single battery could store and deliver. So if your RV requires a lot of 12-volt power, add more batteries! You are only limited by the available space to install the batteries….and your wallet, of course!

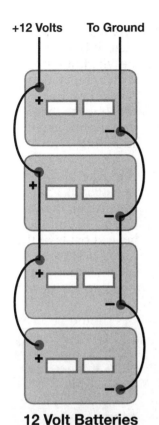

+12 Volts   To Ground

12 Volt Batteries

Fig. 4-14; Multiple 12-volt batteries wired in parallel

Series/Parallel Battery Bank

Like the series connection mentioned above, only 6-volt batteries will be wired into a series/parallel system. Here's what a series/parallel configuration looks like, at left.

In effect, what exists here are two sets of 6-volt batteries. Each set contains two 6-volt batteries wired in series and then the two sets wired together in parallel. As with parallel 12-volt batteries, if more storage capacity is desired, another 6-volt set of batteries can be

Here's another RV Fact of Life – you can never have too much battery capacity! I always recommend having as much capacity as you can fit in. Especially if you dry camp in remote areas often.

But what if your rig is equipped with 6-volt batteries and you want to add to the battery bank? Ah, that involves wiring the batteries into a series/parallel configuration.

+12 Volts   To Ground

6 Volt Batteries

Fig. 4-15; Multiple 6-volt batteries wired in series/parallel

added. In the series/parallel configuration for 6-volt batteries, they must be added in pairs.

And like their 12-volt cousins, for optimum performance, all batteries in any battery bank should be the same type, the same size and the same age. RV batteries are a substantial investment, so it makes perfect sense to be able to get the most out of that investment.

Testing the Battery

Four test procedures can be performed on any battery within the RV, be it a deep cycle or a standard start battery. Of the four tests, one employs common sense, two are tests you can use regularly and one test, though extremely helpful, requires an expensive piece of equipment. That test should be performed by a competent service facility if the other tests fail to make a determination.

Visual Test

The visual test is very basic in its intent. If the battery has cracks, bulges, loose posts or gaping holes then it should be replaced. Some batteries that have experienced extremely low temperatures while in a sulfated condition may become freeze damaged. All such batteries should be replaced accordingly.

Specific Gravity Test

An important, yet often under-emphasized battery test is the hydrometer test, also called the specific gravity test. It can provide a viable method of determining if a battery is charged, and to what extent. Why is this test so critical? When troubleshooting a battery-related problem, one of the first steps is to try to eliminate the battery as the culprit. In order to effectively do this, we must first determine that the battery in question is indeed fully charged.

The term *fully charged* is often misused. Taken literally, it means that any given battery is storing the maximum amount of current it can possibly hold while considering the chemical properties of the contents and the extent to which the battery is sulfated. That sounds like a mouthful, but this merely means that a fully charged battery has as much stored current as it can possibly store at that time, regardless of age or condition.

Fig. 4-16; Battery electrolyte check

One guaranteed way to determine if a typical flooded lead acid battery is fully charged is to carefully monitor the specific gravity while the battery is being charged. When the specific gravity does not continue to rise, but stays constant for a period of two to three hours, then that battery is considered to be fully charged. Any additional charging will be just wasting energy and exposing the battery to unnecessary heat and to possible gassing or boiling of the electrolyte, both of which will lessen its capacity to store current after any further discharge and recharge cycles.

Voltage readings, though important, should not be the prime factor for determining if a battery is fully charged. The exception to this rule is when testing all SLAs. Some batteries are equipped with an internal hydrometer of sorts that monitors the effectiveness of the electrolyte. With no means to apply the aforementioned hydrometer test because of its sealed condition, voltage measurements will, on these batteries, indicate the state of charge when using an accurate digital voltmeter.

Backtracking to specific gravity, just what is it and why is it important? Specific gravity is a number that is used to compare the weight of the electrolyte to the same amount of pure water. It is a number that is not tagged to any unit of measurement. It is a stand-alone ratio to be used for comparison.

To illustrate a specific gravity measurement, for example, pure water has been given a value of

1.000. A charged battery may have a specific gravity of 1.260. This means that the electrolyte in the battery is 1.260 times heavier than the same amount of pure water if the temperature is 80°F. It is actually the sulfuric acid in the electrolyte that enables it to weigh more than water. It could be stated that the specific gravity of a battery will determine the sulfuric acid content of the electrolyte.

Earlier we learned that when a battery is in a sulfated condition (discharged battery), the hydrogen portion of the sulfuric acid combines with the oxygen portion of the lead oxide of the positive plates producing water. In other words, a sulfated battery has more water content than sulfuric acid, resulting in a lower specific gravity reading.

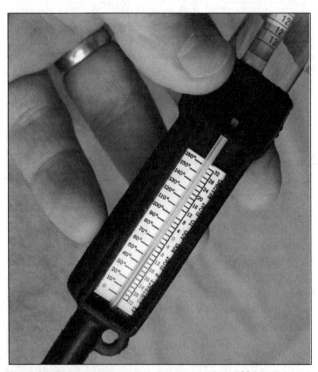

Fig. 4-17; For accuracy use a temperature compensated battery hydrometer

When monitoring the specific gravity during or after charging, it is important to remember that the temperature of the electrolyte also has an impact on the readings taken. The standard for the above chart is always 80°F. If the temperature of the electrolyte varies above or below that 80-degree mark, there must be some compensation for the difference. The industry accepted rule is that for every 10 degrees above 80 degrees, add .004 to your reading. Likewise, for every 10 degrees below 80 degrees, subtract .004 points. Typically, this is of no great importance in the more temperate regions of the country, however, the correction is indeed important in very cold or very hot temperatures as the value can be substantial.

State of Charge (% Charged)	Specific Gravity (Cold Climates)	Specific Gravity (Warn Climates)
100%	1.265	1.225
75%	1.225	1.185
50%	1.190	1.150
25%	1.155	1.115
0% (Depleted)	1.120 and Below	1.080 and Below

Some key points to remember are:

- Do not take a hydrometer reading immediately after adding water.
- Replace any battery that has a 0.050 point difference between any two cells.
- Always use a temperature corrected hydrometer.

Open Circuit Voltage Test

This test is measured at the battery posts with the negative terminal disconnected. Since voltage is what is used to push the current through the circuitry and is not a viable indicator of the capacity of what is actually stored in the battery, this test should be used in conjunction with the specific gravity test. Remember, the amount of current (measured in amps) is what is actually being stored, and that voltage is only the force behind the moving of that current. Though voltage is relative, it should not be construed as the true condition of a battery, except in instances of gel or AGM batteries as mentioned earlier.

Notice the big jumps in the percentage charged compared to the small increments in voltage changes. This drastic difference is why the open circuit voltage test is not viable as a stand-alone method of battery testing. It also validates the rationale of using a digital meter to measure the voltage. It further resolves the misunderstanding that if a 12-volt battery measures 12 full volts, it

Open Circuit Voltage	Percent Charged
12.7 or Higher	100%
12.4-12.6	75-99%
12.2-12.3	50-74%
12.0-12.1	25-49%
11.7-11.9	0-24%%
11.6 or Below	Dead Battery

must be charged or healthy. Actually, if a battery measures just 12.0 volts, it is possible that it is only about 25% charged.

A variation of the open circuit test is to measure the voltage from cell to cell. The open circuit voltage from cell to cell should measure approximately 2.05 to 2.1 volts. If the voltage varies 0.5 volts or greater between any two cells the battery should be replaced.

Load Test

A most effective method of testing the battery on an RV is the carbon pile load test. This test, however, requires specific and expensive equipment usually found only in well-equipped service facilities. Involving the use of a carbon pile tester, this test draws a massive load on the battery that truly determines the interior condition.

Only a high-current tester can apply a variable amount of current that can be dialed in to the specific rate needed depending on the size of the battery to be tested. There are many less expensive, coil-type testers on the market that claim to be battery load testers, however, in actuality they will not effectively load and test

Fig. 4-18; Quality RV service shops will have a battery load tester

the battery as completely as the carbon pile tester. If you are unable to determine if a battery is good by performing the other tests, find a facility in your area that has the capability of performing the carbon pile load test.

Battery Charging Options

In most every RV application, there has been a time or two when electrical woes have led to frustrating downtime during an RV excursion. Although not as common as in earlier years, poorly designed electrical systems, especially within the low voltage, 12-volt DC systems, are still a concern for the active RVer today. Full-time RVers can relate to this fact. Even the casual weekend user has experienced his or her share of dead batteries or appliances that did not function correctly. Ruined batteries, burned out alternators, flickering lights, converter charging problems and erratic appliance operation are just a few examples of the frustrations some have experienced in the past.

In order to keep the 12-volt DC systems charged up, today's RVer has a few options available. Although not all of the alternatives can be used simultaneously, each has a viable statement to be made and a place within the realm of RV battery charging options. Six charging options available to the RVer include:

- Power converter
- Power inverter
- On-board generator
- Portable battery charger
- Automotive alternator
- Photovoltaics (solar panels)

Power converter: A power converter adds an additional voltage source for the 12-volt auxiliary system. A power converter's job is to convert the incoming 120 volts AC to 12 volts DC, nominally speaking. Whenever possible, it is wise to plug the shoreline cord into a source of 120 volts AC. While the converter is activated, it saves the current in the auxiliary battery.

Although not all converters/chargers are created equal, most today will keep some charge going into your batteries while providing the DC current to the appliances, lights, etc. The RV converter is not simply a 12-volt power supply. In actuality, some converters may produce a some-

what unclean form of DC electricity. The battery, wired in parallel with the converter, acts as a filter to smooth out the typically ragged output of the converter. In fact, some converters will not even function at the right voltage unless the battery is in the system.

Converters today are fully automatic. That is, all that is necessary is to simply plug into shore power (or start the generator), and the converter becomes energized automatically. Converters may be configured differently and use different technologies, yet their basic function remains the same. It is important that you know the location of the converter in your rig. If the DC fuses are not directly located within the converter, you need to know where to find them. Be sure to carry spare fuses with you as you travel.

Some converters are built into a distribution panel that features 120-volt AC circuit breakers on one side, and the low voltage, 12-volt fuses on the other side. It can be thought of as sort of an electrical control center. A full section on power converters and converter/chargers follows later in this chapter.

The power converter, with a well-designed charging feature, is a very good method of keeping the RV portion of the 12-volt DC charged, especially if the RV equipped with a sophisticated, three- or four-step converter/charger. The drawback to the AC to DC power converter is that 120-volts AC must be present before the converter can be put to work. That means you must either plug in the shoreline cord or run the generator if so equipped.

Power inverter: There is a charging option on many sophisticated DC to AC inverters that will transpose the inverter into a charger once another form of 120-volt AC is employed. This means the inverter becomes a high-output charger when the shoreline is plugged in, for instance. A more in-depth look at the inverter follows in the next chapter.

On-board generator: As a stand-alone 12-volt battery charger, the generator is a very poor choice. Although some, indeed, may have an inherent trickle charge of sorts, most can rarely charge above 3 amps at best. If a 100-amp battery is 50% discharged, replenishing it at an average 2.5 amps per hour would take at least 25 hours. With the generator consuming an average of a gallon or more of fuel per hour, this option does not seem to make much sense.

However, the value of having access to a power plant in the first place is to be able to produce 120-volt AC. To maximize generator efficiency, use the resultant 120-volt AC voltage to power the charging converter, the charging inverter or the next option, the portable battery charger.

Portable battery charger: The advantage of having a small portable charger is that it can be connected to either of the 12-volt battery systems. Sure, the sophisticated charging converter may be able to pump 50 to 100 amps into the system; most are configured to the RV battery system only. There are some exceptions, however. The automotive battery system sits dormant when parked overnight in a campground or when dry camping in the boondocks. Nothing could be finer than to be able to charge the automotive start battery while connected to shore power. Having a 10- or 15-amp portable charger on board will enable you to keep both systems charging whenever connected to shoreline, running the generator or using the quieter form of 120 volts AC, the inverter.

Automotive alternator: By design, the one element common to both battery systems found on the typical RV is the automotive alternator and its associated charging system. It's not uncommon, however, to discover that the stock automotive alternator supplied by the chassis maker is drastically undersized for the demanding loads attached to the modern RV.

This is probably another good place to mention that you may occasionally spot references throughout this handbook extolling the benefits of the RV aftermarket products. Aftermarket products do offer the RVer various options that include upgrading and improving many aspects of RV life. One of those upgrade areas includes high-performance alternators. Certainly an upgrade to a high-performance, high-output alternator is a wise consideration. Many times these high-performance units are a simple bolt-for-bolt replacement using common hand tools.

Photovoltaics: One of the newest forms of technology to come upon the RV scene within recent years, and certainly one that will become more prevalent as time goes on is the science of photovoltaics (PV) or solar energy. Free electricity from the sun is becoming more integrated into the RV industry each year. In recent years, a valid interest has developed at the manufacturing level as well as in the aftermarket. More on PV to follow in this chapter.

Many manufacturers of RVs implement prewired packages similar to the air conditioner or generator pre-wired packages of years past. Others simply install solar panels and complete systems at the factory level. Most aftermarket service facilities can also install add-on kits for you if you choose not to install it yourself.

Battery Separation
RVs today must keep separate the two distinct battery systems explored earlier; regardless of how many batteries are used in each battery bank. It is important as an owner to know with which type of dual-battery charging system your RV is equipped. It is equally important that it be electrically correct and sized properly in order for you to enjoy that RV to the fullest. The main types of dual-battery charging systems are:

- Isolator
- Solenoid
- Smart solenoid

Isolator: The isolator-type system employs a multi-battery isolator. The battery isolator is a solid state device comprised of a set of diodes; one diode for each battery system in the charging circuit. It distributes the output current of

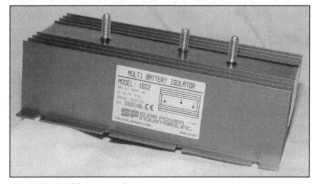

Fig. 4-19; Dual-battery isolator

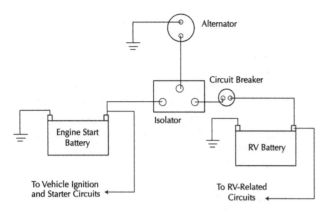

Fig. 4-20; Typical isolator-type dual-battery charging system

the automotive alternator to each battery system independently. It completely separates and isolates the systems from each other at all times. Most common is the two-battery isolator, but there are multi-battery isolators available if you require three or more distinct systems.

You have an isolator type system if you can locate an extruded, finned device usually with three or four individual terminals. Some are painted a bright blue or red, while others are simply aluminum in color. They are usually located either under the hood, in the general vicinity of the battery compartment, or on the firewall of the motorhome. It is vital that the rated capacity of this isolator exceed the rated output capacity of the automotive alternator. Undersized isolators will quickly burn the diodes when exposed to high levels of alternator output.

Solenoid: The solenoid type dual battery charging system uses a heavy duty electromechanical switch that connects the two 12-volt systems together in parallel during the time the engine is running, or during the time that the solenoid is in the closed or energized position. It keeps the two systems truly separated only when de-ener-

Fig. 4-21; Dual-battery solenoids

gized, when the ignition is off. They do not "isolate" the two battery systems from each other. They will still be connected in parallel whenever the solenoid switch is activated.

If you find a round, cylindrical device, silver in color, with two large battery cables attached to two large terminal posts, and either one or two other smaller terminals, you are equipped with the solenoid type dual-battery switch. Usually not available in numerically rated capacities, it must be heavy duty and rated for continuous duty.

Starter solenoids, though similar in design and mechanical movement, are not electrically capable of the high currents commonly found in charging systems. Starter solenoids are designed for momentary duty only and will quickly burn out if used as a dual-battery charging solenoid. Continuous duty, heavy-duty solenoids are often used to complete the "emergency start" circuit on some motorhomes, so don't be surprised if you see a solenoid and an isolator on the same rig.

Some larger RVs will usually be equipped with a very heavy-duty solenoid switch such as the one pictured here. Though solenoids may differ in looks, they are usually identical in function.

Fig. 4-22; Heavy-duty dual-battery solenoid

Smart solenoid: The third type of battery separation is accomplished by the use of "smart" devices such as Sure Power Industries smart solenoid models 1315 and 1314. These devices incorporate a high-capacity, electronically controlled solenoid switch within a well monitored charging system.

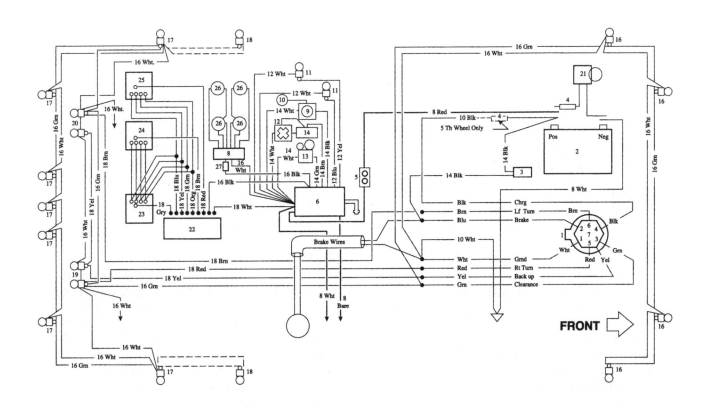

No.	Description	No.	Description
1	Car Connector	15	Refer Light
2	Battery	16	Amber Clearance Lt.
3	Break-A-Way Switch	17	Red Clearance Lt.
4	In-Line Fuse - 30 Amp	18	Amber Clerance Lt.
5	Circuit Breaker - 40 Amp		(Models over 30')
6	40 Amp Converter	19	Right Tail Light
7	Brakes	20	Left Tail Light
8	Stereo	21	Power Jack
9	Furnace	22	Monitor Panel
10	Thermostat	23	Grey Waste Tank
11	Interior Lighting	24	Solid Waste Tank
12	Power Roof Vent	25	Water Tank
13	Water Pump	26	Speakers
14	Range Hood	27	Filter

—— Wire Code ——

Number Designates Gauge

Blk - Black	**Red - Red**
Blu - Blue	**Whit - White**
Brn - Brown	**Gry - Grey**
Org - Orange	**Yel - Yellow**
Grn - Green	

Fig. 4-23; Typical travel trailer DC electrical diagram

The Sure Power smart solenoid comes in two varieties: one begins charging the auxiliary system only after the engine battery has reached a minimum 13.2 volts. The other couples the two systems together in parallel when either battery has reached this pivotal voltage. Until then, the battery systems are kept separate. This is a much better alternative than a standard solenoid.

Troubleshooting 12-Volt DC Systems

When problems arise within the 12-volt DC systems, it is usually at the most inopportune times. Since a large percentage of the amenities found aboard RVs is controlled and powered by the 12-volt DC systems, it stands to reason that there will indeed be a few instances of 12-volt irregularities during the course of RVing travels. However, there is no need to be intimidated by this. A great majority are common-sense related, and many more are regular maintenance items. Having the right tools and applying a few troubleshooting techniques will usually be all that is necessary to find and repair the discrepancy.

One of the most important tools usually provided when the RV is purchased is the owner's manual. Granted, not all RVs are delivered with a detailed owner's manual (that is why the book you are holding is so valuable), but most manufacturers will probably have, at the very least, a wiring diagram for the 12-volt DC circuits somewhere in their files. It is a necessary item for them just to construct the coach. It is also a valuable tool, a "road map," that allows you to follow the electrical path of the voltage and current. Contact your manufacturer and request a copy of the wiring diagram. Be very specific about brand, model number, vehicle identification number (VIN) and other identifying data when you make your request. With wiring diagram in hand is the most effective way to troubleshoot your 12-volt DC system.

Most all 12-volt operational problems fall into one of two categories: battery drains and open circuits. Both can be "flusterating" (that point midway between flustered and frustrated) or worse! When troubleshooting the 12-volt DC

systems, keep in mind the following tips. Consider:

- The system in general
- The circuit in that system
- The component in that circuit

Analyze first, to which system is the problem pertaining: the automotive system or the RV portion? Next, determine which circuit in that system is affected. And finally, pinpoint the component in that circuit that may be the cause. Use the process of elimination. Work from big to little, general to specific. Here are a couple of examples:

Battery Drains

The auxiliary battery keeps going dead. Right away you know the problem is in the RV portion since it is the auxiliary battery in question. By setting your volt-ohm meter (VOM) to the 10-amp scale, you can check for a drain on the battery by unplugging the shoreline if it is plugged in, and removing the negative cable from the battery. You now have an open DC circuit. Connect the red test lead from your VOM to the cable you just disconnected and the black test lead to the negative terminal on the battery. You now have a complete circuit with the meter inserted in series in line with the negative cable. Right away you will see a draw on the battery measured in amps or milliamps (mA).

Next, insure all 12-volt appliances, lamps, etc., are turned off; don't forget those lamps inside the storage bays! If the drain persists, go to the

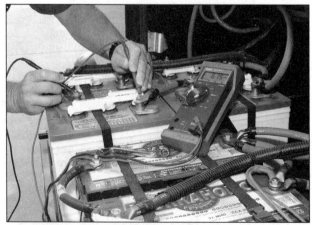

Fig. 4-24; Measuring battery voltage

fuse panel and remove each fuse, one fuse at a time. If the drain disappears while a fuse is removed, the meter will go to zero. When that happens, you know that's the fuse protecting the circuit which contains the problem. Say, for example, that circuit is labeled Right Side, indicating that circuit is situated on the right side of the RV. Now you have at least eliminated the left side and narrowed the search to just those 12-volt items on the right side of the coach.

One by one seek out every 12-volt item. Work from one end to the other in a systematic way. Lo and behold, you finally realize that the booster for the TV antenna was left in the On position creating a small draw that eventually drained the battery. Turning it off, the measured drain on the meter falls to within the acceptable standard of less than 100mA, or one-tenth of one amp. (There are a few parasitic drains on both battery systems that are normal, but if the current loss is greater than 100mA, the system needs more attention.)

Open Circuits

Testing a DC system for an open circuit or a problem that is intermittent is indeed the pinnacle of frustration for most technicians, let alone RV owners. I recommend making a special test cable outfitted with alligator clips at each end of two wires. The length of this jumper cable should be ten feet longer than the RV. I simply used twin 14-gauge, stranded wires taped together. I connect an alligator clip to each end of both wires and keep it coiled and stored in my tool kit. Here's how the pros do it.

Using the systematic logic outlined above, say the power to the 12-volt water pump is somehow lost; the pump will simply not turn on. Again, you know it's the auxiliary battery system and even that it is specifically the pump circuit in question. You've checked the fuse with an Ohmmeter and it tests good; there is voltage leaving the 12-volt distribution panel. You check for voltage at the water pump—there is none. So somehow, somewhere between the panel and the pump, the circuit is open.

Using your alligator-clipped jumper cable, attach one of the wires directly to the water pump and string the test cable to where the fuse

Fig. 4-25; Be sure all DC switches are off when not in use

is located. It can route inside, outside, over cabinets, the sofa, etc., for now. This is just a test. Connect the other end of that same wire to the output of the fuse. But the pump still does not run. And you know you now have good voltage on the jumper cable and at the pump. Ah, but the other wire in the jumper can now be used to test the negative side of that water pump circuit. Connect the other wire directly to the ground wire at the pump and the other end to the ground lug at the 12-volt distribution panel where the fuse is located. Aha! Now the pump runs just fine. You now know you have an open section of wire in the ground side of the water pump circuit.

Some people may now begin pulling drawers, lifting carpeting, disassembling cabinetry, etc., searching for that open section of ground wire. The professional technicians will simply run a new ground wire from the pump to a good chassis ground. It is not necessary to run a new wire all the way to the distribution panel if the problem is on the ground side. Don't even bother looking for the actual open. Simply bypass it by routing a new, properly sized wire to a good chassis ground connection and you've solved the open in that circuit and you'll have free-flowing fresh water once again.

Of course if the pump worked after jumping the hot side of the pump circuit, then you will have to route a new wire from the pump to the distribution panel. But you used the test jumpers as a diagnostic tool to quickly determine the open exists. You can now stop looking for the open and simply run a new wire, cutting off the old wire that contains the open, leaving it in place.

Short Circuits

DC shorts will always result in a blown fuse or a tripped breaker. If the short cannot be easily located, simply run a new wire as outlined above.

Shorts are caused by a myriad of different circumstances; insulation rubbing through, chaffed wires, poor connections, a staple or screw piercing the insulation, etc. Lots of reasons exist and the actual short is almost always located in a portion of the wall or ceiling that is inaccessible. Professional RV service technicians are taught to search for the cause for a limited amount of time and then simply run a new conductor, bypassing the shorted section. You should do the same.

A systematic approach can be applied to any of the 12-volt DC electrical systems. By not becoming overwhelmed at the thought of having to search for a cause, and by using your tools correctly, it can actually be fun and challenging to troubleshoot 12-volt electrical problems. Well, almost!

For a detailed view of RV batteries and a visual explanation of performing the various tests and troubleshooting steps discussed in this chapter, consider ordering the video tape Testing the Battery Systems—The Basics. Contact the author for ordering details.

RV Power Converters

The tireless role of the RV power converter is relatively simple: convert 120-volt AC shoreline or generator power into regulated 12-volt DC to energize all the 12-volt devices found in the RV. Though doing this every single time a unit is plugged in is quite a monumental task.

The power converter is located at the busy intersection of the 12-volt DC system and the 120-volt AC system. Although previous RV power converters were basically simple in design and intent, recent advances in technology have brought new terminology such as MOSFET (metal-oxide semiconductor field effect transistor), high-frequency switching and smart chargers to the RV enthusiast.

Still, by and large, the RV converter is blamed for more electrical problems than for which it is actually accountable. Surveys have approximated that as many as 90 to 95% of all converters returned as defective were in actuality, fault-free. It appears that the real causes for some electrical problems are apparently being overlooked and the finger is often arbitrarily pointed at the converter as the culprit, even though many converter/chargers face unrealistic expectations by RV owners.

Where some converters do fall short, is in the area of effective battery charging. Only rarely and under close monitoring does a battery bank ever approach the 75 to 85% charged level. A true, fully charged system is even rarer. Optimizing the 12-volt battery systems has become one of the most important challenges RVers face. We fear overcharging the batteries yet are confused when the battery bank is rarely charged properly or fast enough to suit our needs.

In recent years, commonplace RV charging converters have been designed in a manner that achieves, at best, a compromised balance between the overcharge/undercharge extremes. The result is that many auxiliary battery banks never attain full capacity during the charging cycles, nor are they ever 100% fully protected from being overcharged. Each result minimizes the useful life of the battery bank and in some cases drastically shortens battery life. There are solutions, but let us first take a look at the basic converter components.

Although considered old technology by today's standards, the design of the most common RV converter is relatively simple. Three main components to a basic converter are:

- Transformer
- Rectifier section
- Method of switching

The transformer is the first step in the conversion process. It decreases the incoming 120 volts AC to 12 volts AC. It is lower voltage, but still alternating current.

The rectifier section then converts or rectifies the 12 volts AC to 12 volts DC. This is done via blocking diodes, silicon controlled rectifier diodes (SCRs) and other related electronic components. Because the voltage that is allowed to pass through the blocking diodes becomes pulsed or erratic in nature during this process, capacitors are sometimes needed to smooth out the delivery of the current.

Since the converter has a 12-volt DC output as does the battery, and they are directly connected, a method of switching must be employed to be able to differentiate between the two. Most converters use automatic relays to accomplish this. In years past and in some special applications today, a manual switch was activated to do this. Although today, most all are fully automatic.

Newer "smart converters" employ many of the same methods, yet utilize different technology. Power supplies and electronic switching devices adapted from the computer industry have varied the voltage transformation process somewhat. In modern, refined converter/chargers, the incoming 120 volts AC is first rectified to 120 volts DC, and then reduced through a much smaller and lighter high-frequency transformer to the lower voltage. The pulsed output of the high-frequency transformer is further rectified to produce an extremely clean and smooth current flow into the batteries.

Types of Converters
Typically four types of converters/chargers are found in RVs today:

- Dual-output
- Single-output ferro-resonant
- Single-output switching
- Single-output multistage

Dual-Output Converter
The dual-output, or split-system, converter employs two distinct DC output formats: one for the various DC circuits found in the coach and a single and a separate output for the battery connection. This type converter has been extremely popular among RV manufacturers for many years, largely for economic reasons. Many models incorporate the 120-volt AC breakers within the same cabinet structure as the converter, so all 120-volt AC breakers are located in the same location as the 12-volt DC fuses. Some of the common characteristics of dual-output converters include:

- Less expensive to replace individual components
- Utilize common parts that are readily obtainable
- Because of heat, are more prone to component failure
- A limited charging capability: 5 to 8 amps maximum
- For large battery banks, charge times may be quite long and relatively ineffective

Single-Output Ferro Resonant Converter
The single-output ferro-resonant design allows for all of its rated output current to be utilized as battery charging current when needed and if the conditions are right. If the branch circuits (lights, water pumps, fans, etc.) are not being used on a 50-amp ferro-resonant converter, for instance, then all 50 of the amps will be available for battery charging purposes. Another advantage is that the ferro-resonant type will compensate for variances in the AC line voltages.

The disadvantages of this type of converter include poor output voltage regulation. Substantial changes in the output voltage can occur with changes in the output current. In other words, as the RV appliances are used, the output voltage drops significantly resulting in an inappropriate voltage for effective battery charging. And like the dual output converter, charging times can become exasperatingly long.

Because of the heat factor, many ferro-resonant converters are equipped with a cooling fan to dissipate the heat generated by the conversion of the voltage. However, all converters are susceptible to heat and, therefore, camping gear and supplies should not be stored in, on or around them. A separate 12-volt DC fuse box or distribution panel is also needed in conjunction with the ferro-resonant converter. Characteristics of the ferro-resonant converter include:

- The ability to charge the RV battery at full-rated output capacity
- It contains no SCRs, diodes or PC boards

- Is more costly for component replacement
- Has higher potential for battery overcharge

Additionally, ferro-resonant converters can utilize the battery as an augmentation if any load so requires. For instance, if when powering a 12-volt electric tongue jack on a travel trailer the load becomes more than the rated capacity of the converter, the current stored in the battery can be utilized and added to the current supplied by the converter. A dual output converter in the same situation would overheat and either trip a breaker or damage other components.

Single-Output Switching Converter
The single-output switching-type converter/charger provides a single circuit connected in parallel with the coach battery and the branch circuits. Again, the rated output current can be split between the charging duties and for powering the coach.

Similar to a stand-alone 12-volt power supply, these types of converters/chargers are able to power the coach even without a battery in place. Another advantage of this type is that the output voltage regulation is quite good and some models offer a user-defined fixed output level. This results in a shorter charging time when compared to the dual output type or the ferro-resonant type, but mandates strict monitoring of the battery charging procedure in order to avoid overcharging the battery. A little of the "automatic" will be compromised with this type.

Single-Output Multistage Converter
The single-output multistage converter/charger is by far the most advantageous. Most all sophisticated, multistage charging converters include, or offer as an option, a highly developed monitor panel for measuring battery voltage and current flow to and from the battery bank. This is a must for the active RVer or full-timer. These converters employ state-of-the-art charging criteria developed specifically for deep cycle batteries while optimizing the charging parameters by taking into account the battery temperature, the total amp-hour capacity of the battery bank and the type of electrolyte used.

Multistage charging converters such as the Xantrex Truecharge 20+ and 40+

(www.xantrex.com) models have an added benefit of a fourth stage, an equalization charge. This breed of charging converter employs the use of microprocessor controlled power MOSFET technology along with PWM for optimum efficiency and performance.

Four Charging Stages
The typical multistage charge sequence involves a bulk charge that basically pours all of the converter's available output into the depleted battery bank until the voltage approaches the gassing point (around 14.2 to 14.4 volts). This bulk stage will bring the battery up to about 75 to 80% capacity in the shortest amount of time. Though the charging current is slowly reduced as the voltage increases, this stage is considered a constant current stage.

Next is the absorption stage, sometimes referred to as the acceptance charge. In this stage, the battery is charged at a constant voltage as the current flow to the battery bank slowly decreases to about 1 amp/100AH capacity of the total bank. Statpower's Truecharge 40+ will charge at 14.4 volts until the current decreases to about 5 amps. At this point the battery bank is considered fully charged.

After the current has been reduced during the absorption stage, it enters a maintenance type of charge sequence called the float stage. This float charge is commonly referred to as a "trickle charge." A constant voltage of about 13.3 to 13.5 volts is applied at a low current of about 1

Fig. 4-26; Multistep charging converter

to 3 amps (some chargers deliver a float current of 1/500 to 1/1,000 of the total battery capacity). This is the point at which many typical converter/chargers begin to boil the electrolyte when left connected to shore power for extended periods since their voltage may remain higher than the gassing voltage limit. Because of its design, the Truecharge 40+ eliminates this fear, and most all RVs can be left plugged in indefinitely when equipped with this newer type of charger. The exception is when the battery bank consists of true deep cycle batteries such as two Trojan T-105, 6-volt golf cart batteries.

Most true deep cycle batteries are best utilized when charged and discharged deeply between charge cycles. They are not designed for prolonged periods of float charge. The Truecharge 40+ considers this and allows the RVer to choose a charging cycle sequence that only includes two steps: the bulk charge and absorption charge. A third, constant output voltage mode can also be selected if necessary.

The fourth stage, the equalization stage, is also available on the Xantrex Truecharge 20+ and 40+ and other similar models. This equalization mode is simply a controlled overcharge designed to minimize or prevent sulfation from occurring in flooded batteries. During normal charge cycles, especially in the hotter climates, higher temperatures and impurities in the electrolyte may prevent some cells from attaining a full charge while allowing a higher degree of sulfation on the plates.

Typically, this is not a problem for most gel batteries as mentioned earlier in the battery section. Since not all batteries require a regular equalization charge (most sealed, lead acid batteries in fact, do not), this feature is user-induced rather than automatic. Close monitoring of the specific gravity is recommended during any equalization charging mode.

One advantage of the CSA and UL-approved Truecharge models is the ability to choose between gel, flooded or AGM battery types. Other features include a 21-day automatic battery top-off cycle which prevents against battery self-discharge, plus it has three separate charging outputs. This is beneficial for charging the engine

start battery of a motorhome, the auxiliary battery bank and perhaps a separate generator starting battery if so equipped. Rarely is a converter ever equipped to properly charge the engine battery while connected to shore power. Over-temperature protection, overload protection and reverse polarity protection are additional benefits.

In most every case, an upgrade to one of these highly efficient, "smart" power converter/chargers is a wise investment and may very well eliminate or at least minimize the 12-volt battery charging woes so prevalent today.

Troubleshooting the Converter

When troubleshooting the power converter, here are five basic steps:

1. Verify the proper incoming AC voltage. Be sure the incoming voltage falls between 103 to 130 volts AC. High and low voltage can have a damaging effect, not only on the converter, but other AC components as well.

2. Verify the correct polarity. Reversed polarity or an open hot or neutral wire somewhere in the 120-volt supply system can indeed be harmful to the converter. Always check the polarity and test the ground fault circuit interrupter (GFCI) each time you enter a new campground. If it is not correct, move to a new site or simply do not plug in the shoreline. Likewise, check the polarity of the DC conductors from the battery. Some components may be damaged if the battery is miswired.

3. Eliminate the battery as the culprit. Because

Fig. 4-27; Measuring converter output

of the close association, oftentimes the converter is blamed for battery or other DC system-caused problems.

4. Make sure all electrical connections are clean, dry and tight. Many electrical problems are associated with loose wires and connections. It is a common occurrence because of the jostling most RVs endure during their lifetimes.

5. Analyze the symptoms closely and carefully. Take notes as you go through the process of checking. Follow a systematic approach by first considering the DC system in general. Next, look at the problem area in specifics. Third, consider the components in the sequence. And finally, accurately measure and record the following voltages:

- The incoming AC line voltage
- The battery voltage in an open circuit test
- The output voltage with the converter without the battery connected to the system
- The output voltage with the battery connected

Should you need to call a service facility or seek advice, having the above voltage information handy will provide a starting point to begin troubleshooting.

Internal Repairs

Due to the level of sophistication in today's power converters, if a problem proves to be interior to the converter, it is recommended that the converter be shipped off for repair. Some well-trained RV service facilities may offer internal converter repairs as a service, but most are probably not fully equipped to handle all possible scenarios. Many components are not field-repairable, yet they can be repaired or replaced relatively inexpensively. (Some do have module boards that are easily replaced if necessary.)

All converter manufacturers have a service and repair facility in-house or one that they can recommend to perform internal converter repairs. Contact your converter manufacturer for the details of its service policy. If your converter has outlived its manufacturer (it does happen), or is out of warranty, contact Master Tech at 800-848-0558. This company is positioned to troubleshoot and repair virtually any RV

converter and return it quickly to you.

Common Complaints

Although not always at fault, many times converters are blamed for a particular ill. The complaints listed below are general complaints followed by possible causes. The possible causes are listed in the following priority:

- Those items easy to check and most likely the problem
- Those items easy to check but least likely the problem
- Those difficult to check but most likely the problem
- Those difficult to check and least likely the problem

1. Converter overcharges the battery:
   » Faulty battery
   » Loose or corroded connections
   » Faulty prototype circuit (PC) board
   » Excessive AC volts
   » Shorted silicon controlled rectifier (SCR) diode
   » Faulty transformer or rectifier section

2. Converter does not charge the battery (not likely with ferro-resonant):
   » Blown fuse
   » Faulty connections
   » No AC input
   » Faulty PC board
   » Faulty light emitting diode (LED) (if equipped)
   » Faulty SCR
   » Faulty transformer
   » Open thermal breaker
   » Open limiting resistor
   » Open diode

3. Converter automatic relay chatters:
   » Low AC volts
   » Reversed AC polarity
   » Very low frequency (should be 60 Hertz)
   » Faulty relay
   » Loose internal connections

4. 12-volt bulbs blow when on converter power but are fine on battery:
   » High AC volts
   » Reversed AC polarity
   » Improper capacitor used
   » Faulty transformer

5. Radio/Television interference with converter on:
   » Radio not wired properly
   » Battery charge line too close to speaker wires
   » Too small radio ground wire
   » Speaker wires in close proximity to 120-volt AC conductors
   » Faulty filter or no filter in system

6. Converter drains battery:
   » Branch circuit drain
   » Weak or faulty battery
   » Faulty PC board
   » Bleeding diode
   » Faulty SCR diode
   » Faulty transformer
   » Above 20mA (All batteries have a normal internal drain and all converters have a normal resistance that does cause some current loss. Anything under 20mA is considered normal.)

7. No converter DC output:
   » No incoming AC voltage
   » Tripped breaker
   » Blown fuse
   » Faulty connections
   » Faulty relay
   » Faulty diode or transformer

Added Thoughts on Converters

The National Electrical Code (NEC) for RVs mandates that power converters be UL-listed for use in an RV. It is not permissible to permanently install a battery charger instead of a converter, for instance. Thermal overload (high temperature cut-off) protection is required on all power converters, not so for simple battery chargers.

The NEC states that power converter cases must be bonded to the chassis of the RV by means of a stranded or solid 8-gauge copper wire. If your converter is a combination converter and 120-volt AC panelboard, then this is not a requirement.

Quite often when troubleshooting 12-volt DC systems or converters, the return path, or ground wire, is often overlooked as a possible cause of a problem. In DC applications, the negative side of the circuit is just as important as the positive side. An "open" can exist on either side of the device. Many 12-volt misfortunes are caused by an undersized or inadequate ground wire.

As a general rule, make sure the ground wire in any 12-volt circuit is at least the same diameter, preferably one size larger, than the positive "hot" wire. This pertains to converters as well. It's always wise to have a large ground wire from the converter firmly attached to the frame of the RV or even directly to the auxiliary battery bank. The ground wire should not be confused with the bonding conductor. The ground wire is a return path for the electron flow; the bonding wire protects and bonds the metal case of the converter to the chassis.

All in all, the power converter of today is an electrical workhorse. Keeping it healthy takes minimal effort. There is no need to perform an abundance of preventive maintenance. Just remember that with any electrical component or connection, it must be clean, dry and tight. Periodically check the terminals and connections—some may loosen over a period of time. Also, make certain the immediate area around the converter is kept clean. Converters do produce heat, so air flow can be crucial with some high-performance, high-output units. And finally, be aware that having a healthy battery will contribute to a healthy power converter. After all, they do work side by side.

Photovoltaics—Solar Power

The terms solar power and RV have indeed been mentioned sporadically in the same paragraph since the 1970s, however, not many people in the RV industry gave solar power much credence. Except by a relatively small group of believers, the value of solar power has not been truly embraced by all.

Fig. 4-28; Roof mounted solar array

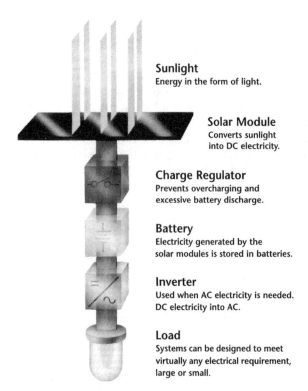

Sunlight
Energy in the form of light.

Solar Module
Converts sunlight into DC electricity.

Charge Regulator
Prevents overcharging and excessive battery discharge.

Battery
Electricity generated by the solar modules is stored in batteries.

Inverter
Used when AC electricity is needed. DC electricity into AC.

Load
Systems can be designed to meet virtually any electrical requirement, large or small.

Fig. 4-29; Typical solar system components (courtesy of Shell Solar)

Recently, though, technology has finally legitimized the viability of adding solar power configurations to the 12-volt DC system found in RVs. Today, more and more RV owners, especially full-timers and those who like to travel off the beaten path and dry camp, are capturing and utilizing that free energy from the sun.

The science behind photovoltaics and the refinement of solar cell technology is quite interesting and warrants additional study should you feel so inclined. For our purposes here though, the instruction will be kept relatively brief. The following diagram illustrates the process of converting light into electrical energy. Keep in mind, improvements occur rapidly within the science of photovoltaics.

Major RV solar equipment manufacturers, such as Shell Solar (formally Siemens Solar), maximize their discipline by using single crystalline silicon technology as opposed to thin film, or amorphous processes. This allows better efficiency overall for RV and other applications.

The making of solar panels begins with the process of melting purified crystalline silicon

and inducing the growth of silicon ingots in a cylindrical mold of sorts. (For an analogy, this is similar to early grade-school experiments of making simple rock candy.) The ingots are then sliced longitudinally into a squared-off shape and sawed into thin wafers that are given their electrical characteristics through a diffusion process of phosphorus-doping the previously boron-doped wafers. These wafers are cut as thin as 200-microns. Silver paste is then applied to each side of the cell, and electrical circuit contacts are formed by the subsequent screen printing process. The cells are electrically connected together, laminated in an embedding medium, sandwiched in glass, secured and framed. Got that? There'll be a test later! Refer to Fig. 4-30.

Major Components of an RV Solar System

Solar Modules and Panels
Mounted on the roof, these collect the sunlight and convert that light energy into DC electrical

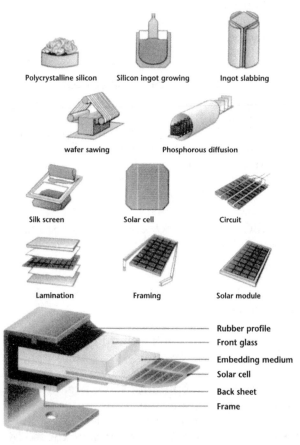

Polycrystalline silicon Silicon ingot growing Ingot slabbing

wafer sawing Phosphorous diffusion

Silk screen Solar cell Circuit

Lamination Framing Solar module

Rubber profile
Front glass
Embedding medium
Solar cell
Back sheet
Frame

Fig. 4-30; Building a solar panel

current. Connecting the panels in parallel alignment will increase the current capacity. Your specific need will dictate how many solar panels will be necessary in the array. In order to produce enough voltage to properly push the current through the system, you will need panels with at least 33 cells each.

Much like a dual-battery isolator that must be sized to the current output of the alternator, or the generator that must be sized to its electrical demands, the same exercise takes place with photovoltaics on RVs. Avoid the common mistake of simply buying the panel that happens to be on sale or the one in stock that the salesperson is pushing. Forethought is required when designing a solar array for RV use.

Remember that each solar panel is an arrangement of individual solar cells. Each cell produces approximately 0.5 volt DC. Therefore, a 33-cell panel will have a voltage output of approximately 16 volts DC, a 36-cell module nearly 18-volts. Although solar panels today are routinely rated in watts, they are easily converted to amps by applying the Power Law that states that power (watts) equals the current (amps) times the voltage (volts).

Each cell in a panel is connected in series. In systems in which more than one panel is needed (an array), the panels are connected in parallel. The variables concerning the output of solar panels are determined by the number of cells in the panel, the degree of light intensity absorbed

by the panel, the cleanliness of the panel and the ambient temperature. Also, panel shading has a reducing effect on a module's ability to produce its rated output. The time of year you predominantly travel also plays an important role in properly sizing a system for the RV. Dry camping in winter, for example, will produce less overall current than the same scenario played out in the summer months in warmer climates. More on sizing appears a little later in this section.

Also, just as charge controllers are not created equal, so it is with solar modules. Varying technologies exist with some manufacturers gaining the edge over others. Shell Solar, a longtime leader of RV solar configurations, has formulated RV kits complete with the module, wiring harness, charge controller, mounting hardware and easy to follow instructions.

Another leader in solar module design is BP Solar. Its highly efficient laser-grooved, buried-grid technology leads the field in the peak power voltage ratings race.

By cutting grooves in the individual cells with a laser and filling them with electro-plated material for the circuitry, efficiency can be increased to

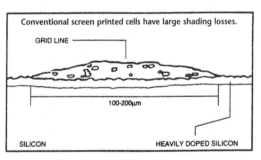
Fig. 4-32; Conventional screen printed cells

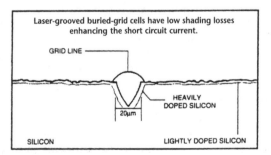
Fig. 4-33; Laser-grooved buried-grid cells

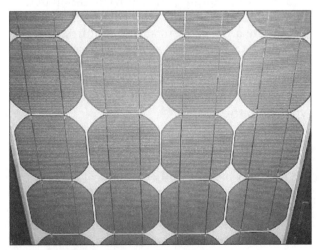
Fig. 4-31; Individual cells are wired in series

17% compared to an average of 12 to 15% for the remainder. The deeply buried grid reduces the occurrences of shadows on the cells resulting in a higher peak power voltage. This is important because of the inherent voltage drop associated with heat. Panel output voltage decreases as the cell temperature increases. In some cases, temperatures nearing 150°F would cause a voltage loss of nearly 2 volts! Power and charging current would suffer as a result.

A typical module with 33 cells has a PPV rating of 16.0 volts at 77°F. A larger module with 36 individual cells will produce 17.0 PPV at the same temperature. But the laser-grooved, buried-grid (LGBG) design of the BP Solar module will produce 18.5 PPV with those same 36 cells.

Storage Batteries
Although most solar panel installations are typically wired directly into the existing auxiliary 12-volt battery system, it is important to note that not all batteries are compatible with photovoltaics. Until recently, one of the most neglected aspects of RV photovoltaics was the lack of capacity to adequately store that free current extracted from the sun. It may be necessary to upgrade the auxiliary 12-volt DC system to store the current your particular array will provide. As mentioned previously, the advances in battery technology have now made solar possibilities more viable than ever. Today, many battery makers produce batteries compatible to solar applications.

Charge Controller
In some inexpensive prepackaged systems, this item may be listed as an optional voltage regulator. In reality, it is a must in order to protect the battery bank from overcharging. If photovoltaics are a consideration to augment dry camping potential, insist on a voltage regulator. Only the very smallest of solar "trickle" chargers should be installed without one. A good rule of thumb is if the peak charging current of the solar panel is greater than 1.5% of the total battery amp-hour capacity, insist on a quality charge controller.

Voltage Regulator
The voltage regulator or charge controller is the device that monitors the voltage and current being passed to the battery. It is an important component in the conscientiously planned

photovoltaic system. Without it, current from the solar panels will flow uncontrolled into the battery system. It is obvious what the result would be. Overcharging is one of the most detrimental forms of 12-volt abuse administered to the battery.

Overcharging causes a heat rise in the battery that not only shortens its potential to store current but it also creates a fire hazard resulting from the manufacture of hydrogen gas at the battery. In most every case, voltage regulation is mandatory.

Four types of photovoltaic voltage regulators/charge controllers can be found in RV applications. They include:

- Shunt-type
- Single-stage
- Dual-stage
- Multistage pulse width modulated

Shunt-type controller: : The shunt-type controller represents the most basic of types and is considered simply an on/off switch at best. It is the least expensive type and simply allows the current generated from the solar module to charge the battery at whatever voltage is available. The regulator monitors the voltage and switches the charging current from the battery through a low-resistance transistor to ground when the battery voltage has reached a predetermined value.

Allowing the charging current to be dissipated and wasted through such a regulator creates an inordinate amount of heat that requires heavy heat sinks to dispel. There also are strict limitations on how much current this type of regulator can handle. Typically, not much more than 2 to 3 amps can be routed through a shunt type regulator.

Single-stage controller: The single-stage controller, also an on/off device, eliminates the need for heavy, cumbersome heat sinks commonly found on the shunt type. With this type, the current is simply shut down when a predetermined value of percent charged is attained. This is by far an improvement over the shunt type of regulation, but not nearly recommendable.

Dual-stage controller: The dual-stage charge controller is more useful, as it eliminates the need to have any solar energy wasted as heat. This type monitors the battery voltage and applies direct charging capability from the solar array to the battery. However, when the full charge limit has been reached (approximately 95%), the regulator switches its circuitry to a trickle mode that slowly tops off the battery and minimizes an overcharging probability. Though energy is seldom wasted, efficiency and battery optimizing are still lacking.

Multistage pulse width modulated: The multistage pulse width modulated charge controller is by far the most sophisticated and most highly recommended. Pulse width modulation (PWM) is a complex method of battery charging that will maintain the battery bank at its highest state of charge at all times. PWM charge controllers pulse on and off literally thousands of times per second. The "off" pulse goes a little longer as the battery voltage rises.

The technology for this type of controller employs the use of highly efficient MOSFET transistors in the circuitry. Power MOSFET technology also prohibits night-time reverse flow battery discharges commonly associated with less sophisticated, inexpensive controllers. Other features of these state of the art controllers include reverse polarity protection, over-temperature protection and an LCD digital readout display for battery voltage, output charging current and an optional current tracking of what is being consumed by the RV systems.

Some controller models incorporate full-time 30-amp charging capability including temperature compensation (extremely important) and automatic battery equalization. The equalization charge is basically a very slight overcharge at regular intervals (30 minutes every 24 hours) to help prevent battery plate sulfation and to allow all cells in the battery to reach the proverbial full charge. Advanced charge controllers employ user-defined parameters for battery voltage, size and type. Typically, the four charging stages found in the top of the line controllers are: bulk charge, taper charge, float charge and the previously mentioned, equalization charge.

Sizing a Solar System

When sizing a system it is important to remember two things: First, the solar components must be sized to your particular RVing requirements; second, the battery bank must be adequately sized to accommodate the current produced by the solar array. Avoid the situation in which the RVer adds an undersized, small solar panel without consideration of the battery size and ends up with too much storage capacity and wonders why the batteries never seem to fully charge, or worse yet, a woefully undersized battery is ruined by too much charging current produced by the solar array. In all cases, the sizing must be closely coordinated. Both the solar array and the battery capacity will be determined by the actual consumption of electricity as predicated by your habits, RVing lifestyle and the equipment found on your RV.

Another factor to remember is that some RV electrical current ratings are listed in amps, while others are rated in watts. To accurately determine the solar requirements, all consumption demands must be made using the same common denominator. Since the typical solar setup is designed to charge the battery bank, it's my recommendation to use amps as that common denominator. All solar brochures will list the common requirements, but in truth, it will ultimately be necessary to go through your RV and calculate exactly what your daily individual requirements truly are. Use the worksheet at the end of this chapter to calculate your DC requirements. There is a separate chart for the AC loads in the following chapter.

Calculate all the DC loads and determine exactly how many hours each day you will use those loads. Additionally, calculate your AC loads, again determining how many hours each day those loads will be activated. List only those AC loads that will be powered by an inverter. The loads covered by the AC on-board generator need not be factored here.

Aside from the measurable DC loads in the rig, it's also prudent to add another 30% to the average daily DC requirements to encompass such parasitic battery circuits such as radio and clock memories, the carbon monoxide (CO) and liquid propane (LP) leak detector and the inverter/converter simmer or stand-by circuits. Additionally, add another 40% to the AC requirements to accommodate those system losses and other deration factors such as local weather patterns and seasonal changes. Finally, add your total usage requirements together to come up with a figure that represents all your loads per day. Keep in mind that every RV will be different. There is no stock answer.

How many solar modules would your RV need? Solar modules are available based on their output rating. Some may be rated in watt-hours, so again, either convert your daily requirements to watts or convert the module output to amp-hours so all formulas have the same common denominator. By dividing your daily requirement by the output values of the modules you are considering, the number of panels in the array can be determined.

A few rules of thumb exist that may be helpful in determining how many panels you should consider depending on your 12-volt DC usage habits and how you actually apply them during your RV excursions. If all you require is simple battery maintenance, consider just a single panel sized about 50 watts. If you use a conservative amount of battery current during a typical outing, say just for the weekend, look at an array that can produce upwards of 250 watts of power. If you watch a lot of television or play a lot of DVDs, you may want to opt for about 500 watts total output. If you tend to use a lot of current, play a lot of CDs or run a computer, consider a solar array approaching 800 watts.

Keep in mind, all solar systems can be added to. Since they are simply wired in parallel, adding panels at any time is quite doable and recommended. The system can grow as your requirements escalate.

How many batteries would your RV need? Once the electrical loads and the number of panels have been determined, the next step is to figure out exactly how many batteries will be needed to store the necessary current for the system. Battery autonomy, or reserve factor, should also be included in the formula. The reserve factor is the number of days you will need current from your batteries without the benefit of having

solar charging capability when dry camping. Usually a factor of two days is average, but take into consideration where you travel, time of year, localized weather conditions, etc. In addition to the reserve factor, an additional 30% of the capacity is recommended as a safety factor.

Again some rules of thumb can be applied for the sizing of the battery bank. If you have decided you need 250 watts worth of solar panels, consider a battery bank that can store about 200 amps of current. Should you choose a 500-watt array, be able to store about 400 amps of current. If, however, you opted for the larger 800-watt array, you'll need to store about 600 amps worth of DC current. As mentioned before, it's always been my recommendation to carry as much battery current as your wallet can endure and your coach can stow.

By taking the daily power or amperage requirement and multiplying it by the reserve factor, plus adding the 30% safety factor, the total battery bank capacity can be calculated. The next step is to consider the type of batteries for the solar array. Remember, not all batteries are adaptable to photovoltaics, especially automotive start batteries. Deep cycle batteries will suffice, however, if you are seriously considering delving into harnessing the free energy from the sun, consider the gel-type battery or the highly rated AGM battery discussed earlier.

Keep in mind that even though some automatic charge controllers allow the user to choose between either a flooded lead acid battery or a sealed lead acid battery, the newer AGM battery, though sealed, is not a gel battery. When using AGM batteries in a solar application, the controller must be set to the same setting as a standard flooded battery. To be sure, check with the manufacturer of the charge controller. Also, keep in mind that AGM batteries do not require as many equalization charges as standard flooded batteries.

Properly calculated, the DC and AC loads on the typical RV can now be adequately covered by applying the newest technology found in the sophisticated advancements of the modern photovoltaic community. Startup costs can be quickly dissipated, especially for the full-time RVer.

The age of harnessing the free energy from the sun is upon us.

Conductors and Overcurrent Protection

All wiring used in RV direct current systems should be stranded conductors; solid copper wire is not permitted in low voltage applications. This is important to remember should you install additional 12-volt DC equipment such as lamps and fans, etc. All wiring installed should be listed by an agency such as UL or CSA. The listing agency will be inked onto the insulation of the wire.

Also, the conductors used should be sized appropriately and according to the load and the overcurrent protection that it provides. It is, however, okay to use a fuse or circuit breaker sized smaller than the conductor recommended. But never use a fuse or breaker sized larger!

Here's a chart that indicates the maximum ampacity for each wire size used in recreation vehicles; from the largest 0000-sized cable down to the smallest 18-gauge wire:

Wire Size (Gauge)	Max Ampacity (Amps)
0000	195
000	165
00	145
0	125
2	95
4	70
6	50
8	40
10	30
12	20
14	15
16	8
18	6

Fig. 4-34; Max amps per wire size

In addition to having the correct size wiring, each 12-volt circuit must be protected by a fuse or a circuit breaker. Such devices are used to protect not only the device installed, but also the conductors. All fuses and low voltage circuit breakers will be sized according the maximum amperage it can safely pass.

If a short develops in that circuit the protection device will protect it by opening or by blowing. Some 12-volt circuit breakers automatically reset while a blown fuse, obviously, will have to be replaced. Take a look at the low voltage circuits in your RV and determine the sizes needed. Be sure to carry spare fuses and circuit breakers as you travel. Again, never substitute a fuse or breaker rated higher than allowed by that individual circuit. When installing new low voltage equipment, always place the circuit protection device as close to the power supply as possible.

Fig. 4-35; Assorted 12-volt fuse types

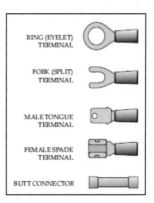

Fig. 4-36; Assorted solderless connectors

Low Voltage Connectors

Solderless connectors used in 12-volt DC wiring come in a variety of sizes and shapes. Many RV owners will be familiar with the ring terminal, spade terminal, butt splice, etc.

It is important to use the correct size

connector for the gauge of wire you are using. Large conductors simply will not fit into a too small connector and you should never trim away a few of the copper strands just to make it fit. A too large connector will not crimp and grab onto the strands properly. Always use the correct size connector. Here's a chart that will help you choose the appropriate connector based on the gauge of the wire.

Wire Size (Gauge)	Color of Connector
8	Red
10 – 12	Yellow
14 – 16	Blue
18 – 22	Red

Fig. 4-37; Choose the correct connector

Be sure to use a high quality crimping tool. The cheap tools will not properly crimp the connector onto the wire and there is a risk it will eventually come loose. In fact, I recommend going one step further and applying heat shrink tubing over the connector and a portion of the insulation on the wire. Take a look at the difference between these two connections.

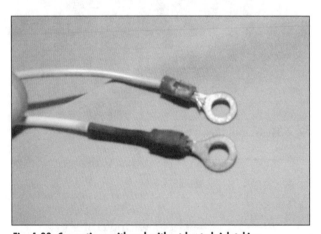

Fig. 4-38; Connections with and without heat shrink tubing

In addition to a secure connection, the heat shrink tubing will protect against moisture intrusion and corrosion build-up. Going the extra mile like this when installing any low voltage add-on equipment will serve you well during your RV travels. Remember, it's your recreational investment and as you've seen through-out this chapter, the 12-volt DC battery systems are indeed vital!

Next up; the 120-volt alternating current (AC) system.

DC Current Usage Worksheet

Resistive Device or Appliance	Approximate Current Draw[1] (Amps)		Approximate Hours Used per Day[2]	Total Current Draw per Device
9" Color Television	3.3	x		
12" B&W Television	1.5	x		
13" Color Television	6.4	x		
VCR/DVD Player	2.5	x		
TV Booster	0.2	x		
Digital Satellite Receiver	2.0	x		
AM/FM Radio	1.0	x		
Radio Amplifier	2.0	x		
Tape/CD Player	2.5	x		
Fluorescent Lamp	1.3-2.0	x		
Incandescent Lamp	1.8 per bulb	x		
Automatic Refer—Gas	0.4	x		
Automatic Refer—12-Volt	35	x		
Range Hood & Lamp	3.5	x		
Fan Motors				
500 CFM	1.3	x		
750 CFM	2.6	x		
1000 CFM	5.5	x		
Evaporative Cooler	9.0	x		
Forced Air Furnace	10.0	x		
Powered Roof Vent	2.5	x		
Water Pump	6.0-8.0	x		
Other		x		
Other		x		
Other		x		
Other		x		
			Total Usage per Day	
			Plus 30% Deration Factor	
			Total per Day Requirement	

1-Actual current draw may vary on your RV. To be 100% accurate it will be necessary to measure the exact current draw for each device on your RV.
2-The more conservative you are, the longer your battery capacity will last.

120-Volt AC Electrical System

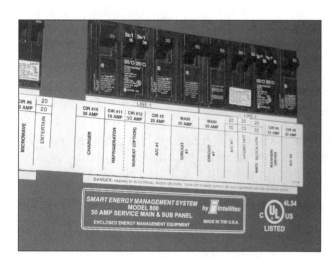

Overview

The system most familiar to you is probably the 120-volt alternating current (AC) system. It is very similar to what you are accustomed to in a typical house. In the RV, 120-volt alternating current is obtained three ways:

- Shoreline connection
- Power inverter
- Generator

The major components typically found in the AC electrical system include the shoreline cord, a distribution panel (breaker box), circuit breakers, resistive units and a host of receptacles strategically placed throughout the living portion of the RV. If the RV is equipped with an on-board power plant or generator, then a means of switching from shoreline to generator would also be included in the list of components. The means of switching can range simply from manually plugging the shoreline cord into a generator output receptacle, to the more common application of utilizing a sophisticated, voltage sensitive automatic relay.

Modern RVs are usually comprised of automatic switching devices to keep these high voltage components in order. All are constructed with safeguards against over-loading and accidental activation of two or more sources of electricity at the same time. In years past, most switching was done manually and required the user to remember the specific when and how. Not so today.

Fig. 5-1; Typical RV campground shoreline pedestal

How and when to use these various electrical sources is usually dictated by the camping environment you find yourself in at any given time. The priority should be if shoreline power is available, such as in the campground or at a permanent campsite, then by all means, plug in. If you are in an area that requires quiet and there is no shoreline connection, then power up the inverter for whatever 120-volt needs you may have. If noise is not a problem, and you have a full fuel tank, fire up the generator.

Regardless of which source you utilize, conservation of energy should always be your foremost thought, even when on shoreline. Get into the habit of good, energy efficient RVing.

Electrical System Safety

Another good habit to embrace is electrical system safety! Safety should be the primary concern when working on any 120-volt electrical device in the RV. An RV Fact of Life is that electrical shocks can be lethal! The human body does conduct electricity! Here are some effects of 120-volt AC electrical currents and the human body. Keep in mind, one milliamp is one, one-thousandths of a single amp (.001-amp).

RV Electricity should indeed be respected, but not feared. Practice safe working precautions while working on the 120-volt AC systems.

- Never work on live or "hot" circuits. Always disable the power source. (When electrical tests must be performed with the power connected, contact a professional RV service technician. Do not attempt yourself!)
- Always use insulated tools (some components may store current and remain charged).
- Always work in a clean, dry space. Never troubleshoot AC circuits while wet or in the rain.
- Wear appropriate clothing such as long sleeves and insulated shoes.
- Remove all metallic jewelry.
- Inspect the VOM and other test devices regularly. Check for defects such as broken insulation on the test leads, bare wires, etc.
- Always hold the probes by their insulators; never touch the metal test points.

Effects of 120-volt (60 Hertz) Current on the Human Body	
Current Flow	**Effect**
1 milliamp (ma) or less	Not usually felt
5 ma	Painful shock
10 ma	Local muscle contractions; with 2.5% of the population, it will not allow a person to let go of the circuit.
15 ma	Local muscle contractions; with 50% of the population, it will not allow a person to let go of the circuit.
30 ma	Difficult to breathe; may cause unconsciousness.
50 – 100 ma	Possible ventricular fibrillation of the heart.
100 – 200 ma	Certain ventricular fibrillation of the heart.
Over 200 ma	Severe burns and muscle contractions. The heart is apt to stop.
A few amps and more	Irreparable damage to body tissue.

A proactive RVer can never be too safe! Especially around 120-volt AC current!

AC Loads

Those amenities in the RV that utilize 120-volt alternating current are called AC "loads." Some may be hard-wired into the system while others, you simply plug in as you would at home. They may include, but certainly are not limited to:

- Air conditioning system
- RV refrigerator
- Power converter
- Microwave oven
- Computer
- Ice maker
- Blender
- Television
- VCR/DVD player
- Hair dryer
  . . . or any other device you wish to simply plug in to any receptacle.

As mentioned, assorted receptacles are located throughout the RV making it very convenient to plug in virtually any electrical accouterment such as a laptop, drill motor, coffee maker, vacuum cleaner, toaster oven, etc. The list, seemingly, is endless.

GFCIs

Another device found in the 120-volt AC system is the ground fault circuit interrupter (GFCI). This device is manifested as either a receptacle (usually located in the bathroom), or as a circuit breaker (located at the breaker box). It is mandated by the electrical code for RVs and protects all receptacles located near sinks and those that are located on the exterior of the RV.

It is a common misconception that the GFCI is a circuit breaker or an over-current protector. Such is not the case. While breakers and some fuses do obviously protect against over-current, they cannot sense or protect against the potentially lethal low-level ground faults.

Fig. 5-2; Testing a GFCI outlet

Push the test button while connected to 120-volt AC power. The reset button should pop out slightly, indicating proper operation. Push the reset button after it pops out to reset.

Fig. 5-3; Receptacle-type GFCI

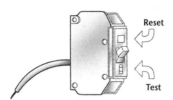

Fig. 5-4; Circuit breaker-type GFCI

Additionally, GFCIs will not sense a direct short to ground. The exception, of course, would be the breaker-type GFCI, which does both.

The benefit of the GFCI is evident in the fact that it will indeed sense the low-level current leakage that might occur in an AC system, lethal

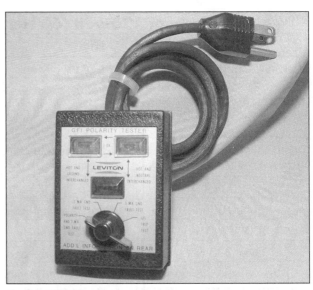

Fig. 5-6; GFCI tester

current that the circuit breaker would naturally overlook. The GFCI used in RVs will sense and monitor current leakage up to 5 milliamps (mA) (.005 of one amp), and then it will interrupt the circuit. Here is how it works:

Current from the shoreline cord, generator or inverter flows through one wire (the hot wire), to a device and back to the power source through the neutral wire. All RVs have a separated and isolated ground wire that is ultimately bonded to the chassis. Unlike conventional household wiring, a common connection between the neutral wire and the ground wire should not occur within the RV system.

In most cases this current to the device and from the device is always equal. The current alternates between the hot and neutral wires in a given circuit. If the current to and from the device is equal, it is said to be balanced. The GFCI constantly monitors this balance between the hot and neutral wire. If the GFCI senses an imbalance between the two currents, and that current differential approaches 4 to 6mA, the GFCI will trip, interrupting the current at that point. Depending on the type of GFCI used and how the

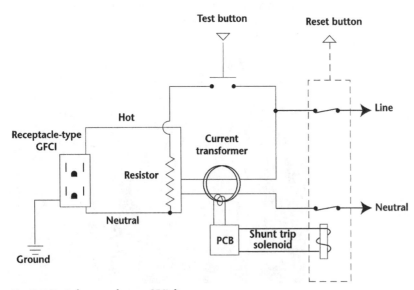

Fig. 5-5; Typical receptacle-type GFCI diagram

GFCI is wired into the circuit, the circuit will be opened and current flow will be stopped to all protected receptacles downstream as well as at the GFCI location.

How the GFCI senses and opens the circuit determines the speed at which it will open the circuit. One method invokes the use of a mechanical relay, such is commonly found in a circuit breaker. Another more common method of sensing is by the use of an electromagnetic, electronic shunt-trip solenoid (see the accompanying wiring diagram). In most cases, both methods will react fast enough that if a shock current is felt at all, the duration will not be enough to injure.

All GFCIs usually contain a bypass or test function that is user-invoked. This test function allows testing of the internal electronic components of the GFCI. It also verifies the integrity of all receptacles on that same branch circuit. The GFCI should be tested regularly.

Independent test devices also exist that allow the user to apply a certain level of current leakage and test the effectiveness of any GFCI. Here's one that can be used to test any GFCI-protected circuit.

Shoreline Connection

Probably the most common method of distributing 120 volts AC throughout the RV is by simply plugging in the shoreline cord to a campground pedestal or any convenient receptacle appropriately sized. All but a very few RVs will have a permanently mounted shoreline cord rated by amperage according to the number of circuits required by that RV. The most common rating is 30-amps. Larger RVs will come equipped with 50-amp service, while some of the smaller folding camping trailers and pick-up campers will have a 15-amp distribution system. The more AC devices and receptacles in the RV, the higher the rating of the shoreline cord. All AC electrical components within the recreation vehicle, the wiring, the loads, the circuit breakers, etc., must all be sized accordingly.

Usually the entire AC distribution system will be

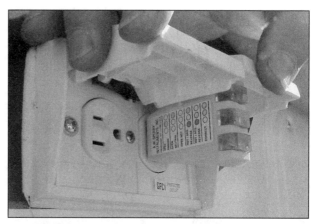

Fig. 5-7; Checking the polarity on an exterior outlet

energized as soon as you plug the shoreline cord into the source power. Some coaches are equipped with an automatic transfer switching device that might entail a short time delay when plugging in or starting the generator. As a general rule, be sure all the heavy loads, (air conditioners, microwave, water heater element, etc.) are in the "Off" position prior to plugging in the shoreline cord.

Seasoned RVers will check for the appropriate supply voltage and correct polarity before subjecting the coach to shore power. It's a good habit to get into. Do not run the risk of damaging sensitive equipment or injuring yourself with exposure to incorrect voltage or reversed polarity. It does happen! Serious RVers may also go as far as checking the frequency of the supplied power before connecting their rigs. You can never be too careful!

The supply voltage should be at or near 120 volts AC, but may be as low as 103 volts or as

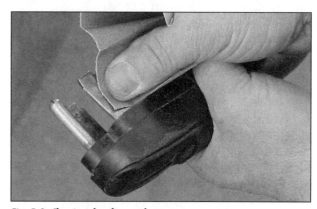

Fig. 5-8; Cleaning shoreline cord contacts

high as 130 volts AC. Damage to equipment will occur if the voltage is too low or too high. Do not plug the coach into the source if the polarity is reversed. Immediately report the discrepancy to the park manager and move to a different site that tests correctly.

The frequency of the AC will measure 59 to 61 Hertz (Hz). In the United States, typically it will correctly measure 60Hz. If you travel to Mexico or remote regions, be sure the frequency is within the correct range.

Inspect the entire length of the shoreline cord periodically for nicks, cuts and damage. Clean and brighten the metal contact points at least yearly. Fine sand paper, 0000 steel wool or emery cloth can accomplish this effectively.

Replace the entire cord if it becomes damaged in any way. Believe it or not, there have been instances of RVers driving away from the camp-site without unplugging the shoreline power cord. If the molded end becomes separated from the remainder of the cord, replace the entire cord. RV Standards mandate the plug end be molded to the cord, though mechanically it's possible to pull it apart should you forget to unplug before driving away. Don't take a chance replacing just the plug cap on the end. Why, you ask? Simple plug caps use screw clamps to secure the conductors in the plug. Over time, those screws will loosen. You could be left with an open ground or an open neutral which could be hazardous. Do not compromise the safety factor! Other than regularly inspecting for damage and keeping the contacts free from corrosion, there is no other maintenance involved with the shoreline cord.

High Resistance Shorts

A high resistance short can exist in an RV that will not trip a circuit breaker or blow a fuse, yet can be lethal. Worn insulation on an AC wire or a pinched conductor anywhere in the system can cause a high resistance short. The same with neutral and ground wire reversed connections. If reversed polarity exists, it's common to have the exterior components become "hot."

Oftentimes RVers experience a slight "buzz" or

shock while touching the ground and a metal component on the RV. This is a good indication that a high resistance short exists somewhere in the AC system. It can be confirmed if the high resistance short disappears when the source of 120-volts is removed. Do not activate the AC system until the source of the short is removed or repaired. To test for high resistance shorts in a recreation vehicle, professional service technicians run a Hot Skin Test.

Hot Skin Test

Some experts consider the Hot Skin Test the most important test performed on any RV. Here's how the pros do it:

- With the RV plugged in to shore power, be sure all the circuit breakers are in the "On" position.
- Set the VOM to the 250-volt AC scale.
- Place one test lead on a bare metal surface on the RV.
- Place the other test lead to a good earth ground. If at your house or in a shop, connect it to a grounded water pipe.
- If the VOM measures "0" there is no high resistance short.
- If there is any voltage measured at all, a high resistance short does exist and must be repaired before putting that RV back into service.
- Reverse the test leads and perform this test again.
- Perform the test a third time but use a different metal component on the RV.
- Repeat the test after all repairs are performed.

But the skin on my RV is fiberglass! I don't need to run the Hot Skin Test, right? Wrong! The chassis, the entry steps and many other parts of the RV are made of metal components. All electrical systems, AC and DC are bonded to the chassis at some point. It's still necessary to perform the Hot Skin Test at least annually. Do not compromise the safety factor!

DC to AC Power Inverters

Like recent advances in photovoltaics and in AC to DC power converter technology, so has the DC to AC power inverter made great technical

Fig. 5-9; DC to AC inverter

strides. The power inverter can now be considered a truly viable alternative for producing 120 volts AC.

As many RVers are aware, campgrounds often restrict the use of efficient yet noisy power generators after certain hours, yet power is still needed for the online RVer equipped with the latest in computer equipment. And whose RV family does not require AC power periodically for ironing, watching television or using a hair dryer? Because of the improved ability to store lots of DC current with the new advances in battery design, inverters are quickly becoming one of the most reliable forms of maintaining true self-containment while maximizing dry camping setups.

The power inverter is the electrical opposite of the power converter. That is, DC power from the auxiliary battery system is inverted to 120 volts AC power output. Electronically processed, this inversion is totally silent. There are no moving parts aside from an occasional cooling fan application.

The sophisticated models even have battery charging capabilities so whenever you plug into shore power at a campground, for instance, the inverter senses another form of 120 volts AC, switches modes and becomes a high-output, three-step battery charger. Other safeguards typically built into the modern inverter include:

- Overcharge protection
- Automatic switching
- Ease of installation
- Simple two-wire hookup

- Overload protection
- Simmer or idle circuit
- Low battery protection

Best installed near the batteries to minimize voltage drop, many inverters can be mounted horizontally or vertically making aftermarket installations a relatively easy task. If you are considering adding an inverter to your present RV, realize that certain upgrades are prerequisite to adding the inverter. It is recommended that the following items be employed with inverter systems:

- High quality, properly sized 12-volt battery bank
- High output automotive alternator (motorhomes)
- Upgraded battery cables and wiring harnesses
- Isolator battery separation
- Accurate battery monitor (voltmeter and ammeter)
- Solar panels to aid in charging
- Advanced AC to DC converter

Waveform Outputs
Inverters designed for RV applications are available in two basic output waveform technologies: quasi-sine wave (sometimes referred to as modified sine wave), produced by low-frequency transformers, and pure sine wave as produced by microprocessor-controlled, high-frequency circuits and components.

Although low-frequency inverters are less expensive and considered efficient devices, they are, however, prone to voltage fluctuations that can cause disturbances in some DC circuits in the RV. Pure sine wave inverters, on the other hand, are extremely sophisticated and can produce AC power at or above the quality levels of shoreline power grids.

Comparisons can be effectuated by looking at the total harmonic distortion (THD) produced by each type. The harmonic difference between the low-frequency RV inverter wave form and true sinusoidal wave shape is a percentage that affects the operation of induction type loads such as motors, compressors or other capacitor-started devices. The higher the percentage, the higher the heat factor; the higher the heat factor, the more damaging to the device. THD (purity of waveform) produced by low-frequency inverters can exceed 40% with some units purported to approach 47%.

The PROsine inverter technology developed by Xantrex produces a true sine wave with less than 3% THD. Additionally, voltage stability is far superior with high frequency inverters. Voltage stability is crucial in many RV applications such as microwave ovens, battery chargers and some televisions. Unpredictable cooking times, buzzing in stereo equipment and video distortion on televisions and computer monitors can be virtually eliminated by installing a high-frequency inverter. If you are one of the many RVers with computer equipment on-board, a high-frequency inverter is a must for laser printers.

Inverter Battery Charging

Battery charging in the PROsine line of inverters employ the much touted three-step charging methods discussed in the power converter section in the previous chapter with the advantage of a higher power factor. A higher power factor rating means that the battery charge circuit draws approximately 30% less AC current to deliver the same DC charging current. This is another area to consider when making comparisons between brands or types of inverters.

Three-step charging by the PROsine line of inverter/chargers will vary the charge rate and voltage depending on the type of battery electrolyte, the size of the batteries and the temperature of the electrolyte. If the incoming AC line voltage varies greatly, that too will affect the charging characteristics.

In the first stage of battery charging, the bulk charge delivers the maximum allowable charge, taking into consideration the variables noted above. It continues this bulk charge until the battery bank voltage reaches about 14.4 volts. This step will charge the batteries to about the 75 to 80% charged level.

The next step is the absorption stage where the voltage is held constant just below the gassing voltage while the current is proportioned down.

The final step is the float stage where the charging voltage is reduced from gassing levels to about 13.5 volts, which continually tops off the charge.

A user-induced equalization charge can also be selected, if necessary, depending on the age and type of batteries in the system.

For RVers who stay connected in one place for an extended time, the PROsine inverter/charger can be left on for long periods without the fear of overcharging the batteries. The sophisticated dynamics of the three-step charger eliminates that concern.

Inverter Sizing

Much like sizing a generator, converter or solar array, it is necessary to evaluate which devices would be operated and powered by the inverter prior to the installation. Each manufacturer produces various models of differing wattage outputs to fit just about every need. It is simply a matter of applying basic mathematics to determine what size inverter is required. Use the worksheet at the end of this chapter to approximate your wattage requirements.

Keep in mind that the listed appliance requirements are approximate and actual running wattage may vary between brands or models. Also make sure that the inverter rating or size you choose exceeds the total wattage requirement based on your needs. There should be a 30% safety factor added to your exact requirements.

If your appliance or device is rated in amps, refer to the Power Law discussion in the previous chapter, or simply multiply the amperage times the voltage; the result is power measured in watts.

Published efficiency graphs and figures can be perused as a method of comparison though real world applications applied by you will determine an inverter's true efficiency. Try not to confuse efficiency with effectiveness. There is a difference. Here's an illustration: A small 12,000 British thermal unit (BTU) furnace installed in an auditorium-sized room may run

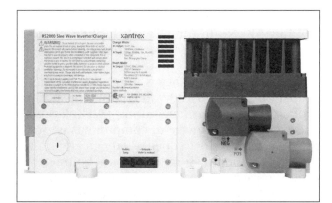

Fig. 5-10; Rear view of an inverter

with a high level of "efficiency." It may use very little current and consume an extremely small portion of liquid propane. It may be very quiet and non-obtrusive - very, very efficient. But, will it be "effective" in heating that room? It is doubtful. For RV inverters, an efficiency rating above 85% is considered exceptional.

When the output AC is not being called for, most inverters will go into a simmer mode until the demand for power is evident again. During this downtime certain monitoring functions must continue. This results in a continuous draining of current from the battery bank. Obviously, the inverter that draws a low amount is preferential.

All 120-volt AC devices in North America are designed to operate at a frequency of 60Hz. The variable should be as low as possible. Plus or minus 0.1Hz is usually considered good.

User maintenance on today's sophisticated inverter/chargers is minimal if at all. As with all electrical devices, though, be sure connections are clean, dry and tight. If troubleshooting procedures point the finger at the inverter as the culprit in a given situation, it will be necessary to return the inverter to the manufacturer since no repairs should be performed by the RVer.

RV Generators

Once considered a luxury, virtually all motorhomes are now factory-equipped with an auxiliary power plant. For total independence, an on-board source of generating 120-volt AC is a mandate. With a generator you can feel confi-

dent of being able to use any of the 120-volt AC appliances at any time, free from the umbilical of a campground shoreline connection or the limits of a power inverter.

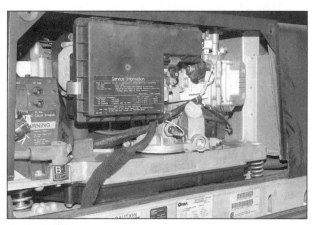

Fig. 5-11; RV generator

Today's RV generator sets have come a long way from the larger, noisier and not-so-reliable precursors of past years. Smaller, lighter, and using state-of-the-art electronics, today's units are extremely reliable. With proper maintenance, the power plant should provide hundreds of hours of AC electricity, which you will soon appreciate when you step out of a 100-degree-plus desert and into the cool confines of an air conditioned bungalow, while your mate drops cubes of freshly made ice into a glass of your favorite beverage, throws a snack into the microwave and turns on your favorite TV show or plops in that movie classic DVD and…well, you get the picture.

With the sophistication of technical achievement, comes the commitment of following

Fig. 5-12; Older style generator

correct and proper preventive maintenance. Though today's RV generator requires less maintenance than in years past, it nonetheless requires some maintenance. It is far too easy to fall prey to the paradigm of "out of sight, out of mind" concerning the RV generator. It does take a concerted effort.

Thankfully, many maintenance tasks can be performed by the RV owner. Yet some tasks are better left to the professional RV technician. Setting up the generator, for instance, requires a special tester called a load bank that usually won't be found in the RVers tool kit (in fact, not all RV dealers have one). Let's look at the RV generator.

Generator Operation

Any device that generates electricity seems somewhat mysterious to the untrained person. Auxiliary generators are probably situated at or near the top of this list. While it is not the goal of this section to delve deeply into the mechanics of the generator, a brief discussion might help in making them seem less intimidating.

The typical RV generator is actually a consolidated unit consisting of a small, air-cooled engine and a second electricity-producing section. The type of RV being equipped with a generator usually dictates whether the engine will have to run on gasoline, liquid propane or diesel fuel. All three fuel types are available.

Electricity is produced inside the generator section through the phenomenon of electromagnetism. One of the reliable physical principles associated with living on Earth is that electrons will flow on a wire whenever it passes through a magnetic field. Greater quantities of electricity can be produced by adding more wires or by increasing the strength of the magnetic field.

The engine has the responsibility of keeping these wires rotating through at least two magnetic fields at specified intervals. Every time a given winding slips past the north magnetic field, current flows in one direction. Continuing through the south field causes it to reverse direction. This represents one cycle, and is where the term alternating current originates. Holding a predetermined engine speed produces the

desired number of cycles per second in the windings. In North America, all appliances are rated for 60Hz, or cycles per second.

This stability of frequency is important for the proper operation of 120-volt equipment such as roof air conditioners, televisions, DVD players and computers. Damage to components is possible should the frequency vary greatly from the 60Hz standard. Since the typical voltmeter cannot measure frequency, it is necessary to have the frequency checked from time to time. One handy device that can check the generator output voltage as well as the frequency is called the Kill-A-Watt, produced by P3 International.

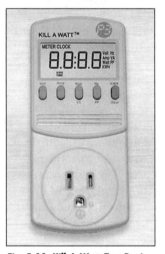

This simple plug-in monitor can be set to measure the line voltage or the frequency at any receptacle in the RV. It is not only valuable to check the output of the onboard generator but this device can verify the incoming line voltage from the campground power source before plugging in the shoreline. If the voltage is too high or too low, if the polarity is reversed, or if the frequency is out of kilter, damage could occur. The cost of the Kill-A-Watt is inexpensive insurance when one considers the costs of electrical damage that could happen. Add this one to the tool kit.

Fig. 5-13; Kill-A-Watt Test Device

Generator Engine

Alternator rotor and generator armature movement is powered by a gasoline or diesel engine. Other than simple oil changes, diesel units, however, are usually beyond the scope of owner-based troubleshooting and repair. Gasoline power plants usually employ a four-stroke engine with one or two cylinders that are cooled by air flow. Generator makers vary in how they place the cylinders (vertical or horizontal), the type of lubrication system (splash or pressurized) and the ease with which to gain access to various components. Size and weight are important factors the coach manufacturer considers as well.

Fuel is supplied by either an electric or mechanical fuel pump. When installed in a motorhome, the fuel line is usually connected to a special take-off tube in the main fuel tank. The lower end of this tube should be situated several inches above the bottom of the tank to prohibit the generator from emptying the fuel tank, thereby rendering the RVer stranded. It is not recommended to simply "tee" into an existing fuel line when installing a generator. This too, could rob the chassis engine of fuel and could possibly create a fuel-starvation situation.

Engine heat produced by the generator must be dissipated. Air circulation and proper installation techniques are crucial to adequate cooling. Also, the generator compartment must be metal-lined and sealed so that toxic exhaust gases cannot gain entry into the interior of the coach.

Most RV generator engines employ the use of a low oil pressure (LOP) switch. The purpose of this switch is to shut down or prohibit the start up of a generator that is low on oil or does not have sufficient crankcase pressure to warrant the starting of the unit. Do not rely on this safety item to be the oil monitor for you. Check the oil level prior to starting the generator each time you use it.

Generator Maintenance

Generators are sturdy units, but extended use can take its toll. This toll is somewhat predictable, however, and manufacturers usually specify maintenance and inspection intervals based on the number of operational running hours such as every 50, 100, 200 and 500 hours. Additionally the RV owner can usually prevent troublesome operation by adopting several good habits. Foremost is the prestart check. Before each startup of the generator, check the oil level, as mentioned above. Then make sure the cooling air intake openings are free of debris, and be sure the generator compartment is clean and free of dirt.

The Golden Rule for all power plants is to never start or stop a generator with a load applied. For

the health of the unit, make sure all AC appliances are turned off prior to starting or stopping the generator.

Also, watch for the effects of vibration. Starting, running and stopping the generator all produce vibration, as does simply driving or pulling the RV down the road. Check and tighten loose mounting bolts periodically. And remember: never use the generator compartment as a storage area. Good air circulation is critical to safe generator operation.

Five important maintenance chores that the RV owner can perform are:

- Keep the unit clean
- Change the oil at specified intervals
- Replace oil, fuel and air filters at specified intervals
- Replace spark plugs as needed or at specific intervals
- Regularly check the battery electrolyte

Cleaning

Dirt, insect nests and debris blocking the cooling fins on the generator can cause overheating. There is no specific time interval for this task, but if you travel in dusty areas, you'll need to clean more often. The best rule of thumb is to simply clean the generator and inside the compartment whenever it needs it.

Also, there should be no oily grime. If you notice a lot of oil blow-by or an accumulation of oil in a specific area or suspect a leak, have it checked immediately.

Fig. 5-14; Clean off oily residue

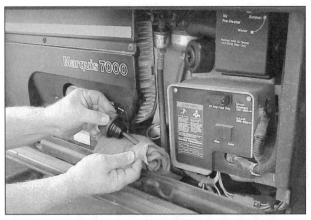

Fig. 5-15; Check the generator oil level daily

Oil Changes

Most generator oil changes should take place between 50 and 100 hours. Different models have different requirements, so check the owner's manual for your particular model if a doubt exists. Unless you will be experiencing temperatures below freezing, use SAE30 oil for your changes. On a brand new unit, change the oil after the first five hours of operation and then every 50 or 100 hours after that. It is further recommended to change the oil filter (if so equipped) each time you change the oil.

Filters

There may be three types of filters to track down and replace periodically: air filter, oil filter and fuel filters. Some units may also have an integral filter screen located inside the fuel pump. Other installations will find an in-line fuel filter somewhere in the system. There may even be a fuel filter attached to the carburetor on some generators. Check the owner's manual to be sure.

Spark Plugs

Spark plugs should be serviced about once a year or every 100 hours. Plugs provide a good indication of just what may be happening inside the cylinders. Badly blackened plugs may indicate a carboned cylinder head or an improperly adjusted carburetor or choke. Always replace the plugs with the same type and heat range. If your unit is equipped with breaker points, always replace the points and condenser at the same time you replace the spark plugs. Be sure to gap the plugs carefully prior to installing them. Check the owner's manual for plug and breaker gap measurements.

Battery

Check your generator start battery at least weekly, preferably as a pre-start check each time you operate the unit. Some generators are wired to the auxiliary 12-volt DC system, while others may be wired to the automotive start battery. All flooded lead acid batteries should have the electrolyte level checked often.

Muffler and Exhaust

A blocked exhaust pipe or damaged muffler may cause the engine to overheat. Many times the muffler and exhaust system on the generator hangs a little lower than anything else underneath the motorhome. Additionally, many installations are behind the rear axle making the generator exhaust system prone to damage by "bottoming out" when entering or leaving driveways or parking lots. Check the muffler system regularly to make sure you have not bottomed out lately. Also, see that the tailpipe extends beyond the edge of the coach. The RV standards call for the exhaust pipe to extend past the vertical plane of the side or rear of an RV, but that it must not terminate under a window that can be opened. Replace all damaged components as soon as you find them.

Maintenance Log

For your convenience, use the log at the end of this chapter to record the tasks that are performed on the generator. It will also provide a track record for a service technician to review should you require deeper troubleshooting and repair procedures at some later point. Duplicate the log and keep it in your RV.

Troubleshooting the RV Generator

Prior to digging into the tool kit, take a close look inside the generator compartment. Do not overlook simple causes by missing something obvious. If it is an electrical problem such as no AC output, check the circuit breakers inside the RV prior to pointing your finger at the generator. Make sure all connections are clean, dry and tight. At the end of this chapter are charts to help track troubleshooting issues. The first chart lists common complaints and possible causes concerning the operation of the engine portion of your generator set. The second chart pertains to the electrical problems you may encounter.

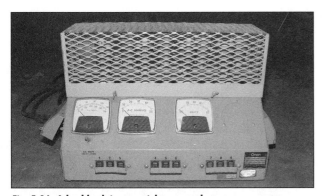

Fig. 5-16; A load bank is essential to correctly tune a generator

Following the prescribed maintenance items listed in the accompanying charts should provide numerous hours of reliable 120-volt AC service by the on-board generator. Periodically, however, it will be necessary to delve deeper and have the choke, governor and carburetor adjusted. Though the adjustment points for these items are quite evident on most units, it is recommended that the generator be taken to a qualified service facility to have them checked. Tuning or setting up the generator requires the use of a specialty load bank that will tax the generator to a specific current limit and have the capability to monitor the output voltage, frequency and current draw at the same time.

If, however, you would be interested in knowing exactly what takes place during a professional generator set-up, order the video tape *RV Generator Tune-Up/Set-Up Procedures* directly from the author.

Multiplexing (Networking)

You've no doubt heard of office computers and even multiple home computers being networked together. In other words, those computers are "wired" together (or in some cases, using Wi-Fi), in order to share the same files or ancillary devices like printers or scanners. File sharing simply allows two or more computers to speak the same language and to communicate with each other. Well, allow me to introduce you to a new protocol adopted by RVIA. Called RV-C, it's the newest technological standard to be embraced by some leading-edge RV manufacturers and product suppliers. The genesis of RV-C began with the idea that certain electronic components could be multiplexed; connected in a

manner that would allow them all to communicate with each other and terminate at one central control panel. The designers of RV-C liken it to an old fashioned telephone "party line." This new standard is being implemented in some RVs now and future growth is expected as more suppliers and manufacturers come on board.

Multiplexing defines a common language for every electronic component on the RV. With this technology, for example, RV makers can now employ sensors to let you know when storage bay doors are open, when the jacks or slideout rooms are not fully retracted, or if the satellite dish is still up, etc. As well as networking the larger electric and electronic devices like the generator, inverter, converter, lamps and appliances, etc. This new technology will likely revolutionize the RV industry.

Your modern automobile is possibly equipped with a central computer and a test port that allows the mechanic to diagnose problems or faults and set operating parameters. Likewise, with RV-C, the professional RV service technician, equipped with a laptop, will be able to configure and diagnose any component on your RV from a single diagnostic test port. Just think, no more misdiagnosis or "guessing" what might be wrong with that furnace or air conditioner! Your troubleshooting and repair costs will be reduced and faster diagnostic speed and accuracy will further reduce your downtime due to a technical issue. Plus, custom configurations such as when the generator should automatically start, or when certain lamps should come on, can be programmed into your RV.

Allow me to quote directly from the RV-C brochure:

> "Multiplexing makes many things possible. With it, you can have multiple controls for the same component - or control multiple components from a single panel. Product controls can be customized for the specific application. The scope for vendors and designers to differentiate their product, refine the controls, and improve the customer experience is expanded exponentially.
>
> Of course, the most powerful reason the

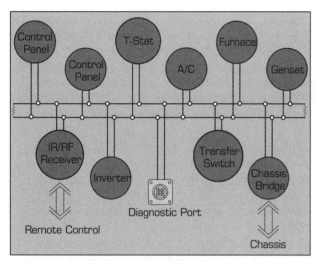

Fig. 5-17; 2-wire multiplexing system using RV-C

RV industry is aggressively adopting this technology is simple: The future demands it. Every similar industry — from automotive to farm equipment, aviation to marine — has already moved to multiplexing. It is becoming a basic customer expectation. Just as no computer beyond the most basic is sold today without a network card, the time shall come when no RV over a certain price point wouldn't be similarly connected. The question is not "Whether", but "When"."

For more information regarding RV-C, please visit: www.rv-c.com

Still relatively new, RV-C devices are quickly finding their way into some of the higher-end coaches and will soon be available in most any fully equipped RV. Electric and electronic in-coach multiplexing is destined to become mainstream very soon. Welcome to the 21st century!

Periodic Maintenance Schedules

Use this maintenance schedule only as a guide. Specifications for your generator may differ. Consult your owner's manual for exact tasks for your generator.

Maintenance Item	Operational Hours Interval				
	Daily	50	100	200	500
Check Oil	X				
Check Battery Electrolytes	X				
Compartment Clean	X				
Cooling Fins Clean	X				
Change Oil & Filter *(if equipped)*		X			
Clean Air Filter Element		X			
Clean Fuel Pump Filter *(if equipped)*		X			
Replace Spark Plug(s)			X		
Replace Breaker Points *(if equipped)*			X		
Check/Tighten All Electrical Connections			X		
Tighten All Mounting Hardware			X		
Check Exhaust/Clean Spark Arrestor			X		
Replace Fuel Filter(s)				X	
Clean Crankcase Breather				X	
Check Tappet Clearance					X
De-carbon Cylinder Heads					X
Other–					

Generator Service and Maintenance Log

Make:		Model:		Serial #:	

	Operating Hours		Service Record	
Date	Hours Run	Cumulative	Task/Maintenance Performed	Performed By

AC Wattage Usage Worksheet				
Device or Appliance	Approximate Wattage[1]		Approximate Hours Used per Day	Total Wattage per Device
Portable Stereo	40	x		
Stereo with Amplifier	150-350	x		
Television	100-300	x		
VCR/DVD Player	30	x		
Video Game Console	10	x		
100-Watt Light Bulb	100	x		
Halogen Work Lamp	100	x		
Halogen Spotlight	1000	x		
Laptop Computer	20-50	x		
Computer with 17" Monitor	400	x		
Cell Phone Charger	15	x		
Coffee Maker	600-800	x		
Microwave Oven	600-900	x		
Refrigerator	700	x		
Toaster	1000	x		
Hair Dryer	300-1600	x		
Air Conditioners	1300-1900 ea.	x		
Electric Drill Motor—Small	250	x		
Circular Saw	1200	x		
Shop Vacuum	800	x		
Other		x		
Other		x		
Other		x		
Other		x		
Other		x		
			Total Usage per Day	
			Plus 30% Deration Factor	
			Total per Day Requirement	

1-Actual wattage may vary with your RV appliances. To be 100% accurate it will be necessary to measure the exact usage for each device on your RV.

Generator Engine Troubleshooting Section	
Symptom	**Possible Cause**
Engine will not crank	Dead battery
	Blown fuse
	Faulty start switch
	Faulty remote wiring
	Defective starter solenoid
Engine cranks, but won't start	No fuel (clogged filter, pinched fuel line)
	Clogged air cleaner element
	Fouled spark plug(s)
	Shorted or open ignition coil
	Improper/damaged ground cable
	Loose plug wire
	Weak battery
	Improper choke adjustment
	Low oil
Engine starts hard, runs rough	Stale fuel
	Clogged air filter element
	Improper carburetor adjustment
	Fouled spark plug(s)
	Weak ignition coil
	Blocked air cooling
	Improper choke adjustment
Engine stops suddenly	Out of fuel
	Clogged air filter element
	Improper governor adjustment
	Fouled plug(s)
	Low oil
	Ignition control fuse blown
No power	Clogged air filter element
	Improper cooling
	Generator overload
	Improper governor adjustment
	Fouled plug(s)
	Improper carburetor settings
	Carbon build-up on cylinder heads
Engine overheats	Improper cooling
	Clogged air filter element
	Carburetor fuel mixture too lean
	Damaged exhaust components

Generator Troubleshooting Section	
Symptom	**Possible Cause**
No AC output	Generator circuit breaker tripped
	RV main circuit breaker tripped
	Branch circuit breaker tripped
	Short inside RV
	Faulty internal component
Low AC output	Engine speed to slow
	Generator overload
	Faulty voltage regulator
	Faulty interal wiring

Overview

Water is a vital part of RVing. It is a crucial commodity for confident self-containment and according to some, second in importance only to the 12-volt direct current (DC) system. As long as there is plenty when we need it and it tastes good, we stay happy. The fresh water system itself does, however, require a certain amount of maintenance in order for RVers to attain trouble-free usage. Certain problems can arise that cannot be ignored. Road vibration may cause fittings to become loosened or even break. Subfreezing temperatures can burst water lines and crack fittings.

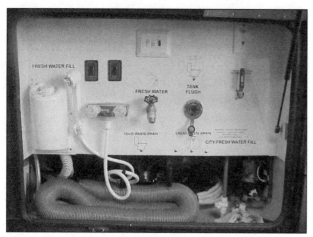

Fig. 6-1; Typical plumbing compartment

Proper inspection, especially during storing and winterizing procedures, may not only minimize, but in some cases, totally prevent many unfortunate situations from developing. All it takes is an understanding of the water systems and a few simple maintenance tasks to keep the water fresh-tasting and free-flowing during your travels.

Two distinct types of self-contained water systems are found in RVs; the older "pressure" system of yesteryear and the predominant favorite among current RV manufacturers, the "demand" system. Though the pressure system is found on some of the older coaches rolling around the countryside and are all but obsolete, we'll explore the intricacies of both types.

Pressure System

With this water system, the entire system is pressurized. Pressure in the system forces the water through the pipes and to the fixtures. The rule here is: if the pressure diminishes, so does the volume of water that can be delivered to the faucets. Two dynamics are used to pressurize this type of fresh water system: air pressure and water pressure. Additionally, there are two methods of administering air pressure to the system.

First, understand that in the pressure system, the fresh water storage container is a rigid, cylindrical container, usually 30-gallon capacity, and is typically located under a couch or dinette. It has a direct rigid pipe connection to the exterior fill assembly. The drain is usually located below the floor level directly under the tank. After the tank has been filled with water, air is forced into the tank. This pressurizes the tank and the system. When a faucet is opened anywhere in the system, the air pressure behind the water pushes it throughout the piping.

Air is pumped into the tank through an air inlet fitting configured into the fill assembly located on the exterior of the coach. Only clean air, from a clean compressor, should be pumped into the fresh tank. It is not advisable to use "gas station air" or "shop air," since it is quite possibly and more than likely contaminated. Avoid using pressurized air that comes from any compressor with a built-in storage tank. Contaminates will always settle in the bottom of such tanks. Compressed air produced from a compressor without a tank is considered best.

Another process of inducing air into the container is with the use of an on-board 12-volt DC air compressor. This device is permanently mounted at or near the pressure tank and is plumbed directly into the tank. The on-board air compressor ensures the RVer of two things: self-containment and a source of clean air.

The second method of pressurizing this type of container is with water pressure. Pressure is pressure, so it does not matter whether the force is predicated by water or air. A city water supply is connected directly to the fill assembly and water is forced into the system and the tank. As long as there is city water pressure present, there will be an ample amount of flow and volume at the faucets and fixtures.

The on-board compressor is usually equipped with an adjustable pressure switch that allows the user to calibrate the pressure up or down depending on how much flow is needed at the faucets. While on city water, this pressure switch is usually bypassed because of the higher incoming pressure, or it is simply turned off.

Demand System

Consisting of a non-pressurized storage tank, the water in a demand system is distributed by pumping the water, drawing it out of the tank and forcing it downstream via a 12-volt DC water pump. This is the preferred method employed today. The various components of a demand system include:

- Storage tank
- Demand pump
- Backflow preventers (check valves)
- Hot/cold low-level drains
- City water inlet
- Fixtures, including the water heater and toilet

Storage Tank

Usually constructed of low density polyethylene, fresh water storage tanks are configured in many shapes and sizes to conform to the installation requirements of the coach manufacturers. Extremely durable, these plastic tanks need little in the form of maintenance. Flushing out the tank periodically by filling, draining and then refilling is usually all that is necessary to keep the water fresh and clean. However, an annual chlorination process to the entire fresh water system is recommended, (more on this later).

All water tanks have a fill opening, a drain fitting, an air vent that aids in filling and drawing water out and an outlet fitting connected to the water pump inlet. Virtually all fresh water storage tanks today are outfitted with a method of monitoring how much water is in the tank at any given time. Electronic sensors affixed to the outside of the tank or through the tank wall using well nuts (see Fig. 6-4) are connected in parallel to sensors mounted in the holding tanks and liquid propane (LP) container. Collectively the tank levels terminate at a centrally located monitor panel inside the RV.

If a crack or leak develops on the fresh water tank, owners must choose to either replace the tank completely or repair the original tank. The only viable method of repairing plastic fresh water tanks is by welding. Plastic welding can be performed on any structural thermoplastic such as acrylonitrile-butadiene-styrene (ABS), polyvinyl chloride (PVC), chlorinated polyvinyl chloride (CPVC), polypropylene or some forms of Plexiglas, among others.

Thermoplastics are unique in that they can be heated and cooled many times, over and over, without changing the chemical make-up or molecular characteristics. That is why they are so useful in the automotive and RV industries.

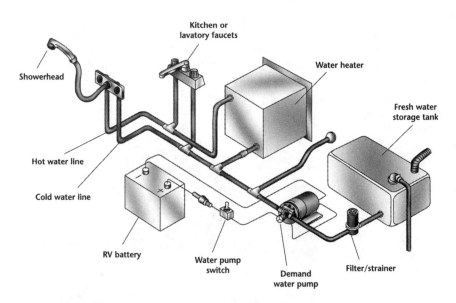

Fig. 6-2; Typical fresh water demand system

Labels in figure: Kitchen or lavatory faucets; Water heater; Showerhead; Fresh water storage tank; Hot water line; Cold water line; RV battery; Water pump switch; Demand water pump; Filter/strainer

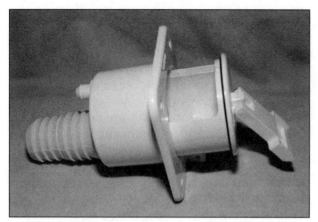

Fig. 6-3; Fresh water tank fill

Fig. 6-4; Well nuts allow the monitor panel to display levels in tanks

Thermo-setting plastics, on the other hand, harden when they are heated and cannot be welded. Professional plastic welding requires an expensive piece of equipment not regularly found in an RVer's tool kit, so if cracks or leaks do develop in the fresh water storage tank, it will be necessary to schedule an appointment with a local RV service professional to evaluate the feasibility of welding the crack. If a replacement tank must be shipped from a warehouse, or if it is an obsolete design no longer available, plastic welding may be just the cure. (To see how effective plastic welding can be on RV components, order the training video *Plastic Welding Techniques* from the author.)

Demand Pump
The demand pump is so named because it is constructed in such a manner that enables the pump to run only on demand. The demand pump is wired with an integral pressure switch that will become activated when the pressure drops below a certain setting, as when a faucet is

Fig. 6-5; Demand water pump

opened, and will continue to run until the pressure rises to another preset point.

Today's pressure switches are preset at the factory and are nonadjustable. An interesting side note is that there are fewer problems concerning pressure switches now than when the switches were adjustable in years past. The demand pump is powered by the 12-volt DC system. Today's demand water pump requires only simple maintenance. A later section in this chapter will detail water pump troubleshooting and repair.

Backflow Preventers
In order to keep unwanted water from backfilling into the fresh water storage tank while connected to city water, backflow preventers are installed in the fresh water system. Unchecked, city water could burst the fresh water tank and damage water lines. Backflow preventers permit water flow in one direction only. There should be three backflow preventers, or check valves, located in the system. They are typically placed:

Fig. 6-6; City water inlet check valve

Fig. 6-7; City water inlet check valve, rear

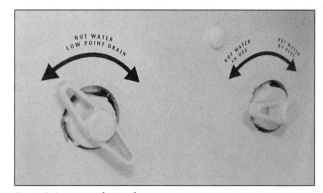

Fig. 6-9; Low point drain valves

- At the city water inlet: This keeps the water pump from pumping water from the tank and out the city water inlet when running the demand pump.

- At the demand pump: This is usually an integral portion of the outlet fitting at the pump. This check valve keeps the city pressure from backfilling the tank through the water pump.

- At the cold inlet to the water heater: This one prohibits the already heated water from being siphoned out or migrating to the cold water piping when another faucet is opened or when the toilet is flushed. This backflow preventer may be absent on some coaches. If so, it is recommended that one be installed.

Hot/Cold Low-Level Drains

Hot/cold low-level drains may be situated anywhere in the fresh water system. Their purpose is to aid in draining the entire system of water for winterizing purposes. They are usually located at

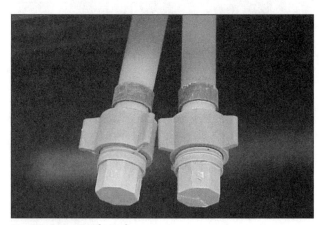

Fig. 6-8; Low point drain plugs

the floor level inside a cabinet or underneath the coach. Some may be situated in a compartment bay. Check your owner's manual for their exact location on your RV.

City Water Inlet

Usually located on the side of the RV, under the coach or in a compartment, the city water inlet fitting is for connecting a hose to the campground or city water supply. Always taste the water before connecting. Caution here will minimize the chance of contaminating the entire system with foul tasting water.

Fig. 6-10; City water inlets

It is always wise to use a pressure regulator when connecting to any city water source. Some parks and campgrounds may have unrestricted pressure and could burst fittings or rupture lines inside the RV. The city connection may "tee" into the system anywhere in the cold water side of the system, downstream of the water pump. The city pressure will distribute the water

Fig. 6-11; City water pressure regulator

equally to every fixture and appliance.

Be sure to use an approved RV water hose for making this connection to the city water supply. Common garden hoses may impart an unpleasant taste to the water.

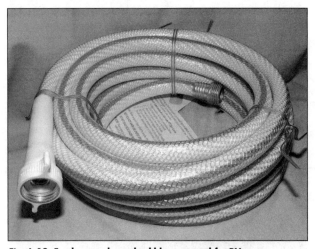

Fig. 6-12; Fresh water hose should be approved for RV use

Some RVs may be equipped with what is termed a manual quick fill valve to be used in conjunction with the city water inlet. This valve, when opened, will allow the city water pressure to fill the fresh water storage tank without having to disconnect the city water and fill through the tank's normal gravity fill port. Care should be exercised when using this valve. Lack of attention can cause the soft, pliable fresh water tank to expand and possibly rupture if the quick fill valve is left on too long.

Fixtures
Fixtures within the fresh water system include all hot and cold faucets located in the galley, the lavatory and the tub/shower area. Additionally, water is fed to the toilet and the water heater.

Many RVs are equipped with an exterior auxiliary shower head or set of faucets which are handy for rinsing off those sandy feet during a visit to the beach. Though these are considered an added plus, in reality, they are also another location for a potential water leak if not checked periodically. Do not overlook these items when checking the fresh water system or while winterizing the RV.

Fig. 6-13; Exterior shower door

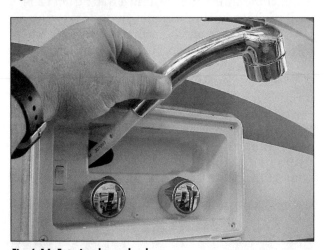

Fig. 6-14; Exterior shower head

An important fitting in the fresh water systems is the vacuum breaker associated with the tub/shower enclosure or the lavatory faucets. If the shower hose is long enough to reach into the sink or toilet, the vacuum breaker attachment is necessary for sanitary reasons. The vacuum breaker fitting will drain all the water from inside the hose after shutting off the faucet. This is a normal occurrence but can be annoying.

As an alternative it is permissible to replace the vacuum breaker assembly on the faucet with a fitting called a D-spud. When a D-spud is used instead of a vacuum breaker, a D-ring must also be installed so the shower hose will not be able to reach the sink, tub or toilet. The D-ring is simply a D-shaped wall bracket through which the shower hose is run. The D-spud will eliminate that apparent leakage of water back down the shower hose once the faucet is turned off.

Fig. 6-15; Fresh water D-spud fitting

Additional plumbing fixtures may be included, such as a water filtration system. A point-of-use (POU) water filtration system is the most viable, the most convenient and the most readily available. Many fine companies have jumped to the forefront with an assortment of effective filtration products.

Fig. 6-16; In-line fresh water filter

Filtration systems can run the gamut from simple mechanical strainers to the more exotic reverse osmosis and super-chlorination systems. The best system for you depends on your traveling habits and the cleanliness of the water you are likely to run into.

Many POU systems are installed under the galley sink and deliver fresh water directly to a dedicated faucet for cooking and drinking. However, some RVers prefer the very popular in-line external units such as this one from Hydro-Life, (www.hydrolife.com), which allow finite filtration without losing that precious under-the-counter storage space. The added plus is that all the incoming city water is processed, so you can enjoy RV showers without the heavy metals and odors sometimes found in park systems. As an additional precaution, use an in-line filter as you fill the fresh water tank on the RV. As water is processed through the filter just before it enters the city water inlet or the inlet to the fresh water tank, submicron particles, bacteria, cysts and unwanted chemicals are removed by the active filtering media, usually activated carbon.

The process by which activated carbon removes impurities is called adsorption. Adsorption is the physical process that occurs when dissolved molecules, bacteria and other particles are attracted to and attach themselves to the surface of the adsorbent, the carbon. Kind of like a magnet sticking to a metal surface. Quite different from the more familiar process of absorption, which can be likened to a paper towel soaking up water.

As an adsorbent, especially when filtering trihalomethanes (THMs), volatile organic contaminates (VOCs), pesticides and fungicides, activated carbon is quite effective because its surface area is enormous: about 1,000 square meters per gram. To put that into perspective, a piece of carbon the size of a single pea will yield a surface area a little over the size of half a football field. But as with many good things, there is a downside to using carbon as the sole filtering media. Exposure to chlorine in water supplies will quickly deteriorate the adsorbing qualities of carbon, rendering it minimized or useless in as little as 200 gallons, so when chlorinating the fresh water system, be sure to remove or bypass the filter first.

Hydro-Life is but one company that utilizes the benefits of a filtering media known as KDF. KDF is a National Sanitation Foundation (NSF)-certified bacteriostatic. It has very high purity of copper/zinc that can reduce contaminants and heavy metals from water. KDF causes an electro-chemical reaction that neutralizes harmful chemicals and dangerous metals such as lead. As an example, chlorine is broken down into a harmless chloride after being zapped with the .04 volts produced when the water passes through the KDF. The water then passes through the carbon to complete the filtering process. KDF basically reduces the overall chlorine content enabling the activated carbon to last much longer.

Another name synonymous with RVing is SHURflo (www.shurflo.com). Aside from their very popular water pump, SHURflo also offers the Waterguard Water Filter Kit. This cartridge-type filter can be mounted inside, under the counter or used as an in-line, exterior filter. One Waterguard model incorporates a handy bypass valve for easy cartridge replacement or for winterizing purposes. Like any canister-type filter, the Waterguard replacement cartridges are available with an assortment of filtration media depending on the degree of filtration needed.

When choosing a filtration system, look for one that satisfies the requirements of Standard 53: Drinking Water Treatment Units - Health Effects, as determined by NSF, a third-party certifying agency. Though no official standard exists for POU filters, virtually all public health officials have adopted the standards of the NSF.

To ensure proper filtration efficiency, always replace the filter media or cartridge as least once a year. Keep in mind, the longer a filter is in service, the less effective it becomes. At some point, an exhausted filter media will begin dumping contaminates back into the system. In severe cases or when tainted water has been encountered, it may be necessary to replace the filters more often.

Another fixture common to the fresh water plumbing system is the accumulator. The water accumulator tank is used to hold a cushion of air in the system to eliminate knocking or clanging of the pipes when a faucet is abruptly turned off. The accumulator tank houses an entrapment of air that acts as a shock absorber and eliminates this annoying effect.

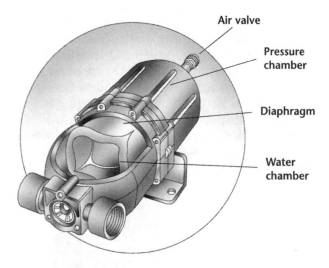

Fig. 6-17; Fresh water accumulator tank

In past years, it was necessary to remove and drain the accumulator when it filled completely with water. The oxygen (air) inside became totally absorbed into the water, eliminating that cushion of air. Today, SHURflo produces an accumulator that is constructed with a flexible diaphragm that effectively isolates the air chamber from the water area negating the need to remove and drain it. The pressurized air and the water never mix.

Repairing the Demand Water Pump

Compared to earlier years, the modern demand water pump is a technological wonder. Today's pump manufacturers have water pumps so finely tuned that, short of blatant abuse, little can go wrong. Out of sight and usually out of mind day in and day out, most water pumps will faithfully continue to provide running water.

Fig. 6-18; Demand water pump installation

Pump Components

Demand pumps, although somewhat complex internally, are basic in function and major components. Most 12-volt DC demand pumps can be broken down into these basic components:

- 12-volt DC motor
- Pumping mechanism
- Pressure switch
- Check valve
- Mounting assembly

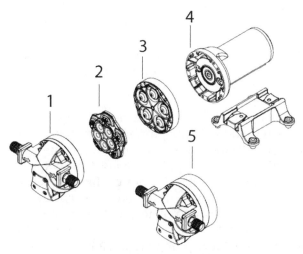

Fig. 6-19; Demand water pump components: 1. upper housing with pressure switch; 2. valve assembly; 3. drive housing; 4. motor; and 5. pump head repair kit.

There are a few different pump designs on the market, but virtually all contain these five basic components. The method of pumping may differ, but elemental operation and the principle goal are the same.

The demand principle revolves around the thought of the pump being a dormant component until we either turn on a hot or cold water faucet or flush the toilet. It is upon this call or demand for water that the pump will immediately spring to life and provide a nice, steady stream of water.

The modern pump has individual components that are easily replaced. All major component groups for each manufacturer can be individually replaced. RVers with extremely old demand pumps may want to purchase a newer style simply to upgrade the system.

The purpose of the 12-volt DC motor, the pumping mechanism and the mounting base are pretty obvious, but let's explore the reason why a pressure switch and a check valve are integral components of the demand water pump system.

The pressure switch is simply an on/off 12-volt switch. It is a normally closed switch, which means sitting on the bench by itself, there is continuity across the two terminals. Once pressure is applied to the switch, the contacts open and there is no continuity. It is the switch's purpose to provide 12-volt DC current to the pump motor whenever the pressure against the switch falls below approximately 40 pounds per square inch (psi). This is exactly what will happen when a faucet is opened or the toilet is flushed.

Unfortunately, this is also exactly what happens if a leak exists anywhere in the fresh water plumbing system. Remember, the demand for water can be either intentional or unintentional. For this reason, it is a good idea to turn off the main water pump switch if you are going to be away from the RV for any length of time.

Today's pressure switches are nonadjustable but extremely reliable. Some pressure switches in past decades were very temperamental and required constant adjusting and frequent replacing. Most of today's pressure switches are manufactured to keep the water pressure at or very near 40psi. Additionally, the modern RV water pump is quite stingy with the amount of current it uses. Here's a chart provided by SHURflo, the leading supplier of water pumps for the RV industry, which details the current draw/water flow relationship of their Aqua King Premium demand water pump.

Pressure (PSI)	Flow (GPM)	Current (Amps)
0	4.0	4.1
10	3.3	6.3
20	2.9	7.6
30	2.7	8.8
40	2.4	10.0

Fig. 6-20; SHURflo current/flow rates

The built-in check valve is a necessary and required item that prohibits backfilling of the water tank through the pump while connected to city water. Though it rarely happens with the newer pumps, if you suddenly realize the fresh water storage tank is full or overflowing, and your rig is connected to city water, chances are the check valve inside the demand pump is defective. In most cases, the check valve assembly can be purchased separately or as part of a repair kit.

Familiarize yourself with all the repair kits available for your particular pump. If you frequently travel off the beaten track and enjoy the benefits and solitude of dry camping often, you may want to consider carrying a water pump repair kit with you, just in case. There is no reason why the confident RV owner should not be able to perform all repairs to the demand water pump.

Fig. 6-21; Demand water pump.

Troubleshooting Suggestions

Though water pumps are quite reliable, there are times when the water pump just may not perform as expected. Here are a few instances of water pump failure and how to effectively troubleshoot the cause.

If the pump will not run at all, open any two faucets, turn the master pump switch on and with a 12-volt test light, pierce the red wire that is attached directly to the pump motor. Attach the negative lead of the test light to a good ground connection. If there is voltage present on the wire at the motor, check the ground wire for the pump motor. If that wire is sufficiently grounded, the motor is faulty.

If there is no voltage indicated on the red wire, touch the test light to both wires attached to the pressure switch. If one is hot, remove them both and touch them together. If the pump runs, the pressure switch is faulty.

Obviously, if no voltage is indicated anywhere at the pump, check that circuit until the reason for the lack of voltage can be determined. If there is no voltage anywhere in the coach, suspect the battery. If there is plenty of 12-volt DC electricity in the RV, check the pump fuse, the master pump switch and the wires that electrically connect each of these components to the pump.

If you smell what appears to be burning electrical wires, and find the pump is extremely hot to the touch, remove the pump portion from the 12-volt motor and apply 12 volts directly to the motor. If it runs but does not get hot, suspect binding components in the pump assembly. If it continues to get hot replace the motor.

Intermittent water pump cycling has traditionally been the indicator of a water leak. The leak may be internal to the pump, but in most cases the leak will exist somewhere in the fresh water system. A faucet may drip, the toilet ball valve may be passing water into the bowl, a fitting may be seeping, the water heater pressure and temperature (P&T) relief valve may be dripping or any of a couple of dozen other possibilities.

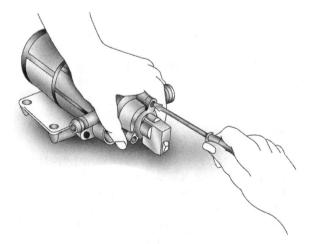

Fig. 6-22; Carefully tighten any loose screws on the upper housing

Troubleshooting the Fresh Water System	
Symptom	**Possible Causes**
Pump motor will not operate	Dead battery of no voltage
	Blown fuse
	Faulty master switch
	Faulty pressure switch
	Loose or disconnected wire
	Faulty ground wire
	Burned out motor
	No demand for water
Motor runs, but is very hot	Insufficient wire size
	Low voltage
	Motor shaft binding
	Faulty motor bearings
Pump cycles periodically	Water leak in fresh water system
	Internal leak in pump
Pump runs, but is noisy	Loose screws/components in pump
	Faulty bearings in motor
	Binding components in pump
	Faulty motor windings
Pump runs, but water spatters	Low or no water in tank
	Inlet line to pump is kinked
	Water filter is dirty
	Air leak inlet to pump
	Outlet hose is kinked
	Faulty motor bearings
	Loose mechanical connections
Pump runs continuously	Pressure switch miswired
	Low battery voltage
	Stuck pressure switch
	Loose or faulty internal components

If the cycling vanishes, the leak is somewhere in the rest of the system, downstream of the pump.

If water is not seen readily pooling anywhere, strongly suspect the toilet. Other than the water pump, the toilet is the only other component that could possibly leak without a telltale wet spot giving away the location of the leak. Do not forget to look outside and underneath the coach as well. If the city water inlet check valve is stuck open, for instance, the same symptom will result.

Also keep in mind, the faster the pump cycles, the larger the leak. If it only "burps" every five minutes or so, it is probably a very small leak. Large leaks should be easier to spot than small leaks. As each leak is located and repaired, run the test again.

Some demand pumps are noisier than others, but if a pump is extremely noisy, tighten any screws that are exposed. If the noise continues, remove the pump and bench test it to determine which component may be causing the noise. Separate the pump assembly from the motor itself and apply 12 volts directly to the motor. If it continues to run noisily replace the motor. If the motor runs fine by itself, check the individual pumping mechanism components. Be sure the mounting base attaching screws are not too tight. The rubber mounts should be intact and not compressed too much.

To determine if the leak is internal to the pump, turn off the pump and disconnect the output water line on the pump. Plug or cap the outlet port directly on the pump. Turn on the pump. If it continues to cycle periodically, the pump has an internal leak and will need to be removed and disassembled for further repair.

If the pump runs, but the water simply sputters out of each faucet, suspect an air leak on the inlet side of the pump. The nonpressurized connections between the tank and the inlet to the pump are prone to having hose clamps become loosened. Tighten all clamps and make sure the hose is not kinked anywhere along its entire length. If there is an in-line filter or strainer positioned between the tank and the pump, clean it or replace it, depending on the type. In some cases the problem may be a faulty motor, but these instances are somewhat rare.

If the only way to prohibit the demand pump from running is to shut off the master switch, suspect a stuck or miswired pressure switch. First make sure all the faucets in the RV are closed and the water heater is full. Then check the wiring from the master switch to the pressure switch and finally to the pump motor. The voltage should follow that same path. If the wiring appears correct, chances are the pressure switch is faulty and will have to be replaced.

The quick reference table on page 93 may be helpful. By following these simple troubleshooting procedures, you should be able to quickly determine if a condition is relative to the demand pump or to the rest of the fresh water system.

General Fresh Water System Maintenance

General fresh water system maintenance usually involves three items:

- Checking for leaks
- Chlorinating the system
- Cleaning/replacing the filter/strainer

Checking for Leaks

Obviously, water leaks are to be avoided. To prevent water leaks, periodically check in and around all cabinets, fixtures, tank area, and behind the toilet for any indication of a leak. Seemingly small amounts of moisture can quickly escalate into a major crisis if left unattended.

Use the water pump as a troubleshooting tool. Close all faucets firmly and turn the water pump on. If the pump cycles or "burps" periodically, a leak could exist somewhere in the system. Be sure to check inside all exterior storage compartments and underneath the coach. In rare instances, the leak could be internal to the pump.

Chlorinating the Water

Foul or stale tasting water can not only ruin a vacation but may even be harmful. There is usually sufficient chlorine in most city water supply systems, but if foul tasting water persists, it may be necessary to treat the fresh water system. Of course, the fresh water container only stores the quality of water put in there, so be sure to taste it prior to filling up. Here's the approved method of chlorinating the entire fresh water system:

1. Drain and flush the fresh water tank; leave empty.
2. Mix 1/4-cup of liquid household bleach (sodium hypochlorite) solution with one gallon of fresh water.
3. Pour directly into the fresh water tank.
4. Pour in one gallon of the chlorine/water solution for every 15 gallons of fresh water tank capacity.
5. Top off the tank with fresh water.
6. Remove or bypass water purification equipment and/or filtering cartridges. (Note: Remove the anode rod and install a pipe plug if the water heater is a Suburban).
7. Turn on the water pump and open every faucet in the RV, including exterior faucets or showerheads.
8. Allow the solution to pump through the system to the toilet, through the water heater and to every hot and cold faucet at each sink until the distinct odor of the chlorine is present at every fixture.
9. At the city water inlet, using the eraser end of a pencil, push in on the check valve spring allowing the solution to pump out through the city water inlet until the chlorine odor is detected in the discharge.
10. Close all the faucets and turn off the water pump.
11. Allow the system to stand for four hours. This will chlorinate and disinfect the system, including the fresh water tank, the water heater, the faucets, the complete piping system and all fittings to a residual level of 50 ppm (parts per million).
12. At four hours, drain and flush the system once again and top off the water tank with fresh water.

If 100 ppm residual concentration is required or desired, use 1/2-cup of bleach instead of 1/4-cup with each gallon of the solution and let it stand for at least one to two hours. Do not allow the chlorinated solution to sit longer than four hours in the fresh water system to avoid damage to some delicate plumbing components found in some water pumps. If the odor of the chlorine is still too strong for your tastes, drain, flush and refill the tank until you are satisfied.

This process should be performed after any period of nonuse, such as during the spring shakedown after storage, or whenever stale or distasteful water is experienced.

Cleaning/Replacing the Filter/Strainer

Most fresh water systems will usually have one filter/strainer located between the fresh water tank and the water pump. At least once a year, clean or replace the filter element or screen. This filter protects the demand pump from debris that may be inadvertently induced into the fresh tank. Plastic chips from drilling during the manufacturing process may have fallen inside the tank also. This filter can save repair dollars and more importantly, downtime, by simply keeping it clean.

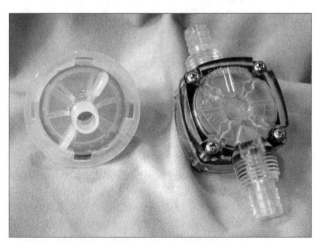

Fig. 6-23; Fresh water pump strainers

Fresh Water System Repairs

Modern fresh water plumbing systems have endured many changes over the years and have evolved into one of the most durable, least problematic and easiest to work with group of

components found on RVs today. That is not to say repairs are never required, but when proper maintenance practices are employed, they are minimized.

Fresh water system damage is most likely to occur due to freeze damage (a lack of proper winterizing techniques) or by an errant staple or a misdirected mounting screw piercing a water line. The good news is that regardless of the types of damage that may occur the RV owner is more than likely capable of repairing them with relative ease. The hardest part may simply be gaining access to the piping. Prior to attacking a repair, however, the RVer must first understand the basic differences among fresh water system components. First let's explore the types of water tubing used in RVs today.

Types of Water Tubing

In years past, the most popular type of fresh water line was a semi-flexible plastic tubing called polybutylene (PB). However, developments concerning the manufacture of PB tubing have rendered this type extinct in RVs being produced today. After a rash of lawsuits, Shell Chemical Company, provider of the resin for the manufacture of PB tubing, abruptly withdrew the resin and its formula from the plumbing industry some ten years ago, effectively stopping all production of PB tubing. That led to the adaptation and integration of cross-linked polyethylene (PEX) as the main type of tubing used in RV manufacture since the new millennium.

PEX is produced by three basic methods: radiation, silane and Engel. The differences in manufacturing methods have proven the Engel method as having an advantage over the other types. One example is the tubing produced by Uponor. Their "hot" cross-linked Engel-produced tubing has an inherent property called thermal memory that permits kinked tubing to be repaired by simply heating the affected kink with a heat gun or a high-powered hair dryer.

Thermal memory allows the tubing to return to its original shape and more importantly, its original strength. This characteristic can be handy for the RVer who discovers a kinked section under a gaucho for instance, even though it goes against the common plumbing practice of

Fig. 6-24; Installed tubing on a PEX fitting

always replacing damaged tubing. Testing, however, has proven that only Engle-produced PEX has this advantage. With silane or radiation-manufactured PEX, replacement is still mandatory. Uponor's Plumb-Pex system, with its unique clamping method, allows RVers and professional service technicians an easy way to facilitate repairs and/or upgrades.

Adapter fittings are readily available for RVers splicing PEX tubing into a system previously plumbed with PB. Adapters are necessary since internal PB and PEX fittings are not compatible. The wall dimensions are thicker on PEX even though the outside diameter of the tubing is the same.

In previous years, other types of water lines besides PB have appeared in RVs. Some still are seen today even though cross-linked PEX is found in much greater numbers. Other types used include:

- Copper tubing
- PVC
- CPVC
- Flexible vinyl hose

Copper tubing connections must be either flared connections or "sweat" connections (those that are soldered with a portable propane torch). Brass compression fitting connections should be avoided for fresh water plumbing use.

PVC and CPVC are cemented, semi-rigid plastic pipes that some manufacturers also use. Exactly the same as a typical home sprinkler system,

PVC can only be used for cold water lines, while CPVC is permissible for either hot or cold lines. A flexible hose-type water line is permissible, as mentioned above, between the water tank and the pump, and sometimes it is used on the outlet or pressure side of the pump, but only for the first eighteen inches so a connection can be made to the rest of the system. This is common if semi-rigid plastic piping is used throughout the system. Pump vibration could possibly lead to a cracked fitting if a solid connection were to be made between the pump and the system. Any flexible hose utilized must be approved for RV use. This includes the hose used for the city water hookup in the campground.

Flexible hoses are also utilized between the faucet and the shower head in the bathroom. You will also find them in slideout rooms that contain fresh water plumbing and with some washer/dryer installations.

Definitions of Fittings

When purchasing or referring to the various kinds of fittings available, it is important to know the correct nomenclature for each. Even professional RV technicians become confused while pondering the different kinds of fittings and just what they should be called. Invariably, the wrong type is purchased on that first trip to the hardware store only because you thought you needed a coupling when you really needed a union. Here's a quick glossary of a few common fittings that should keep the differences clear in your mind.

Fitting Descriptions
- <u>Union</u>: Two like male ends. The sizes may differ, but each end is the same type.
- <u>Coupling</u>: Two like female ends, with each end the same type.
- <u>Elbow</u>: Usually 45 or 90 degrees. A variation is called a "street ell." This type has one female end and one male end of the same type.
- <u>Adapter</u>: Always connects two different types of pipe or tubing.
- <u>Nipple</u>: Two like male ends of threaded pipe. Similar to a union but available in varying lengths.
- <u>Tee</u>: A connection for three separate lines. They could all be alike or one or more may be a different type. The "branch" is always at a 90-degree angle to the "run."

- Cross: Similar to the tee but has four separate branches.
- Wye: A connection for three individual lines similar to a tee, but the "branch" portion is positioned at something other than a 90-degree angle.
- Bushing: Male end reduced to an always smaller female end. Usually bushings are threaded but also may have a slip connection.
- Plug: Male end method to terminate a fitting.
- Cap: Female end method to terminate a line or pipe.
- Nut: Female threaded fitting used as a method of attachment, e.g., flare nut or compression nut. An exception would be an inverted flare nut, common to the LP system, which consists of male threads instead of female threads.

Sealants

When using sealants such as pipe dope or Teflon tape on fresh water system fittings, be sure it is approved for such use. Some sealants may be harmful if ingested. Check the label before purchasing. It must be suitable for fresh water systems.

Never use pipe sealants or tape on flare fittings or any plastic-to-plastic connection in the fresh water plumbing system. Sealants may be used on barbed fittings or threaded fittings other than those in the fresh water system.

Common Piping Problems

If fittings are knocked loose or broken, they will have to be replaced. If a puncture occurs anywhere in a length of tubing, cut the tubing at

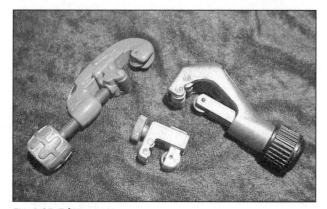

Fig. 6-25; Tubing cutters

that point and install a simple union or coupling. If damage occurs to a length of tubing, the entire length will have to be replaced, but Engle-produced PEX lines, remember, can be repaired if crushed or kinked.

To cut copper tubing, a special tubing cutter will be necessary. Three different types are pictured here. Additionally, be sure to de-burr the inside and outside of the tubing prior to attaching the fitting. Burrs left on the end of the tubing may cause an improper flare that could result in a leak.

PB and PEX tubing can be cut with a special scissors-like tubing cutter or with a common razor knife. All cut ends should be square with the tubing. It is not necessary to ream PB or PEX tubing after cutting. Tube cutting tools are readily available at local hardware stores.

If rigid piping is used such as PVC or CPVC be sure to carefully follow the directions on the can of cement for those types of plastic pipes. For best results when cementing plastic pipe to a fitting apply a liberal amount of cement to the fitting and to the pipe itself. Insert the pipe fully into the fitting with a quarter-turn twisting motion.

When replacing cemented fittings and subsequent piping, precut the pieces and dry fit them before cementing. If the alignment is not quite correct, changes can only be made before cementing. PVC and CPVC fittings cannot be reused.

Rigid plastic water lines are more prone to freeze damage than the more flexible PB and cross-linked PEX. If your coach has rigid lines, and you live in the colder climates, proper winterizing procedures are mandatory. Be sure to study the winterizing chapter carefully.

With proper care, frequent inspections and diligent use, the modern RV fresh water plumbing system should provide many years of quality service.

Waste Systems

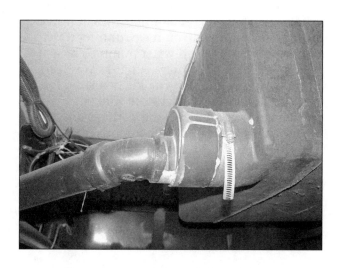

Overview

As distasteful as some might proclaim waste systems to be, waste systems on RVs are a necessity in order to be truly self-contained. In reality, the simplicity of waste systems usually means not many problems actually arise — as long as a little preventive maintenance and care is employed, that is. As with any major system within the RV, a certain amount of attention and proactive prevention at varying intervals can help in minimizing any unpleasantness or downtime that takes away from the direct enjoyment of the RV.

Health Issues

Always take precautions when working on the RV waste plumbing systems; even when simply evacuating the holding tanks. Always wear disposable gloves when handling sewer hoses and connections. Many RVers have added a glove dispenser right in the waste systems compartment as a reminder.

When using tools and working on the waste systems, be sure to clean and disinfect them after each use. Those same tools may be working on the fresh water system next! A can of spray disinfectant is a handy item to carry with you as you travel. Good hygiene goes a long way. Hopefully I don't need to remind everyone to thoroughly wash your hands with plenty of soap and hot water after working on the waste systems.

Types of Systems

There are two distinct types of RV waste systems: the "gray" water system and the "black" water system. The gray water system is typically the liquid waste from the kitchen sink, the lavatory sink, the shower or tub and perhaps a washer/dryer drain.

The black water system is the solid waste associated primarily with the toilet. The black and gray systems should not be interconnected, that is, they must each have a dedicated method of storing the waste (holding tanks), and each

must have its own waste termination valve (dump valve). There are, however, a few exceptions to this rule. For instance, in some cases it is permissible to have one other fixture drain into the black water tank. For all practical purposes, however, and also for the ease of understanding, the two systems should remain separate.

Gray Water System

The gray water system in an RV will be quite similar to what you are familiar with at home. Turn a faucet on and you have running water either via the on-board water pump or by a hose-connected city water source, as you learned in the previous chapter. The kitchen sink, the bathtub or shower, the lavatory sink, a washer/dryer connection and perhaps an exterior shower head are all comprised of easily identifiable components. On larger fifth-wheel travel trailers or large motorhomes the shower and lavatory drains may have a dedicated holding tank separate from the kitchen galley sink and/or the washer/dryer connection. Still, everything other than the toilet waste is considered gray water.

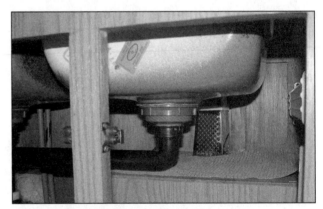

Fig. 7-1; Under-cabinet view of a RV sink drain

The sink drains, P traps, vents and drain pipes are similar to what you would find in a residential home and are important components of the gray water system. All are made of acrylonitrile-butadiene-styrene (ABS) plastic and are quite easily maintained. It is important, however, to know exactly where drain lines are situated throughout the RV.

All P traps must be removable for cleaning; none will be cemented in place and all are

Fig. 7-2; Typical P trap

situated directly under the sink or tub/shower or behind the washer/dryer. Those under the tub or shower enclosure may have to be accessed from behind a removable panel or from inside a below-the-floor compartment. Maintenance is identical on RV P traps to those found in a residential home; remove and clean them once a year. Care must be taken when stowing camping gear and personal items around drain pipes and P traps. Fig. 7-3 shows how not to stow your pots and pans. Yes, somewhere in there is a P trap. Such items bouncing around under the sink could damage drain lines.

The sizing of the plumbing lines and pipes may vary from RV to RV though all must comply with NFPA 1192, Standard for Recreational Vehicles. The drain piping in the gray waste system from each of the sinks to the gray water holding tank typically range from 1-1/4 to 2-

Fig. 7-3; P traps should be free of clutter

inches in diameter depending on the overall size of the plumbing system. The tank outlet from the gray water tank to the termination assembly can be from 1-1/2 to 3-inches in diameter. All vents from each tank must be at least 1-1/2 inches in diameter. Periodically check the positioning of the vent pipe under the roof vent cap. Additionally, realize that constant exposure to the elements will eventually deteriorate plastic plumbing vent caps.

All waste piping should flow gradually downhill from each fixture to the holding tank. Supports are required every four feet in order for the piping to maintain this downward slant. When replacing horizontal sections of ABS drain piping, be sure to keep the proper slope in mind; a minimum of 1/8-inch per foot.

Black Water System
All waste introduced into the system through the RV toilet is considered the black water system. Additionally, as previously mentioned, maybe another fixture will also drain into the black water holding tank. We'll take a closer look at RV toilets a little later in this chapter.

Waste Systems Venting
The importance of venting, for both the gray and the black systems, cannot be overstated. Without proper venting, fixtures will not drain properly, odors can propagate and the holding tanks will not drain quickly or properly.

As any tank empties, air must enter the container which enables the contents to flow freely and quickly. Remember, RV holding tanks rely solely on gravity for emptying; the same for fixtures. Additionally, stored waste in the holding tanks creates a biological wonderland with bio-action going on non-stop. Odors are a natural by-product and as such, must be vented to the atmosphere. Most plumbing vents allow air into and out of the waste tanks, thereby allowing faster and easier evacuations and draining. There are two types of vents used in RV waste systems: direct exterior vents and anti-siphon trap vent devices (ASTVDs).

Direct Vents
Direct vents connect the waste systems (either within the drain piping or in the tank) to the

Fig. 7-4; Common roof sewer vent cap

atmosphere outside. It is a vertical section of ABS piping that protrudes from the piping system or the holding tank up and through the roof of the RV; simply a common, open-ended pipe usually covered by a roof vent cap.

Another type of direct vent is the side vent. Side venting is only permissible in the liquid waste system, (typically a single fixture), which must also be equipped with a specialty fitting called a diverter tee. The diverter tee is partitioned internally so that air is vented at the same time water is draining. As the water goes downhill, the air travels uphill.

Through-the-side venting is common to smaller RVs such as pickup campers and folding camping trailers. By far, the most common and most effective waste system direct vent, however, is the one that goes through the roof.

Anti-Siphon Trap Vent Devices (ASTVD)
Another type of vent is the anti-siphon trap vent. These handy devices are used as a secondary vent to aid in draining fixtures. They are not to be considered a replacement for a direct vent, however. These devices are a type of "check vent" whereby air is allowed into the system (to aid in draining a sink full of water, for example), but not allowing air to pass out of the system. You'll find an ASTVD installed in the liquid drain

Fig. 7-5; Anti-siphon trap vent device

piping system, usually at or near a P trap inside a cabinet. They should be mounted at least 6-inches above the P trap horizontal arm. ASTVDs do not allow odors to escape into the living portion of the RV because of an integral atmospheric pressure-controlled, one-way valve. Air in, but not out.

In addition to individual ASTVDs used in the liquid waste drainage system, there still must be at least one vent protruding through the roof to allow sewer gases out of the tank. The better designed waste systems will have ASTVDs installed at every P trap as well as a direct vent running from each holding tank up and through the roof.

RV Toilets
We want our travels to be as trouble-free as possible, knowing all along that just by virtue of having a house on wheels bouncing along the highway things are going to happen. We really do not mind washing the coach, repairing a small window leak or even performing a lengthy winterizing procedure. Shoot, we do not even mind taking out the garbage every day. But please! Let's not have any malfunction with the toilet!

Having an understanding of the different types of toilets, along with basic knowledge of maintenance procedures, can prevent inconveniences with relative ease. Each RV toilet has individual characteristics and varying applications. The four types are:

- Recirculating toilet
- Portable toilet
- Marine toilet
- Vacuum Flush

Recirculating Toilet
Totally self-contained, recirculating toilets do not require a holding tank or a fresh water supply, although some can be plumbed into the fresh system for ease in filling or "charging." This type is commonly found in smaller travel trailers, folding camping trailers and pickup campers where design limitations prohibit the placement of a holding tank. The predominant benefit of having a recirculating toilet is that no holding tank is necessary.

This type of toilet is "charged" with its own supply of specifically treated water that circulates again and again to flush the contents from the bowl. Only the treated liquid is recirculated. A filtering device inside the main housing traps the solid waste. Recirculation is typically facilitated by a 12-volt direct current (DC) motor attached to an internal submerged pump. A timer mechanism regulates each flush cycle.

The waste is held in an internal reservoir until full, and then the unit is flushed through a typical floor flange and flexible sewer hose into either the campground sewer connection or a standard dump station. A full-flow slide valve is usually an integral component of the recirculating toilet. Additionally, a standard three-inch termination valve will be attached to the dump assembly on the exterior of the RV.

To dump a recirculating toilet, attach the flexible sewer hose to the campground sewer and to the dump assembly on the RV. Open the RV dump valve. Next, inside the coach, open the slide valve on the toilet. It is recommended to pour additional fresh water through the toilet to rinse out the drain piping and the flexible sewer hose before closing the valves. Repair kits and spare parts are available for each of the models currently on the market.

Portable Toilet

Smaller trailers and van campers may come equipped with a portable toilet. A common design has two compartments: a fresh water

Fig. 7-6; Portable RV toilet

storage tank and a separate holding tank. A hand-operated bellows pumps fresh water from the tank into the bowl and rinses the waste (some may be battery operated as well). A foot pedal then operates the flushing mechanism to dump the bowl contents into the lower compartment. When the lower holding tank is in need of evacuating, it can be easily removed and carried to the dump station. While in the RV, the toilet is attached to the floor with quick release brackets for ease of removal when dumping is necessary. As with any RV toilet, it is wise to rinse and flush the bowl and the flushing mechanism thoroughly after each evacuation at the dump station.

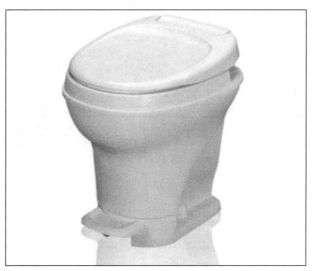

Fig. 7-7; RV marine toilet

Marine Toilet

By far the most common type of toilet in today's RV is the marine toilet. It is permanently mounted and plumbed into the fresh water piping system. Most are gravity-flushed by operating a mechanical seal that typically opens the drain and turns the water on at the same time.

The marine toilet requires a holding tank. The toilet is simply bolted to the floor flange and connected through the floor to the tank below. Marine toilets are compact and fit well into the varying RV floorplans. They are constructed without the typical back tank found on most common household toilets. Water enters the bowl directly from the fresh water system. The swirling motion of the incoming water rinses and flushes the toilet into the holding tank.

All marine toilets have a positive water seal to prevent holding tank odors from entering the coach. As an RV owner, it is important to check this water seal daily. Doing so will pinpoint potential problem areas before they actually develop. Always make sure a small amount of water actually stays in the bowl after the flushing cycle has completed. Fig. 7-8 shows the seal that keeps water in the bowl on the popular Thetford Aqua Magic.

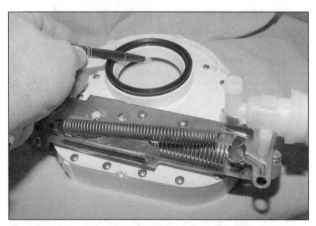

Fig. 7-8; Toilet water seal mechanism

The common RV marine toilets utilize an internal vacuum breaker, which is basically a back-flow device. Without the breaker, water being drawn at a distant galley sink, for instance, could theoretically create a partial vacuum that may cause water to be siphoned from the toilet. The vacuum breaker serves as a one-way check valve of sorts.

Fig. 7-9; Standard toilet floor flange

Fig. 7-10; Toilet flange gasket

All marine toilets mount to a standard floor flange that is secured to the RV floor. A toilet-to-flange seal or gasket is required in all instances. Additionally, all rough-in dimensions are virtually the same, which means the RVer can upgrade or otherwise replace toilets at any time. The only consideration would be the base design and the position of the flange closet bolts. Not all marine toilets have the same pedestal or base construction, so flooring, carpeting, tile or linoleum cut-outs may not match.

Fig. 7-11; Vacuum flush toilet

Vacuum Flush Toilets

One of the newest design innovations in RV waste technology is the emergence of the vacuum flush toilet. Though accurately described as a marine toilet, it is quite unique in its design. This new toilet system consists of the toilet, a vacuum pump and a reservoir tank. A vacuum exists at all times within the system. When flushed, (by foot pedal or electronic push-button control), the stored vacuum is released and the toilet bowl is instantly cleared. The waste along with very little water is forced through the pump and into the holding tank at about 7-feet per second. And because of the vacuum system, the toilet does not have to be positioned directly over a holding tank. Once flushed, the vacuum pump starts and builds up the vacuum level once again, thereby recharging the system. As with most marine toilets, additional water can be introduced into the bowl before or after flushing by lifting up on the foot pedal.

Vacuum operated toilets are available in all ceramic or a combination of ceramic bowl with a plastic base assembly. The advantages to this new vacuum system are many, including possible aftermarket upgrades to existing systems. If you're a serious RVer, it may be a good idea to check one out at your next RV show.

User Maintenance

Common sense is important when using any of the different types of RV toilets. Never flush solid objects down the toilet. Do not flush cigarette butts or gum wrappers, etc. Use only biodegradable toilet tissue.

Two types of base-to-flange seals are available for permanently-mounted RV toilets: rubber and wax. It is wise to carry a spare seal. Rubber seals (Fig. 7-10) have the advantage because they are not drastically affected by heat. If travel is predominantly in the Sun Belt areas, a loosening of the toilet may occur during the hot summer months.

Regarding wax seals, ambient or radiated heat can actually melt a wax seal. In effect, as the seal collapses, it appears the toilet mounting bolts have loosened and the toilet wobbles on its base. It will be necessary to tighten the bolts periodically should the toilet be equipped with a wax seal. Wax seals can also be quite messy when doing repairs on some specific models of toilets. The rubber seal, on the other hand, is spongier and is not as affected by hot weather. Regardless of which seal is preferred, always replace the seal each time the toilet is removed from the floor flange.

Recirculating and portable toilets will require a treatment for odor control and solid waste breakdown. Do not use formaldehyde- or alcohol-based substances. Recirculating toilets especially need a method of odor control since there is no vapor barrier or positive water seal between the stored waste and the interior of the RV in most cases. Familiarize yourself with the specific maintenance tasks associated with recirculating and portable toilets as directed by the manufacturer supplier. Because of the design

and operating characteristics of the vacuum flush toilet there is no need for odor control additives.

When cleaning the toilet during the camping season, avoid using abrasive cleansers. RV toilets are constructed of either ABS plastic, ceramic or china, so choose the cleanser that is friendly to the construction material of the toilet. Remember, most RV toilets have rubber or Teflon seals, so care must be taken not to introduce harmful cleaning agents that will damage the seals.

Troubleshooting and Repair

Yearly maintenance can eliminate or at least minimize certain repairs. However, when repetitive mechanical movement of parts takes place, a certain amount of wear begins. This continues until a component fatigues and a repair is in order.

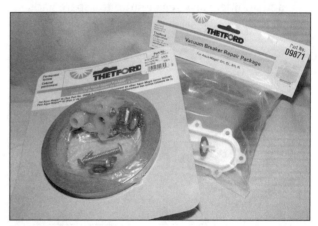

Fig. 7-12; Toilet repair kits

The most common RV toilet, the marine-type, is relatively free from operational troubles. However, without a few maintenance procedures problems can still develop. Not unlike the RV demand water pump, most toilet makers have individual replacement parts and repair kits that are readily available at most RV parts and accessory stores. As a general rule, all repair kits come with well-written instructions along with all the parts needed for a replacement task. The only job you really have to do is troubleshoot the symptoms correctly. First, let's look at the basic components of the RV marine toilet.

Marine Toilet Components

Although toilet design and component construction materials may differ among the various manufacturers, the same basic components are found in each. They are:

- Water inlet valve
- Vacuum breaker assembly
- Flushing mechanism
- Flange attachment

Water Inlet Valve

This is the fresh water connection point at the rear of the toilet. On some Thetford models it is also called a ball valve because the valve-closing device is actually a small steel ball with a hole machined through which rotates in a plastic housing. Since this device could corrode or simply wear out over a period of time, it might be a wise decision for full-timers and dry campers to add an inlet valve repair kit to the spare parts inventory.

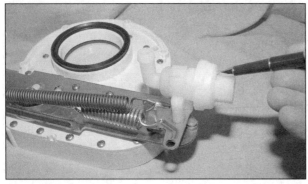

Fig. 7-13; Water inlet valve

Vacuum Breaker Assembly

The vacuum breaker prevents water from being siphoned out of the toilet bowl due to a pressure drop caused by water being used somewhere else in the fresh water system. Vacuum breakers contain a float assembly, a seat and an assortment of seals. Some are repairable, while others must be replaced. Check with the manufacturer of your toilet to determine the availability of a repair kit for the vacuum breaker.

Flushing Mechanism

Flushing mechanism designs differ, but the two most popular include Thetford's flat-blade slide mechanism and SeaLand's half-round flush ball

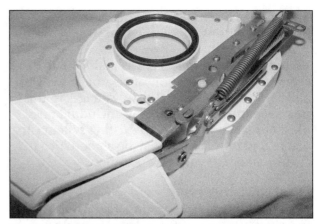

Fig. 7-14; Toilet flushing mechanism

with a Teflon seal. Both are initiated by activating a foot pedal. Foot pedal flushing on these common units also automatically opens the water inlet valve and allows fresh water to enter and circulate in the bowl as it flushes the contents into the holding tank.

Both Thetford (www.thetford.com) and SeaLand have made it possible to add more water to the bowl after the flush, if desired. Thetford's popular units including the Aurora model, have a separate foot pedal that opens the ball valve only, allowing more water to enter the bowl. By lifting up on SeaLand's foot pedal instead of pressing down, the water inlet valve is opened and likewise, water fills into the bowl. Typically, the flushing mechanism and the water inlet valve will account for the majority of user complaints with marine toilets.

Flange Attachment

All toilets attach to a standard floor flange, which is secured to the floor of the RV. Attached to the floor flange are two or four closet bolts that secure the toilet to the flange. A gasket is positioned between the flange and the base of the toilet.

The position of the closet bolts will vary between brand and even model of the same manufacturer. A popular model by Thetford uses two bolts located at the five and eleven o'clock positions on the floor flange. Other Thetford models have bolts positioned at three and nine o'clock. SeaLand, meanwhile, uses four mounting bolts, two in the front and two at the rear of the flange.

Common Complaints

Problems associated with the marine toilet are few, but over time, they do crop up. The most common complaints will center on these issues:

- Water leaks
- Excessive odor
- Water continues to run
- Flushing mechanism sticks

Water Leaks

There are four reasons why water may be leaking at or near a marine toilet. By checking where the water is coming from and exactly when the water appears, RVers can pinpoint which of the four main causes is the culprit.

If water drips to the floor from the upper portion of the toilet during only the flushing cycle, the problem is most likely the vacuum breaker. Usually a float seal is not sealing properly. On some units, the float can be disassembled and cleaned. Other models will require a repair kit. Still others may require a completely new vacuum breaker. To make sure, check the user's manual.

If water leaks onto the floor after the flush cycle has completed, or without flushing the toilet at all, the culprit is the water inlet valve.

Sometimes water will appear to be leaking only if the bowl is filled to capacity. There is a slight possibility the bowl is cracked at a point above the normal water level. This is not a very common situation, but it does happen occasionally and is usually caused by improper winterizing techniques. This is only possible with toilets made with plastic bowls.

Water may also be noticed around the base of the toilet with no apparent or visible dripping from above. Chances are the seal between the flange and the base assembly is faulty. Remove the toilet and replace the flange gasket.

Excessive Odor

Odor coming from the holding tank directly below the toilet is usually a sign there is not enough residual water left in the bowl after a flush cycle, or that the water has leaked past the flushing mechanism and into the holding tank.

This water seal is crucial for keeping the tank odors from permeating the interior of the RV. This situation is caused, in most cases, by foreign matter becoming trapped in the groove for the slide blade on Thetford's Aqua Magic units. On SeaLand's unit, a typical cause is a worn seal or a clamp ring (on some models) that is too loose.

On the Aqua Magic, fashion a hook out of a coat hanger or a bent screwdriver that will reach into the groove to scrape out the residue. Take special care not to damage the seal. In severe cases it will be necessary to remove and disassemble the complete flushing mechanism to remove the debris which can be substantial in some neglected situations.

To rectify the situation on the SeaLand toilet, simply tighten the clamp ring. In some cases, a complete seal kit may have to be installed in either brand if water still continues to seep past the seal and into the holding tank. It is imperative that some water stay in the bowl at all times.

Water Continues to Run

The predominant cause of this situation is a stubborn slide valve that keeps the water inlet valve open. In some cases, the water inlet valve itself may be faulty, allowing water to continually enter the bowl. If the water that continues to run does not stay in the bowl but flows on through to the holding tank, the problem is usually a slide valve or flush ball that is held partially open. It is either stuck or is kept open by foreign matter wedged between the seal and the half ball or the slide. If it is obvious the slide mechanism or half ball is fully shut yet water simply continues to enter the bowl, chances are the cause is a faulty water inlet valve.

Flushing Mechanism Sticks

If the Thetford toilet is mounted too tightly to the floor flange, the base of the mechanism becomes distorted and the blade will not slide smoothly in the housing. Loosening the closet bolts and lubricating the slide blade will usually eradicate this symptom.

Occasionally, abrasive cleaners can accumulate as deposits inside the slide mechanism impeding the movement of the blade. In this instance, a complete removal and cleaning is in order.

Again, be sure to liberally lubricate all slide blade components.

As previously mentioned, many repair kits and replacement parts are readily available for all RV toilets. Parts that are not available in kit form can be ordered through any RV parts and accessory store or directly from the toilet manufacturer.

Holding Tanks

All waste, liquid and solid eventually reach one of the on-board holding tanks. Holding tanks are usually constructed of either ABS or polyethylene plastic. Polypropylene, fiberglass and metal have also been used in the manufacture of holding tanks in years past. Today's plastic tanks, however, have proven to be extremely durable.

Location of Tanks

Many holding tanks are mounted below floor level. Some tanks are sandwiched between the upper floor and a subfloor; still others may be located between the floor and a belly pan on those units with sealed bottoms. Others may be placed in a large storage bay. Some may be mounted in a midlevel storage area of a large fifth-wheel travel trailer. The coach construction and the layout of the floorplan are two determining factors as to where the holding tanks are actually placed. The black tank, however, is usually positioned directly under the toilet. Some floorplans mandate the use of 45-degree elbows from the toilet to the holding tank when such an off-set is dictated by the floorplan or the presence of structural members. Since gravity is the method of draining, high marks are given to those coaches with a straight drop from the toilet into the holding tank. Decidedly less blockage problems exist with straight drop connections.

All holding tanks, however, must be removable. That is, other components such as floors, subfloors, undercarriage trailer hitch receiver or any aftermarket add-on device must permit the removal of the holding tanks for repair or replacement. A fairly common occurrence in years past was to find a damaged holding tank

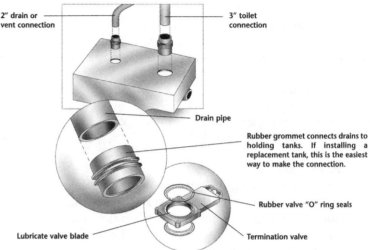

Fig. 7-15; Holding tank connectors

that needed to be removed only to find out some unknowing installer welded a permanent hitch receiver directly below the tank prohibiting its removal. Thankfully, this is not usually the case today.

Not all RVs have both gray and black water holding tanks. Some small camping trailers and slide-in truck campers may not be equipped with a gray water tank. The gray water may terminate through the side of the coach and be connected to a sewer drain connection prior to being used, or the waste is collected in a portable container and then manually emptied. Additionally, some small RVs do not have a black holding tank. They may be equipped with a recirculating-type toilet that is evacuated periodically through a three-inch outlet connected directly into the campground sewer connection.

Size of Tanks

The size of each holding tank will vary from manufacturer to manufacturer. Often a tank's size is dictated by the space that is available, the capacity of the fresh water storage tank and the design of the floorplan. Obviously, the larger the capacity of the holding tank, the longer the intervals between evacuations. This is especially appreciated when dry camping.

Dump Outlets

The outlets from the holding tanks are usually configured into a single termination assembly comprised of one main outlet for connecting to

Fig. 7-16; Holding tank termination valves

the campground sewer and two inlets, one from each tank. Between each tank outlet and the inlet to the termination assembly are the termination valves or "dump" valves. The gray water tank termination valve must be a minimum 1-1/4-inch diameter, while the black tank must be plumbed with a 3-inch inlet and a 3-inch outlet. A flexible sewer hose with an appropriate adapter is attached to the termination assembly, connected to the campground or dump station, and the tanks are emptied.

Correct Evacuation Procedures

1. Always wear disposable protective gloves. When handling any waste system component, always wear throwaway latex or rubber gloves and be sure to wash your hands thoroughly afterwards. No need to take undue risks.

2. Connect the sewer hose to the termination outlet and the sewer inlet. You'll need to remove the sewer cap and attach the sewer hose adapter. Make sure the seals are in good shape. Inspect the seal on the cap and the adapter periodically. Seals are easily replaced so there is no excuse for having dripping hose connections.

I recommend using a clear sewer adapter at the hose connection or a clear fitting at the sewer inlet in order to check the cleanliness of the water as you flush each tank after evacuation.

Be sure you have the correct elbow adapters on hand to securely affix the bitter end (open end) of the hose into the park's sewer inlet. No leaks allowed here either! Keep in mind there is no

standard size sewer inlet mandated for RV parks or dump sites; you'll find everything from 3-inch to 4-inch to even 5-inch or larger inlets. Be prepared! Do not just simply stick the open end of the hose down the sewer inlet allowing tank odors and park septic odors to escape.

Also, use the shortest sewer hose as possible. Do not use that 20-footer for a 6-foot run and have it snake back and forth between the coach and the sewer inlet. And be sure to maintain the proper slope of the drain hose. Remember water and waste cannot flow uphill!

3. Only evacuate a holding tank (black or gray) when it is over 3/4 full. Yes, this means not leaving the gray valve open while in the campground – the total opposite of what we've been taught for years. Filling each tank above the 3/4 mark before evacuating will ensure you'll have enough volume (and velocity) to thoroughly drain that tank and flush the hose at the same time. A slow flow of a small amount of water will not gather much steam or be able to rinse away any stubborn deposits in either holding tank.

Here's another reason for keeping the gray holding tank valve completely closed except while evacuating – ever walk through a beautiful, scenic campground and catch a whiff of sewer odor wafting through the park? Kind of ruins the moment, huh? All those coaches with the gray tank valve in the open position (sewer hoses obviously connected), are simply acting as a direct conduit to the park's sewer system. Each coach becomes a mini-vent system for the septic system of that campground. No wonder sewer

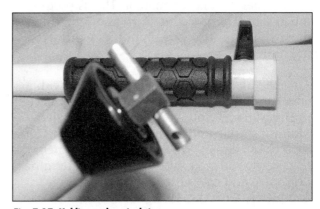

Fig. 7-17; Holding tank swivel rinser

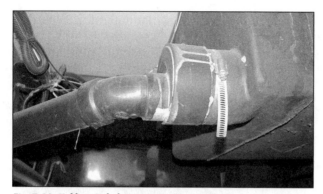

Fig. 7-18; Holding tank drain connection, gray water

odors still abound in the nicest of destination locations!

Follow the logic; a large septic tank or waste management system in a campground will have intrinsic venting designed into it for sure, but with numerous motorhomes and travel trailers connected to that system with their gray tank valves open, odors rise up through the septic system, through the sewer hoses of those RVs, through the empty gray holding tanks and up the vents of those holding tanks. Remember, it may be your gray tank, but it's the campground's black and gray odors coming up and through! The only problem with this scenario is that the gray tank vents on the RVs are a lot closer to the ground than the park's own sewer vent so odors are more noticeable. But by keeping the gray tank valve closed until the tank is almost full you will eliminate the localized (at your site) venting of the park's sewer gasses. The more people who follow suit, the less likely we'll have to endure septic odors in and around the campsite.

4. Evacuate the black tank first. This is pretty much standard procedure now and something most all RVers are aware of, but it's worthy to mention it again.

After the black tank empties flush it out with a large amount of fresh water if you are connected to city water. Simply keep flushing the toilet. Monitor the cleanliness of the water through the clear hose adapter. When the draining water is relatively clear, stop flushing, close the termination valve and cover the bottom of the tank completely with fresh water.

Permanently installed holding tank spray kits are available that attach to each holding tank thereby allowing fresh water to be directly induced into the tank after dumping, but I'm hesitant to drill mounting holes into holding tanks. Plus I like to flush all components of the waste system including the toilet, sink drains, etc., so I prefer to simply flush the toilet and run water in the sinks.

5. Evacuate the gray tank last. After the black tank has completely emptied and the termination valve is closed, open the gray water valve and empty that holding tank. Be sure to rinse this tank as well and cover the complete bottom of the tank with fresh water afterward. Dumping the gray tank last utilizes its liquid contents as well as the fresh water added after dumping to help clean any solid waste that may remain in the sewer hose.

6. Drain the sewer hose. After both tanks have been emptied for the last time at that location, take the time to "milk the hose." Raise the hose at the closest point near the termination outlet on the RV and walk it towards the sewer inlet. Keep raising the hose as you walk, thereby "milking" the hose and emptying it completely of water and waste. Even a properly sloped flexible sewer hose will have residual water and waste particles left inside. These particles will become an odor generator over time, so it's imperative in an open system, (one without a positive shut-off valve at the sewer inlet), to completely remove as much moisture as possible.

Fig. 7-19; An aftermarket electric valve

7. Check the "P" traps. Every month or so, look down each sink drain and the tub/shower drain to ensure the water seal is still there. You'll probably have to use a flashlight, but it is crucial that a water lock remains at all times. This is the principle method of preventing gray holding tank odors from entering the interior of the RV. In some waste system designs, a quickly draining tank can cause that water lock to be siphoned out of the trap. Remember, a dry "P" trap is nothing more than a shortcut for odors to gain entry into your RV.

8. Be sure the toilet bowl contains water at all times. An empty toilet bowl will allow black tank odors into the RV. If water can leak past the seal, vapors can also!

As mentioned earlier, many RV makers choose to install gray water holding tanks with only a 1-1/2- or 2-inch drain outlet. Even though the tank outlet in the photo to the right is a 3-inch outlet, the tank drain line has been reduced to 1-1/2 inches. This practice can actually contribute to the proliferation of gray tank odors and false monitor panel readings. It is my opinion it would benefit every segment of the RV industry if manufacturers choose instead to use only 3-inch outlets on both gray and black holding tanks. RVers would benefit by realizing a quicker exit flow rate during dumping. Tests have proven that faster dumping sequences will increase the flushing action resulting in all waste, residue and sludge being quickly washed away rather than having them slowly recede down the tank walls and trickle through a 1-1/2-inch opening. Thankfully, some RV manufacturers have now adopted this as common practice.

One company has even taken this line of reasoning yet further. Phase Four Industries (www.phasefourindustries.com) has developed a complete RV waste evacuation system by incorporating its unique electric termination valve, the Drain Master, on both holding tanks. With this concept, both tanks are constructed with three-inch outlets and each is equipped with an electric Drain Master located very near the outlet of each tank. Both tank outlets can be quickly brought to a termination assembly and then a single three-inch drain pipe routed to a side or rear connection point.

Odor Control

Previously, it was common practice to simply mask the odors in the holding tanks and to combat the consolidation of the solid waste by using strong chemicals. In some cases, it seemed these chemicals were more obtrusive than the odor from the waste.

Many different chemicals were formulated to aid in the dual task of masking the odor and breaking down the solids. For many years, formaldehyde-based chemicals seemed to work the best. However, as technology progressed and the dangers of formaldehyde poisoning came to be understood, other options became a reality. Today, formaldehyde- and other alcohol-based chemicals are no longer recommended for use in either holding tank. Many RV campgrounds and state parks, in fact, now prohibit the dumping of formaldehyde-laced holding tanks into their waste systems.

Be aware that tank odors are not exclusive to the black water holding tank. Oils, soaps and other residue co-mingling and fermenting in the gray tank can also produce their own olfactory objections. This is especially true when old habits have us leave the gray termination valve open while connected in the campsite. Gray tank matter will adhere to the walls of the tank and quickly dry out, leaving us to the mercy of nature's own method for biodegradation, which is smelly at best.

Fig. 7-20; Xtreme Vent

Aftermarket products such as the Xtreme Vent produced by Coil n' Wrap, (www.coilnwrap.com), can provide further remedy to the odor issue. This unique roof vent operates around the Venturi Effect which, in simple terms, states that as air is passed through the vent, it decreases the static atmospheric pressure inside the holding tank and literally draws vapors and subsequent odors out of the tank through the vent pipe.

The vent rotates 360-degrees and is made of heavy duty metal as opposed to plastic. The pivoting action is very smooth and it captures even the slightest wind. A 1-MPH breeze entering the vent opening creates 4-MPH air movement inside the vent pipe. The air moving through the vent actually sucks odors and vapors out of each holding tank. The faster the incoming air, the quicker vapors are drawn out of the holding tank. Installation is very simple; any handyman can replace an existing sewer vent with an Xtreme Vent.

Another added benefit is that the lowered static pressure creates on oxygen rich environment inside the holding tank, thereby maximizing the efforts of the natural (or added) enzymes breaking down the solids and tissues faster.

Treating the Tanks
The safest way to protect and treat the holding tanks and to minimize odors is to use a non-chemical, enzyme-based product, preferably one that contains live bacteria. The live bacteria actually digest the odor-causing molecules and break down the solid waste quickly.

TriSynergy (www.trisyn.com) has a product called RM Tank Care that has met with success in breaking down solid wastes and eliminating odors. There are many suppliers who also have produced an additive that contains no formaldehyde. Thetford Corporation has a complete line of products specifically designed for both gray and black holding tanks. Carefully read the product label before purchasing any additive for the waste system.

To effectively treat both holding tanks, add four or five ounces of RM Tank Care (or equivalent) to the tanks, along with enough fresh water to cover the bottom of each tank. After subsequent evacuations of each tank add another four or five ounces. This will ensure the tanks remain fresh and you are doing your part to help protect the environment.

Another process of rinsing and cleaning RV holding tanks has been perfected by All Pro Water-Flow (www.allprowaterflow.com). This process is based on hydro-jetting the tank interiors with very high water pressure. No chemicals or additives are needed to combat obnoxious odors since literally all of the odor-

causing bacteria build-up and sludge residue is totally removed during this one-hour procedure. Custom nozzles have been designed to completely flush and clean each tank with clean water pressures between 1,750psi and 6,000psi. Interestingly, the nozzle and hose remain centered inside each tank during the process so that all interior surfaces are cleaned completely. Performance is monitored by a small camera inserted into the tanks before and after the service. This process is recommended at least once per camping season.

Termination Valve Maintenance
Periodically, the dump valves, especially the black water valve, will need to be serviced. Usually dump valves are bolted in place between two adapter fittings. After draining and flushing the tanks, these bolts can be taken out and the valve removed from in between the adapter fittings.

On both sides of the dump valve are rubber seals that periodically need to be replaced. Also, occasionally waste will accumulate in the groove for the slide portion of the valve. To avoid crisis repairs while traveling, once a year, remove, disassemble, clean and lubricate both termination valves. I recommend Dow Chemical's 111 lube. This little bit of yearly maintenance will eliminate most dump valve problems encountered.

Also, during the camping season use a slide valve lubricant such as Thetford's Drain Valve Lubricant. Two to four ounces of this water-soluble additive is poured down a sink drain into the gray tank and flushed down the toilet into the black tank to lubricate the inside of the dump valve blades and to coat the inside of the

Fig. 7-21; Replacement dump valve kit

tank drain outlets to aid in complete draining and trouble-free valve operation. One of the most disagreeable RV repairs is replacing a stuck or broken dump valve with a full holding tank. RV technicians hate it and they get paid to do it. It is certainly no fun when it happens to you, miles from nowhere, in the middle of the vacation getaway. A little attention to the waste systems can avoid such scenarios.

Flexible Sewer Hoses

It pays to purchase a quality sewer hose. Avoid the temptation to obtain the cheapest vinyl hose on the market. The best ones are made from polypropylene and are a minimum 20-mil thick. Pinholes can develop quickly even in a relatively new vinyl hose. Vinyl hoses are no match for weed-wackers or other ground-keeping implements.

Interestingly, the RV must conform to rigid codes of design and construction and the RV campground dump station or sewer inlet must conform to the standards of sewer design and construction, yet the crucial link between those two is not even considered. That gray area (no pun intended), is not governed by any standard or code. Both entities, the RV manufacturer and the campground, leave that totally up to the discretion of the user. And quite frankly (again, no pun intended), there are some crappy sewer hoses on the market. Hopefully a new, minimum design standard will be forthcoming in the near future.

The best sewer hoses (such as Phase Four's Sewer Master), have an inherent memory. They are extendable only as far as need be. Bend graceful turns and it stays in place. If you only need eight feet to reach the sewer inlet, just extend it that far. There is no reason to struggle with a floppy, accordion-like vinyl hose.

Another commendable product from Phase Four is the Waste Master, a manual shut-off nozzle attached to the end of the sewer hose. Currently, most RV manufacturers do not supply a safe, clean, positive shut-off method of connecting the RV sewer hose to the sewer inlet in the campground. The Waste Master hose (available up to 25-feet in length) is permanently attached to the termination assembly.

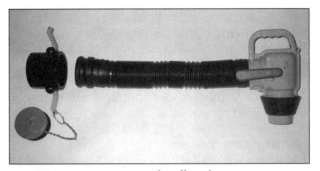

Fig. 7-22; Waste Master positive shut-off nozzle

This eliminates the need to waste copious amounts of fresh water rinsing out the hose after dumping. With a positive shut-off at the nozzle and a positive shut-off at each termination valve, there is never a mess to contend with, or odors emanating from a filthy, open-ended hose jammed into a storage compartment.

Always a point of contention with typical RV waste systems is the method of attaching the sewer hose adapter as well as the sewer cap; the dreaded bayonet fitting. This method has (sadly) been around since day one and relies on only two attaching points to compress a circular seal around the 3-inch opening. And to secure those two points, the whole assembly must be twisted against the rubber seal. Leaks and drips are inevitable as the seal becomes distorted by the twisting motion.

Thankfully there is a new method of attaching the sewer hose adapter and cap. This new method employs an industrial cam-type locking mechanism whereby the adapter (or cap) is inserted straight into the fitting without a

Fig. 7-23; Cam Loc termination attachment

twisting motion and is held firm by heavy duty, opposing cams. Currently, the Cam Loc method is only available from Phase Four. Adapters are available to modify any existing bayonet-style attachment point to the new Cam Loc method. A welcome upgrade for any serious RVer.

Holding Tank Repair

Today, virtually all RV holding tanks are made from thermoplastic. The two most common plastics used are ABS and polyethylene. Thermoplastics are extremely durable and they can be formed into a myriad of specific shapes to fit into most locations. They are also highly resistant to freeze damage. Additionally, thermoplastics are relatively inexpensive, and they are readily available from an abundance of suppliers.

However, many RV waste holding tanks are located underneath the coach and as such, are susceptible to road debris, tall speed bumps and most curbs. Additionally, a not-so-careful approach to steep driveways can quickly separate the RV from its waste dump assemblies leaving a pungent, telltale trail all the way to the RV.

Holding tanks do incur periodic damage such as stress cracks, broken outlets and leaky fittings that can, for the most part, be repaired by the assertive RV owner.

Repair or Replace?

This is the dilemma faced by many RVers. The fine line between these two ideals sometimes becomes difficult to discern. The predominant question when considering repair or replacement is, "To what extent is the damage?" Clearly a holding tank with major damage, large pieces missing or simply too many cracks should be replaced.

For the most part, however, many cracks and leaks in a holding tank can be repaired. This is a noteworthy option, especially when traveling. Additionally, if you have an older RV, perhaps the exact tank is no longer offered. There are many obsolete components, termed orphan parts, which are simply no longer available at any cost.

The first step in determining the damage is to completely inspect the tank. If the damage was caused by rocks or road debris, chances are the crack will be on the bottom of the tank, already exposed and easily inspected. If a collision caused a holding tank leak that appears to be coming from somewhere on top of the tank, or on the side, it may or may not be readily visible. You can try using a mirror and a flashlight to find a leak. However, to be sure, it is recommended that the tank be completely removed from the coach.

Black and gray water tanks installed underneath the coach are usually attached by similar methods. The only glaring difference is the black water tank will obviously have the toilet attached to it. All toilets attach to the tank via a 3-inch drainpipe. The gray water tank, on the other hand, will have a 2-inch pipe, as its largest possible drain entry into the tank; more typically it will be a 1-1/2-inch drain from the sinks into the top of the tank. Both tanks will typically have a vent that protrudes through the roof of the RV. Other drains and vents may attach at any location on top of either holding tank. In most cases, the holding tank will have to be removed. For typical black water tank installations, here is how:

Removing the Tanks

1. First and foremost, be sure the tank has been emptied prior to even starting to think about dropping the tank. (If the damage was substantial enough to automatically empty the tank through a large, gaping hole, order a replacement tank. With damage that significant, a repair should not even be considered.) Flush the tank with fresh water to clean it as best as possible.

2. Turn off the water pump or the city water and disconnect the water line to the toilet.

3. Locate the closet bolts and remove the toilet. After the toilet has been removed, remove the screws that hold the floor flange in place and remove the flange. Many times the flange is threaded into the top of the holding tank. Otherwise, it just slips into a rubber grommet affixed to the top of the tank.

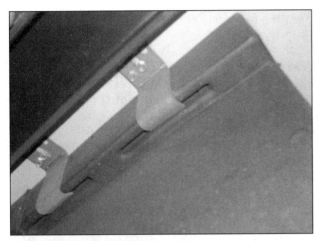

Fig. 7-24; Holding tank bracket mount

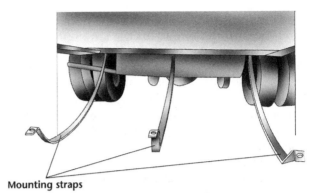

Mounting straps

Fig. 7-25; Holding tank, strap mount

4. On the roof, locate the vent for that tank. Remove the vent cover and see if the vent pipe will unscrew. Keep in mind, however, not all vents go straight from the tank to the roof. Some, called wet vents, have a drain from a sink also connected. Others may have 45-degree elbows in place, prohibiting them from turning. If the vent will not unscrew, locate the point where the vent enters the tank at or near floor level. Look inside closets, under cabinets, etc. until the ABS piping is located in an area that can be reached with a hacksaw blade. In some instances, access to the drain connection can be realized from under the coach, yet on top of the tank. The bottom line is that all drains and vents, as well as the toilet, must be removed, disconnected or severed in order to allow the tank to be dropped straight down or removed from the bay.

5. Locate and determine just how the tank is secured to the RV. Many installations utilize mounting straps or metal bands that completely support the bottom of the tank. Some may have an upper flange that is bolted or screwed to the underside of the coach. Still others may be suspended by structural supports or angle iron. Many methods are used to secure holding tanks. Some are simply secured into the basement portion of a compartment; some are just set and blocked into a storage bay. Look over the installation carefully to determine which method was used.

6. Remove any electrical wires attached to well nuts, or probes that connect the monitor panel to the tank. Be sure to mark the exact location

for any such wires and to note their respective colors. (If your tank has external, glued-on sensors, it may be necessary to order replacements if they are not salvageable).

7. Remove the dump assembly located at the outlet of the holding tank. Typically, the fitting or pipe is clamped, cemented or screwed into the outlet of the tank. If the pipe is cemented, it will be necessary to cut the pipe at a convenient location close enough to the tank outlet to have enough clearance for the tank to drop straight down. Clamped or threaded connections can be removed and reused. Many times there is only one dump outlet shared by both holding tanks; therefore, be sure both tanks are emptied in Step 1 since both dump assemblies may have to be removed.

8. Support the tank and remove the mounting screws, supports or straps, and carefully lower

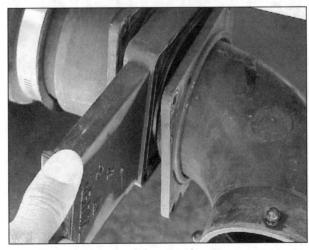

Fig. 7-26; Termination valve, bolts removed

the tank to the ground. On basement or storage bay installations, simply lift the tank out. Once removed, the tank can be closely inspected to determine the exact source of the leak or damage.

In some cases, it may be necessary to plug the outlet and fill the tank with fresh water in order to spot a small hairline crack or other hard-to-find leaks.

Some holding tank installations are better left to professional RV technicians. Those that are encased between the floors of an RV with a solid underbelly may prove too difficult for the average RVer to repair. Likewise, those that are buried in the confines of some basement model motorhomes or buses are probably a little too much to tackle. Use your own judgment.

Method of Repair

Once the crack has been located, and it is determined to indeed be repairable, choose which method should be used to make the repair. There are basically two viable options:

- Aftermarket patch kit
- Plastic welding

Aftermarket patch kits are available for today's plastic tanks, however, they work best with tanks made of ABS plastic. They will, however, perform as a satisfactory, though temporary, patch on polyethylene tanks. They can be used anywhere on an ABS tank, but are only recom-

Fig. 7-27; Plastic welding kit

mended for cracks located on the top of polyethylene tanks.

Like the fresh water tank mentioned in an earlier chapter, the only true and permanent method for repairing polyethylene holding tanks is by plastic welding. Plastic welding is also recommended for repairing ABS tanks, as well as any other type of thermoplastic, including polypropylene, polyvinyl chloride (PVC) and Plexiglas. Plastic welding requires specialized equipment found only in well-outfitted service shops. (For a detailed look at plastic welding procedures, order the training video Plastic Welding Techniques by contacting the author.)

So how do you decide whether to use a patch kit or to have the crack welded? For ABS tanks, if the crack is in a portion of the tank that is less than 3/16 inches thick, use a patch kit. If the thickness of the ABS tank is greater than 3/16 inches, or if the crack is in a position of tension when the tank is installed or filled, take the tank to a repair center proficient at plastic welding.

For polyethylene tanks, only use a patch kit if the crack is located on top of the tank or on a side within two inches of the top. Avoid using a patch kit if the crack is located at or near the bottom of the tank or near an outlet fitting, except in an emergency.

Many patch kits come with easy-to-use tubes of epoxy and strips of webbing that can be used to reinforce the area to be patched. Carefully read the instructions on the package. Be sure to take all the necessary precautions when making the repair.

A temporary patch for ABS tanks can easily be fashioned by mixing minute shavings of ABS plastic with some ABS cement, roughing up the area around the flaw, and quickly applying a thin layer of this mixture to the crack and surrounding area. Next, work in a thin strip of cotton fabric and apply another layer or coating of ABS cement. Allow this patch to completely dry, then repeat the process. Gradually add layer upon layer until the area over and around the crack appears thicker and stronger. Finally, allow the entire patch to cure for 24 hours before filling with water. Keep in mind that this may only prove to be a temporary fix, and it may be necessary to eventually have the crack welded by a professional.

Testing the Results

Always allow ample time for curing or drying after a repair to a holding tank. Typically, 24 hours for ABS and polyethylene tanks is sufficient when an aftermarket patch kit is employed. If either tank was professionally welded using a plastic welding machine and welding rod, the tank can be tested immediately.

It is recommended that a static leak test be performed prior to reinstalling any holding tank after a repair. Carefully support or suspend the holding tank between two supports and plug the outlet. A method of plugging the outlet is to temporarily reinstall the dump assembly and simply close the dump valve. Fill the tank with fresh water through one of the openings in the top of the tank. Allow the filled tank to sit for 30 minutes while you closely monitor the area that originally leaked. If no moisture appears during the 30-minute test, the repair was successful. If a leak persists, try the repair again. In some cases, the crack may be in a location that is under stress when installed and simply cannot be sealed. In those instances, welding or replacement may be the only viable options.

Once successful, drain the water from the tank and reinstall the holding tank in the reverse manner in which it was removed. Any ABS drain or vent pipe that had to be cut in order to remove the tank will now have to be reconnected by using ABS cement and a common ABS coupling of that particular diameter.

Connect the dump assemblies, taking care to align all parts so that both termination valves operate smoothly. Now is a good time to clean and lubricate the dump valves. Be sure each is fully closed and the sewer cap is in place.

Reconnect all monitor panel wires that were previously disconnected.

Align the toilet flange and secure it to the top of the holding tank through the opening in the floor. Be sure to use pipe sealant on any threaded fitting, and ABS cement on any glue-type slip

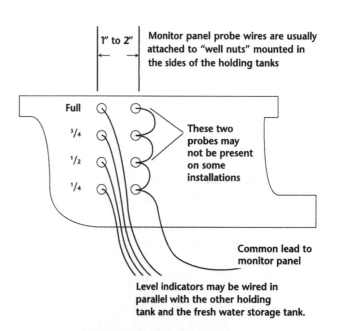

Level indicators may be wired in parallel with the other holding tank and the fresh water storage tank.

Fig. 7-28; Well nut locations on the holding tank

fitting. If the tank is equipped with the rubber grommet-type of connection, like those pictured here, use either pipe sealant, tube silicone or a spray lubricant to assist in the reinstallation. Coat the inside of the grommet and the outside of the three-inch ABS down pipe.

Reinstall the toilet being certain to use a new flange gasket. Attach the water line and check for leaks at that point by subjecting the inlet fitting to city water pressure.

Once again, fill the tank through the toilet and allow the water to completely fill and back up into the toilet itself. By overfilling the tank in

Fig. 7-29; Holding tank rubber grommets

this manner, every component is effectively tested. If there are no leaks, drain the tank through the dump assembly as usual.

Allow plenty of time for making holding tank repairs. Rushed jobs are often unsuccessful. Those owners who exhibit patience and persistence usually succeed.

General Waste System Maintenance and Repairs

All drain pipes must be suspended or supported in the RV. Periodically, inspect the entire length of the drain piping system inside and underneath the coach. Look for road damage and broken supports. Also, if the configuration warrants, visually inspect the bottom of each holding tank. Check in and around all P traps, sink drains, etc. for any moisture. Store only soft goods and lightweight supplies under sinks or in areas where plumbing drain pipes run.

Pay close attention to the termination assembly area. Make sure the outlet cap is firmly attached before traveling. If liquid is present when this cap is removed prior to connecting to the park sewer, a leaky termination valve seal may exist. Be certain all valves are closed tight.

In cold climates, be aware of freeze damage, especially when storing the RV. Avoid using extremely caustic drain cleaners. Because of the proliferation of plastic drain pipes in the housing industry all household-type drain cleaners used today are usually acceptable in RVs as well.

Rigid, Schedule 40 ABS drain pipes are pretty

Fig. 7-30; Drain pipe hanger strap

durable under normal use. However, ABS dump assemblies are no match for curbs, speed bumps or dips in the roadway. The most common damage to ABS drain lines are caused by the RV bottoming out. Any impact will result in a few broken or cracked plastic fittings or dump valves. In some cases, the entire waste piping system below the floor line can be wiped out, including the holding tanks. Unprotected waste drain plumbing must be foremost in your mind as the RV enters and departs steep driveways, crosses speed bumps or dodges road debris and potholes. A little too much speed, a too-steep approach angle or a too quick or slow reaction time can all lead to an additional repair and a not-so-pleasant one at that, in an olfactory sense.

Other than P traps and an occasional fitting, all other ABS fittings are usually cemented throughout the RV. If a pipe or fitting needs to be replaced, it will be necessary to first cut out the bad section with a hacksaw and then to insert a new section. When making ABS pipe repairs, keep these items in mind:

- Protect the work area. Spilled ABS cement will ruin virtually any floor covering.
- Have all pieces cut and sized to fit before cementing. Cut the pipe square. Avoid angling the hacksaw during the cut.
- Lightly sand or bevel the edges of a cut section of pipe for easy insertion into the fitting.
- Dry fit all the components to confirm the correct alignment.
- Disassemble and apply the ABS cement to both pipe and fitting and insert quickly and fully.
- Immediately after inserting the pipe into the fitting, slowly rotate the pipe or the fitting 90 degrees.
- Allow freshly cemented fittings to cure before running water in the lines. Refer to the instructions listed on the side of the cement container for specific details.

The bottom line is simple: unpleasant as it may appear, unattended RV waste systems will increasingly become more unpleasant unless a few straightforward preventive maintenance tasks are performed each year. Doing so will enhance the enjoyment of the RV (and your camping neighbors will appreciate it too)!

Chapter 8

Liquid Propane System

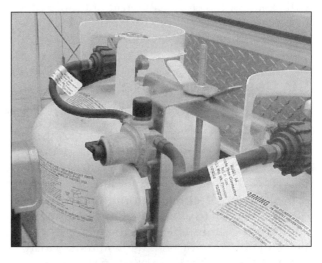

Overview

Liquefied petroleum gas, commonly referred to as liquid propane or LP, is a remarkable fuel. Stored as a liquid but used as a vapor, LP is extremely proficient at satisfying our need for the creature comforts of home while traveling. Self-contained cooking, heating, refrigeration and hot water are all possible because of the direct compatibility of LP with the RVing concept. One remarkable fact about LP is that a lot of it can be compressed into a relatively small container. For every gallon stored as a liquid, LP will expand to over 36 cubic feet of usable gas to be burned at the appliances. For RVing purposes alone, it is a very effective fuel.

LP Usage and Storage

The most important factor concerning LP is safety. Safety in filling, handling, storing and using must remain paramount in the minds of every RVer. LP is considered a safe and reliable product, yet it is flammable, so care must be taken at every juncture. If, when performing any procedure detailed in this handbook, you do not feel completely comfortable with the safety aspect of the situation, do not proceed. You must satisfy yourself thoroughly that neither personal nor equipment safety will be jeopardized before proceeding. Never compromise the safety factor!

Fig. 8-1; DOT LP cylinder

Propane, butane, ethane, methane and natural gas are all classified as liquefied petroleum gases. All but natural gas are hydrocarbons, and each will give off heat as a byproduct. In this vein, propane is most closely related to butane. The chemical formula for propane is C3H8, while butane is C4H10. Notice the two gases are very similar. Butane consists of one more molecule of carbon and two additional molecules of hydrogen, making butane a slightly heavier gas. Natural gas is also often compared to LP. For those familiar with natural gas used as a fuel, this chart provides some comparisons.

Property	Propane	Natural Gas
Chemical Formula	C_3H_8	CH_4
Specific Gravity		
(As a Vapor)	1.225	1.185
Boiling Point	$-44\,°F$	$-258\,°F$
BTU per Gallon	91,600	—
BTU per Pound	21,600	—
BTU per Cubic Foot	2,520	1,000

The fact that propane has a dew point (boiling point) of $-44\,°F$ makes it the perfect fuel for the appliances found on RVs. In years past, butane was also used as a fuel in RVs. Its boiling point is only $32\,°F$, which meant it was virtually useless when the temperature dipped below freezing; not unheard of for those who enjoy winter RVing. Propane, though, is the favored choice of fuel today. Different blends do exist, but by and large, it is all propane.

LP is inherently odorless. An odorant called ethyl mercaptan is added during the distilling process. Its distinct smell leaves no doubt when LP is present. If this odorant is evident at any time during any RVing excursion, immediately extinguish all appliances and turn off the LP service valve. Have the RV thoroughly checked to be sure there are no leaks prior to operating the appliances again. Remember, never compromise the safety factor!

A clear and distinct odor does not necessarily indicate there is a LP leak, however. It is common after refilling the LP container to experience a residual odor for a while, but it should soon subside. If it persists, however, a leak test is in order. Additionally, when a container of LP is completely emptied during usage, it is common

smell of the odorant, which remains behind in the empty tank—the odor becomes accentuated due to absence of LP.

Types of LP Containers

So how is liquid propane safely stored and carried in the RV? Two types of LP containers are used in RVs; DOT cylinders and ASME tanks. Both types must comply with rigid codes pertaining to their construction. One is built to the specifications of the American Society of Mechanical Engineers (ASME). The other conforms to the specs formulated by the Department of Transportation (DOT). Both types are subject to the codes and standards governed by the RV Industry Association (RVIA). Understanding the differences between the two types of LP storage containers and their individual components will help gain insight into using the RV effectively and efficiently.

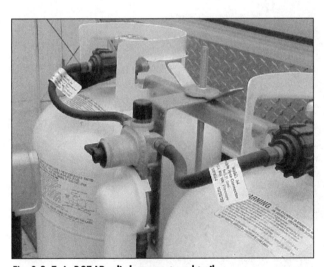

Fig. 8-2; Twin DOT LP cylinders on a travel trailer

DOT Cylinders

The DOT cylinder is common to travel trailers and some motorhomes, most pickup campers and pop-up folding tent trailers. These cylinders are usually secured to the A frame on the tongue of the trailer. In some instances, they may be found in a separate compartment accessed from the exterior of the RV. Such compartments must be sealed from the living portion of the RV. Typically they are manufactured for use in either an upright or horizontal position, though some

are specially manufactured to be used in either position. Check the data plate to be sure. Additionally, they should be transported in their respective positions at all times, especially when filled. Always use a safety plug or cap on the outlet valve when transporting LP containers.

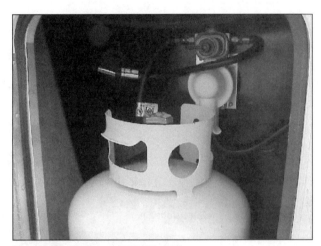

Fig. 8-3; Single connected DOT LP cylinder

The sizing of DOT cylinders can be somewhat confusing, and the method of filling varies as well. In some parts of the country, LP is sold by the gallon (remember, it is stored as a liquid); in others, it is sold by the pound. So what may be a five-gallon container in California may very well be a 20-pound cylinder in Illinois. In some areas, the LP is pumped into the tank and measured by the gallon. In others, the container is weighed before and after filling, and you pay for the weight in pounds of LP transferred into the cylinder.

This chart shows the amount of British thermal units (BTUs) available in each cylinder size.

Gallons of Liquid	Pounds of Gas	BTU
1.0	5	91,600
2.5	11	229,000
4.8	20	439,680
7.2	30	659,520
9.2	40	842,720

One advantage to DOT cylinders is they can be easily removed and transported to the filling location. On a typical dual-tank setup, such as on a standard travel trailer, it is possible to remove and fill one cylinder while the RV appliances operate off the other. ASME tanks, on the other hand, are permanently mounted and are seldom, if ever, removed. To fill an ASME tank, the motorhome must be driven to a filling location.

ASME Tanks

Another type of LP storage vessel found on RVs is the frame-mounted ASME container. Usually installed on motorhomes, the ASME tank is always mounted horizontally and usually permanently. Traditionally, these types of tanks

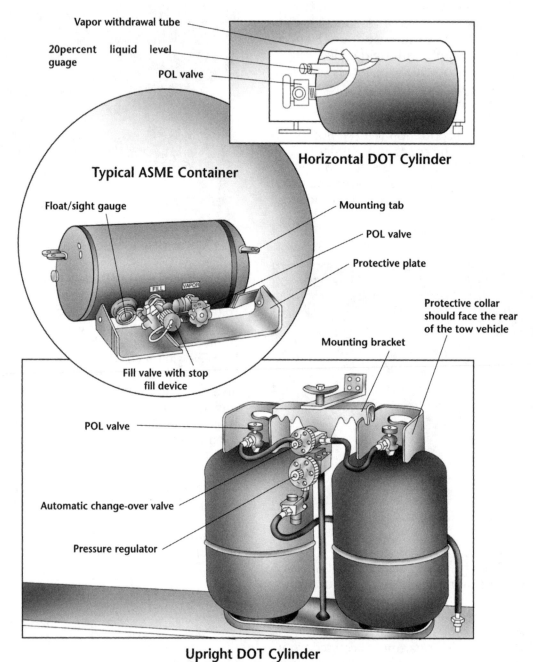

Fig. 8-4; DOT and ASME cylinder components

have a larger capacity than that of their DOT cousins; hence, they are found on the larger Class A motorhomes and bus conversions. RV manufacturers must comply with strict guidelines as to where ASME tanks can be located.

Fig. 8-5; A permanently mounted ASME container

Fig. 8-6; Another example of a mounted ASME container

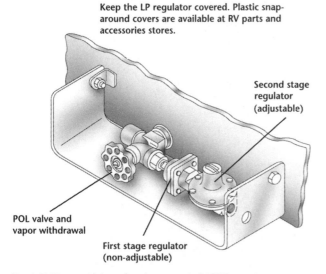

Keep the LP regulator covered. Plastic snap-around covers are available at RV parts and accessories stores.

Second stage regulator (adjustable)

POL valve and vapor withdrawal

First stage regulator (non-adjustable)

Fig. 8-7; Vapor withdrawal path on a typical ASME container

Container Components

A few basic components are found on all LP containers. Some are associated with both types, while others are unique to a particular vessel type.

Service Valves

Both types of LP containers have service valves, and the main outlet remains the most manipulated component on the container. In the past, all LP containers were equipped with a service valve commonly referred to as the POL valve. The term POL has been around for a long time, but you may not know its origin. Originally, POL was an abbreviation for a California manufacturer of gas-related fittings and products called Prest-O-Lite. Later, POL became known as the acronym for "put on left" since the fitting that mates with it is a left-hand threaded fitting. Currently only the horizontal ASME tanks are equipped with the old-style POL valves.

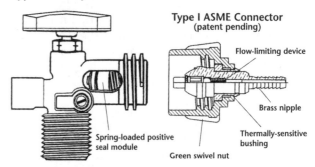

Type I ASME Cylinder Valve

Type I ASME Connector (patent pending)

Flow-limiting device

Brass nipple

Spring-loaded positive seal module

Thermally-sensitive bushing

Green swivel nut

Fig. 8-8; Type I DOT cylinder valve

Beginning April 2002, however, a new industry standard was adopted for upright DOT cylinders. Instead of the tried and true POL-type service valve, the new RV Type I CGA 791 service valve was introduced. The new pigtail connector that mates to the newer valve features a wrenchless, green swivel nut that can be tightened and loosened by hand. You may be familiar with a similar setup on your home LP barbeque grill. Additionally, the 1-5/16-inch ACME threads are right-handed threads. The newer valve contains an internal, spring-loaded component that prohibits all gas flow from the container until a positive, leak-free connection has been made. Since April 2002, LP gas retailers will only refill DOT cylinders with the Type I service valve.

Let's fully explore the Type I valve fitting used with today's DOT cylinders; there are two versions of the Type I valve connector currently in use. The older version will have a black thermal sensitive bushing found between the green nut and the flexible hose.

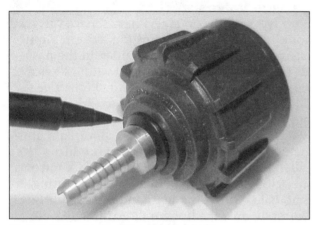

Fig. 8-9; LP Type I valve fitting with black bushing

When this bushing is exposed to temperatures over 240°F, it will melt and allow the brass nipple inside the nut to shift about 1/4 inch (See photo). The forward movement of the nipple will close a small piston inside the cylinder valve, and all LP will stop flowing.

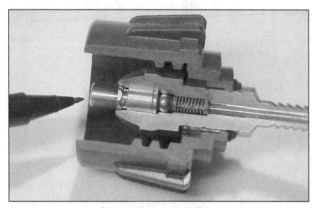

Fig. 8-10; Cutaway of the LP Type I excess flow plunger

The newer Type I valve fitting does not have this visible black bushing. As seen in the photo, the thermal sensitive device is located behind the four slits located at the rear of the green nut. Still, the flow will be stopped when the brass nipple moves forward and trips the piston located in the service valve on the cylinder.

Fig. 8-11; Newer LP Type I valve fitting without the black bushing

Inside the green nut, machined into the brass nipple, is found the flow-limiting device. The purpose of the flow-limiting portion of the ACME connector nut is to restrict the flow of LP should an excessive leak develop anywhere in the LP system. Just about every time the DOT cylinder service valve is opened, the small ball bearing in the nut assembly moves towards the piping system and into a brass seat, restricting the flow of gas. It does not, however, fully shut off the gas flow; the ball bearing only restricts it.

By design, a small amount of LP is allowed to bypass the ball and flow into the LP piping system. As long as all the appliances are turned off and there are no LP leaks anywhere in the system, this small amount of bypass flow quickly builds up enough back pressure that it eventually equals the bypass flow pressure coming through the device. When that happens, the small spring pushes the ball bearing back and

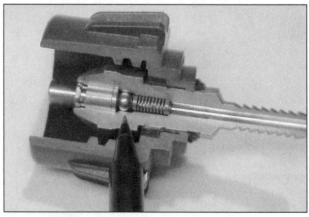

Fig. 8-12; Cutaway of the LP Type I excess flow ball

off the seat and permits unrestricted flow of LP into the system. This whole process takes about five seconds and is the way the system is supposed to work.

If, however, a burner is inadvertently left on somewhere in the system (perhaps the oven thermostat is set to the Pilots On position), or if a small leak is in the piping or at any connection, here's what happens that leads many RVers and service technicians to erroneously believe the regulator is faulty.

The cylinder valve is opened, the ball bearing shifts into its seat and the bypass flow passes into the system. This time, however, the back pressure cannot equalize because of the escaping LP through the open burner or leak. Without this pressure equalization, remember, unrestricted flow will not be permitted through the flow-limiting device. The bypass flow, however, may be sufficient to operate one or two stove burners, so you may think everything is operating normally, until you try to light a larger appliance like the furnace or the water heater.

Quite rapidly the volume of available bypass LP is used up, and any burner flame at that appliance will be quickly drawn down to virtually nothing. In other words, not enough LP exists to support furnace or water heater operation, and one would presume the regulator is not functioning properly. The fact is, nonetheless, the flow-limiting safety feature in the ACME nut is working properly and signifying a leak somewhere in the system.

To reset the flow-limiting device, completely turn off all LP burning appliances and close the service valve on the cylinder. Wait about 30 seconds and fully reopen the service valve. Light a stove burner and try to ignite the furnace. If the stove burner flame shows evidence of fuel starvation, it means the back pressure still has not equalized the bypass flow and a leak still exists somewhere in the piping system. Further troubleshooting is in order.

20% Liquid Level Gauge

Sometimes mistakenly called a 10% valve, a 20% liquid level gauge is a separate component on all ASME tanks, and is usually built into the

Fig. 8-13; LP Type I service valve

service valve on upright DOT cylinders. (It's the slotted set-screw with the hole in the center in the photo below.) This valve is employed to properly fill the container and is a requirement in most states. Also, it is a virtual necessity when dispensing the LP fuel by the gallon; it lets the attendant know when the container is 80% full. Note that you should never top off the tank to the maximum capacity. The container should only be filled to 80% of the maximum capacity. The top 20% of every LP container is for the vapor area and to accommodate the expansion of the LP. By far the most common type of abuse associated with LP containers is overfilling.

Vapor Withdrawal Tube

Integral to horizontal containers only, the vapor withdrawal tube is an internal tube positioned in the upper 20% of the container - the vapor space. It assures that only vapor is withdrawn and processed through the regulator and into the piping system. Remember, LP is stored as a liquid, but burned in the appliances as a gas. Overfilling of the container causes liquid to fill this tube and be delivered through the regulator to the system. This condition will ruin the regulator and cause serious damage to the LP appliances. In severe cases, the entire piping system must be replaced.

Safety Valve

A safety valve is a component built into all service valves. This is a preset spring-loaded device that monitors the interior pressure of the container. In the photo, it's the component at the far left on the service valve labeled "safety." If the pressure rises too high, the safety valve will open and release container pressure to the atmosphere during any of the following three conditions:

• Containers not properly purged of air
• Overfilled containers
• Containers exposed to excessive heat

Avoid all three conditions. The pressure relief valve on ASME containers is a separate component attached directly to the tank and is not an integral portion of the service valve as on the DOT cylinder.

Fill Valve

On DOT cylinders, the fill valve is actually the Type I service valve. Filling and withdrawing LP is effectuated through the same valve on DOT cylinders. On ASME containers, however, it is a separate component. Currently all LP containers, ASME and DOT alike, must be equipped with an overfill protection device, referred to as OPD. This listed and approved safety mechanism makes certain the tank will not be overfilled.

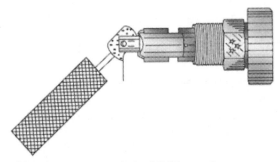

Mounts permanently in ASME containers. Automatically shuts off incoming LP during the filling process once container is 80 percent full.

Fig. 8-14; Automatic stop fill device, required on all ASME containers

Float/Sight Gauge

The float gauge, or sight gauge as some call it, may be common to both types of containers. This device provides a visual indication of how much fuel remains in the container. Outfitted with a sending unit, it can be remotely connected to the monitor panel inside the RV. Usually only associated with ASME tanks, an aftermarket replacement service valve assembly for DOT

Fig. 8-15; LP container with sight gauge and sending unit

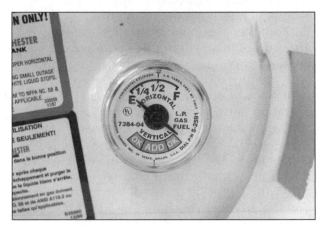

Fig. 8-16; Horizontal DOT cylinder sight gauge

cylinders can be installed that has a float gauge as an integral portion of that assembly as well. Some DOT cylinders do have a mounted sight gauge separate from the service valve.

Mounting Brackets/Collars

Bracket and collars protect the service valve and other components from flying road debris such as rocks and gravel. The brackets also provide the method of secure attachment to the RV in most instances.

Data Plate

Located on each container, the data plate provides specific information regarding that particular vessel. On ASME tanks, it will be located on a plate welded to the tank; on the DOT cylinders, it is simply stamped into the protective collar. Stamped information includes tare weight (TW), which is the weight of the empty container and main shutoff valve assembly. Other data include the water capacity rating, which is the capacity of the container if filled with water, the maximum it can hold. This figure, minus 20%, is considered the maximum LP content when properly filled.

An easy way to determine how much LP remains in a partially emptied DOT cylinder is to remove the cylinder and weigh it. Subtract the tare weight (stamped on the collar) and divide the remaining figure by 4.2, which is approximately how much LP weighs per gallon. The resulting figure will be how many gallons are left in the cylinder.

Each gallon can provide about 91,600 BTUs of energy. To determine how long the LP will last, add up all the input BTU ratings of the four LP burning appliances. The input rating per hour can be found on the data plate of each appliance or by looking in the owner's manual of each appliance. Approximate the length of time each appliance will be operated that day and divide that figure into the 91,600. This final figure will be the approximate daily LP consumption.

Requalification of DOT Cylinders

The date of manufacture can also be found on the collar of the DOT cylinder. This is important since federal regulations now require periodic requalification of all DOT cylinders. One approved requalification method is a complete external visual inspection. When the visual inspection method is used, the first inspection and requalification is due 12 years after the original date of manufacture. Subsequent inspections and requalification are required every 5 years after that.

If the RV is equipped with DOT cylinders, check the date on the collar. Refilling may be refused if the cylinder is due for requalification. Do not use an older cylinder until it has been properly inspected, requalified and stamped accordingly.

The National Propane Gas Association and the Compressed Gas Association has outlined spe-

cific instructions for inspectors to follow to properly requalify DOT cylinders. What can be done to be sure DOT containers will pass the mandated visual inspection for requalification?

First, do not allow rust to build up on the LP cylinders, especially around the bottom base ring. Since many cylinders are continuously exposed to the weather, they are susceptible to rust. Remove any evidence of rust or corrosion yearly and maintain a good covering of paint. During the visual inspection, each bottle will be scrutinized for pits caused by corrosion, so the more attention provided in this area, the more likely it will pass the inspection.

Two terms to be remembered when considering the requalification inspection are: condemned and rejected. Any bottle that is condemned due to its physical condition cannot under any circumstances be utilized further. It must be scrapped. If a cylinder is rejected, it simply means that it cannot be used until adequate repairs have been made. However, such repairs must be made by either the manufacturer of that cylinder or by a facility authorized by the Bureau of Explosives. It will, in all honesty, be easier (and more cost effective) to simply replace the cylinder with a new one should it be rejected.

The inspection of cylinders includes looking for, measuring and analyzing dents, cuts or gouges in the metal of the container. Bulges or damages due to exposure to fire or abuse are also considered. Different types of corrosion will be checked: isolated pitting, line corrosion and general corrosion. In addition, close inspection around the neck area where the POL service valve is threaded into the bottle will take place. The collar and cylinder ring will also be inspected for corrosion and pitting.

There are specific condemnation rules that apply to each of the aforementioned areas of concern. RVers can eliminate early cylinder replacement and retain structural integrity by removing rust and applying a primer and coat of paint on a yearly basis.

Purging LP Containers

All new, and in some cases used, LP containers may contain combined elements of water, air and other contaminants that are not conducive to LP and appliances. All contaminates should be removed prior to placing that container into service. This pertains to DOT and ASME vessels alike. Water vapor present in the gas vapor may cause erratic regulator performance. It also makes the regulator more susceptible to freeze-ups. Additionally, it will have an effect on the odorant that is added to the LP.

Air inside the container may cause an abnormally high tank pressure, which in turn can cause the pressure relief valve to open. Poor combustion and erratic appliance operation are sure to result from either water or air being inside any LP container if allowed to remain in the vessel. If reduced performance is associated with any two or more of the appliances, it may indicate the LP container is in need of purging. Normally, purging of LP containers is performed by an LP dealer. All RVers should, however, be aware of the purging procedures:

• Determine if the container pressure is zero. Should it hold only air pressure (as in new tanks, which are leak-tested at the manufacturer and usually shipped containing air), the air can simply be released to the atmosphere. If the container is a used bottle and contains LP, the local LP retailer should have a large burner that can be connected to the container and the remaining contents burned off. Never release filled LP containers into the atmosphere.

• Drain any water that may have settled in the bottom of the container. This is no problem with DOT cylinders; however, ASME tanks will have to be removed from the coach in order to drain the water.

• Next, pressurize the container with approximately 15 pounds per square inch (psi) of LP vapor. Containers should never be purged with liquid. Water vapor will freeze and remain in the container if the purging is done with liquid LP.

• Vent this small amount of vapor in a safe area through the service valve.

• Repeat this vapor filling and venting process four more times. As each tank is vented, more moisture is removed.

• Methanol is then added to the container to absorb any remaining molecules of moisture. Another 15psi of LP vapor is then introduced into the container.

• The container is now ready for liquid filling and regular usage. Leak tests should be performed on all fittings before putting the container into service.

LP Regulator

As the LP vapor exits any container it passes to the component at the theoretical center of the LP system - the pressure regulator. In order to appreciate the how-to of LP system maintenance, one must truly understand the inner workings of the LP pressure regulator. Probably the hardest working component found on the RV, the regulator is appropriately self-descriptive. It must keep up with fluctuating internal LP container pressures, then regulate and deliver a nice smooth, even flow of LP vapor to each of the appliances. And it must do this continually whenever the service valve is opened. If it stumbles or skips a beat, internal damage to delicate components found on some appliances could result.

The pressure regulator is truly the heart of the system, and a relatively inexpensive component

Fig. 8-17; LP regulator

as well. Being affordable, it is highly suggested that all RVers carry a spare regulator whenever and wherever they travel. In the event of regulator failure, in most cases, replacement is usually mandatory. Regardless, it is definitely cheap insurance just in case.

LP Regulator Operation

What makes the LP regulator such a workhorse? Here's what happens inside the regulator when you open the service valve on your LP container. The fuel vaporizes and enters the first of two stages. In this first stage, the incoming container pressure is reduced to approximately 10psi. The actual pressure inside your LP container will vary depending on the amount of fuel in the container, the temperature and a few other factors. Suffice it to say that the pressure is quite high—upwards of 250psi or greater. Not only is the pressure high, but it is also fairly unstable, fluctuating up and down as factoring conditions change. Remember that there is no pressure regulation going on inside your LP tank, simply containment. It's also important to note that we store LP as a liquid, yet use it at the appliances as a vapor. But let's continue.

Fuel enters a chamber below a rubber diaphragm that is held steady by the opposing force of a coiled spring positioned above it. As the fuel is induced into the chamber, the diaphragm is expanded and pushed up against the opposing strength of the coil spring, compressing it. An equivalent here would be like trying to blow up a balloon inside a shoebox. The sides of the box would give way to the expanding balloon until the strength of the box sides can overcome the pressure inside the balloon.

Attached to the spring/diaphragm connection is a mechanical pivot and arm that connects to a seat assembly and the first-stage orifice. As the diaphragm moves against the spring when the fuel enters, the pivoting arm moves the seat closer to the orifice, impeding the flow of fuel.

On all two-stage LP regulators, this first stage is preset to approximately 10psi, a nonadjustable setting. However, as the fuel passes through the first-stage orifice of the regulator and enters the second-stage chamber, regulation takes on a more definitive approach.

For years the four LP burning appliances found on typical RVs have been designed and manufactured to operate with a delivery pressure of between 10 and 14 water column (WC) inches. For optimum appliance operation, therefore, the operating line pressure is set at 11 inches WC, which falls about in the middle of this designed spectrum. From this stage on we think of pressure in terms of water column inches instead of pounds per square inch.

A water column inch is a much smaller unit of measurement employed to measure the rather slight LP operating line pressure. The analogy would be like measuring distances in either miles or inches. Each would be accurate, but the inch measurement would be more finite. For vapor pressure measurements, 11 inches WC is the equivalent of 4/10 of a single psi (0.4psi). Not a whole lot of pressure! Then again, not that much is needed, but it does have to be steady, which is the job of that hardworking regulator.

Fig. 8-18; Dual-stage LP regulator

(labels: Non-adjustable first stage; Adjustable second stage; Main spring; Vent; Inlet (supply pressure); Diaphragm; Outlet; Orifice; Mechanical linkage)

Many of today's newer, more efficient appliances require even less pressure and less fuel to operate at their optimum than previously. In these appliances, an additional regulator is often at work internally to the appliance. These individual appliance regulators further reduce the 11 inches WC pressure on the system to even less pressure required by that appliance. These so-called third-stage regulators are of the nonadjustable variety. The common denominator, therefore, among the four LP burning

Fig. 8-19; Example of a third-stage/appliance regulator

appliances is the main regulator located at the LP container.

In the second stage of a typical two-stage regulator, much the same mechanical action and reaction takes place between the diaphragm, a pivoting linkage and a coiled spring as in the first stage. The main difference here is that the orifice opening is much smaller (more restricting), which reduces the incoming 10-psi from the first stage to the correct operating pressure of 11-inches of water column. Also, the spring tension on the second stage is adjustable so finite pressure adjustments can be made. The second-stage adjustment point is positioned under a protective cap on the regulator.

When no burners are lit in the RV and therefore, no need for fuel to be flowing, the second-stage orifice will be shut off completely, effectively stopping the flow of fuel inside the regulator. At this juncture, the spring tension has overcome the pressure exerted against the diaphragm by the incoming LP.

When a burner is lit anywhere in the system, however, the drop in pressure inside the regulator body allows the springs to push the diaphragm back down. This movement will allow the linkage to move the seat away from the orifices in each stage, allowing more fuel to enter the regulator. As more fuel enters, the incoming LP pressure once again overcomes the spring strength, and the orifice is again impeded by the seat. As more fuel is consumed at a burner, the pressure drops inside the regulator once again, and (pause), I think you get the

picture, the cycle simply continues.

Therefore, the bottom line is this: regulator operation is basically a balance between the strength of the springs and the flexibility of the diaphragm as fuel constantly enters and exits the regulator body. An exact LP pressure setting is attainable because the second-stage spring strength is adjustable.

Regulator Freeze-Up

Moisture inside the LP container periodically freezes in the orifice at the inlet to the regulator, stopping the LP flow. Remember, the LP is vaporizing at –44°F, far lower than is necessary to freeze moisture. This is why contaminated LP containers need purging. Regulator freeze-up is all but a thing of the past since two-stage regulators are now required on all newly built RVs.

Another type of regulator freezing takes place when external moisture freezes and blocks the vent portion of the regulator. The vent opening of all regulators must be pointed downward to avoid any blockage. Inspect and keep the regulator's protective cover in place.

On travel trailer installations with twin DOT cylinders, an automatic change-over valve is usually used in conjunction with a dual-stage regulator assembly. This device allows automatic switching between cylinders when one cylinder is emptied. Uninterrupted flow of LP is realized using the automatic change-over device. Additionally, the empty cylinder can then be removed and transported to the filling station while the remaining cylinder provides fuel to the system.

Always transport DOT cylinders with a POL plug or a QCC1 ACME cap installed on the service valve. Also, be sure the cylinder is transported in the same position as it is utilized; horizontal cylinders must remain horizontal, upright cylinders must remain upright. This will minimize the chance of inducing the liquid version of LP into the service valve or vapor withdrawal tube, which could damage the regulator and possibly an appliance control valve.

Other Regulator Factors

An important feature to understand about LP

regulators is a phenomenon called lockout pressure. Lockout pressure is that pressure necessary to fully seat the orifice in the second stage of the regulator, effectively stopping the flow of LP through the body of the regulator. This only becomes a factor when the service valve on the LP container is open (pressure is in the system), yet no burners are lit anywhere in the RV.

Here's the important point to remember; lockout pressure is always slightly higher than the set pressure as determined by the second-stage adjustment. Why is this important, you ask? When measuring the operating line pressure and after correctly adjusting the regulator, if the lockout pressure continues to rise significantly, beyond 14 inches WC, or will not fully come to a stop, a faulty regulator exists. It's a quick test to determine how healthy the internal components of the regulator actually are. More on this later.

Another important fact to remember: each stage of the regulator must be able to "breathe" as the diaphragm expands and contracts inside the regulator body. That is, as fuel enters, the diaphragm expands slightly into an upper chamber above the diaphragm. These upper chambers are exposed to the outside atmosphere through a vent in each stage. If the upper diaphragm chambers were not vented allowing air to be expelled as it flexes, the diaphragm would simply not be able to move.

Here's the key: the vent openings for each stage must be kept clean and free from moisture, dirt, mud, snow or any other type of muck that may plug or block them. This is equally crucial for both the first and second stages. Typically the first-stage vent is a fairly tiny hole in the regulator housing. It doesn't take much to plug it. Likewise the vent portion of the second stage, though more prominent, is also critical for proper operation and must be kept clean. In fact, it is a mandate that the vent portion of the second stage always be positioned downward (within 45 degrees of vertical). This position minimizes the possibility of dirt or mud collecting directly onto the vent screen. When purchasing replacement regulators, be sure the vent configuration is correct for your application.

Fig. 8-20; Regulator cover

Finally, always keep your regulator covered with a plastic cover. If yours has become lost or damaged, pick up another during your next visit to your dealer or service center. This is the single-most effective method of protecting the LP regulator.

Okay, you say, now I have an idea of what goes on inside the regulator, but whenever I turn the adjustment screw on the regulator, I see no difference in any of the burner flames I check. Stop! Major rule number two: Never attempt to adjust the LP regulator without the proper knowledge of how to do it, or without having the proper test equipment on hand. Once you have studied this chapter and have obtained the necessary equipment yet to be discussed, then and only then should you even consider adjusting the LP pressure on your RV. Okay, but if that's major rule number two, what's number one? Never compromise the safety factor. Like electricity, LP must be respected. In order to be respected, it must be understood. In order to be understood it must be studied. So we continue.

Manometer

Since we are now accustomed to seeing LP pressure referred to in units of measurement called water column inches, here's what that actually means. A correctly set LP regulator in a typical RV allows just enough pressure to raise an actual column of water 11 inches. A device called a manometer is used to measure the LP pressure after regulation.

One type of manometer is the spring gauge type that has a dial indicator and a short piece of

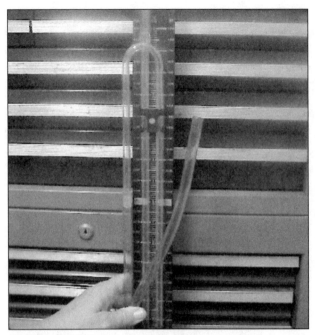

Fig. 8-21; A U tube manometer

rubber tubing attached to it. It will measure directly in water column inches.

Another type of manometer employs an actual column of water attached to a ruler marked off in inches. Also known as a U tube manometer, it too, has a rubber hose to facilitate connecting it to the LP system. Be sure to prepare this manometer correctly by filling the tube with water until the level on each side of the manometer is at the zero point in the middle of the scale. The scale itself will slide up or down in order to get it right on the mark. This preparatory step is crucial to the accuracy of the

Fig. 8-22; A gauge-type manometer

measurement. Filled properly, the U tube or water column manometer is 100% accurate as mentioned earlier.

A third, electronic LP manometer is also available though not widely used by RV owners because of their higher initial cost. Here are a few more random manometer attributes.

The spring/dial type of manometer is compact and can be easily stored. The true water column U tube manometer is 100% accurate. It's a little more cumbersome, but less expensive to purchase. The dial type needs periodic calibration. (Hint: The water column type is used to calibrate the dial type.) The bottom line, however, is this: You must have a manometer in order to set your LP pressure regulator correctly. Remember, the operating pressure is so slight that virtually any changes or adjustments that are made will not be visually apparent in any flame structure on any of the appliances in the RV. Only by accurately measuring with a manometer will differences in operating line pressures be detected. In fact, damage could easily occur in some appliances if attempts are made to adjust the LP regulator without the use of a manometer. Do not take the risk.

A manometer is a wise investment if you are sincere about performing your own preventive maintenance on your coach. Manometers can be purchased through well-stocked appliance repair stores.

LP Test Device

A manometer is but one of two "tools" required to correctly set the operating line pressure of the LP system. In addition, an LP test device apparatus will be necessary. This test device cannot be store bought, but is constructed using common brass fittings and components. (Completed LP test devices are available by contacting the author).

To construct the LP test device you'll need the following components:

- 1/4" FPT brass cross
- 1/4" MPT brass plug

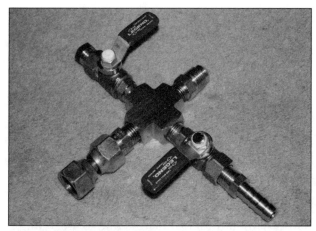

Fig. 8-23; LP test device apparatus

- (2) 1/4″ MPT X 3/8″ flare adapters
- 3/8″ X 3/8″ female flare swivel
- 1/4" MPT X 5/16″ barbed adapter
- (2) 1/4" MPT X 1/4" FPT gas valves

A length of rubber low pressure flexible hose with 3/8″ female flare swivels on each end can be substituted for the short, rigid 3/8″ female flare swivel for ease of attaching to the regulator if necessary. The professional service technician will have both in his tool kit.

For proper accuracy, the LP regulator should only be adjusted while it is under a load of approximately 50% of the RV's installed appliances. As such, it will be necessary to drill a 3/32″ (or #41 drill bit) hole through the end of the 1/4″ brass plug before assembling the test device. A #41 orifice is rated at 75,000 Btu/hour which equates to approximately 50% of the

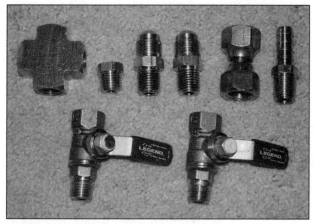

Fig. 8-24; LP test device; individual components

overall coach requirement. Be sure to use an LP approved thread sealant when putting the LP test device together (for assembly, refer to the photo above).

Okay, so how do we actually measure the pressure and adjust the regulator? What follows is a detailed, step-by-step set of procedures that safely and accurately sets the pressure and effectively tests the entire LP system for leaks. It will not locate a leak, but it will indicate if one exists. It is recommended to perform these steps at least once per camping season. For full-time RVers, I would opt to check the system at least quarterly. And immediately if you suspect a leak anywhere in the system.

Setting the LP Pressure and Testing for Leaks

It is paramount that the ambient air and the LP piping system are at the same approximate temperature before setting the LP pressure at the regulator. If you bring a motorhome into a garage or shop on a cold day, be sure to allow the temperature of the piping system to adjust to the room temperature before setting the pressure. Pressure and temperature have a direct effect on the LP system and any disparity between the two will have negative results. Here are the procedures:

1. Completely turn off all the LP appliances and the service valve on the LP container.

2. Connect the test device apparatus to the system directly at the output of the regulator. That way the container valve, the test device, the manometer and the regulator adjustment point are all within easy reach at the same time.

   a. Disconnect the RV's low pressure rubber hose connection from the flare fitting at the outlet of the regulator and attach the test device to the regulator using the female flare swivel (or optional flexible hose). Be sure to use a backup wrench!

   b. Reconnect the RV's low pressure hose to the adapter fitting on the opposite side of the test device.

c. Attach the manometer to the barbed fitting on the test device. If using a true water column manometer, be sure it is filled to the correct level.

3. Turn on the LP at the container by rotating the service valve counter-clockwise. Always open the service valve slowly and completely. Never force the valve beyond the wide-open position, but do open it all the way.

4. Slowly open the gas valve on the test device for the manometer connection.

5. Slowly open the gas valve on the test device for the #41 orifice while reading the pressure measurement on the manometer. The pressure should be at 11.0-inches of water column. If you are using a dial type manometer, water column inches can be read directly from the gauge. If you are using a U tube manometer, the incoming LP pressure will force the water down one side of the U and up the other side. The actual measurement is obtained by adding the two sides of each column of water together.

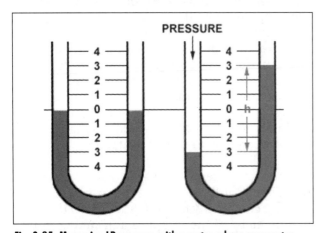

Fig. 8-25; Measuring LP pressure with a water column manometer

6. Adjust the regulator to obtain 11.0″ of water column with the regulator under a load via the #41 orifice. Turning the adjustment screw clockwise will increase the pressure; counter-clockwise will decrease the pressure on the manometer. Do not move the adjustment point more than one-quarter to one-half turn at a time. Be sure to let the manometer settle between adjustments. The movement of the water will take a few seconds to settle.

Don't rush this step. This is where accuracy is important. Get it right on 11.0″.

7. After obtaining the correct 11.0″ of water column measurement, close the gas valve on the test device for the #41 orifice. Be cognizant of the measured pressure on the manometer when closing the orifice valve. Remember that the lockout pressure needed to fully seat the regulator will be more than the 11″ you just set. Keep an eye on the manometer. If the pressure rises significantly past 12″ of water column, or simply keeps slowly rising, the regulator is faulty. Any number of factors may contribute to a faulty LP regulator condition, including age. In any case, replace the regulator if the lockout pressure rises above 14″ within three minutes.

8. Completely turn off the main service valve thereby trapping LP within the entire piping system and the manometer. The pressure reflected on the manometer is the total of the set pressure plus the lockout pressure (14″ maximum).

9. Bleed the pressure down to about 6 or 8 inches by slowly opening the gas valve on the test device for the #41 orifice. The actual number really doesn't matter as long as it is below that of the set pressure. Just find a reference point below the set pressure and then quickly close the valve on the test device for the orifice. Make note of this reading.

10. Next, set a timer for three minutes.

a. If after three minutes there is a decrease in pressure from the previous reading, a leak exists somewhere in the system and further troubleshooting is needed. Do not use any LP appliance until the leak has been located and eliminated. Keep the service valve turned off at the LP container.

b. If after three minutes there is an increase in the reading, LP is leaking through the service valve and into the piping system. In other words, when you think the service valve is off, it isn't. This could be hazardous, and the container valve should be replaced as soon as possible, after which the entire LP leak test and lockup test must be run again to insure that the coach is indeed leak-free. This is imperative. If the leak through the service valve is greater in volume than any leak into the atmosphere that may exist in the system, it will never be detected in this manner.

c. If after three minutes absolutely no drop in pressure is indicated, the RV is leak-free.

11. Bleed the pressure from the system by opening the gas valve on the test device for the #41 orifice and remove the manometer and the test device. Reconnect the RV's low pressure rubber hose to the outlet of the regulator, returning the LP system to full operation.

12. Open the service valve and bubble test that fitting to be sure a leak was not created by removing and reconnecting the hose. Never use a soap solution that contains ammonia or any derivative.

13. Once you are certain no leaks exist in the entire system, test fire each appliance letting each run through at least one cycle of operation. Be sure the water heater is filled with water and that the refrigerator is level before lighting those appliances. During this step, see if you can smell the presence of LP in, at or near each appliance as it is running. Remember, the LP leak test only checks the system up to but not including the individual appliances. If you suspect any appliance leaking internally, immediately shut it off and call your local RV service facility. It is not recommended that you attempt any internal appliance repairs yourself.

It is easily appreciated just how much work a manometer actually performs. Additionally, I cannot overstate the importance of maintaining a leak-free RV while traveling and enjoying this style of living. Likewise we cannot nor should not minimize the safety concerns of a neglected LP system. Regularly checking the LP system in this manner will guarantee the appliances are being fed a quality diet of fuel at the correct line pressure. Plus, verifying the system to be leak-free is an added benefit of having the cost-effective manometer and test device apparatus as a valuable portion of the tool kit.

Finding LP Leaks

If the manometer leak test detected a drop in pressure during the three minute test, a leak exists somewhere in the LP system. It is necessary now to troubleshoot the system and pinpoint exactly which component is leaking. It could be a cracked or loose flare nut, a hole in the copper tubing, a leaky regulator, or a faulty component in an appliance.

The first thing to do is eliminate the appliances as the source of the leak. It is possible, in some instances, to have LP leak through an appliance even though the appliance is off. To eliminate each appliance, disconnect the 3/8″ flare nut at each appliance, one at a time and plug the line with a flare plug. Run the above test again after plugging off each appliance.

If the leak disappears after disconnecting the furnace and plugging the line, for instance, then the problem lies somewhere in the furnace. If the leak persists after disconnecting each appliance and plugging the incoming copper lines with flare plugs, it will then be necessary to troubleshoot further.

At this point, turn the LP back on and spray or daub a leak detector solution on each fitting and pipe joint in the system. Start at the valve fitting at the LP container and bubble test each fitting and connection point. Although they do exist, it is not necessary to purchase a special leak detector solution. Simple dish washing

Fig. 8-26; A set of 3/8″ flare plugs and caps for LP testing

soap mixed and diluted with water, or better yet, a child's bottle of blowing bubbles works extremely well. As mentioned above, avoid using dish soap that contains ammonia products.

If bubbles appear around any fitting after a few seconds, try tightening that fitting. Always use a backup wrench when tightening any LP fitting. Daub a little more solution to verify the leak has been eliminated. Also, while going through the system, fitting by fitting, keep a sharp nose for the unmistakable presence of the LP odorant. Many times your nose will determine the culprit fitting before even applying the soap bubbles.

After checking each fitting in the system, perform the full three minute manometer leak test again. Remember, to be leak-free there should be no drop in pressure during the three minute test.

If the LP leak is isolated to one of the four LP burning appliances, call the local RV service center as further internal diagnosing of that appliance will be necessary. Some modern furnaces control valves permit a slight but intentional LP flow through the valve even when the unit is not running. This is a normal occurrence, but to be sure call a professional RV service technician.

Periodically test the on-board LP leak detector. Be sure to follow the instructions in the owner's manual. If at any time there appears to be no LP flowing, check the operation of the leak detector. Most will have a positive fuel shut-off solenoid located at or near the service valve. It is possible that the detector is simply doing its job and has shut off the flow of LP.

LP Combustion

All four of the major LP burning appliances found on RVs require the proper amounts of air and LP gas to be mixed for optimum operating efficiency. Understanding this simple fact, and making sure it occurs, could save repair dollars and costly downtime while traveling. A brief discussion follows on the attributes of proper combustion as it relates to RV appliances. It will further emphasize the importance of a strong preventive maintenance program concerning the coach.

The burners in the appliances each perform the same general function. They mix specific amounts of air with the incoming LP gas prior to a burner being ignited or burned. This mixture is crucial to the operation of the appliances as it relates to efficiency. In most cases, there are no adjustments that can be made to the incoming air. Some earlier RV appliances, which were adapted from the mobile home industry, were equipped with adjustable air shutters. However, the advent of electronic ignition and the gradual decline in the use of the common standing pilot burner flame virtually eliminated the usefulness of air adjustments. The water heater is the only exception today.

The LP regulator controls the pressure of the LP gas as it is delivered to the burners of the appliances. The adjustment of the LP pressure is very critical for proper operation of the appliances.

The individual burner orifice or jet controls the amount of LP gas that enters the burner. This is a predetermined amount that defines the BTU capacity of that particular appliance. RVers have no control over how large this opening is, nor do we need to be. However, we can be responsible for how small this opening can get. Dirt, dust and spider webs coagulate regularly in burner orifices. We have all heard the campfire stories of insect nests in the orifices. Well, they are very true indeed. Partially blocked orifices, in effect, restrict the flow of LP that mixes with the air, resulting in an improper mixture that creates carbon deposits (soot) and a poor running appliance. Remember seeing that large black stain on the side of the RV above your neighbor's water heater?

To combat this situation and to get the most out of LP burning appliances, make it a point to clean the burners and check the LP pressure periodically. It should be done, at the very least, once a camping season. If travel is predominantly in dusty climates, consider cleaning the burners more often, perhaps twice per camping season. More details on this in later chapters.

Flame Failure Safety Devices

With the exception of the range, LP appliances

rely on a built-in safety method that will shut off the incoming LP should the flame be extinguished. In past years, all appliances utilized a pilot flame that ignited a larger, main flame. If the pilot flame blew out, the main burner could not ignite, and gas flow would cease.

An integral portion of most safety valves and pilot burners is the thermocouple. Although the industry has progressed technically by leaps and bounds, some things just never become 100% outdated. The typical thermocouple is one of those items.

In 1806 the inventor of the thermocouple discovered that when two different metals were heated to a certain temperature, an electrical voltage was produced. This is but one of the facets behind the principle of thermal electricity.

Twenty or so years later, a couple of inventing geniuses invented the common electromagnet. Now the thermocouple had a purpose. When combined with the electromagnet, the thermocouple could produce the voltage needed to power the magnet, which in turn was used in an assortment of configurations to control the flow of gases and vapors. This was the beginning of the flame failure safety system.

The thermocouple as we know it consists of two

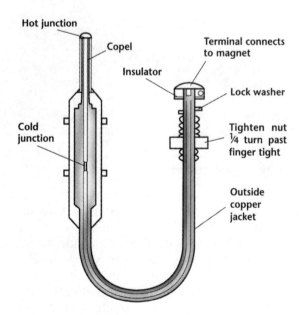

Fig. 8-27; A typical thermocouple

unlike or dissimilar metals. Today's thermocouples utilize stainless steel and a variant of copper called copel. They are fused together at one end. This is called the hot junction, which is the portion that is actually in the pilot flame. In fact, to work at optimum performance, only the first 3/8 inches of the thermocouple should actually be in the flame. In order to produce the voltage necessary at least a 400-degree temperature difference must exist between this hot junction and the cold junction. If too much of the thermocouple is positioned in the flame, a higher temperature will be realized at the cold junction since it will be physically closer to the flame. If that condition exists, the required voltage difference will not be present and subsequent appliance problems will result. Concerning pilot flame size, bigger is not always better.

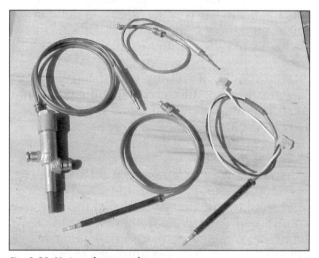

Fig. 8-28; Various thermocouples

At the opposite end of the thermocouple is the terminal attachment that screws into the flame failure safety device or gas control valve. Always use caution when tightening this terminal. Only tighten it one-quarter turn past finger tight or damage may result.

The principle of operation of the thermocouple is that as the tip of the thermocouple containing the two dissimilar metals is heated in a common flame, a direct current (DC) voltage is produced that gets sent along the insulated wire encased in the copper tube to the terminal that is attached to the electromagnet in the gas valve.

The voltage produced energizes the electromagnet, which allows the gas to continue to flow to the appliance. If the pilot flame were to go out, the tip, or hot junction, cools and the voltage stops. When the voltage stops being produced, the electromagnet portion of the gas control valve becomes de-energized, the gas flow stops and the flame goes out. It is now necessary to relight the burner.

So how much voltage are we talking about anyway? Approximately 25 to 30 millivolts are produced by the typical RV thermocouple. It will vary somewhat with its overall length. One millivolt is one one-thousandths of one volt, so it is a relatively small output voltage.

Occasionally, thermocouples become faulty and must be replaced. Less frequently, electromagnets may also fail. Some gas control valves have replaceable magnets while others do not. On those appliances with non-replaceable magnets, the entire gas valve must be replaced.

Thermocouples are relatively inexpensive items. It is recommended to carry an extra thermocouple for each RV appliance. It could very well be cheap insurance and will guarantee a smooth flowing LP gas system during the trip.

What can you do to help extend the life of the thermocouples? Once a year use a wad of fine steel wool to brighten up the tip of the thermocouple. Carbon buildup from the open pilot flame can cause erratic temperature differences between the hot and cold junctions in the thermocouple resulting in intermittent operation of that appliance.

Fig. 8-29 shows a thermocouple with a distinctive carbon buildup near the hot junction.

Rub gently with fine steel wool (see Fig. 8-30).

The thermocouple tip is now clean (Fig. 8-31).

Inexpensive aftermarket thermocouple testers are available that test the effectiveness of thermocouples. Also, if the volt-ohm meter (VOM) in your tool kit incorporates a millivolt scale, you can perform an open circuit voltage test or bench test on the thermocouples to test their output.

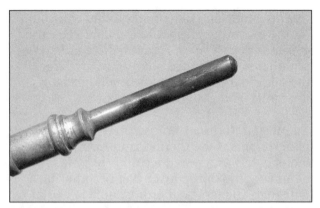

Fig. 8-29; Thermocouple with carbon buildup

Fig. 8-30; Cleaning a thermocouple that has carbon buildup

Fig. 8-31; A clean thermcouple

To test a thermocouple's output, first disconnect the terminal of the thermocouple from the gas valve. Attach the negative lead from the VOM to the outer copper tube casing anywhere along the length of the thermocouple. Attach the positive lead from the meter to the terminal button at the very end of the thermocouple. Second, apply a flame to the hot junction until the voltage

Fig. 8-32; Using an aftermarket thermocouple tester

reaches between 25 and 30 millivolts. If a thermocouple cannot produce that much, chances are it is faulty and should be replaced. After the test, only tighten the terminal one-quarter turn past finger tight.

On pilotless appliances, a printed circuit board controls the gas flow. The flame failure safety device on these direct spark units is considered integrated into the electronics of the board, coupled with a flame sense probe positioned in the flame much like a thermocouple. These, too, can be tested but it requires special equipment not likely to be carried by the average RVer. Therefore, testing of direct spark ignited appliances is best left to the professional service technician.

Additional Notes About LP Usage

• Always remain safety conscious. Never compromise the safety factor.

• Never overfill any LP container. Do not allow an LP retailer to fill any container more than 80% full. Avoid topping off the tank.

• The POL fitting is a left-hand thread; the ACME Type I (green) nut is a right-hand thread. Do not use any pipe dope or sealant on either fitting. Adding a sealant may actually cause a leak. The ACME Type I fitting is to be hand-tightened only.

• Always bubble test any fitting that has been disconnected, loosened and reconnected.

• Never use a flame to test for leaks. Always use a soapy solution that does not contain ammonia or chlorine derivatives.

• On twin DOT cylinder installations, such as on a travel trailer, install the cylinders with the open portion of the collar ring facing the trailer, not the tow vehicle. The closed collar will protect each tank's service valve from road debris kicked up by the tow vehicle.

• Never store LP containers indoors. Do not expose the containers to heat and always plug or cap the service valve when not in use.

• The safest way to travel with LP containers is with the service valve turned off. This is especially true when filling up at a gas station. Never have appliances lit while refueling with gasoline or diesel.

• Leak test the complete system at least once per camping season.

• Use common sense. If you smell LP, immediately turn off the supply of gas.

• If in doubt - don't. If you do not feel comfortable performing any procedure on the LP system or any of the appliances, turn off the LP container and call the local RV service center.

A detailed DVD showing the preventive maintenance procedures for the LP system, including setting the delivery line pressure and testing the RV for leaks, is available directly from the author or through RVIA:

http://www.rvdoctor.com/dvd.html

As crucial as the LP system is to enjoying the advantages of self-contained RVing, possessing a thorough knowledge of the system and its components will further enhance your ability to stay on the road. Next, let's explore the individual RV appliances.

Chapter 9

Range: Stovetop/Oven

Overview

Of all the RV appliances, LP range, consisting typically of a combination cooktop and oven, requires the least behavioral modifications for owners in their transition from house to RV. The largest hurdle to get over is simply the smaller size and possibly the differences in cooking times for some meals.

Fig. 9-1; Typical LP range

The only LP burning appliance that is not directly vented to the exterior of the RV, the range is considered so trouble-free that many owners only take the time to learn how to light the pilots and operate the oven. By learning slightly more than that, you can minimize downtime and loss of repair dollars by simply being acquainted with the sequence of operation and knowing how to test a couple of the components.

Pilot Model Ranges

As mentioned, the range consists of two appliances in one. The cooktop usually consists of three or four burners, much like a residential house range, that may or may not be lighted by a pilot assembly. Many manufacturers offer both models. The other component to the range is the oven. Some older ovens were situated above the cooktop, the so called "eye level" units, while some are configured with the oven positioned below the stove. Usually, the only shared component is the incoming gas line. Some models also share a portion of the thermostat.

Yet others are stand-alone cooktops.

The pilot model cooktop is the only LP appliance without a 100% safety shutoff device. Unlike all the other appliances, if the pilot flame were to be extinguished on the stove, the pilot gas would continue to flow. Granted, there would not be a great deal of gas flowing but caution must still prevail. If the stove pilot is extinguished, turn the gas off at the LP container and wait a minimum of five minutes before attempting to light the pilot again. If the RV has been closed up for any length of time, open the windows and allow the RV to air out.

Safety Note: Some RVs are equipped with just a gas cooktop and a separate electrically operated convection and/or microwave oven. It is not recommended for RVers to troubleshoot and repair convection or microwave ovens. These are better left to the professionals.

Stove Components

The components found on a typical pilot model cooktop include:

- Internal or third-stage regulator
- Manifold
- Burner valves
- Stove burner
- Flash tubes or ignitor assembly
- Pilot burner
- Manual pilot valve
- Thermostat control assembly

On some units, an internal LP regulator, which further reduces the delivered line pressure, is

Fig. 9-2; Appliance regulator on a range

positioned at the point where the LP line enters the range and connects to the main manifold. This third stage typically reduces the 11 inches water column (WC) that is set at the main regulator at the LP container to a point below 10 inches WC. The regulator is secured to the manifold pipe. The manifold pipe is that portion of the range to which the burner valves and the thermostat are attached. The manifold distributes the LP to each of the burners. Each burner valve controls one of the three or four stove burners commonly found on RV cooktops. Each burner valve also houses the orifice for that burner as well.

The cooktop burners usually consist of the burner head, a mixing tube or venturi and the primary air inlet. The mixing tube is positioned over the orifice fitting on the burner valve. As incoming LP is passed through the orifice, it draws in primary air through the opening in the mixing tube. The air and the LP are mixed in the tube and burned at the burner head. On rare occasions the primary air inlet may include adjustable air shutters. In those instances, position the shutter so the flame is predominantly blue with a hint of orange or yellow on the tips of the flame.

Fig. 9-4; Manifolds with round and square tubing

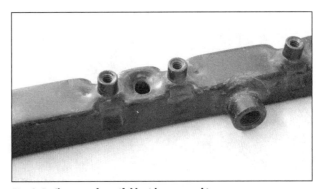

Fig. 9-5; Close up of manifold with square tubing

The close-up view in Fig. 9-5 shows a square manifold. The burner valves bolt to this manifold. On the round pipe manifold, the valves are threaded into pretapped holes.

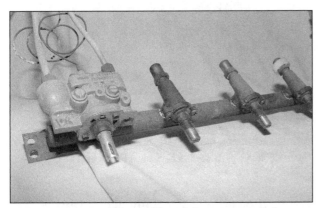

Fig. 9-3; Cooktop manifold assembly with thermostat attached

Fig. 9-3 shows the manifold piping assembly with burner valves and attached thermostat.

Some manifolds are made of round piping while others are formed with square tubing as shown in Fig. 9-4.

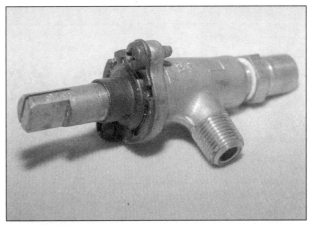

Fig. 9-6; Cooktop burner valve

Each stove burner will have a dedicated burner valve attached to the manifold pipe.

Fig. 9-7; Cooktop burner

Most RV cooktops usually have three or four individual burners.

Fig. 9-8; Burner valve orifice hood

Each burner valve contains an orifice hood with a precisely machined orifice opening. The size of the orifice opening determines the British thermal unit (BTU) rating of that burner. Many cooktops today will have burners of varying ratings.

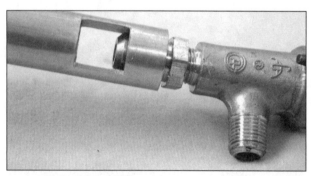

Fig. 9-9; Burner valve and burner tube

Fig. 9-9 shows the relational positioning of an individual burner valve and its burner tube. The orifice hood extends into the mixing tube portion of the burner near the primary air inlet.

As the LP flows through the burner valve into the mixing tube, air is drawn in through the primary air inlet and mixed with the LP on its way to the burner head as shown in Fig. 9-10.

Fig. 9-10; Air inlet mixes air with the incoming LP

Stove burner ports occasionally become clogged with cooking grease. Remove the burners and soak them in a mild solution of liquid detergent and water. Lightly scrub them with a soft bristle brush. Use a wooden toothpick for stubborn areas in and around the burner openings. Take care not to distort or otherwise enlarge the burner ports. Many are constructed of soft aluminum and are easily damaged.

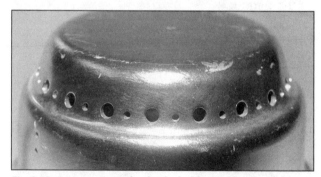

Fig. 9-11; Burner ports need to be checked for blockages

The methods used to actually light a stove burner run the gamut from simple manual methods such as kitchen matches or butane lighter to automatic devices. Some are equipped with a push-button piezo (pee-AY-zo) ignitor, individual automatic piezo-activated burner valves, electronic ignition modules or a standing pilot assembly.

Pilotless stove burners ignited manually are lit by simply opening the burner valve and lighting

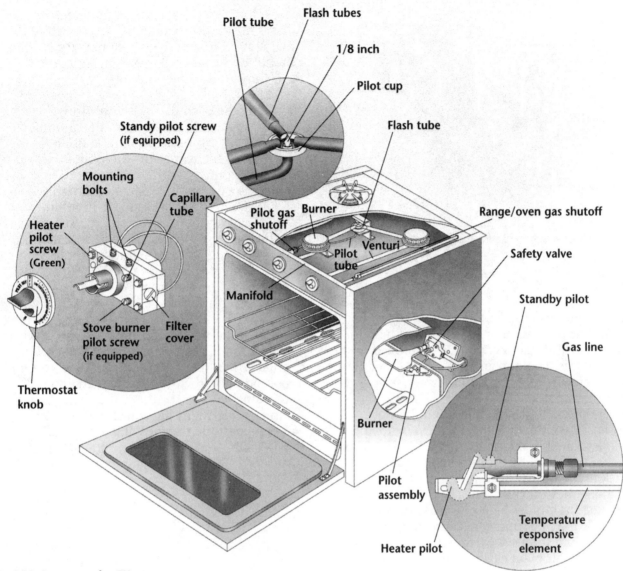

Fig. 9-12; Components of an RV range

a match near the burner head. If the stove is equipped with a push-button piezo ignitor, open the burner valve and push the ignitor rapidly until the burner is lit. The piezo produces a high-voltage spark that will ignite the incoming LP at the burner head.

Some burner valves engage an automatic piezo ignitor integral to each valve on the stove. Turning the valve allows LP to flow to the burner head at the same time an automatic spark is produced. This method is common to household cooktops as well. Still others may be equipped with electronic ignition modules.

The photo below shows a common push-button piezo ignitor.

Fig. 9-13; Typical push-button piezo ignitor

Fig. 9-14; A burner valve with integral piezo

A burner valve with an integral piezo ignitor is shown in Fig. 9-14.

A very common method of lighting the stove burners is by a centrally located standing pilot assembly. The standing pilot is positioned in the center of the cooktop and has tubes, called flash tubes, attached to each burner head (see photo).

Flash tubes allow LP to flow from the stove burner down the tube to be ignited by the pilot flame located in the center of the burners. This gas is consumed by the pilot flame and burns back to the burner head where the flashback flame ignites the burner head. It is imperative that the flash tubes be positioned downward towards the pilot burner because LP is heavier than air and it must flow down to the pilot flame. If a problem exists prohibiting any of the burners from being ignited by the pilot flame, chances are the flash tubes are misaligned.

Fig. 9-15; Flash tubes

The pilot burner itself is an open-flame burner that is positioned equidistant from each of the four stove burners. The height of the pilot flame should be no taller than 3/8 inches above the rim surrounding the pilot tube.

Typically the oven thermostat controls the cooktop pilot. On those units, the pilot tube runs directly from the oven pilot assembly in the oven to the rear of the thermostat located on the front control section of the oven. On such units, the oven pilot is usually adjustable via a small adjusting screw located behind the thermostat knob. To access the adjustment simply pull the thermostat knob straight off the shaft. There will be corresponding holes in the bezel through which the adjustment screw is accessible. If no holes are visible, it's of the nonadjustable variety.

The oven thermostat control assembly attaches directly to the gas pipe manifold as mentioned earlier. When the oven thermostat controls the cooktop pilot, the dial will be marked accordingly.

In years past the thermostat dial was labeled "Pilots Off" and a separate position that simply read "Off." Though not graphically displayed,

Fig. 9-16; Oven thermostat control, pilot on

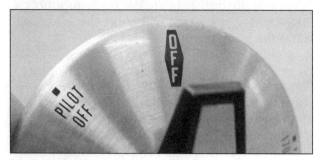

Fig. 9-17; Oven thermostat control, pilot off

the off position really meant pilots on. On this type of thermostat, when the dial is set to "Off," pilot gas is actually being fed to the cooktop pilot and the oven pilot at the same time. With this type, when the thermostat is turned to the "Off" position you should immediately light the two pilot flames. RVers have inadvertently left the thermostat in the "Off" position during a period of storage only to find the LP tank drained of all fuel. Because of the confusion of the "Off" position actually meaning pilots on, thermostat dials were reconfigured to reflect a more logical labeling method. Here are two examples of oven thermostat dials:

Just be aware of the type thermostat dial you have so no confusion abounds!

Oven Components

The components of the range pertinent to the oven include:

- Thermostat control assembly
- Safety valve
- Pilot assembly
- Main burner assembly

The oven thermostat control assembly allows LP to flow to the cooktop pilot, the oven pilot and ultimately, to the main burner assembly in the oven. Attached to the thermostat is the temperature sensing probe, positioned inside the oven. This is the portion of the thermostat that monitors the inside temperature and allows the thermostat to ignite the main burner when more heat is called for.

Fig. 9-19; Typical oven with door open

Fig. 9-20; An oven thermostat

Many times a thermostat is wrongly accused of being faulty when, in fact, the temperature sensing probe may simply be covered with cooking oils, grease or even oven cleaner, and is simply not sensing the temperature correctly. Keeping this sensing element clean will eliminate many problems associated with false oven temperatures.

Take care when handling the temperature sensing probe. It attaches to the thermostat by the use of a small capillary tube that is an integral part of the thermostat. This capillary tube is somewhat fragile and will kink easily. If kinked or broken it will mandate a complete thermostat replacement.

Fig. 9-18; Oven temperature sensing probe

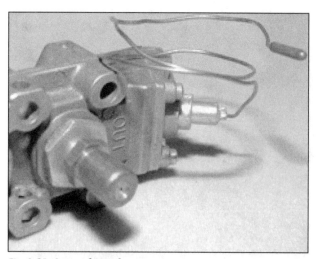

Fig. 9-21; Oven saftey valve

The safety valve is second in line after the thermostat to receive the LP fuel intended for the main burner in the oven. The oven safety valve is equipped with a capillary tube filled with mercury on older ranges. On newer units, because of a ban on mercury by some US states, the safety valve contains an electromagnet. In either case, the operating principle remains the same. Once heated by an extended pilot flame, the safety valve opens and fuel flows to the main burner where it is ignited by the pilot.

The oven pilot assembly is typically match lit. To light the pilot flame, turn the thermostat dial to either the "Off" position or the "Pilots On" position (if that confuses you, refer to the thermostat knob discussion above) and position a match near the pilot assembly. Once the pilot is lit the oven thermostat can be set to the desired cooking temperature.

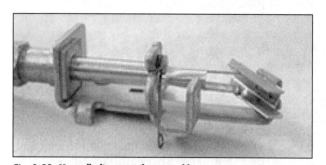

Fig. 9-22; Manually lit oven pilot assembly

Sequence of Operation

After the thermostat is set to a temperature

(assuming the pilot flame is lit in the oven), the oven pilot becomes slightly larger and begins to heat a thermal bulb attached to the safety valve. This photo shows a thermal bulb attached to the pilot assembly. This thermal bulb, when heated by the pilot flame, expands a bellows in the safety valve or energizes an electromagnet and allows the LP to flow through the safety valve and on to the main burner where it is ignited. This results in a time delay from when the oven thermostat is first set to a desired temperature until the main burner actually ignites.

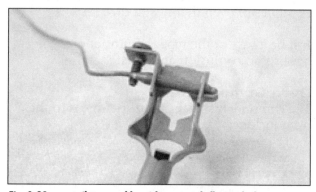

Fig. 9-23; oven pilot assembly with mercury bulb attached

A good way to tell which component may be faulty in a situation where the main burner will not ignite at all is to carefully watch the oven pilot. While watching the pilot flame, turn the oven thermostat knob above 300° F. Immediately the standing pilot should expand and envelope the thermal bulb portion of the safety valve. If it fails to gain in size, replace the thermostat. If it indeed becomes bigger and engulfs the thermal bulb, then the safety valve is faulty and needs replacing. The positioning of the thermal bulb in the secondary pilot flame is crucial. It has to be in the fire of the secondary pilot in order to activate the safety valve.

The main burner varies in design among manufacturers. Some burners are straight tubes with burner ports on either side. Others are flat, plate-like devices that configure the main flame into somewhat of a circular pattern.

In either case, the main burner will remain ignited until the desired temperature is attained inside the oven as sensed by the oven temperature sensing probe portion of the thermostat.

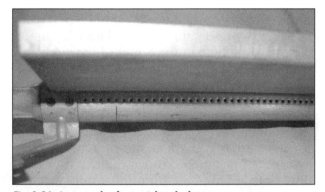

Fig. 9-24; An example of a straight tube burner

Fig. 9-25; An example of a flat burner

The broil setting on the thermostat bypasses the limit of the thermostat. In this setting the burner will remain ignited until the oven knob is repositioned to a different setting or turned to the "Off" position.

The RV oven can take a little getting used to. It has happened that the thermostat actually falls out of calibration and cooking times are not the same as in the house oven. In many instances, using the same ingredients, same recipe, same duration and the same set temperature will yield different cooking results.

If oven problems occur, the first item to check is the oven door seal. However, some ovens found in RVs are susceptible to fluctuating LP gas inlet pressures or other phenomena which varies the way a favorite dish will emerge from the oven. In some cases, it may be possible to compensate by calibrating the oven thermostat. It will be necessary to first determine if the thermostat can be calibrated. Not all oven thermostats have that ability.

All thermostats found on RVs that can be calibrated will have a slotted screw adjustment inside the shaft, located behind the thermostat knob. Remove the knob and look into the shaft. If no slot is visible, that thermostat cannot be field calibrated; it must be replaced.

There is no screwdriver slot inside this thermostat shaft; this one cannot be calibrated.

Fig. 9-26; A thermostat that cannot be calibrated

You can clearly see the screwdriver slot inside this thermostat shaft. This one is easily calibrated.

Fig. 9-27; A thermostat that can be calibrated

Oven Calibration Procedures

If the oven is deemed inaccurate, measure the temperature to test the thermostat. Calibrate if the actual temperature varies more than plus or minus ten degrees of the set thermostat temperature. Be sure normal convection air flow inside the oven is not blocked by the use of wide baking sheets, tin foil, etc.

Calibrating an adjustable thermostat requires a good, accurate oven thermometer. The small cooking, spring-type thermometers are neither accurate nor reliable enough for the task of calibrating. Some digital models are relatively inexpensive.

Check to see that the oven temperature sensing bulb is positioned correctly in the oven and that no grease or oven cleaner is coating the bulb, either of which could result in abnormal operation of the thermostat as previously mentioned.

Set the thermostat to 300° F and cycle the oven two or three times to warm the unit. Note: When actually setting the thermostat do not go past the desired temperature, but turn the knob just up to it. Place the thermometer in the center of the empty oven.

Note the first measurement or reading when the main burner ignites again. You should be able to hear it ignite. Continue to let the burner operate. Take the second reading as soon as the main burner flame goes out and reverts back to the pilot. Again, listen closely. This completes one cycle.

The thermostat will need to be calibrated if the average temperature varies more than 10 degrees from the original 300-degree setting. To obtain the average temperature, subtract the lesser of the above readings from the greater. Add one third of that difference to the lesser number. This final average should be within plus or minus 10 degrees of 300.

To illustrate thermostat calibration, for example, when the oven reignites, assume the first temperature reading is 307° F. After one cycle, the second reading is 319° F. The difference between the two is 12. One third of that difference is 4, added to the lower reading (307 plus 4 equals 311 degrees). This thermostat exceeds the plus or minus ten degrees and is in need of calibration.

To illustrate conversely, when the oven reignites, assume the temperature reading 302° F. After one cycle the second reading is 311° F. The difference between the two is 9. One third of that difference is 3, added to the lower reading (302 plus 3 equals 305 degrees). This thermostat is within the tolerance of plus or minus ten degrees and does not need calibrating.

If the oven thermostat needs calibrating, it will be necessary to obtain a second knob for that range. Drill a hole in the center of the knob and install this test knob on the thermostat shaft taking care not to rotate the shaft. Insert a flat blade screwdriver through the knob into the adjusting slot in the shaft of the thermostat. Again be careful not to rotate the shaft. Holding the screwdriver still, rotate the knob only to the average temperature recorded in the test procedure noted above. It is critical that only the knob rotate, and the screwdriver and shaft remain steady. Using the above example, rotate the knob as close to 311° F as possible.

After calibrating, test the results by again measuring the temperatures. If the thermostat is of the nonadjustable convention, it will be necessary to replace that thermostat in order to have correct cooking times.

Troubleshooting

The chart will help determine the cause of some common symptoms with the RV range. Be sure to record the model number and serial number of the range for future reference when ordering parts or discussing a problem with a service facility.

Preventive Maintenance

Owner maintenance for the RV range is relatively simple. The only items to check in advance of operational problems are the following:

- Be sure the LP pressure is set correctly
- Keep the temperature sensing probe clean and free from cooking oils and oven cleaners
- Periodically check the door seal
- Perform the ten-degree temperature differentiation test at least every two years
- Keep the pilot assemblies clean
- Keep the ports on the stove burners clean

Like other LP appliances, all manufacturers will provide an owner's manual detailing operational and safety issues. The wise RVer always reads the owner's manual. Very few problems will arise when RVers follow these mandates.

Troubleshooting the RV Range	
Symptom	**Possible Causes**
Stove pilot will not stay lit	Insufficient LP supply
	Incorrect LP pressure
	Blocked pilot orifice
	Pilot flame too large or too low
Stove burners will not ignite	Incorrect LP pressure
	Incorrect fuel/air mixture
	Flash tubes bent or mispositioned
	Blocked burner charge ports
	Faulty ignitor
Flame lifts off burner head	Too much LP pressure
	Incorrect fuel/air mixture
Oven burner will not ignite	Incorrect LP pressure
	Incorrect fuel/air mixture
	Blocked oven pilot orifice
	Temperature probe mispositioned
	Faulty safety valve
	Faulty oven thermostat

Fig. 9-28; Check for worn seals on the oven door

Chapter 10

Water Heater

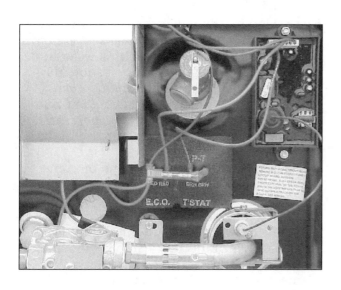

Overview

Prolonged hot showers when at home are predominantly taken for granted by most of us, but while traveling in an RV a hot shower involves an interesting test of timing. It is truly an experienced RVer who is aware of just how long it takes for six to ten gallons of hot water to trickle down the drain. The goal is to have all remnants of soap suds accompany that last drop of hot water at precisely the same time. However, within less than an hour, fresh, hot water will once again be available to stream forth from that shower head.

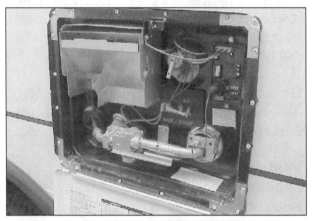

Fig. 10-1; Installed water heater with open access door

The RV water heater is a most welcomed appliance to the family of liquid propane burning appliances found on just about every RV. Hot water for bathing and for washing dishes makes life on the road much easier. Hot water has certainly been endearing to many novice RVers who would never go "camping" unless shower facilities are available.

The RV water heater, as with any of the LP-fired appliances, needs occasional maintenance to keep it in shape. Fortunately, the water heater is the easiest of the appliances on which to work. Usually situated at a comfortable height, most components are located on the outside of the RV, easily accessed behind the vented door. Some older models have printed circuit boards and thermostats located on the rear of the unit, but for the most part most have all newer units have the controls and components on the exterior.

Water Heater Types

The predominant model today is the automatic spark model, commonly referred to as the direct spark ignition (DSI) model. This unit is fully automatic. All that is necessary for the owner to do is simply make sure the heater is filled with water and then flip a switch. All components and related functions are controlled by a printed circuit board.

The second most popular choice found today is the standard pilot-type water heater. These units are the latest versions of the earliest water heater models. Simple in design and operation, they have been a mainstay for many years. Even though they are less expensive than their automatic cousins, they are slightly less popular. It appears automation wins out over economics.

Another type of water heater found on some earlier RVs is the electric-only version. Powered by 120 volts alternating current (AC), these units are only operated when plugged into shoreline or when on-board generator power is available. Some units today are a combination of LP gas and electric. An electric heating element is emerged in the tank portion of the water heater. This format allows the RVer to operate the water heater on LP while dry camping or traveling and on 120 volts AC while plugged in overnight at the campground.

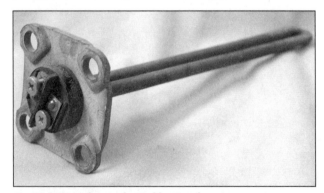

Fig. 10-2; Water heater electrical heating element

Another feature that is available on some water heaters on motorhomes is the motor-aid or heat exchanger kit. This feature allows the engine cooling lines to be routed through a pipe that circulates inside the water heater tank, thereby heating the stored water while driving. By the time the motorhomer reaches his or her destination or a stop for lunch, hot water is already present at the faucet. This kit conserves LP fuel while traveling. However, the maintenance factor becomes greater with the motor-aid models. Periodically, the hoses will need to be replaced. On some of the larger Class A motorhomes or conversion buses, this could be an expensive yet necessary venture.

Yet another type of water heater is the space-saving tankless (not thankless!) water heater; commonly called an instantaneous water heater. In this design there is no actual storage tank. Incoming water flows through a coil as it is heated by an LP flame. The burner is only lit when there is a demand for water. As soon as the hot faucet is turned off, the burner goes off as well. The burner heats the water only as the water flows; activation is automatic via an impeller-type switching valve.

Some earlier tankless models utilized a pilot flame, but the majority of water heaters available today are automatically ignited much like the standard DSI RV water heater. Since there is no storage tank, there is no recovery time associated with the instantaneous water heaters, hence the name. Also, since there is no storage tank, some components normally associated with water heaters are eliminated such as the thermostat. There are multiple safety features built in, however.

The British thermal unit (BTU) input is quite high on instantaneous units, sometimes up to 50,000 BTUs depending on the design of the burner ports. There is virtually no owner maintenance required by an instantaneous water heater; simply keep the LP regulator set properly. If your RV is equipped with an instantaneous water heater, consult the manufacturer should operational problems arise.

Common Components

The DSI automatic ignition water heater and the pilot water heater both have many of the same components and some that are pertinent to just one or the other type of heater. The components common to both types of water heaters are:

- Inner tank
- Pressure and temperature (P&T) relief valve
- Drain
- Main burner orifice
- Mixing tube
- Primary air adjustment

The inner tank of a water heater is surrounded with insulation and typically covered with a cardboard, foam or a metal covering. Since water heaters are usually installed under a cabinet or another structure, external aesthetics are not necessarily a consideration.

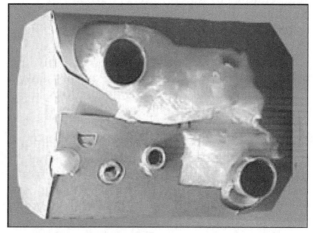

Fig. 10-3; Water heater inner tank

The P&T relief valve is an interesting device. As a safety component, the P&T valve has often been viewed by RVers as an item of mystery. Many P&T valves have been unnecessarily replaced, thought to be defective because they dripped water every day. By design and intent, however, the P&T relief valve will usually drip some water during each heating cycle.

The P&T relief valve will drip water occasionally because as any containerized liquid is heated, that liquid will expand, causing not only a rise in temperature but also a rise in pressure. Since the RV water heater is a tank filled with water, if there were no method to regulate or control this expansion during the heating cycle the unchecked pressures and temperature could rupture the tank within the water heater resulting in serious injury.

Fig. 10-4; Pressure and temperature (P&T) relief valve

Temperatures in water heaters above 210° F are considered unsafe. Therefore, all P&T valves on today's water heaters are preset (nonadjustable) to open at 210° F. In the small confines of the RV water heater, the water is heated very quickly with a rather inordinately large LP burner flame, so keeping up with the drastic fluctuations of both temperature and pressure is no easy task.

In RV water heaters, or any pressurized tank for that matter, there is usually a cushion of air at the very top above the water level that acts as an accumulator and buffers the water. It also allows space for the water to expand into while being heated. This air (oxygen) is eventually absorbed into the oxygen portion of the water. At this point, there is no place for the expanding water to move into since the tank is literally completely full. The P&T valve then does its job of becoming a virtual hot water faucet - it opens. Expelling hot water from the outlet of the P&T valve allows more cold water to enter the tank (lowering the temperature), and the relief valve snaps shut.

Usually, draining some water from the water heater tank will reinstate this cushion of air if excessive dripping is encountered. To accomplish this, remove the water source (either turn the demand pump off or interrupt the city water flow), and open any two hot water faucets in the coach. Next, open the manual lever on the relief valve until the water flow stops. Close the valve and the faucets, then turn the pressure back on.

The fact that this dripping of the relief valve seems to be more prevalent today is justified by the design and the sophistication level of the

modern water heater. Back in the good ol' days all water heaters were thermostatically controlled manually. Today, with the prominence of electronic ignition and circuit boards, control of the temperature of the water is removed from the RVer. On many units the thermostat is a preset, temperature sensing, normally closed thermal switch that electrically turns off the water heating sequence when the preset temperature has been reached.

There will continue to be P&T valves that simply fail, not seal or otherwise become faulty, but by and large all will drip occasionally. They must, however, drip slightly only during the heating cycle. If indeed they drip or weep during non-heating phases and the pressure within the fresh water system is less than 150 pounds per square inch (psi), then the relief valve may be faulty.

Since heating water within the confines of a closed tank will result in the expansion of that water and virtually all P&T relief valves will drip a little during the normal heating cycle, it must be determined how much is excessive. How much should a P&T valve drip? And how much is a little bit? Why doesn't it drip every single time? Why only sometimes? There are basically seven reasons why the P&T relief valve might drip that also govern how much water it will drip. When and how much water the P&T valve drips is determined by:

1. The temperature and the pressure of the incoming water from within the fresh water system to the water heater. Once the temperature or pressure rating of the relief valve has been exceeded, the disc valve opens, expelling the hot water. As the cold water comes into the tank, how cold that water is and at what pressure it is being forced into the water heater will determine how long the disc valve portion stays open. The longer the disc valve portion stays open, the more water will drip. As the water temperature inside the water heater is cooled by the incoming water, the disc valve closes.

2. The cleanliness of the thermostat or probe portion of the relief valve. Mineral deposits and galvanic corrosion will leave a residue on the probe that could slow the temperature sensing process slightly.

3. The pressure setting of the relief valve. Though mandated at not more than 150psi, some replacement P&T valves are rated at 125psi. Though certainly not dangerous, it will tend to drip more often than one rated for 150psi.

4. How much of a cushion of air is on top of the water inside the tank. If most or all of the air space or expansion space has been absorbed into the water, the relief valve will drip more often. Reinstate this expansion area and the relief valve will not drip as much.

5. The age and condition of the spring assembly inside the P&T relief valve. Constant usage of the manual lever on the valve will, over time, weaken the spring or cause mineral deposits to possibly get between the seat and the disc causing excessive dripping. The manual lever is best left undisturbed.

6. The temperature rating of the preset thermostat found on the electronic ignition water heaters, or the positioning of the manual thermostat. Lowering the manual thermostat setting or exchanging the preset thermostat for one that is rated at a lower temperature will lessen the frequency of the dripping.

7. The elevation and the atmospheric pressure at which the water heater is utilized. Although very slight, this will affect how much pressure occurs.

All water heaters have a drain of some type. Located on the front of the water heater towards the bottom left corner, some drains may have an actual valve, while others may simply be a

common pipe plug. Remove the plug or open the valve to drain the water heater. Open the hot water faucets inside the RV to aid in this draining.

The main burner orifice is threaded into either the gas control valve (in a pilot system) or the gas solenoid valve (in a DSI unit). This orifice directs the LP into the next component, the mixing tube.

Fig. 10-6; Main burner orifice

The mixing tube is where the LP and the primary air are mixed just prior to burning at the main burner. This tube, though not a precision component, must be kept clean, and more importantly, properly aligned. More often than not, misalignment of the mixing tube contributes to the majority of service-related ills with the LP water heater.

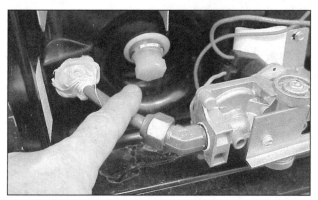

Fig. 10-5; Drain plug

Fig. 10-7; Air shutter/mixing tube

Fig. 10-8; Air shutter inlet adjustment

To understand how the LP and air are mixed, read on. As LP gas is projected through the main burner orifice, air is drawn in through the openings in the mixing tube. A "venturi effect" brings in a precise amount of air that is needed to mix with the LP in order to have safe and complete combustion. The LP pressure is set at 11 inches of water column (WC). The orifice has a specific opening, so the only variable is the amount of primary air allowed to enter. The primary air adjustment controls the volume of this incoming air.

The primary air adjustment is adjusted while the main burner flame is burning. The flame should appear mostly blue in color with some orange or yellow tinges. The adjustment is considered correct when the flame is the correct color and also when the flame is not a loud roaring flame. If you can hear the burner more than five feet away with the door closed, chances are the mixture is incorrect and further adjustment is necessary.

Suburban Manufacturing Company (www.rvcomfort.com) incorporates a component called an anode rod into its line of water heaters. The anode is a long cylindrical bar of magnesium alloy that is threaded into the inner tank at the rear of the heater on some older water heaters. Newer Suburban models configure the anode rod as a portion of the drain plug, making annual inspections easy. Designed as a sacrificial element, it keeps electrolysis to a minimum and extends the life of the inner tank. All chemical and mineral reactions taking place inside the tank will attack the "weaker" molecules of the magnesium anode instead of the aluminum or glass lining in the inner tank.

Periodically, this sacrificial anode will have to be replaced. A deteriorated anode rod will produce a less than favorable odor that permeates the water system and is released through the faucets. Most RVers assume this "rotten egg" smell is caused by something in the fresh water tank, but rarely do they consider the water heater tank an extension of the fresh water system. If a terrible odor is present at any of the faucets in the RV, seriously consider the anode rod in the water heater as the culprit. Full-timers should add an anode rod to the spare parts kit if their water heater is equipped with one. Atwood water heaters do not require an anode.

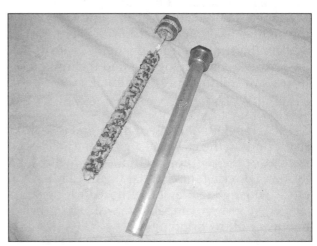

Fig. 10-9; Partially sacrificed anode rod and a brand new one

Pilot Model Components

The components that are common only to pilot model water heaters include:

- Pilot assembly
- Gas control valve
- Thermocouple

Fig. 10-10; Pilot assembly

The pilot assembly consists of the pilot orifice and the pilot burner. The pilot orifice is typically the location where spiders and other insects love to build their nests. It is one of the smallest LP components found on RVs, and since it is constantly exposed to outdoor conditions, it is most susceptible to blockages. Periodically, the pilot orifice should be removed, soaked in a solution such as acetone and simply air-dried. As with any orifice, never poke anything into or through it to clean it. They are usually made of very soft aluminum or brass and are easily damaged.

In some instances, tough blockages in the pilot orifice may need a little assistance. In those cases, soak the orifice and blow through it with compressed air in the opposite direction of the normal flow of the LP. After using compressed air, always soak the orifice again in acetone and let it air dry. Avoid using compressed air alone since some air compressors contain vast amounts of moisture that may cause erratic flame characteristics at some LP burners.

Using acetone, which displaces water and quickly evaporates, will usually eliminate any moisture concerns. Take care, though, when using chemicals such as acetone. Wear proper protection for the skin and eyes.

Two common pilot assemblies are found in use today. One type has a separate thermocouple and pilot assembly (Robertshaw). The other type has a combination thermocouple and pilot assembly (Baso). They are not interchangeable.

Fig. 10-11; Unitrol control valve

The gas control valve is a complex unit that performs nine different functions for the water heater. They are:

- Water heater thermostat
- 100% safety gas valve
- High temperature energy cut-off (ECO)
- Main burner LP pressure regulator
- Internal LP gas filter
- Main burner gas valve
- Pilot burner gas valve and adjustment point
- LP pressure test tap
- Pilot burner pressure regulator

The control valve accommodates the manual knob that allows the owner to light the pilot flame, set the water temperature and shut off the appliance completely. The lower section of the gas control usually has an elbow fitting along with a threaded main burner orifice. Additionally, the incoming LP line attaches to this control as does the pilot tube and thermocouple.

Fig. 10-12; Note the position of the knob for lighting the pilot

The gas control valve threads into the inner tank portion of the water heater, immersing the temperature sensing tube portion into the tank of water. Internal to this temperature sensing probe is the ECO. This is a normally closed, thermally controlled device that will open the circuit, interrupting the voltage being produced by the thermocouple when the water temperature exceeds a safe limit. When this circuit is broken, the electromagnet portion of the built-in safety device snaps shut, effectively shutting off the LP supply to the pilot and main burners.

The temperature sensing probe also houses the thermostat probe that will shut off the main burner gas supply once the temperature of the water has reached the setting established by the user. In this instance, the pilot flame will remain lit as long as the thermocouple is positioned correctly in the flame and continues to produce at least eight millivolts.

The thermocouple is positioned in the pilot flame and is attached to the electromagnet portion of the 100% safety valve located in the gas control assembly. Remember to keep the tip of the thermocouple cleaned and positioned in the pilot flame.

DSI Model Components

The following components pertain only to the automatic ignition water heaters activated by the flip of a switch from inside the RV. Aside from the common components listed above, the DSI models also have:

- Thermostat
- ECO switch
- LP solenoid gas valve
- Printed circuit board
- Electrode assembly

The nonadjustable thermostat is a thermal disc device secured to the front or rear of the water heater in direct contact with the inner tank. Most thermostats for DSI water heaters are preset for temperatures between 120 and 140° F. Wired in line between the PC board and the

solenoid gas valve is the ECO switch. A thermal disc device is affixed to the inner tank. Some may contain a resettable push-button; others will automatically reset once the water temperature drops below the preset temperature rating of the ECO. The ECO and the thermostat are additional safety devices to help protect the appliance.

The LP solenoid gas valve is ultimately controlled by the circuit board. The incoming gas line attaches to one end of this valve while the main burner fitting and orifice attach to the other end. Energized by 12 volts direct current (DC) from the board, the gas valve will remain open as long as it is receiving voltage. This valve will close under the following conditions:

- Water temperature reaches thermostat setting
- ECO opens the circuit to the board
- 12 volts DC is not supplied by the circuit board

The circuit board is the heart of any DSI appliance. Similar to the furnace, the board on DSI water heaters performs the following three functions:

- Provides 12 volts DC to the LP solenoid gas valve allowing gas flow to the main burner.

Fig. 10-14; Circuit board

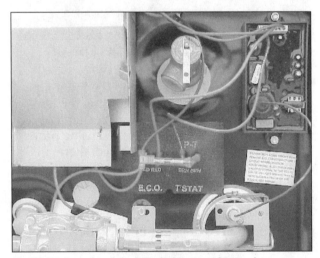

Fig. 10-13; Examples of the ECO, thermostat and P&T valve

• Creates a high-voltage output spark that ignites the LP at the main burner.

• Monitors the flame sense current from the electrode assembly and sends the unit into lockout when it fails to detect a flame; some water heaters are equipped with three-try circuit boards that will go into lockout after three failed attempts to ignite the burner. Additionally, the board permits a timed purge cycle prior to sending a spark to the electrode assembly.

The electrode assembly receives the high-voltage output from the circuit board and creates an electrical arc to ground. At the same time, the LP and air mixture is forced to flow through this electrical arc causing ignition of the fuel at the main burner. The electrode probe also "senses" the presence of the fire and sends a micro-amp signal back to the board allowing the gas valve to remain open. If the flame is unstable or is extinguished for any reason, the micro-amp circuit between the electrode and board is opened and the board shuts off the voltage to the gas valve and it closes.

This electrode assembly is susceptible to carbon buildup and heat stresses over a period of time. Many circuit boards have been replaced in error when the cause of an outage has simply been a carboned electrode assembly. In fact, a recent poll determined that the majority of water heater service problems are caused by the electrode assembly, more so than any other component on the water heater. For this reason, it is advisable to carry a spare water heater electrode assembly in the spare parts kit.

Sequences of Operation

Though the two major RV water heater manufacturers (Atwood and Suburban) utilize much of the same technology and methodology, each brand of water heater has some distinct variances in the order of operation. What follows are the sequences of operation for each manufacturer.

Both Atwood and Suburban start their sequences at the water heater switch located inside the RV. This switch is equipped with a red lamp, commonly referred to as the "failure to

ignite" lamp. The sequence begins by turning on this switch. Typically the lamp will light immediately and then go out during the attempt to ignite the burner. Once the burner ignites, the lamp stays extinguished. If it fails to ignite properly, or if the flame blows out, the lamp is illuminated indicating a failure to the RVer.

Atwood Sequence
• When the water heater switch is activated, voltage is passed to the thermostat.
• The normally closed thermostat passes the voltage on to a thermal cutoff.
• The thermal cutoff passes the voltage to the circuit board.
• Once the board is energized, ignition spark is produced and voltage is passed to the ECO switch.
• Voltage then passes through the ECO to the gas valve, opening the valve.
• LP is passed through the valve into the burner where it is ignited by the spark from the circuit board.
• Once a flame is established, the flame sense circuit on the circuit board stops the sparking and the board keeps the gas valve open.
• Once the designated water temperature is reached the thermostat opens the circuit and power is stopped and the flame goes out.
• As you use hot water, the temperature drops and the thermostat closes and the cycle starts over.
• The cycles continue until you turn off the water heater switch or a problem develops with the flame, the thermostat or the thermal cutoff.

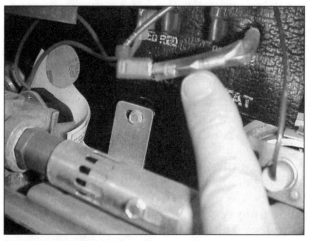

Fig. 10-15; Atwood thermal cutoff

Suburban Sequence

- When the water heater switch is activated, voltage is passed to the ECO switch.
- Voltage passes through the normally closed ECO and on to the thermostat.
- From the thermostat the voltage is directed to the circuit board.
- Once energized, the circuit board creates the spark and opens the gas valve.
- LP is passed through the valve into the burner where it is ignited by the spark from the circuit board.
- Once a flame is established, the flame sense circuit on the circuit board stops the sparking and the board keeps the gas valve open.
- Once the water temperature is reached the thermostat opens the circuit and power is stopped and the flame goes out.
- As you use hot water, the temperature drops and the thermostat closes and the cycle starts over.
- The cycles continue until you turn off the water heater switch or a flame failure problem develops.

With both Atwood and Suburban, if the flame fails to ignite, (after one to three tries), the circuit board puts the water heater into lockout. To eliminate a lockout condition, the RVer must turn the master water heater switch off and then back on.

Water Heater Maintenance

At least once, maybe twice during the camping season it will be necessary to clean and service the RV water heater. The water heater is exposed to the elements, therefore, road grime, dust and dirt have ample opportunity to gather in and around the various components (see photo). Periodically blowing the front area with compressed air will help minimize this condition. Likewise, soot and remnants of the products of combustion will gather in the flue portion of the water heater. Blow through the flue occasionally with compressed air as well. Be sure to wear eye protection when performing this step, as flying debris will be present.

Aside from general cleaning and blowing with compressed air, the following components will need periodic attention as well.

Fig. 10-16; Neglected main burner assembly

Electrode Assembly

Carbon deposits can be cleaned off and the probes brightened with steel wool. Inspect the probes and replace the assembly when the probes become pitted or if a portion of the ceramic insulator is broken. Check the gap between the probes. If the electrode assembly has three probes, the gap between the spark probe and the ground should be half as much as the gap between the ground probe and the flame sense probe. Adjust or move only the center ground probe to achieve this spacing. Additionally, never allow the spark to jump from the spark probe to the flame sense probe; it could damage the PC board. If the electrode assembly has only two probes, the gap should be approximately 1/8-inch. Take care when adjusting these probes. If any portion of the ceramic

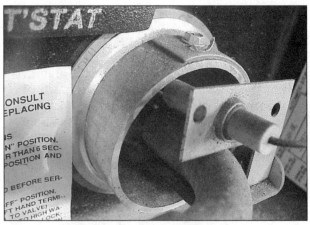

Fig. 10-17; Dirty burner and electrode assembly

insulator becomes cracked or broken, the entire electrode assembly will have to be replaced.

Pilot Assembly

If the water heater is a pilot model, as mentioned above, it will be necessary to disassemble and clean the orifice and the pilot burner periodically. Be sure the flame spreader for both the pilot flame and the main burner flame are positioned correctly. Note the photos.

Fig. 10-18; Main burner flame spreader

Thermocouple

Clean the thermocouple tip or hot junction with steel wool or emery cloth. Keep the tip brightened and free from carbon build-up. This thermocouple is heavily coated with carbon.

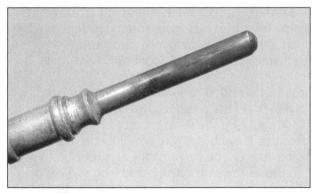

Fig. 10-19; Thermocouple with carbon buildup

Rub the end of the thermocouple with fine steel wool to remove the carbon buildup.

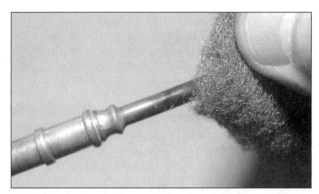

Fig. 10-20; Cleaning the thermocouple with steel wool

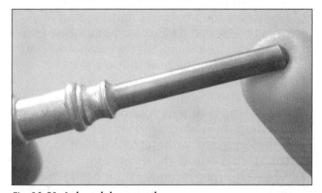

Fig. 10-21; A cleaned thermocouple

After cleaning, the tip should be smooth and have a brighter look to it.

Circuit Board

Clean the contact strip where the multi-pin connector plugs in. I used to recommend using a simple pencil eraser to brighten the contact strips until I ran across a product called DeoxIT (www.caig.com). Cleaning and preserving electrical contact strips in this manner is a much

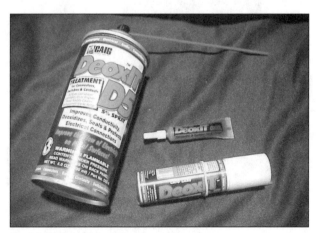

Fig. 10-22; DeoxIT circuit board contact preserver

better method. Small amounts of corrosion, invisible to the naked eye, can prohibit proper conducting of current and strange operational characteristics may develop. Keeping the board contacts clean will minimize erratic operation.

Gas Control Valve

Occasionally, it may be necessary to lightly lubricate the main control knob located on top of the gas control valve. Do this only when the water heater is shut off completely. Never spray cleaners or lubricants near the water heater while it is in operation. Many cleaners and lubricants are flammable. A light coating of petroleum jelly can be applied under the cap to the portion of the shank that revolves and can also be applied to the push button.

Mixing Tube

Make sure the U tube or mixing tube is properly centered on the main burner orifice fitting and that the alignment with the gas control valve is correct. This is one of the most common reasons for improper combustion in both types of water heaters today. The mixing tube should be straight with the flow of LP gas coming from the control valve and positioned so the orifice is centered in the opening of the mixing tube. Position the air adjustment shutter to about one-quarter open to begin with, and then adjust accordingly after lighting the main burner. The roar of the main burner should not be heard from farther than five feet away with the water heater door closed. The fire should be mostly blue with tinges of yellow or orange at the tips.

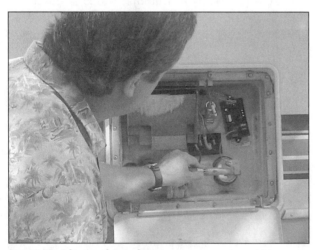

Fig. 10-23; Adjusting the air shutter

LP Gas Pressure

Be sure the LP line pressure is set to 11 inches WC. Refer to Chapter 8.

Fig. 10-24; Be sure to check all ground connections

Battery Voltage

To operate correctly the incoming DC voltage must be minimum 10.5 volts, but for optimum operation, be sure the battery is fully charged or the converter output is sufficient. Also, do not overlook the negative side of a DC circuit. A faulty ground connection at the water heater can cause erratic operation and outages. Be sure this ground screw connection is secure on your DSI water heater.

Additional Tips on the Water Heater

If the pilot model unit is prone to pilot outage, consider adding an automatic reignitor kit. All pilot models can be retrofitted with an electronic kit that will automatically reignite the pilot flame should it be extinguished while parked. Contact the water heater manufacturer or a well-stocked parts and accessory store.

It is further advised to install a water heater bypass kit. This is especially useful when storing or winterizing the RV during cold winter months. Permanently attached to the rear of the water heater, the valve configuration of a bypass kit allows the water heater to be closed off from the rest of the fresh water plumbing system. This is helpful when RV antifreeze is used during the winterizing procedures. With the kit, the water heater can simply be emptied and bypassed, thereby, saving a substantial amount

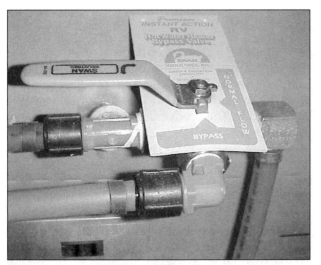

Fig. 10-25; Water heater bypass valves

Fig. 10-26; Water heater cleanout probe

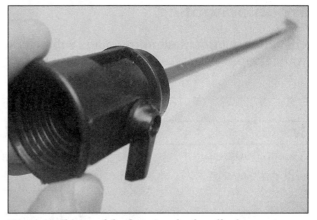

Fig. 10-27; Close-up of the cleanout probe shut-off valve

of antifreeze. Many RVs come equipped with a bypass kit from the factory.

To extend the life of the inner tank and to eliminate the buildup of mineral deposits inside the water heater, backflush the heater two or three times a year. This is especially helpful when you travel extensively and encounter a varying quality of water. Mineral deposits settle to the bottom of the tank, so simply draining the tank will not usually rinse out these deposits. A copper tube with a short bend on the tip, a handy tool available at RV supply centers, can help remove mineral deposit buildup. The one pictured here comes equipped with a garden hose connection and shut-off valve.

Follow these ten steps for a good flushing procedure:

1. Make sure all energy sources to the water heater are turned off and that the water inside has cooled.

2. Turn off all sources of water pressure; the onboard pump and the city water connection.

3. Drain the water heater by opening the drain valve (or removing the plug). To aid in draining, open all hot water faucets throughout the RV.

4. If water barely trickles out of the drain, remove the drain valve completely and carefully insert a straightened coat hanger into the drain

opening in the tank to help break up any calcified deposits. Thoroughly flush out the tank using the tool in the photos above.

5. Close all hot water faucets opened earlier and turn on the city water or the water pump (the higher the pressure, the better). If a pressure regulator is normally used in-line with the city connection, temporarily remove it for this step.

6. Open the P&T relief valve and allow water to gush from the drain opening as fresh water rushes in.

7. Allow this flushing to continue for five to ten minutes. This will remove any stagnant water along with any residual mineral deposits that may remain.

8. After about ten minutes of flushing, turn off the water source, reinstall the drain plug (or close the drain valve) and close the P&T valve by allowing the lever to snap shut.

9. Turn on a water pressure source once again and open all the hot water faucets inside the coach until water flows freely from all hot faucets.

10. Finally, turn off the water source and all but one of the hot faucets, then open the P&T valve once more to release any water and to establish a cushion of air on top of the water in the water heater. When water stops dripping from the P&T valve, close the last hot faucet inside the RV and the P&T valve. The heater is now prepared for use.

Troubleshooting

The following troubleshooting charts will help you determine the cause of many common complaints with the RV water heater.

As with all LP burning appliances, record the model number, serial number and any specification number that is included on the data plate or in the owner's manual. This information will be needed by the service facility when ordering parts or seeking assistance.

Remember to leak check any LP fittings that may have been removed and to regularly leak test the entire LP system using the manometer and test device as outlined in Chapter 8.

Troubleshooting the Pilot Model Water Heater	
Symptom	**Possible Causes**
Water heater pilot will not stay lit	Incorrect LP pressure
	Faulty, loose or weak thermocouple
	Faulty magnet in control valve
	Pilot flame too large or too low
	Dirty pilot orifice
	Faulty control valve
Main burner will not ignite	Dirty or blocked main burner orifice
	Obstruction in mixing tube
	Insufficient LP pressure
	Misalignment of mixing tube
	Improper air shutter adjustment
	Water already at set temperature
Erratic main burner flame	Orifice partially blocked
	Misalignment of mixing tube
	Mixing tube damaged or blocked
	Improper air shutter adjustment
	Flame spreader mispositioned
	Incorrect LP pressure
	Moisture in LP container
	Exhaust obstruction
Flame flashback in mixing tube	Incorrect LP pressure
	Misalignment of mixing tube
	Improper air adjustment

Troubleshooting the Direct Spark Model Water Heater	
Symptom	**Possible Causes**
Water heater goes into lockout– spark present but no LP	Incorrect LP pressure
	Low voltage
	Blocked orifice
	Mixing tube obstruction
	Loose wires on ECO
	Loose wires on solenoid valve
	Faulty ECO
	Faulty circuit board
	Faulty solenoid valve
	Dirty contact on circuit board
	No LP
Water heater goes into lockout– LP present but no spark	High tension lead wire loose
	Electrode assembly loose
	Incorrect electrode gapping
	Dirty electrodes
	Cracked porcelain insulator
	Faulty circuit board
Water heater goes into lockout– LP and spark present	Incorrect LP pressure
	Poor ground connection
	Electrodes not in flame
	Electrodes erratically sparking
	Dirty electrodes
	Partial obstruction in main burner
	Low voltage
	Partial obstruction in burner orifice
	Improper air adjustment
	Flame spreader mispositioned
	Mixing tube mispositioned
	Faulty solenoid valve
	Faulty circuit board
Excessive or insufficient water temperatures	Bypass kit not set properly
	Thermostat not seated against tank
	Faulty thermostat

Troubleshooting the Direct Spark Model Water Heater (continued)	
Symptom	**Possible Causes**
Erratic burner flame (sooting)	Low LP pressure
	Contaminated LP supply
	Improper air adjustment
	Mixing tube misaligned or blocked
	Misaligned flame spreader
	Blocked orifice
	Obstructed main burner
	Exhaust obstruction
No spark and no LP	No voltage
	Dirty contacts on circuit board
	Faulty ECO or thermal cut-off
	Faulty on/off switch
	Faulty thermostat
	Faulty circuit board
Intermittent ignition– fails to ignite	Cracked porcelain insulator
	Fluctuating thermostat
	Damaged insulation of spark wire
	Loose ground screw
	Loose ground on gas valve
	Electrode assembly not grounded

Overview

Ahh! The comforts of home. Cold beverages, hot water, home cooked meals and a warm, cozy bungalow to take the nip out of the cool fall air. The RV furnace can particularly be appreciated during those chilly fall and spring evenings. For those who RV on a full-time basis, it can literally be a mandate on a cold winter's night. Today's RV furnace and heating system has come a long way since the early days of RVing.

Fig. 11-1; RV furnace access door

Early RV furnaces were really nothing more than scaled down versions of the heaters and furnaces found in mobile homes. In fact, some were the exact same unit. Those early heaters were big and bulky, as well as heavy users of liquid propane (LP) fuel. Today, more British thermal units (BTUs) of heating efficiency can be packaged into a much smaller unit, weighing a fraction of

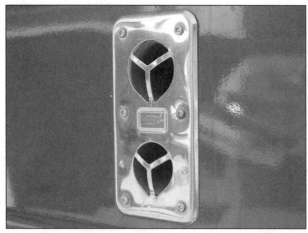

Fig. 11-2; RV furnace intake/exhaust vent

what the earlier units weighed, and at the same time, be installed in a non-obtrusive, out-of-the-way location within the floorplan. Additionally, today's units require only nominal preventive maintenance compared to what seemed like constant attention demanded by the earlier furnaces. The RV furnace and heating system has progressed both technically and functionally.

Types of Heating Systems

Four main types of heating systems are found in RVs:

- Forced air
- Radiant or gravity
- Catalytic
- Central Heating System (Hydronic)

Like the water heater discussed in the previous chapter, most furnaces today are ignited by an automatic electronic principle that has come to be known as DSI, direct spark ignition. Pilot models still exist, though they are not as popular as the DSI models.

In the pilot system, a constant standing pilot must be maintained in order to ignite the much larger main burner whenever there is a call for heat. The lighting of this pilot involves manually holding a gas valve open while a small amount of LP is drawn into the pilot area. Actual ignition of the pilot flame is effected by a match, a flint ignitor, a glow coil or a piezo (pee-AY-zo) ignitor. Maintenance tasks and most troubleshooting tips will pertain to both pilot and DSI models alike with a few exceptions. The operating principle of each type of furnace, however, remains basically the same regardless of the means of ignition. The purpose of a pilot flame is solely to light the main burner when a call for heat comes from the thermostat.

Forced Air Furnace
By far the most popular choice among RV manufacturers today is the forced air furnace. The forced air furnace draws in fresh air from outside the vehicle, mixes it with the LP, burns that mixture in a sealed combustion chamber and blows air over the heated chamber and into the living portions of the RV through a system of

Fig. 11-3; Forced air type of furnace

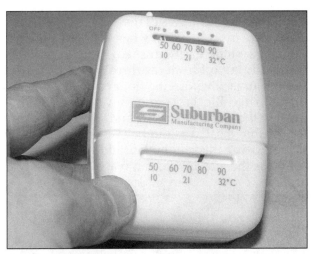

Fig. 11-4; Wall thermostat

ducts or directly out the front of the furnace grill (blow-through design).

Most forced air furnace manufacturers use this same design strategy for their units. Some may have slightly different components and possibly a different sequence of operation, but by and large, most follow the same basic principle.

An important aspect concerning forced air furnaces that is often overlooked is return air. Insufficient return air will cause the furnace to overheat, and performance will be hindered. If the furnace is installed under a bed or a cabinet, there should typically be a minimum of 48 to 55 square inches of grill area in order to have enough air returned to the cabinet of the furnace. Never store supplies on or around the furnace cabinet. Refer to the specific owner's manual for a detailed explanation for a particular unit.

Components

The following basic components represent a typical RV forced air furnace. Your furnace may or may not have all these parts:

Thermostat
Usually mounted on the wall, typically in the living or dining area of the coach. A built-in thermometer senses the room temperature and calls for heat when the temperature drops below the setting.

Relay
The relay receives the signal from the wall thermostat and sends current to the 12-volt DC

motor. This is usually called a time-delay relay. Sometimes it is also referred to as the fan switch. The relay is a device that allows the furnace fan to continue running after a heating cycle in order to purge the combustion chamber of any unused gases as the furnace cools down.

Motor
The 12-volt direct current (DC) motor usually performs two functions. First, it draws in fresh air from outside the RV through an internal venting system. All appliances mix air with the LP for proper and complete combustion. The fresh air blower, attached to the shaft of the motor, draws this primary air into the combustion chamber. Once the internal conditions are right, LP will enter the chamber to be mixed with the air for burning. Another blower wheel is also attached to this motor usually at the opposite end of the shaft. The other main function the motor performs is powering the blower fan. This blower fan, much larger than the fresh air blower, circulates the heated air throughout the ducting system to all areas of the RV.

Ducting System
Consisting typically of flexible heater duct hose, the ducting on smaller recreation vehicles runs throughout the rig, usually into every area. Some larger RVs will have a more elaborate ducting system with four or five outlets encased within the floor area and feature flat floor vents.

All ducts begin at the furnace housing, also called a distribution plenum. Those outlets closest to the furnace will disseminate the heat first. Care must be taken when routing a flexible ducting system. Easily crushed, some ducts can be totally cut off from the distribution network. Ducts encased within the floor cavity are usually trouble-free. Blockages and obstructions in any duct will cause overheating and erratic operation of the furnace. Ducts can be cleaned periodically by removing the vent outlets and vacuuming in as far as the attachment can reach.

Fig. 11-5; Central heat floor register

Vent System

There are usually two segments of the venting system associated with modern furnaces: the fresh air intake vent and the hot exhaust vent. All byproducts of burning LP, including carbon monoxide and other extremely hot gases, must be exhausted from the furnace combustion chamber and delivered to the outside atmosphere. A rigid piping exhaust system carries these harmful gases to the exterior of the RV. Never touch the exterior exhaust vent during furnace operation. Very high stack temperatures

Fig. 11-6; New exhaust assembly

exist that can be dangerous. Typically, the fresh air intake and the hot air exhaust are coupled into one outside vent assembly. The fresh air intake portion must be kept separate from the exhaust portion if the two are combined into one vent. It is vital that the exhaust vent be totally sealed from the interior of the RV.

Sail Switch

Also called an air prover switch, this microswitch is positioned in the direct flow of air from the blower fan. It performs two basic functions. First, it will only close if there is enough air being brought into the combustion chamber to support combustion. It "proves" there is sufficient air to mix with the LP before the fuel is allowed into the combustion chamber. Second, it concurrently delivers the voltage sent from the relay on to the next electrical component.

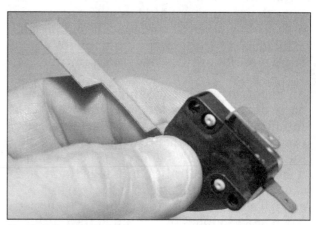

Fig. 11-7; Typical sail switch

Circuit Board

Electronic circuit boards now control the majority of LP appliances. The circuit board performs four basic functions in the furnace:

• Monitors a timing circuit to make sure the chamber is purged of any unused gas before allowing more LP to enter.

• Powers the LP gas valve on the furnace, which starts the flow of LP to the combustion chamber.

• Emits a high output voltage that creates an ignition spark that lights the burner in the chamber.

• Creates a lockout condition if flame does not ignite in the prescribed number of tries. Usually the board continually sparks until a flame is sensed. In some cases, the board may try three times to light the burner. Lockout stops any of the remaining events from happening until the wall thermostat contacts have been manually opened and reset. The fan may continue to run, but there will be no heat. (See the end of this Forced Air Furnace section in this chapter for information on preventing lockout.)

Fig. 11-8; DSI circuit board

Limit Switch

The limit switch performs another safety function, just as its name implies. It will allow the current flow to continue through the circuit only if the internal case temperature is below a certain setting. This thermal switch will interrupt current flow to the circuit board if the internal temperature rises above this preset limit.

Fig. 11-9; Assorted limit switches

Gas Valve

Electrically controlled by the circuit board, the gas valve can have one or two solenoid valves that must open in order for the LP to reach the burner area. Usually quite durable, gas valves do, however, sometimes fail.

Fig. 11-10; Redundant gas valve

Electrode Assembly

Situated in the combustion chamber, this device receives the high voltage output from the circuit board and creates an electrical arc to ground. At the same time, the LP/air mixture is forced to flow through this electrical arc causing ignition of the fuel at the burner assembly. The electrode assembly also "senses" the presence of the fire and sends a micro-amp signal back to the board allowing the gas valve to remain open. If the flame is unstable, or is extinguished for any reason, the micro-amp circuit between the electrode and circuit board is broken and the board

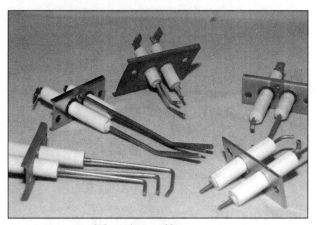

Fig. 11-11; Assorted electrode assemblies

shuts off the current to the gas valve. This electrode assembly is susceptible to carbon buildup and heat stresses over a period of time. Many circuit boards have been replaced in error when the cause of an outage has simply been a carboned electrode assembly.

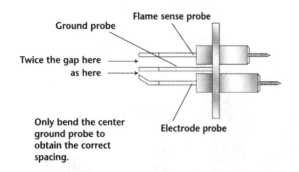

Fig. 11-12; Electrode assembly components

Burner

The LP/air mixture passes through an orifice and into the sealed combustion chamber and ultimately is consumed by the fire at the burner assembly. The burner design will vary among manufacturers, yet the purpose is the same. It will burn the fuel to create the heat that the fan then distributes through the ducting system. All main burners are situated inside the combustion chamber, therefore, it is not recommended to remove the burner. Gaskets sealed against the combustion chamber cannot be reused due to the threat of carbon monoxide poisoning. Always have replacement gaskets on hand prior to working on any component attached directly to the combustion chamber.

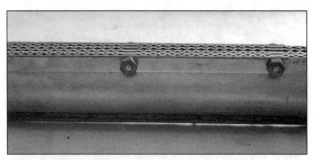

Fig. 11-13; Typical aluminum burner

Sequence of Operation

Since the whole sequence is usually automatic on modern RV furnaces, here is a detailed account of what happens when the thermostat calls for heat.

If the room temperature drops below the set temperature on the thermostat, a 12-volt DC current is sent to the time delay relay, or fan switch. The relay has three main components – a heater coil, a set of contacts and a thermal disc – that open and close the contacts at a certain temperature.

The relay receives the current from the thermostat and passes this current to the built-in switch inside the relay. This is accomplished by the heater coil which then puts into motion the bimetal thermal disc which closes the contacts.

Current is then passed to the 12-volt DC motor which spins two blower wheels simultaneously. One begins drawing fresh air into the combustion chamber from outside the RV while the other wheel begins blowing unheated air through the distribution ducting system.

The blower wheel blows against a large paddle attached to the sail switch that closes its contacts once the blower has reached approximately 75% of its normal speed. Once the sail switch closes, the current is next passed to the limit switch. The limit switch is a normally closed thermal switch that will only open the circuit if high casing temperatures are experienced. If a normal condition exists, the current passes through the limit switch to the printed circuit board.

Here is where things become slightly more complicated as the circuit board next performs simultaneous tasks. The circuit board has a built-in timer that allows the blower fan to purge the combustion chamber of any unused gases or other byproducts of combustion. After this time has elapsed, the board will then send current to the gas valve, which opens, and gas flows to the burner.

At the same time, a high-voltage spark is produced by the board and sent along what looks like a spark plug wire to the electrode assembly. As the gas mixture flows through the spark created by the board, it ignites and burns. The electrode then will sense this flame by sending a

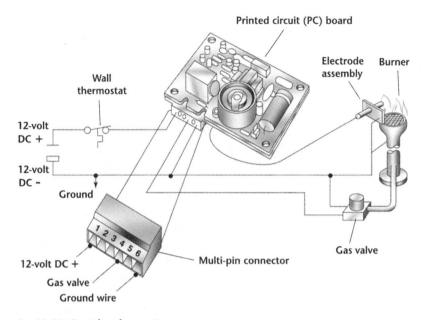

Fig. 11-14; Circuit board connections

very small current, measured in micro-amps, back to the board confirming the presence of the flame. The flame itself acts as a conductor to complete this sense circuit. If the flame did not ignite, the circuit is opened and the board either tries for a second or third time to light the burner or it goes into a lockout condition.

This lockout condition is a safety feature that is not alterable. Circuit boards, although all look identical, can actually be quite different by having shorter or longer purge times, one or more tries for ignition before lockout, etc. Using an incorrect board to remedy a faulty furnace condition may result in damage to the new board. Newer aftermarket boards, specifically those designed by Dinosaur Electronics

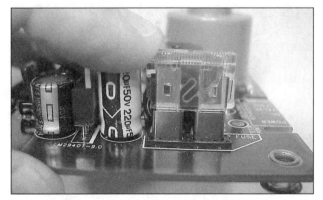

Fig. 11-15; DSI circuit board fuse

(www. dinosaurelectronics.com), have been developed to eliminate many of the common burnout problems associated with some appliance boards. As an added benefit, Dinosaur boards are wired with a protecting fuse (Fig. 11-15).

If a flame ignited the main burner and the heating cycle began, the wall thermostat will open its contacts when the temperature setting has been satisfied. If the unit went into lockout, the wall thermostat contacts must be manually opened and then closed to start the process over again. In a lockout condition, the blower fan will continue to run until the thermostat contacts are manually opened.

After a normal heating cycle, the blower fan will remain running, purging the combustion chamber of unused gases and venting any remaining byproducts of combustion. The fan will continue to run until the heater coil, located in the relay, cools anywhere from three to five minutes, then the contacts are opened and the blower motor stops.

Maintenance

All LP burning appliances require periodic maintenance. Some procedures are probably beyond the scope of the average RVer, so if you are not comfortable performing any maintenance task, call a nearby RV service facility. Although you may decide not to perform maintenance yourself, it still is a requirement for trouble-free operation. What follows is a generic list of tasks that are applicable to the majority of forced air furnaces found on today's RVs. Keep in mind, the model in your RV may differ slightly. Consult the owner's manual for exact location of the components discussed.

Additionally, it will probably be necessary to remove the inner furnace assembly from the outer casing in order to clean and service the unit. Usually only two or three screws need to be removed in order to pull the furnace. Again, consult the owner's manual for specifics.

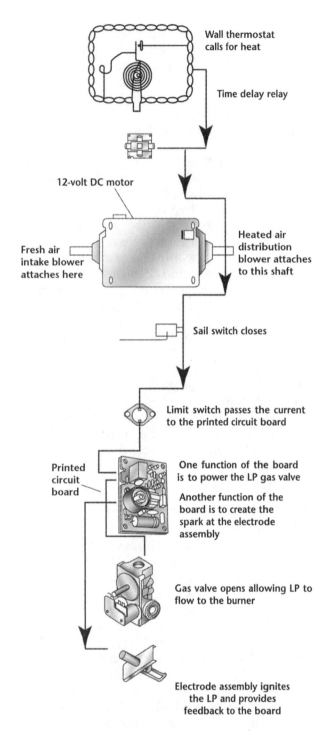

Wall thermostat calls for heat

Time delay relay

12-volt DC motor

Fresh air intake blower attaches here

Heated air distribution blower attaches to this shaft

Sail switch closes

Limit switch passes the current to the printed circuit board

Printed circuit board

One function of the board is to power the LP gas valve

Another function of the board is to create the spark at the electrode assembly

Gas valve opens allowing LP to flow to the burner

Electrode assembly ignites the LP and provides feedback to the board

Fig. 11-16; Sequence of operation of the forced air furnace

The LP gas line and 12-volt power supply will also have to be removed. Turn off the LP at the container and plug the 3/8-inch copper line with an appropriately sized flare plug once it is removed from the furnace. After servicing the

furnace, be sure to leak-test the system prior to lighting any LP appliance.

Areas that typically need annual attention are listed below:

Electrode Assembly

Carbon deposits can be brushed off and the electrodes brightened with steel wool or emery cloth. Inspect the ceramic insulator if so equipped. Any cracks or chips will necessitate electrode replacement. It is recommended to keep a spare electrode assembly in the spare parts kit. If the electrode has three probes, make sure there is twice the gap between the center probe and the flame sense probe than there is between the center probe and the spark probe.

In instances of extreme neglect, the carbon deposits can render the electrode assembly unusable. This assembly is beyond a simple cleaning; it must be replaced.

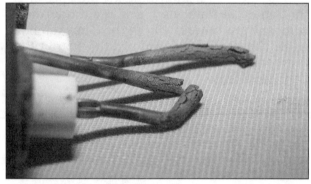

Fig. 11-17; Neglected electrode assembly

Here's what the electrode assembly should look like. Notice any difference?

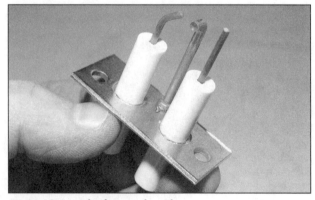

Fig. 11-18; Example of a new electrode

Here's an electrode assembly with a cracked ceramic insulator. This assembly also cannot be repaired and must be replaced.

Fig. 11-19; Electrode assembly with a chipped insulator

Pilot Assembly

If the furnace is a pilot model, it will be necessary to clean the pilot orifice. It is recommended that the orifice be soaked in a solution of acetone and then air-dried. Never insert anything into or through the orifice.

Fig. 11-20; Two different pilot assemblies

Main Burner

Dust, lint or any other debris should be cleaned from the main burner and the main burner orifice at least once a camping season. However, most are located interior to the sealed combustion chamber. This is one job for a professional service technician. Remember, gaskets cannot be reused.

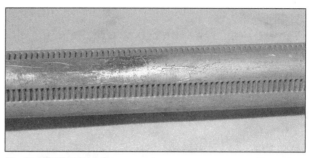

Fig. 11-21; Dirty main burner

Thermocouple

If the furnace is a pilot model, clean the thermocouple hot junction by lightly brushing or brightening with fine steel wool.

Fig. 11-22; Clean the thermocouple with fine steel wool

Blower Wheels

Dust and lint will congregate in the corners of these "squirrel cages" if not cleaned at least once a year. In some cases, this accumulation can actually slow the fan speed so that the sail switch will not close. Disassemble and wash and clean the blower wheels thoroughly.

Fig. 11-23; Assorted furnace blower wheels

Circuit Board

Annually clean the contacts where the multi-pin connector attaches. If you haven't already, take a look at the product I always use on electrical contacts, DeoxIT (www.caig.com). But at the very least, use the eraser portion of a common #2 pencil to at least clean the surface of the contact strip.

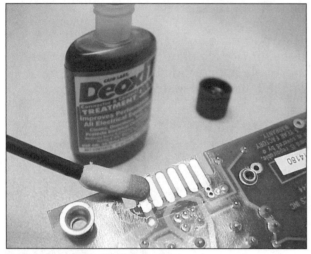

Fig. 11-24; DSI circuit board contact cleaner

Vent Tubes

Check and clean yearly or more often if necessary. It is crucial that the exhaust vent remain clean and clear of any obstructions. Often wasps or other insects will build nests in the vent tubes, especially during times of lengthy storage.

Interior Casing

Vacuum in and about the casing the furnace slides into. Reach into the distribution ducts as

Fig. 11-25; Check intake/exhaust vent regularly for obstructions

far as possible. Cleanliness and furnace performance are proportionally related.

Wall Thermostat

Clean the contacts on the older, spring-type wall thermostat by simply inserting a small piece of paper between the contacts, closing the contacts and then slowly pulling out the paper. Never file or sand thermostat contact points. Clean only with dry, plain paper. Any typical business card will suffice. On this thermostat it will be necessary to unsnap the opaque plastic cover to gain access to the actual contacts. There is no user maintenance involved with electronic thermostats. And yes, the old type wall thermostat can be replaced with any 12-volt DC programmable thermostat. A simple upgrade to bring your unit into the 21st century.

Fig. 11-26; Clean the contacts on wall thermostats

Duct System

Inspect all ducting throughout the RV. Straighten any sharp bends or turns. Look for crushed ducts under gauchos or where ducts pass through walls or partitions under cabinets, etc. Shorten any lengths that appear too long. Many installers have simply snaked excess ducting under cabinets rather than taking the time to cut them to the proper lengths. This can create an overheated situation in the furnace or insufficient heat delivery in the RV.

LP Pressure

Be sure the LP delivery pressure is set to 11 inches of water column (WC).

For a detailed technical training videotape that shows all the various procedures for cleaning and servicing the RV furnace, please contact the author.

Troubleshooting
The following chart will help determine which components may be at fault when the operation of the furnace falls below normal expectations.

Preventing Lockout
Lockout can occur if the gas pressure happens to fluctuate at the time the thermostat calls for heat. Pressure fluctuations can be caused by a faulty pressure regulator located at the LP container. It could also be caused by a kink or obstruction in the delivery tubing or gas lines. Isolating the furnace from the coach piping system can determine if the LP system is the cause.

Connect a separate LP bottle and regulator and run the furnace on a test bench. If the furnace performs properly on the bench, then the coach LP system should be checked. (It may be necessary, on some furnaces, to install the furnace in the outer casing and to install the fresh air and exhaust vents in order to safely bench test the unit.)

If lockout persists, check the return air flow areas. Refer to the owner's manual for the details on the minimum amount of return air space. Also, check the operation of the sail switch and be sure the electrode and burners are cleaned and free of carbon deposits. Finally, have the LP supply checked for excessive moisture. It may be time to purge the LP container.

Radiant Heater
Radiant heaters, also called gravity heaters, are

Troubleshooting the Forced Air Furnace	
Symptom	**Possible Causes**
Blower does not run	No voltage at furnace
	Loose/faulty electrical connections
	Faulty relay
	Faulty blower motor
Blower is noisy	Squirrel cage out of balance
	Excessive DC volage
	Reversed DC polarity
	Squirrel cage hitting casing
	Foreign matter in squirrel cage
	Worn motor bushings or bearings
Blower runs, burner does not ignite	No LP
	Inadequate LP pressure
	Reversed DC polarity
	Blockages in ducting
	Open limit switch
	Faulty circuit board
	Faulty gas valve
	Improper electrode gap spacing
	Faulty electrode assembly
	Loose or disconnected wiring
	Faulty relay
Burner ignites then shuts down	Flame sense probe mispositioned
	Faulty wiring
	Carbonated electrode assembly
	Faulty circuit board
Main burner will not shut off	Thermostat contacts not opening
	Faulty gas valve
	Shorted relay
Repeated circuit board failures	Spark jumps to flame sense probe
	Board or wires shorted to casing
	DC voltage spikes from converter

not used in the RV industry today, but many older units are still out there and they, too, need periodic maintenance. Radiant heaters operate on the simple principle of convection - hot air rises, cold air falls. Normally, all radiant heaters are pilot models with the same methods of lighting as mentioned in the sections above. The main burner is ignited by the pilot and the heat generated simply radiates to all areas of the RV.

Radiant heaters are usually positioned near the floor of the coach to take advantage of the convection principle. As the hot air rises, it heats the interior of the RV.

Sequence of Operation

When the room temperature falls below the set temperature or setting on the thermostat (most thermostats are built in to the gas control valve mounted at the heater instead of on the wall), there is a call for heat. Air is brought in from outside the RV by a small fan located at the rear of the heater. The LP and fresh air mix in the combustion chamber, commonly called a firebox on radiant heaters, and is ignited by the constant pilot flame.

Some radiant heaters may have an additional fan that helps blow air past the firebox to aid in the distribution of heat throughout the coach. Once the room is heated to adequately satisfy the thermostat, the main burner is extinguished, but the constant pilot remains lit. A blower fan may continue to run in order to purge the firebox of any unburned fuel and other byproducts that may still linger. Usually though, any unburned fuel is simply consumed by the pilot.

Maintenance

Normal cleaning and servicing procedures can be followed for the radiant heater as well as the forced air furnace. The three main areas of concern are:

- Cleanliness: Cleaner components mean less downtime.

- Correct LP pressure: Always a mandate with any LP appliance.

- Venting: The exhaust vent and intake vent should be clean and cleared of any obstructions, such as wasp nests.

Radiant heaters are very simple in design. By attending to the above three items, the RVer will experience few problems with this type of heater.

Catalytic Heater

Similar to how radiant heaters employ the convection principle, catalytic heaters are unique in the manner in which the LP fuel is burned. Catalytic heaters have a combustion process that burns LP without a flame and at uncommonly low temperatures. Additionally, all radiant heat produced by the catalytic heater is usable. Very little energy is wasted. The heat is directed to people and to objects and only heats the surrounding air space by radiant transfer after first warming the occupants.

The catalytic process burns the LP in the air to produce infrared heat without a flame. The flameless process mixes the gas and the air within the presence of a platinum-based catalyst pad, which is the primary feature of the catalytic heater. LP enters and permeates the pad from rear to front, mixes with the air at the front surfaces and burns without a flame. Sometimes a slight flame may be visible at the heater face on the initial lighting from a cold start. This is normal during the time the catalyst pad heats up. Also, there may be a slight odor of propane during this cold start-up.

Catalytic heaters may be vented through the side wall of the RV, or simply surface-mounted on any wall inside the coach with no direct vent to the outside. Some are thermostatically controlled. All heaters must be listed and approved for RV use.

Fig. 11-27; Typical catalytic heater

In the past, non-vented catalytic heaters were allowed in RVs only under strict guidelines. As the technology has progressed and improved safety features have been implemented, the non-vented catalytic heater has since proven itself to be an extremely efficient method of comfort heating in smaller RVs. They are now allowed to be installed anywhere inside the RV, however, since the catalytic process heats people and objects rather than air, it is best to mount the heater in an area with no obstructions, such as furniture or cabinetry.

One of the current safety features of a catalytic heater is the oxygen depletion sensor (ODS), which will shut down the heater if the oxygen level in the RV falls below a safe level. Additionally, today's heaters are equipped with a 100% safety shut-off system in the event the flame extinguishes or when nonignition occurs.

Components

Very basic in design, the catalytic heater has few parts other than the pad, housing and the method of controlling the LP flow. Since no venting is required on some models, installation is relatively simple. Only an LP gas line is required at the mounting location.

The major components of a typical catalytic heater are:

- Catalytic pad
- Method of ignition
- Thermocouple
- Gas valve
- Thermostat

Catalytic pad: The pad is the main component on the catalytic heater. It is fragile and sensitive; never touch the pad itself. It is possible to experience what is called "catalytic pad poisoning," in which the pad can get damaged by being cleaned or by being exposed to impurities. The catalytic pad can only be used with propane. Airborne contamination from motor fuels, cooking oils and aerosol compounds can all contribute to a shortened pad life. Pads should be replaced about every three years under normal use.

Method of ignition: The recommended catalytic heaters use a piezo or an electronic ignition system for lighting the fuel.

Thermocouple: As a portion of the safety system, the thermocouple produces the millivolts necessary to keep the gas control valve open and the LP flowing into the unit.

Gas valve: The gas valve permits the flow of LP as long as the thermocouple produces voltage.

Thermostat: Models that are thermostatically controlled require a 12-volt DC source. Usually when 12 volts are required for the thermostat, the heater is equipped with electronic ignition.

Maintenance

Very little maintenance is needed to perform directly on the catalytic heater. The primary concern is to make sure the incoming LP pressure is maintained at 11-inches of water column and that the surrounding area is kept clean and free from lint or other airborne contaminates. Never touch or wash the pad itself. Maintenance is limited to simply vacuuming the outer grill in front of the pad.

Since non-vented catalytic heaters consume air from inside the room, it is recommended that a window or two stay slightly opened in the RV in order to provide sufficient fresh air. The coach must have a minimum of at least one square inch of free fresh air opening for every 1,000 BTUs the heater is rated for. Do not operate the heater in coaches that are tightly sealed or closed off.

Keep in mind that other than checking the LP pressure and testing the thermocouple, all repairs to catalytic heaters must be performed by the factory. Also, be sure to read the cautions and warnings in the owner's manual. Each model may have specific information that is not listed here.

Central Heating Systems (Hydronic)

Typically found on diesel-powered motorhomes, the central hot water heating system provides a continuous supply of hot water for the plumbing system plus heat for interior comfort heating. That's correct; it's not only a

Fig. 11-28; Hydronic heating system

comfort heater, it's also a water heater. Employing a diesel-fired burner and a 120-volt AC heating element, this "on-demand" system usually is segregated into different heating zones within the RV. For slightly chilly mornings, the diesel burner can be bypassed and the heat supplied solely by the electric heating element, thereby conserving fuel.

With the diesel burner operating, a solution of 50% water and 50% anti-freeze is kept at temperatures between 175 and 200-degrees F. Individual circulating pumps in each zone allow for separate temperature settings on different thermostats so heating can be regulated closely and independently from the main living area to the bedroom to the bathroom. In some of the larger motorhomes, a separate zone may include the storage bay where the fresh water tank is located to keep it from freezing in the cold winter months. There is also a heat exchanger for motorhome engine preheating during cold weather start-ups.

Maintenance
About the only regular maintenance required by the user is to keep an eye on the level of the 50/50 solution in the expansion tank. The only caution is to check and add solution when the unit is already hot.

Once a year the diesel nozzle needs to cleaned, as does the main combustion chamber. Under heavy use, the fuel nozzle may need replacing

periodically. Also once a year, the fuel filter should be replaced. Though not out of the realm of "do-it-yourself," these procedures are usually performed by a professional RV service technician.

The preeminent manufacturer of hydronic central heating systems is Aqua-Hot Heating Systems, Inc. They have provided a detailed maintenance and repair manual on their website should you like more information.

http://www.aqua-hot.com/b2c/ecom/ecomEnduser/default/Manuals.aspx

Additional Notes About Heating Systems

In some applications, the cooling and heating of the RV is controlled by either a centralized mechanical or a digital comfort control thermostat. Some will control an independent forced air furnace in conjunction with the air conditioning system, while others may employ heat strips or a heat pump in direct association with the air conditioner (more about this in Chapter 13, Roof Air Conditioning).

Regardless of which type of furnace or heater is installed in the RV, take the time to record the model number, serial number and any specification number that may be pertinent to the unit. This information will be needed to answer questions or to order replacement parts when contacting the manufacturer or service center. With proper yearly maintenance, the heating system in your RV should provide many years of comfortable RVing in the colder climates.

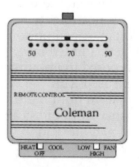

Fig. 11-29; Mechanical heating/cooling thermostat

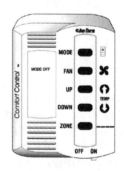

Fig. 11-30; Digital comfort control center

Chapter 12

Absorption Refrigerator

Overview

Of the four LP appliances found in today's recreation vehicle, the one that is probably the most perplexing to the RVer is the absorption refrigerator. Understanding the theory of absorption and why it takes heat in order to make cold can be baffling at best. Then toss in the fact that this is all accomplished silently with no moving parts and very quickly we resort to just simply shaking our heads while grabbing another cool beverage from the fridge.

Regardless of the complexity of the absorption refrigerator, periodic maintenance is still a mandate concerning all LP burning appliances, especially the refrigerator. Most are fully automatic today, but the RV refrigerator just may also be the one appliance that is most neglected.

By grasping a basic view of the theory of absorption and understanding the importance of leveling, ventilation and cleanliness, the RV refrigerator can provide many years of RVing enjoyment and unfettered independence.

Fig. 12-1; Modern RV refrigerators provide plenty of storage

Heat Sources

The RV refrigerator uses three energy sources: 12 volts direct current (DC), 120 volts alternating current (AC) and LP. As mentioned earlier, refrigeration revolves around using heat in order to make cold. All three energy sources are employed as heat producers. The 12-volt DC and 120-volt AC electricity are used to energize heating elements, while the LP is burned at an open burner at the rear of the refrigerator.

Cooling Unit Operation

The main component of any RV absorption refrigerator is the cooling unit. The cooling unit is that item most visible on the back of the refrigerator. It is a complex device consisting of a series of tubes within tubes; its coils are seen when the outside service door at the rear of the refrigerator is opened. All cooling units consist of four major sections:

- Boiler
- Condenser
- Evaporators
- Absorber

Through these four main components the contents are circulated. All cooling units are sealed and, therefore, are not field-repairable. Specialized charging machinery and unique

Fig. 12-2; Refurbished refrigerator cooling cores

material handling procedures make it mandatory that if a cooling unit is determined to be at fault in a nonworking refrigerator, it must be replaced. (For a detailed pictorial of cooling unit charging procedures, contact the author).

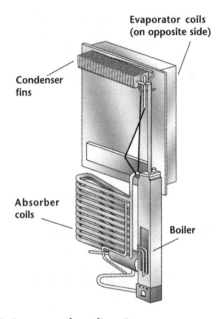

Fig. 12-3; Components of a cooling unit

Inside the cooling unit precise amounts of materials are added during manufacture. Water, liquid ammonia, hydrogen gas and a chemical compound called sodium chromate are all present inside the sealed cooling core. As temperature and pressure act on the contents, they undergo various states of evaporation and condensation, all within the confines of the sealed unit. Because of the caustic nature of liquid ammonia, the sodium chromate is added to protect the insides of the tubing during the refrigerati on cycle.

Refrigeration Cycle

When heat is applied to the boiler portion of the cooling unit, the ammonia and water begin to boil. Bubbles of ammonia gas are produced, which rise into the percolator tube (see Fig. 12-4), along with an accumulation of weak ammonia and water. As the ammonia and water solution pass into the tube, the ammonia vapor continues into the water separator. Any water vapor reaching this point is condensed and falls

back into the boiler section, thereby separating the water and leaving dry ammonia vapor to pass to the condenser. As air circulates over the condenser fins from the outside of the unit, it removes heat from the ammonia vapor inside causing it to condense into a liquid that flows to the low temperature evaporator. The low temperature evaporator portion of the cooling unit is positioned in the wall or shelf of the freezer section of the refrigerator.

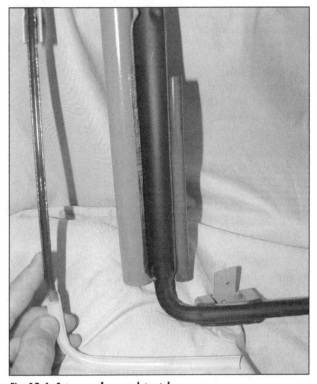

Fig. 12-4; Cutaway of a percolator tube

The evaporator is internally fed hydrogen gas, which passes across the surface of the incoming ammonia and subsequently causes the vapor pressure to evaporate the liquid ammonia. The evaporation of the ammonia removes heat from the evaporator section through the walls of the freezer and through the tubing, removing heat from the freezer section of the refrigerator, including any food stored there. The net result is that through the theory of absorption and its principles, the RV refrigerator is not really making cold, but basically removing heat. Cold, in this context, is simply the absence of heat.

From the low temperature evaporator, any remaining remnants of liquid ammonia and

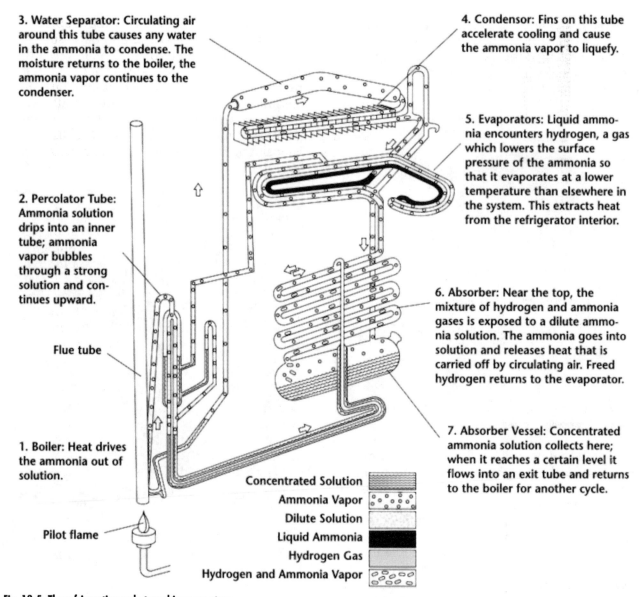

3. Water Separator: Circulating air around this tube causes any water in the ammonia to condense. The moisture returns to the boiler, the ammonia vapor continues to the condenser.

4. Condensor: Fins on this tube accelerate cooling and cause the ammonia vapor to liquefy.

5. Evaporators: Liquid ammonia encounters hydrogen, a gas which lowers the surface pressure of the ammonia so that it evaporates at a lower temperature than elsewhere in the system. This extracts heat from the refrigerator interior.

2. Percolator Tube: Ammonia solution drips into an inner tube; ammonia vapor bubbles through a strong solution and continues upward.

Flue tube

6. Absorber: Near the top, the mixture of hydrogen and ammonia gases is exposed to a dilute ammonia solution. The ammonia goes into solution and releases heat that is carried off by circulating air. Freed hydrogen returns to the evaporator.

1. Boiler: Heat drives the ammonia out of solution.

7. Absorber Vessel: Concentrated ammonia solution collects here; when it reaches a certain level it flows into an exit tube and returns to the boiler for another cycle.

Pilot flame

Concentrated Solution
Ammonia Vapor
Dilute Solution
Liquid Ammonia
Hydrogen Gas
Hydrogen and Ammonia Vapor

Fig. 12-5; The refrigeration cycle traced in seven steps

hydrogen gas are passed lower into the high temperature evaporator, which is positioned in the lower food section of the refrigerator. This process continues to remove and transfer heat from inside the box to the outside, but not as much heat is removed. That is why it is warmer in the food section, or lower portion, than in the upper freezer section.

After the ammonia and hydrogen gas pass through the evaporator, the contents flow to the absorber section. Upon entering the upper portion of the absorber, a continuous trickle of weak ammonia solution comes into contact

with the mixed ammonia and hydrogen gas, which readily absorbs the ammonia from the mixture, freeing the hydrogen gas and allowing it to rise back through the absorber coil and to the evaporator section. The hydrogen gas effectively moves back and forth between the absorber and the evaporator sections.

The strong ammonia solution produced in the absorber flows down to the absorber where it is held, mixed with water and fed into the boiler section, and the process starts all over again.

The low temperature evaporator tubing is

Fig. 12-6; Secondary evaporator fins inside a refrigerator

hidden inside the freezer compartment while the high temperature evaporator is positioned in the lower food section of the refrigerator. The fins inside the lower compartment are secured directly to this component through the back of the refrigerator. A thermistor, or in some cases individual thermostat capillary tubes, are secured to the fins inside the refrigerator.

Leveling

Though leveling of today's absorption cooling is not as crucial as in years past, the term "relatively level" can swiftly move the casual RVer into a false sense of security if taken with a cavalier attitude. It is my advice to get the unit as level as possible to avoid the costs of premature cooling core replacement. The motivational force in moving the liquid contents throughout the system is nothing more than gravity. From the point where liquid is first produced in the condenser section until the liquid reaches the boiler section, gravity is employed. Since liquids cannot flow uphill, the importance of running the refrigerator only while level is fully appreciated.

The prevailing attitude is that if the RV is comfortably level for living, the refrigerator is level enough for operation. If eggs don't roll off the countertop, you're probably okay. If

doubts exist, simply place a round bubble level inside the freezer compartment to be sure. Better to be safe than sorry!

Leveling is important during any operational mode (12 volts DC, 120 volts AC or LP) while the RV is stationary. While physically moving down the road, there is enough jostling and movement to keep the liquids safely flowing through the system. It is only crucial when the vehicle is not in motion.

Operating the refrigerator off level creates an inordinate amount of heat at the rear of the unit, especially in the boiler area. Coupled with improper ventilation, this extra heat can escalate very quickly into potential costly troubles. When overheating occurs over a period of time, the sodium chromate inside the pipes begins to crystallize. The percolator tube inside the boiler section can become impassable because of a blockage caused by the crystallized sodium chromate. When this happens, the cooling unit is blocked and cannot be repaired. It must be replaced. Typically the blockage will occur in the percolator tube, one of the smallest of the internal pipes inside the cooling core. This photo shows an actual crystallized sodium chromate blockage cut from a defective cooling core.

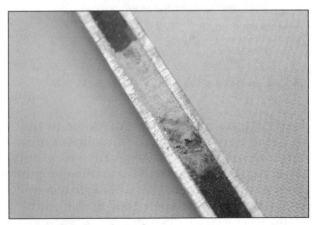

Fig. 12-7; Blocked percolator tube

Leveling is one of the two most important factors to consider when using the RV absorption refrigerator. The other is ventilation.

Ventilation

Improperly vented heat is probably the predom-inant cause of improper cooling of the refrigera-tor. As heat is removed from the interior of the refrigerator, it is relocated to the rear of the cooling unit by the actions and reactions of the boiler, condenser, evaporators and absorber coils as described above. Heat created by the three heat sources, including the products of LP combustion, as well as heat generated by the condensing of the ammonia vapor, must dissi-pate quickly and efficiently in order to make sure the refrigeration cycle is not hindered.

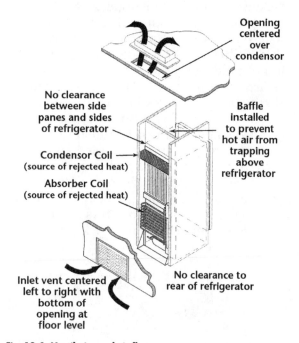

Fig. 12-8; Ventilation and air flow

To accomplish trouble-free refrigeration in an RV absorption refrigerator, a continuous supply of free-flowing fresh air is required to pass over the heat-producing areas of the cooling unit to safely remove unwanted heat. The refrigerator installation must include a good drafting tech-nique for evacuating this heat.

A natural draft is created by installing the refrigerator into a cabinet opening with close tolerances allowing for a flue system to be employed. This flue, or drafting chimney, must be continuous from the bottom of the cabinet, up the back of the cooling unit and out the roof

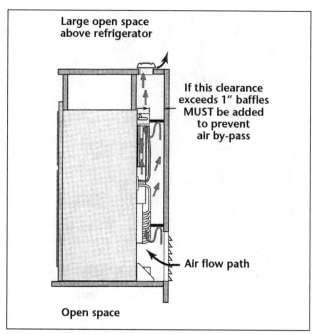

Fig. 12-9; Air flow chimney

vent. Proper clearances must be adhered to. Check the owner's manual for the specifics and verify the installation of your unit. Some instal-lations allow for smaller refrigerators to be vented solely through the side of the RV with vents placed at lower and upper locations. Each size and each brand of refrigerator may have different installation requirements. Check the installation against the manufacturer's requirements.

The natural draft method of ventilation begins by inducing air from outside the RV. This outside air must be at a temperature lower than the cooling unit components. A natural draft is created when the cooler intake air entering through the lower vent is heated and becomes lighter and rises up through the roof vent. The greater the difference between the removed or rejected heat and the intake air, the stronger the draft will be. This is called thermosiphoning. (To ensure the integrity of the natural thermosi-phoning effect, never store camping gear or other objects behind the lower refrigerator compartment door.)

A good installation encourages as much air as possible to flow over the cooling unit, thereby preventing the intake air from bypassing the heat generating components altogether. Any bypassed air tends to cool the heated air, which counteracts the draft effect. The drafting compartment at the rear of the refrigerator should be totally sealed from the interior of the RV. Strictly adhering to the clearance guidelines for proper installation, as set forth by each refrigerator manufacturer, will indeed maximize its performance.

Aftermarket fans can be added to those units that do not appear to have good ventilation. The bottom line is: The more heat given up to the exterior of the RV in the fastest amount of time, the better the overall cooling performance. This is why the ambient heat has a direct impact on the effectiveness of the refrigerator. Since there is no compressor to quickly facilitate refrigeration, the inside of the refrigerator will be warmer while operating in the high desert at noon, than when operating at night at sea level.

Refrigerator Controls

So far, the cooling unit components, the theory of absorption, proper leveling and proper ventilation all pertain to virtually every single RV absorption refrigerator ever made. The differences between brands and models are strictly in the controlling of the heat sources as they relate

Fig. 12-10; Reinstallation after repair

to the absorption principle. All the bells and whistles, the aesthetics of design and unique features are secondary to the basic principle of operation discussed above.

Today's refrigerators fall into two basic categories: those that are fully automatic and those that are not. Fully automatic units only require the user to set the thermostat to the desired setting and simply flip a switch or push a touch pad. Electronic controls will automatically choose the appropriate heat source and begin the refrigeration cycle.

The priority for automatically choosing the mode of heat source for Dometic refrigerators is 120 volts AC, 12 volts DC and then LP gas. Norcold models have a slightly different priority for their automatic models: 120 volts AC, then LP gas and finally 12 volts DC. Some models allow the user to choose a particular mode of operation and override the typical priority. Those refrigerators that are not fully automatic require the RVer to choose the heat source manually. All units have built-in and fully automatic safeguards making the RV refrigerator an extremely safe appliance to operate.

Importance of DC Voltage

With the proliferation of 12-volt DC components and electronic circuitry employed on the modern RV refrigerator it is crucial to have and maintain a fully charged battery bank. In past years it was feasible to light the refrigerator on LP and have refrigeration without a battery even in the system. Not so today; without a healthy battery system it is not possible to operate the modern absorption refrigerator on any mode.

It is equally important not to neglect the negative side of the DC circuit as well. Poor ground connections contribute to many electrically related ills associated with RV refrigerators. Be sure all electrical contacts are secure

Manual Refrigerator Components

When dissecting the manually operated absorption RV refrigerator it is best to divide the components into two camps, LP-related and those that pertain to the electric mode of operation. First, let's explore the LP side of absorption refrigeration.

LP Components

Though differences abound in the design of the LP components found in most RV refrigerators, their function is fairly standardized. In other words, a thermostat senses temperature and directs the refrigerator when to cool and when not to cool. There are many different types of thermostats, but don't let this confuse you. Keep in mind your refrigerator may or may not have all the following components. Check the owner's manual for your specific brand and model to be sure.

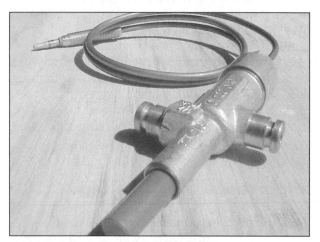

Fig. 12-11; Typical safety valve and thermocouple

Manual Shut-Off Gas Valve

All LP-fired refrigerators will have some type of manual gas valve that can be utilized to completely shut off the gas flow to the refrigerator. On most models the gas valve is located at the rear of the unit (as are most all the major components), even though the method of operating this valve may be located at the front of the refrigerator, accessible from the interior of the RV.

LP Safety Valve

The LP safety valve on the manual RV refrigerator is also called a flame failure safety device. Consisting of a valved gas port, a thermocouple connection, an electromagnet and an activation button, the safety valve will effectively shut off the LP supply should the burner flame be extin-

guished for any reason. The safety valve is situated at the rear of the unit as viewed from the exterior access panel. The thermocouple is positioned in the actual burner flame. As in pilot model furnaces and water heaters, when heated, the thermocouple produces a voltage that powers the electromagnet. If the flame is extinguished, voltage stops being produced, the electromagnet shuts down and the safety valve closes.

LP Filter

Some older refrigerators may be equipped with an LP filter located somewhere in the system. Non-existent today, these filters may become partially blocked if exposed to contaminates in LP fuel sources. They are packed with a cotton-like material that cannot be rejuvenated; the filter itself must be replaced.

Fig. 12-12; Old style LP filter

Burner

The LP burner is situated directly below the flue pipe at the rear of the unit. The LP burner on the manual refrigerator is a constant burner flame, meaning the flame is always lit. When the thermostat calls for more cooling inside the refrigerator, the burner receives full LP pressure and the flame is a strong bright blue — also called high fire.

After the thermostat has been satisfied the burner flame is reduced to what is called the bypass flame. The burner remains lit, but the flame size is much reduced because the thermostat allows only a minimal amount of LP flow to reach the burner. Another term for bypass flame is low fire.

As depicted above, LP burners come in many shapes, sizes and designs. All are rated for a specific British thermal unit (BTU) input based

Fig. 12-13; Assorted LP burners

a like solution and then simply letting them air dry. Never insert any object into a burner orifice and do not use compressed air. Some orifices contain a delicate, laser-drilled ruby that can be damaged by air pressure or intruding probes. The orifice opening is precisely milled to allow a specific amount of LP to enter the burner. Do not arbitrarily change orifice sizes.

Methods of Ignition

As with any LP burner, there must be a way to ignite the incoming fuel. The RV refrigerator has seen a plethora of devices and methods employed over the years. The most common method today for lighting the manual RV refrigerator is the piezo (pee-AY-zo) ignitor. The same type piezo as discussed in previous chapters, it basically is a self-contained, spring-loaded device that creates a high-voltage spark directly over the burner as LP enters.

on the size and design of that refrigerator. Because of its positioning, the burner is often subjected to falling rust and debris from inside the flue assembly. Partially blocked burners can be rectified by performing a refrigerator "clean and service" procedure annually.

Burner Orifice

Affixed to the LP burner is a precisely manufactured burner orifice. This is the component most likely to be blocked by dirt, dust or a spider's web. We've all heard the stories of spiders and other critters being attracted to the odorant in the LP fuel. The stories are true! Since the orifice contains the smallest opening through which the LP must flow, it stands to reason this will become one of the first components to become clogged if not maintained properly.

Orifices are easily cleaned by removing them from the burner and soaking them in acetone or

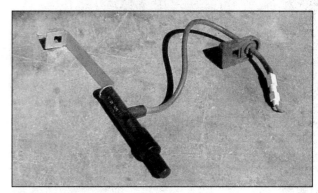
Fig. 12-15; Piezo ignitor

Here's a little history for you. Prior to the advent of the piezo, other means of refrigerator ignition included:

Flint ignitor: The flint ignitor consisted of a typical old-style cigarette lighter flint coupled with a knurled knob that rotated on a shaft that traversed from the front controls of the refrigerator to the burner area. Interestingly, some were right-handed and some were left-handed. This required an opposite rotation and a different knurled knob to strike the flint correctly.

Glow coil: The glow coil ignitor was powered by a single D-size dry cell battery and required the RVer to keep a watchful eye in case the battery became depleted. It heated a small element

Fig. 12-14; Assorted LP burner orifices

Fig. 12-16; A Flint ignitor

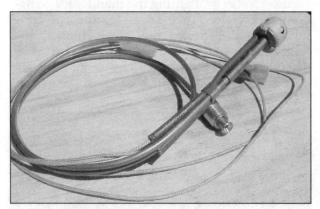
Fig. 12-17; A Glow coil ignitor

Fig. 12-18; A Zip tube ignitor and burner assembly

of LP was fed through a ported tube from the front of the unit back to the burner area. The user held an open flame (Yikes!) at the start end of this tube and an open flame spread itself from the front of the refrigerator, directly underneath a protective shield, to the burner. The flame "zipped" along the open ports in the tube, hence the name. It was necessary to hold the button in until the thermocouple produced enough voltage to keep the safety valve open. The open flame continued to burn all along the zip tube until the button was released.

Believe it or not, as obsolete as some of these methods may seem, they are all still out there. This proves the point that well-maintained LP appliances can last a very long time indeed.

Flue Assembly
Positioned directly above the burner is the flue assembly, which consists of the flue pipe (open pipe in photo below), a flue baffle and possibly a flue cap. The heat produced by the burner rises up the flue pipe and eventually out the top where it is released to the atmosphere through the vent attached to the roof. The purpose of the flue baffle is to restrict this escaping heat from

positioned over the burner; when it reached a certain temperature it ignited the LP at the burner.

Zip tube ignitor: The zip tube ignitor was a scary looking device for some users. Accessed from the front of the refrigerator inside the RV, the zip tube method involved depressing a gas valve button that allowed LP to enter the burner at the rear of the unit. At the same time a small portion

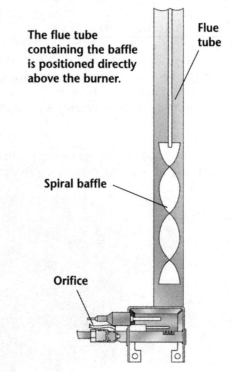
Fig. 12-19; Flue baffle positioning

Fig. 12-20; Heavily insulated flue pipe

Fig. 12-22; LP/120-volt switch mechanism

the burner and keep it concentrated at the boiler section of the cooling unit so the process of absorption can begin. Without the baffle, the heat would dissipate too quickly for refrigeration to take place.

The positioning of the baffle inside the flue is crucial. The length of the hanger wire should never be modified. The baffle should, however, be cleaned periodically, as should the flue itself. Soot, scale and carbon deposits should be removed at least once annually.

LP Thermostat

When the temperature of the air inside the refrigerator compartment is higher than the setting on the thermostat, this is the device that calls for more heat in the burner area. Some LP thermostats are configured as stand-alone

Fig. 12-21; Gas and electric thermostat combination unit

thermostats just for the controlling of the LP flow. Others are combination thermostats like the combo gas and electric thermostat pictured here. Like burners, many configurations of thermostats are found on RV refrigerators.

The bypass screw is an integral component of the manual LP thermostat. This is the device through which the bypass level of LP flows to provide fuel burned as the low fire. The bypass screw is nothing more than a small brass screw with a precise hole drilled through it. It is secured to the body of the thermostat within the bypass flow of LP. One common malfunction of an older manual-style refrigerator is the temperature inside the box getting too cold, even on the lowest setting of the thermostat. Typically this is because the amount of bypass LP flowing to the burner is too much; the hole in the bypass screw is too large. The repair is to simply replace the existing bypass screw with one containing a smaller hole.

Also attached to the LP thermostat is a tiny capillary tube. The capillary tube is an integral part of the thermostat also and is not replaceable. If bent, kinked or damaged in any way the entire thermostat must be replaced. The capillary tube routes from the thermostat housing at the rear of the refrigerator up and into the lower food storage compartment. The loose end is attached to the secondary evaporator fins inside the storage compartment. It must be secured to a specific fin, depending on make and model. This component actually senses the temperature inside the refrigerator. Filled with an inert gas, it expands and contracts with the interior temperature changes and dictates the workings of the thermostat as it responds to the cooling demands of the high temperature evaporator section of the cooling core. Take extreme care when handling any capillary tube.

Electric Components

Remember, it takes a source of heat to begin the absorption process. A burning LP flame creates heat as does an electric heating element. When the electric mode of the manual RV refrigeration is selected, the LP components become dormant and all control processes are via electrical devices. Let's explore that side of the manual RV refrigerator.

Power Cord

The refrigerator is equipped with a standard, three-prong, 120-volt AC power cord, usually wired to a junction block at the rear of the refrigerator. As with any power cord, be sure the contacts are straight and undamaged. It will plug into a standard simplex or duplex receptacle at the rear of the refrigerator compartment.

Electrical Switch

Each model will have some method of turning the electricity on and off. Selector switches come in a myriad of designs depending on the brand and model of the refrigerator. Most are activated by turning a knob inside the refrigerator, accessed from the front of the unit. A long rod runs to the rear of the unit where the switch is actually located. This assembly, found on older Dometic refrigerators actually turns off the LP

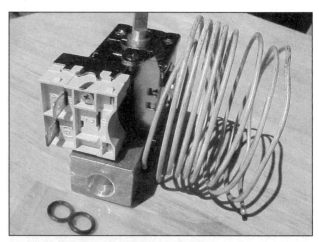

Fig. 12-24; LP/120-volt combination thermostat

valve at the same time it turns on the electric switch and vice versa.

Electric Thermostat

As with the LP mode, the electric mode of operation must be regulated through a thermostat. Some models are equipped with a thermostat dedicated solely for the electric operation, while others are outfitted with a combination electric/LP thermostat. The function of the electric thermostat is the same as its LP counterpart except it does not contain any method of bypass; it simply allows current to flow to the heating element or not. The thermostat pictured here is a combination electric/LP thermostat.

Heating Element

As the temperature is sensed by the thermostat, it opens and closes internal contacts, and controls the electricity supplied to the actual heat source, the electric heating element. The heating element is rated in watts specific to that refrigerator.

Fig. 12-23; LP/electricity switch mechanism

Fig. 12-25; Older style heating element

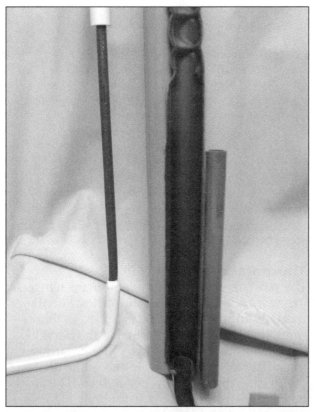

Fig. 12-26; Cutaway view of the boiler tube

The two most common designs of heating elements include the cartridge type pictured here and an L-shaped, thinner, pencil type. Heating elements are either 120 volts AC, 12 volts DC or a combination of both. Resistance measurements can be taken on any heating element and compared to published charts to determine their electrical health. AC voltage can also be measured at the heating element while the refrigerator is running on shoreline power or generator.

The heating element slips into a pocket welded to the boiler section of the cooling core. The heating element must fit snugly into this pocket and be the correct height in order to obtain the proper temperature levels needed at the boiler. The heating pocket in this photo is the short vertical tube on the far right of the assembly.

Automatic Refrigerator Components

By far the most common type of absorption refrigerator found today is the fully automatic model. Norcold (www.norcold.com) and Dometic (www.dometic.com) both produce

fine automatic refrigerators making it quite easy for the RVer. Add automatic levelers to the mix and today's active RVer can be set up perfectly level and operating the absorption refrigerator within minutes.

The process of cooling remains the same regardless of the type of refrigerator. As mentioned earlier, fully automatic units choose the best energy source by utilizing circuit boards and other electronic components.

The priority for automatically choosing the heat source for Dometic refrigerators is 120 volts AC, 12 volts DC and then LP gas. In other words, if the coach is connected to the campground pedestal the refrigerator automatically chooses the AC mode of operation. If 120 volts AC is not available, it switches to 12 volts DC as long as battery power is sufficient. The 12-volt mode on some Dometic models, however, is an option. On their AES line of refrigerators, the 12-volt option is automatic, while on the AMES models, the 12-volt DC mode must be manually selected.

Norcold models have a slightly different priority for their automatic models: 120 volts AC, then LP gas and finally 12 volts DC. However, the principle remains the same.

Typically 12-volt DC operation on any RV absorption refrigerator should be considered a maintenance mode only; viable only after the refrigerator has been cooled down on either 120 volts AC or LP.

Circuit Board(s)

Dometic and Norcold both use printed circuitry to control the operation of their respective models. Some units have more than one board, so be sure to check the owner's manual for the location of the boards on your specific model.

As with other automatic LP appliances, the main circuit board is the brain of the refrigerator and controls all functions of operation. There is very little for the RVer to be concerned about with troubleshooting and repairing of circuit boards. Specialty testers are necessary in most instances to diagnose operational faults. About all the owner can do is keep the unit clean and periodi-

Fig. 12-27; Circuit board mounted on rear of refrigerator

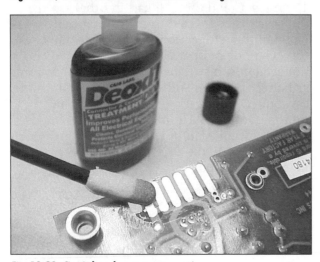

Fig. 12-28; Circuit board contact preservative

cally treat the contacts on the multi-pin connector strip of the board with a contact preservative like DeoxIT, as mentioned in previous chapters. As always, take care when handling any circuit board. Dropping or mishandling it can be an expensive mistake.

Ignitor Assembly

Two of the many functions of the circuit board are to create a spark at the burner and open the gas solenoid valve. This results in the automatic lighting of the burner when the refrigerator is operated utilizing the LP source of heat.

Some electrode assemblies make do with a single probe that creates the spark to the burner and monitors the presence of the flame. Others incorporate a spark probe and a separate flame sense probe.

Fig. 12-29; Burner and electrode.

Thermister

Thermostatic control of most automatic refrigerators invokes the use of thermistors instead of thermostats outfitted with capillary tubes. In those units, the thermistor is attached to the interior cooling fins at the secondary evaporator instead of a capillary tube. The opposite end of the thermistor attaches directly to the circuit board. Pictured here is a thermistor assembly for both a Dometic and a Norcold refrigerator.

Typically the thermistor cable is routed from the board location and enters the refrigerator storage compartment through the rear wall of the unit. It attaches to either a specific holder mounted to the sidewall of the lower food storage area or to a specific fin on the secondary evaporator.

Like capillary tubes, thermistors must be treated with care to avoid damage to it or the circuit

Fig. 12-30; Dirty burner and electrode assembly

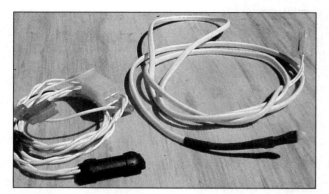

Fig. 12-31; Two types of thermistors

board itself. Since the thermistor takes the place of the thermostat, a defective one will manifest itself as either a refrigerator that overcools on both LP and electric operation or one that does not cool at all.

Thermistors can be easily tested by disconnecting them from the circuit board and measuring the resistance between the two wires in the cable.

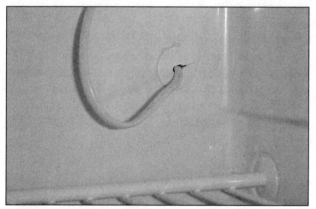

Fig. 12-32; Thermistor entering through refrigerator wall

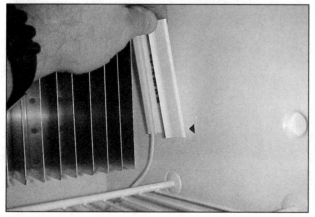

Fig. 12-33; Thermistor wall mount

A proper reading will be approximately 7,000 to 10,000 ohms.

Maintenance
Due to the complexity of the electronics of controlling the operation of the RV refrigerator, the owner is somewhat limited in many troubleshooting and maintenance procedures. As mentioned above, most ignition, operating and monitoring functions are now electronically controlled with very little consumer responsibility. There still exists, however, some owner-related steps to be performed.

Cleaning
Keep the rear of the refrigerator as clean as possible. Once or twice a year, vacuum in and around the burner area. Reach up to the absorber coils with the vacuum attachment, or simply wipe down the pipes with a damp cloth. Be sure to do this when the refrigerator is not operating.

From the roof, remove the roof vent and inspect the condenser fins. Because of the warmth generated by the refrigerator, many creatures, including birds, are prone to construct nests on top of the condenser, effectively blocking the flow of draft air. This can easily cause an overheated condition for the cooling unit and make it a fire hazard. Stack temperatures located at the flue extension on top of the boiler are extremely hot. Most all refrigerator roof vents today are equipped with a protective screen to prevent critters from nesting on the

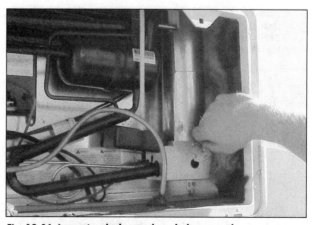

Fig. 12-34; Inspecting the burner through the access door

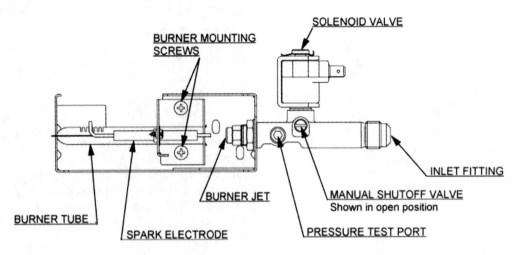

Fig. 12-35; Typical LP components

fins. But check to be sure it is in good condition. If not, it is recommended to install hardware cloth inside the roof vent as prevention.

Like all LP burning appliances, the burner and burner jet must be kept clean. During periods of nonuse, spiders and other insects build webs and nests in and around LP burners. The refrigerator burner is no exception. Inspect the burner assembly by opening the access door. Carefully remove and disassemble the burner. Refer to the owner's manual for specific instructions, but

typically it is not a daunting process. Once disassembled, soak the burner jet in acetone and let air dry. As mentioned previously in this chapter, do not insert anything into the jet. If the unit is equipped with a thermocouple or electrode, remove carbon deposits and brighten the tip with emery cloth. Position and gap the spark electrode according to that model's requirements.

If the unit is equipped with a direct spark ignition (DSI) board similar to the boards on the furnace and water heater, clean the multi-pin connector strip. All other circuit boards require special testing equipment, and no owner testing is recommended.

Check to make sure the flue baffle is in place above the burner and inside the flue pipe. Remove the flue baffle and clean it. It will probably be necessary to remove an aluminum flue extension or cap to gain access to the flue baffle hanger. Never shorten or lengthen this hanger. Remember, each hanger is made to a certain length for each model refrigerator.

While the burner assembly and flue baffle are removed, clean the inside of the flue pipe with a flue brush. A flue brush is available through an

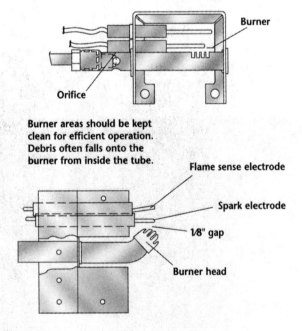

Fig. 12-36; Two styles of refrigerator burners

Fig. 12-37; Circuit board location will vary depending on make and model

Fig. 12-38; Barb adapter used to measure LP pressure at the refrigerator

appliance repair facility. Measure the diameter of the flue pipe in order to obtain the correct size brush. It must make contact with the complete inside wall of the flue pipe.

After all components have been cleaned, carefully reassemble them in the reverse order from which they were removed. Take special care when tightening LP gas tubing and fittings. Always use two wrenches so components do not twist or distort from their intended position. (This is especially crucial with the older manual models.)

Leak-test any LP fitting that was disconnected. When it is certain there are no leaks in the system, attach a manometer to the pressure test port and check the LP pressure with the refrigerator burner lit. Be sure the pressure is set to 11-inches of water column. To attach the manometer directly to the refrigerator test port, a barb fitting with 1/8-inch male pipe threads will be needed. For checking and adjusting the LP pressure, refer to Chapter 8.

For information on how to order the companion video tape on refrigerator maintenance, Cleaning and Servicing the RV Absorption Refrigerator, please contact the author.

Troubleshooting

Since all brands and models differ in components, sequences of operation and troubleshooting paths, it is virtually impossible to cover all the possible scenarios within the confines of these pages. By and large, if a specific problem is in the area of refrigerator controls, i.e., the check light keeps coming on, the heat source chronically malfunctions, etc., the cause is usually a circuit board.

If there appears to be an operational problem such as insufficient cooling, over-cooling or absolutely no cooling, here are a few items to check before making that appointment at the service facility.

First and foremost, be sure the refrigerator is comfortably level during operation. Habitually running the unit out of level may cause a little more chromate to become crystallized. This may slowly continue until one day there will be no cooling at all. Nothing can clear a crystallized percolator tube. The cooling unit will need to be replaced.

Second, make sure no obstructions are in the ventilation and drafting chimney at the rear of the cooling unit. Overheating can cause a multitude of operational problems and lead to a shortened life of the cooling unit. Here's an example of a boiler section in a refrigerator that was run off-level for some time. The two heating elements were virtually welded into their respective pockets. Needless to say, this was an expensive repair involving a new cooling core and two new heating elements.

Fig. 12-39; Overheated boiler section

Third, remember the LP delivery pressure must be set at 11 inches WC.

If an operational problem arises, try operating the refrigerator on another heat source. The purpose of switching modes is to try to isolate the problem area and eliminate the cooling unit as the culprit. If the cooling unit can be ruled out as a possible cause then the RV technician will only have to concentrate on the problem mode. If the exact symptoms occur on both LP and 120-volt AC, the problem is probably the cooling core itself.

In some instances, various control components are shared between each of the heat sources, such as those older models that have only one thermostat. In that case, additional trouble-shooting will have to be performed by the service technician. But the goal is to eliminate the cooling unit as the cause of the proble if possible.

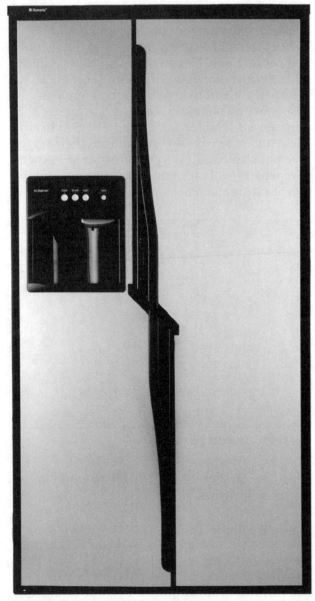

Fig. 12-40; Dometic NDA 1402

Fourth, never block the rear vent opening of the refrigerator. Some owners assume that doing so will eliminate flame outage on those units that are not automatic. As discussed earlier, proper ventilation is crucial.

Fifth, periodically check the seal on the refrigerator doors. Worn gaskets will allow cool air inside the refrigerator to escape. Gaskets may be checked by closing each refrigerator door on a slip of paper at various points around the gasket. If the paper can be pulled out with very little resistance or if it simply falls out, the gasket is faulty. A good indication of a faulty door gasket is the formation of frost or ice on the secondary evaporator fins located inside the lower food storage section.

Finally, proper storage of food inside the refrigerator will enable the air inside to circulate freely. Never block off a shelf with a large tray or pan. The principle of convection is employed to keep the air circulating inside the refrigerator, thereby maintaining an even temperature throughout the entire food section.

Refrigerator Run Tests

It is recommended that a refrigerator run test be performed before any major excursion or at least once per year. Give yourself plenty of time; they require about 24 hours to complete.

Begin the run test by first inspecting the rear of the refrigerator cooling unit. Look for evidence of ammonia leaks. On visible tubing, a yellow residue will indicate a leak. The odor of ammonia will be prevalent if a leak exists in hidden sections of tubing. If you smell ammonia, do not operate the refrigerator. Open all windows and vents inside the RV and allow it to air out. Ammonia leaks mandate a cooling unit replacement.

Be sure all door gaskets are in good shape and check for a proper ventilation chimney at the rear of the refrigerator.

Plug the RV into a shoreline connection and place the refrigerator to the 120-volt AC mode. Set the thermostat to the highest possible setting.

Place one or two quarts of water in an open bowl in the lower food compartment and insert an accurate thermometer in the bowl. Water is used to simulate food storage during the test.

Allow the refrigerator to run on AC electric for 24 hours at which point the water temperature should be between 32 and 43-degrees F. (Some refrigerators may obtain this temperature within the first 12 hours, but the 24 hour timeframe will cover all brands and models).

Note: High temperatures and high humidity levels will reduce the effectiveness of the cooling process. If the test is performed under these conditions, expect a higher water temperature.

If the refrigerator falls within the correct temperature range noted above, it can now be loaded with lobster tails and adult beverages! It's good to go!

Remember, the four important areas to consider with the modern RV absorption refrigerator, to have safe, reliable, silent operation are:

- Leveling
- Ventilation
- LP gas pressure
- Cleanliness of components

By maintaining a watchful eye in these four areas, the RV absorption refrigerator will provide many years of reliable service.

Roof Air Conditioning

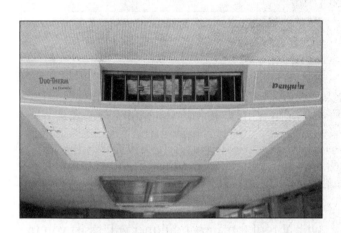

Overview

Today virtually all but a handful of RVs are shipped with at least one, oftentimes two, rooftop air conditioners. It's not uncommon to see three units on the roof of some of the larger 45-foot motorhomes! Yes, as RV owners we've come to expect automatic climate control as part of the whole RV package, especially during the hot summer months.

Thermodynamics

When one ponders the science behind the operation of air conditioners (or refrigeration for that matter), one can quickly become buried within the technicalities of how they actually work. At the risk of boring many readers, a very small look into those dynamics is necessary to fully understand what an air conditioner is doing and how to keep it running smoothly and coolly while we enjoy the climate inside the rig as we travel and camp. We certainly are perplexed and annoyed when it doesn't perform as it should; let's explore a little of what makes it tick.

All RV air conditioners operate on the varied principles of thermodynamics. Thermodynamics is the study of heat (thermo) and how it is moved about (dynamics). It is ruled by laws. The first law of thermodynamics states that energy (heat in this case) cannot be created or destroyed. The second law of thermodynamics is the realization that heat always moves or flows from hot places to cold places. It will never move from cold to hot. Because of this dynamic, the roof air conditioner on the RV must move the heat from inside the coach to the outside of the RV. Through the application of condensation and evaporation, the components of the air conditioner simply transfer the heat to the outside atmosphere.

Now if you really wanted to dig deeper, you could delve into the study of such terms as the latent heat of freezing, of vaporization, of condensation, of sublimation, of fusion, etc. Unless you have an interest in such studies, you will quickly become so entrenched you'd think you were on a technical track with no end. If you think you might have the stomach for it, (and you have absolutely no other hobbies or interests) let me know and I will recommend some

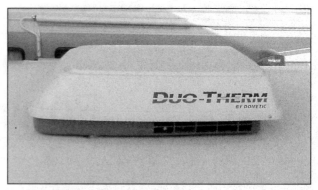

Fig. 13-1; Typical roof top air conditioner

good books for you. For our purposes here, however, only a little appreciation is necessary.

It's important to realize the roof air conditioner on the RV simply removes heat from inside the coach and transfers it to the exterior of the RV. This process makes the inside temperature cooler. It's primary job, however, is to reduce the moisture content of the air first. A basic understanding of the components and operation of a typical roof top air conditioner will assist you in preventing potential problems and will further underscore the need for regular maintenance.

Major Components of RV Air Conditioners

Most RV air conditioners consist of six major component parts or groups of parts:

- Compressor
- Condenser
- Evaporator
- Blower assembly
- Capillary tube
- Control devices

Okay, with that small taste of thermodynamics and the above list of the major components, let's now explore how the roof air conditioner actually does what it does.

How the Air Conditioning System Works

RV manufacturers constantly search for new ways to improve the aesthetics of their products, including air conditioners. Modern advances regarding the air conditioner include "split system" air conditioners that eliminate that superstructure on top of your RV. Also, some models incorporate a heat pump that will both heat and cool the RV. With the popularity of basement-style motorhome designs, basement model air conditioners are on the rise.

All air conditioners have one common goal: keep the RVer cool. Roof-top air conditioners, however, are still the preferred favorite among the majority of coach manufacturers and retail customers. Though many of the dynamics discussed here apply to all types of air conditioners, the crux of this chapter deals with the roof air conditioner.

To transfer heat, the air conditioner takes advantage of one of the natural properties of all liquids; namely, that whenever a liquid vaporizes, heat is absorbed. In the motor-driven compressor air conditioner, the application of this ideal is sophisticated, employing a circulating refrigerant that boils at a low temperature and can be used over and over. The fact that the refrigerant inside the sealed system of the roof air conditioner can change its form allows the transfer of heat to take place.

Fig. 13-3; Penguin horizontal compressor

The entire air conditioning system is sealed and pressurized with a refrigerant, typically R-22. Each refrigeration cycle starts with the compressor. Its purpose is to take in low-pressure refrigerant and, just as the name implies, compress it and discharge it as a high-pressure vapor. When the refrigerant is compressed, heat radiates, which causes the discharge line to become rather warm. Since temperature directly impacts pressure, on hot, sunny days the pressure inside this discharge line can be as high as 360 pounds per square inch (psi) or more.

The next component in the system to see this high-pressure vapor is the condenser coil. The condenser is the finned coil located on the roof and visible at the rear of most air conditioners. In the condenser, the vaporized refrigerant is cooled by air passing through the coil, which condenses the refrigerant back into a liquid. When it leaves the condenser on the way to the capillary tube, the refrigerant stays in a liquid state.

The capillary tube is a metering device used in controlling the flow of the refrigerant. The typical roof top air conditioner is said to be capillary-tube controlled. This capillary, or cap tube determines the amount and the force at which the refrigerant enters the evaporator. All cap tubes are a specific length for that particular air conditioner. They must never be altered.

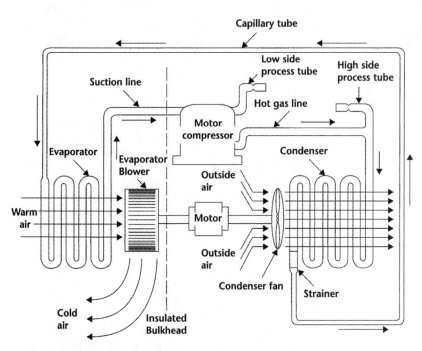

Fig. 13-2; Typical RV air conditioning cycle

Fig. 13-4; Exposed air conditioner condenser

The high-pressure liquid refrigerant next enters the evaporator coil in a controlled amount as determined by the capillary tube. When the high-pressure liquid enters the low-pressure atmosphere of the evaporator, the refrigerant evaporates rapidly into a gas. When this evaporation takes place, heat is absorbed from the air, which is being blown over the evaporator coil.

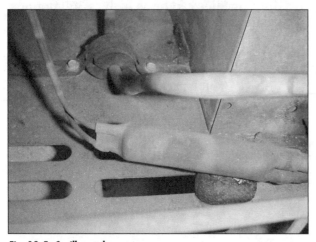

Fig. 13-5; Capillary tubes

That air with the heat removed is delivered to the inside of the RV through the discharge ducts on the ceiling plate. Some applications include a central duct mounted in the ceiling.

The blower motor and fan distribute the now cooled air throughout the coach. Additionally, the same motor draws air across the condenser fins with the addition of a fan attached to the opposite end of the motor shaft.

Fig. 13-6; Air discharge ducts, flat design

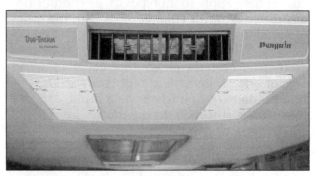

Fig. 13-7; Air conditioner discharge duct

After the refrigerant passes through the evaporator, the low-pressure vapor is then returned to the compressor through the suction side or low-pressure line to begin the cooling cycle again. As long as there are no breaks or cracks in the tubing, joints or the various components, this process will continue as long as the compressor is running.

Controlling the Climate
Many of today's RV air conditioning systems incorporate the advantages of electronic methods of thermostatic control. Beyond the scope of the average RVer, this chapter will steer clear of electronic controls and only include the main control components of the standard, analog roof air conditioner. Specialty testers and devices are necessary to service electronic thermostats and control centers.

Fan Switch
This switch simply controls the speed of the blower fan. Different brands and models abound with various features but most will have at least two speeds. Many today are controlled electronically.

Fig. 13-8; Blower motor and fan

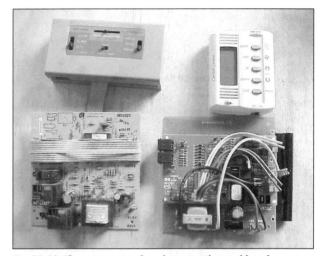
Fig. 13-10; Thermostat controls and associated control boards

Fig. 13-9; Assorted air conditioner control boards

and a run capacitor (that takes over for the start capacitor after the unit is running) are associated with the typical roof-top air conditioner. They are predictably located inside the roof top shroud. The fan motor may also have a capacitor in its circuit. All testing should be performed by a qualified air conditioning technician, but just knowing what they are and where the components are located will help you understand the importance of preventive maintenance.

Fig. 13-11; Various types of capacitors

Thermostat

The air conditioning thermostat controls the operation of the compressor by sensing the need for cooling and the room temperature. The sensing element is positioned in the path of the return air being drawn back into the air conditioner. The thermostat typically has a temperature range from 90° F down to about 62° F. That is, the thermostat will close causing the compressor to become activated only if the temperature at the sensing element is within this parameter. Rarely will a roof-top air conditioner cool at temperatures below 62° F.

Capacitors

Usually a start capacitor (to help jump-start the compressor and motor from a standing start)

Compressor Overload

The compressor is protected by an overload thermal protective device If the temperature of the compressor casing goes beyond a safe limit, the overload device will open the circuit, thereby shutting down the compressor. The overload thermal protective device is located on top of the compressor. The overload device can be tested by

Fig. 13-12; Overload protective devices

measuring for continuity between the two contacts.

Relay

This relay is often referred to as the start relay and is usually located in the electrical control box near the start capacitor. This normally closed relay controls the current sent to the start capacitor. It also disconnects the start capacitor from the system once the compressor has started, allowing the run capacitor to take over. Some relays may be classified as time-delay relays. This means that the compressor is delayed from initial start-up for a short period of time to allow the head pressure to equalize in the closed refrigerant system. This greatly extends the life of the compressor.

Fig. 13-13; Start relay devices

Fig. 13-14; Typical heating coil component

Some units have a Positive Temperature Coefficient Resistor (PTCR) instead of a compressor start relay. Though a solid state device, the PTCR performs the same function as the start relay. In some cases, the PTCR replaces the start capacitor as well.

Cold Control (Freeze Protection)

When coil temperatures of the evaporator approach freezing, a thermistor device (on electronic units) or a thermal switch (on analog units), will shut-off power to the compressor and switch the fan to the highest setting in order to bring the coils to a higher temperature and eliminate compressor freeze-up. The location of the sensor on the evaporator coil is very specific to each air conditioner. Take care not to alter or move the remote sensor during inspections and cleaning.

The electronic thermistor can be checked for continuity to a good frame ground. If either of the two conductors have continuity to ground, the thermistor is faulty and needs to be replaced.

On analog units the cold control switch is a normally open thermal device that closes when the coil temperature falls to a point somewhere between 41 and 49° F. It can be tested by checking for continuity between the two conductors. If the ambient temperature is above 70° while testing, there should be no continuity through the device. When testing in temperatures below 49° F., there should indeed be continuity. Replace the cold control switch if results differ.

Heat Producing Air Conditioners

Some roof-top air conditioners are equipped, (perhaps as an option), with a separate heating coil that allows the RVer to use the roof air conditioner to take the chill off a cool morning without having to fire up the LP furnace. Heat strips are a nice addition, but do require additional AC voltage and current to operate the heating coil and the blower motor on the unit. Attached to the interior plenum of the roof air conditioner, warm air is delivered through the same ducts as the cool air when the air conditioner operates in that mode.

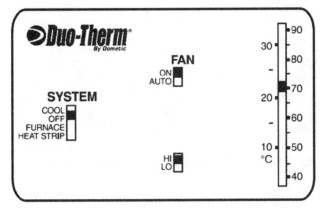

Fig. 13-15; Electronic wall thermostat with heat strip and furnace option

Heat Pumps

Some RV air conditioners may be equipped with a heat pump feature. Different from the electrical heating coils mentioned above, the heat pump feature utilizes the same components as the air conditioner, only a reversing valve is included which simply reverses the flow of the refrigerant through the compressor. Depending on the positioning of the reversing valve, the unit will either cool or heat the RV. During a heat cycle, heat is removed from the outside air, processed and released to the interior of the RV.

There will be a heat pump selection switch featured on the main wall thermostat. There is no owner maintenance necessary for the reversing valve on a heat pump. If problems develop, it will be necessary to make an appointment at a qualified RV service shop.

Maintenance

Periodic inspection and regular maintenance will keep you informed as to the condition of the air conditioner. If, at any time, a drastic decrease in cooling is noticed or a refrigerant leak is suspected, do not operate the unit until it has been thoroughly checked by a qualified RV service technician. Damage to other components may result. Performing the following steps once or twice a year will yield many years of conditioned air. Be sure to perform all of these checks with the power off. The final step listed is the only one when the air conditioner should be running.

1. Remove and clean the filter. The filter is usually accessible from inside the RV. Most can be rinsed out with warm water, however, consult the owner's manual for that particular brand to be sure. Never operate the air conditioner with the filter removed.

You may want to consider replacing the original air conditioning filter(s) with electrostatic air filters. By virtue of air moving through the

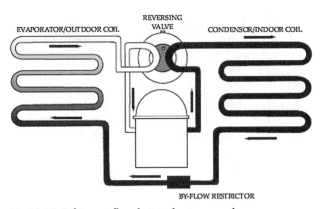

Fig. 13-16; Refrigerant flow during a heat pump cycle

Fig. 13-17; A dirty air filter can inhibit air flow

Fig. 13-18; Electrostatic filters actually attract debris

filtering element, the electrostatic filter attracts dirt particles easier, resulting in cleaner air being drawn in across the evaporator. Cleaner air means less chance of blockages occurring in the fins.

While the filters are removed, check the positioning of the thermostat sense probe. That's the thin, pencil-like, copper-looking device attached to the tiny tubing leading to the thermostat. Be sure it is situated in the direct flow of return air to the unit. Look closely for grime or a film that may have accumulated from cooking oils and/or cigarette smoke. Gently clean the sense probe with a warm rag if contaminates are found. Take special care not to kink the small capillary tubing leading to the probe.

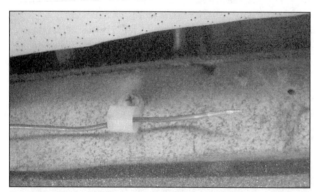

Fig. 13-19; Check and clean the thermostat sense probe

2. With the interior shroud removed, check the condition of the mounting gasket located between the bottom of the roof top unit and the roof itself. It will be visible from inside the RV by looking up and into the 14-inch opening in the roof. If the gasket has been compressed beyond usefulness or there is evidence of water leaks, it's time to have a new gasket installed. Now is also the time to tighten the mounting bolts if they have become loosened.

3. On the roof, remove the shroud and inspect all refrigerant tubing lines for cracks or leaks. If any are found, do not operate the unit until a complete repair, evacuation and recharge has taken place. A refrigerant leak is often accompanied by an oily stain.

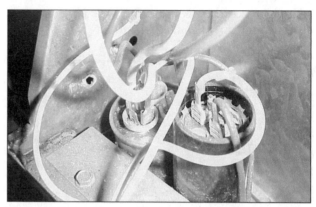

Fig. 13-20; Examine the capacitors for abnormalities and loose wires

While the shroud is off, now is the time to check the drain holes in the air conditioner pan. Remove any debris if found. Plugged drain holes may permit moisture to drip inside the RV while operating the air conditioner.

4. Check all electrical wiring. Look for loose connections, wear and missing or burned insulation. Make sure all wire nuts are taped to prevent them from coming loose while enduring the vibrations that occur with roof air conditioners and by normal driving.

5. Inspect the fan blades and motor assembly for free mobility and to make sure the blades or "squirrel cage" do not rub or hit any other portion of the housing.

6. Inspect and clean the condenser coil and the evaporator coil. If any of the fins are damaged on the exposed condenser coil, carefully straighten them as best as possible. A fin comb can be purchased at a heating, ventilation and air conditioning (HVAC) supply store if the condenser has sustained denting or damage. Take care not to disturb the cold control

Fig. 13-21; Check for damaged fins and debris

Fig. 13-22; Assorted fin combs

thermistor on the evaporator if so equipped.

7. Regularly inspect the roof-top shroud. Roof air conditioner shrouds are traditionally made of plastic and are pretty durable; however, such durability has its limits. Besides normal degradation due to the ultraviolet (UV) rays of the sun, low hanging branches can literally leave their mark on the air conditioner exterior shroud.

Damaged shrouds can sometimes be cemented; if the shroud is constructed of acrylonitrile-butadiene-styrene (ABS) plastic, patch kits are available for minor cracks. Replacement shrouds are always available from the manufacturer in those instances of major damage. Another option is to replace the plastic shroud with a stronger and more durable one made of fiberglass. Bri-Rus, (www.brirus.com), a West Coast supplier manufacturers assorted replacement shrouds for all current and most discontinued roof air conditioners.

8. Keep the 12-volt batteries charged. Wait, isn't

this the air conditioning chapter? The air conditioner compressor and fan indeed are powered only by 120-volts AC, but modern control circuits in the thermostat and circuit boards are powered by 12-volt DC low voltage. Operational problems with various relays, circuit boards and the wall thermostat can develop under low battery conditions.

Checking the Refrigerant Charge

Overall, the average handyman or handywoman with a few hand tools can effectively perform the above maintenance procedures in a relatively short period of time. But for you RV technicians-in-waiting here's an additional step that will provide an indication of the effectiveness of the refrigerant charge in the roof unit. This step requires a probe-type pocket thermometer. (Many are available, but even the simplest will suffice.) The goal isn't so much an accurate reading, but rather a method of obtaining the difference in temperature readings between the cold air and the return air.

To obtain the difference in temperature readings, begin by running the air conditioner on "high cool" or the maximum setting for a minimum of 30 minutes. Be sure all the RV windows and vents are closed. Position the thermometer directly in the flow of the cool air being discharged into the RV. After the temperature stabilizes, note this reading.

Next, place the thermometer probe in the path of return air to the unit. The return air path is that path of air that goes directly through the filters. The probe can actually be inserted into the filter element. Note this reading as well. On "high cool," a temperature differential of 18

Fig. 13-23; Pocket thermometer for measuring temperature differential

Fig. 13-24; A Pocket thermometer inserted into the return air cavity

to 22° F indicates a system with the proper charge of refrigerant. In areas of high humidity, remember, the temperature differential will be somewhat less.

Also realize that on extremely hot days, the RV air conditioner can only reduce the ambient temperature by this differential. If it's 105° outside, you'll be fortunate to obtain an inside comfort level around 85°. For lower temperatures during hot spells, a very large capacity system is required. Because of their relative size and capacity, most RV air conditioners are simply no match for extremely high temperatures.

If the temperature differential is substantially less than 20°, contact your local RV service facility; further troubleshooting may be necessary. There may be a slow refrigerant leak somewhere in the closed system or a faulty component may have reduced the overall cooling efficiency. Though the RV owner can safely perform rooftop air conditioner maintenance, air conditioner repairs should be handled professionally. In the event the unit needs to be evacuated and recharged, special recovery equipment and licensing is necessary. Gone are the days of simply adding refrigerant.

Troubleshooting
The following troubleshooting chart lists the common causes for a few operating symptoms of a typical analog roof top air conditioner. Due to the complexity of modern RV air conditioners, it is recommended to always refer to the specific owner's manual for your unit. Not all operational ills are listed here.

Troubleshooting the RV Roof Air Conditioner	
Symptom	**Possible Causes**
Blower motor will not run	No voltage at air conditioner
	Circuit breaker tripped
	Open winding in motor
	Loose connection
	Faulty fan switch
	Faulty motor
Blower motor runs very slowly	Low voltage
	Loose wires or connection
	Fan or squirrel cage misaligned
Compressor will not start	Open compressor windings
	Thermostat setting already attained
	Overload device tripped
	Faulty thermostat
	Faulty or dislocated cold control device
Compressor turns, but will not start	Low voltage
	Faulty start capacitor
	Faulty run capacitor
	Faulty compressor motor
	Defective start relay
	Unequalized pressure in system
Compressor starts, runs, then trips overload	Low voltage
	Defective start relay
	Faulty start capacitor
	Faulty run capacitor
	Overly high compressor head pressure
	Shorted compressor wiring
	Internal damage to compressor
	Faulty overload device
Air conditioner short cycles	Thermostat at or near desired setting
	Partial loss of refrigerant charge
	Faulty compressor bearings
	Discharge pressure too high
	Too much refrigerant charge
	Thermostat sense probe not in position

Troubleshooting the RV Roof Air Conditioner (continued)	
Symptom	**Possible Causes**
Compressor runs continuously	Low refrigerant charge
	Refrigerant leak in system
	Dirty or blocked condenser
	Faulty thermostat
	Contaminated system
	Damaged or blocked evaporator coil
	Thermostat sense probe not in position
	Coach doors and windows open
Insufficient cooling	Low refrigerant charge
	Refrigerant leak in system
	Restricted or damaged cap tube
	Blocked evaporator coil
	Faulty compressor
Frost build-up on evaporator coils	Low refrigerant charge
	Plugged capillary tube
	Defective cold control device
	Improper placement of cold control device
	Defective circuit board
	Improper air flow
	Poor air flow separation (return/discharge air mixing)

Chapter 14

Hitches and Towing

Overview

Even though the equipment and techniques involved in towing are not overly complex at the surface level, accurate research, thoughtful planning and the proper setup of the towing gear are mandates for safe and enjoyable travel. It takes a professional shop with experience in such installations of towing equipment to accomplish the latter of these prerequisites, and many RV dealers and service centers are capable of performing them. It is wise, however, to shop around for the best expertise available. This is one area you do not want to choose simply by the best price. And certainly the initial installation is not a do-it-yourself job.

Fig. 14-1; Ball mount with sway control

To the uninitiated, the breadth of the information available on towing can be rather daunting unless you have direction in your planning. The pages in this chapter break down into three typical towing scenarios: towing conventional travel trailers, towing fifth-wheel travel trailers and finally, towing a small vehicle behind a motorhome, often referred to as dinghy towing. Information regarding electric brakes on travel trailers and auxiliary braking for the dinghy will be addressed in the following chapter.

Towing a Travel Trailer

Though the ideal scenario will find the fortunate RVer purchasing the travel trailer and the tow

Fig. 14-2; Perfectly aligned towing package *(photo courtesy W. Aldridge)*

vehicle at the same time in order find the perfect match between requirements and equipment, however, this does not always happen. Often the RVer will already own a pickup or suitable tow vehicle and search around for a travel trailer that can safely be towed behind this existing vehicle. Other times, the RVing family may have found the perfect floorplan with all the necessary accoutrements and now must choose the tow vehicle that will safely haul that unit down the road. In every case, however, the tow vehicle and travel trailer must be suited for one another. For our instructional purposes here, let's assume you have chosen the perfect travel trailer for your family and its interests, hobbies and habits. Now what? Find the appropriate tow vehicle.

Choosing the Tow Vehicle

To properly choose a tow vehicle, first closely check the trailer you have in mind. Exactly what is required to safely move that trailer down the road? Think of the loaded trailer not as an RV, but rather as one huge mass of poundage that you will be dragging along behind you as you cruise down the highway. The operative word here is weight: a body of weight that you must get rolling and more importantly, be able to eventually stop.

A later chapter will detail how to weigh your towing combination using a platform scale. Knowing the gross vehicle weight (GVW) will enable you to pare down the list of potential tow vehicles. (The gross vehicle weight rating (GVWR) for all travel trailers will be conspicuously posted inside the RV and in the owner's literature that will be included in all new trailers.)

Towing specs have been published along with a listing of the extra equipment needed to safely tow a travel trailer and are available from an automobile dealer selling suitable tow vehicles. These extras, commonly referred to as "trailer packages," such include a larger radiator, a higher output alternator and larger battery, auxiliary transmission cooling and a prewired harness for the electrical connections. Remember, not all vehicles can safely tow a trailer. Some may actually be damaged if you attempt to tow. Ask the dealer for the manufacturer's rated towing capacity of the vehicles on your short list.

Aside from your wallet dictating what tow vehicle to purchase, ponder what you personally look for in a vehicle. Do you favor gasoline-powered or diesel? What creature comforts do you need and indeed cannot live without? Also, unless you choose to become a full-time RVer, consider what else the tow vehicle will be doing when not hauling your belongings down the road. Will it second as a work truck? Can it be used as a family vehicle? Only you can answer these questions, as well as the question of aesthetics and accouterments.

Travel Trailer Hitches

Once you have settled on a tow vehicle, it is imperative that you be aware of the many different types and styles of equipment available. Here is where you need some expert advice and a little homework. Although variations exist, some vehicles may be better suited than others for your particular towing combination. An examination of some of the more common options concerning towing equipment is in order, but it is important also to understand that final decisions can only be ascertained after knowing the specifics of your particular tow vehicle and trailer. It is highly advisable to develop a relationship with a local RV service facility. Make certain the service facility is capable of installing the equipment you consider. If necessary, contact the manufacturer of the equipment and ask the company for its recommendation of a good shop in your area. More often than not the manufacturer will be happy to oblige you. After all, its reputation also rides on the quality of work by the shop that installs its product.

Obviously, a hitch is that crucial connection between tow vehicle and trailer. Just as in choosing a tow vehicle, choosing a hitch is also determined by weight rating. Since you now

know what your trailer weighs and the capacity of your tow vehicle, simply choose a hitch that falls within those parameters. Is it that simple? Just about; it's a matter of doing the math. All good service facilities that install hitches will first ask you about the total weight you will be towing. Next, they will ask you about tongue weight. Tongue weight is that percentage of the total weight that will be placed directly on the hitch assembly. It usually amounts to approximately 12 to 17% of the total weight of the trailer. Any cargo stowed in the tow vehicle behind the rear axle must also be considered and added to the tongue weight when trying to determine the hitch required. The key is to ensure the gross weight of the trailer remains less than the tow vehicle's maximum load rating. That, plus each component in the towing configuration must also be rated appropriately.

Hitch Types

There are two basic types of hitches: weight carrying and weight distributing. Weight carrying hitches literally carry the weight of the trailer on the hitch and rear axle of the tow vehicle.

By far the most common type of hitch today is the weight distributing, or load equalizing, hitch. Always mounted directly to the frame of the tow vehicle, this type of hitch, by its design, distributes the towed weight to both axles of the tow vehicle. A weight distributing hitch is the preferred method of towing all but the lightest forms of travel trailers.

Hitch Classifications

All hitches are rated to tow within a specific weight limit, termed classifications. It is vital to understand that some hitches may indeed fit a multitude of vehicles, so it is paramount that all components of the chosen hitch be rated for that specific load. The following chart depicts the various classes and their maximum capacities.

Class	Type	Capacity
I	Weight Carrying	2,000 GVW
II	Weight Carrying	3,500 GVW
II (torsional)	Weight Distributing	3,500 GVW
III	Weight Carrying	5,000 GVW
III	Weight Distributing	10,000 GVW
IV	Weight Distributing	10,000 GVW
V	Weight Distributing	15,000 GVW

Weight Distributing Hitch Components

What most call "the hitch" is actually comprised of several components, not including the coupler of the trailer. Weight distributing hitch assemblies include three main components:

- Receiver
- Ball mount
- Spring bar assembly

The main component of a weight distributing hitch is the receiver. The receiver is, in most cases, bolted to the frame at various strategic points underneath the tow vehicle. Some may be custom fabricated and welded into place. Hitch manufacturers today produce a myriad of hitch receivers for specific tow vehicles that are custom designed just for that vehicle. All the bends and mounting holes are in the correct place. It will mate perfectly with the frame of the tow vehicle. For older, obsolete vehicles, custom hitch receivers can be fabricated from scratch by a quality hitch shop.

The ball mount is the actual link between the trailer and the tow vehicle. It, too, is available as a bolt-together unit or it can be fully welded. Installation of the ball mount is not as simple as it may appear. Careful measurements must be taken on the tow vehicle and also on the trailer. Ball mount tilt angle and ball height are two important measurements that are necessary to ensure a proper hitch setup. Tilt angle is best left up to the professional hitch shop. The result of correct ball mount tilt angle will find the spring bars parallel with the bottom of the trailer coupler when fully hitched and connected.

Ball mount height, however, can be determined by leveling the trailer on a hard surface street or parking lot. The trailer must be fully loaded to its traveling weight. Measure the distance at the axle (or in between tandem axles) from the road surface to the top of the frame. If the trailer has a solid underbelly, defer to a professional hitch shop for proper measuring. The top of the frame should coincide with the top of the coupler on the A frame. Next, add 1/8 inch for every 100 pounds of trailer tongue weight. The final calculation will be the correct ball height needed at the ball mount. Since ball mount height is specific to just one trailer, it is not wise to borrow someone else's ball mount. Chances are the ball height or the tilt angle will be different.

Also be aware that not all ball mounts are created equal. Hitch ratings and ball mount ratings must be compatible. Remember, the overall tow rating is based on the weakest link in the configuration. If, for example, a Class V hitch receiver has a weight rating of up to 7,500 pounds, be sure the ball mount is like-rated. If the ball mount is only rated for 5,000 total pounds, then the overall rating is reduced to 5,000 pounds even if the Class V receiver is rated significantly higher.

The third component of a weight distributing setup is the spring bar assembly. Using the dynamics of leverage as its theory, spring bars are like the handles on a wheelbarrow. By lifting up on the bars, the weight is distributed or shifted toward the front axle. This component adds a new dimension to the handling characteristics of the tow vehicle. Steering and turning become improved and safer while towing.

Other items located at or near the hitch connection include:

- Safety chains: In case the trailer and tow vehicle should prematurely part company
- Breakaway switch: Applies full power to all electric trailer brakes in case of unintentional separation (electric brakes are detailed in the following chapter)
- Electrical connector: Connects the tow vehicle lights and other circuits to the trailer (See Tow Wiring, later in this chapter)

Alternative Hitch Designs

Another type of hitch is available that virtually eliminates any of the effects of trailer sway. Called the PullRite hitch (www.pullrite.com), its unique design takes advantage of the fifth-wheel principle and puts it to use when towing a conventional travel trailer.

When towing, the location of the pivot point (the ball mount) is directly proportional to the amount of sway felt by the driver. The closer the pivot point is to the rear axle of the tow vehicle, the less sway will be evident. While the conventional hitch has its pivot point six to eight

Fig. 14-3; PullRite hitch

inches behind the vehicle, the PullRite's pivot point is located immediately behind the rear axle of the tow vehicle, similar to a fifth-wheel hitch installation, where the pivot point is located almost directly above the rear axle in most cases. There is also a large radius bar formed into a 140-degree arc. The long draw bar glides through this arc on sealed roller bearings. A larger 180-degree design is also available for a tighter turning radius; a nice option for tow vehicles with a longer wheelbase.

Tests have shown travel trailers making a complete U turn on a narrow street using the PullRite hitch without having to back up. Hitching up can take place anywhere along the arc. The draw bar can be positioned to the far left, for example, allowing the driver full vision of the ball mount while backing the tow vehicle under the trailer coupler.

The Hensley Arrow (www.nosway.com) is another unconventional piece of equipment used for towing conventional travel trailers. Not so much an alternative hitch per se, it is probably better described as an engineered and well thought out anti-sway ball mount of sorts. It still will slide into the typical two-inch receiver

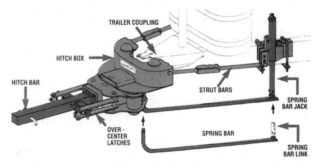

Fig. 14-4; Hensley Arrow hitch assembly

mounted under the tow vehicle. The design of this type hitch makes use of converging linkages that form a flexible trapezoid framework which gives the tow vehicle complete control over the actions of the towed trailer. It basically locks the two vehicles into a single unit as it travels down the highway. In other words, it eliminates the tail-wagging-the-dog syndrome sometimes associated with trailer sway

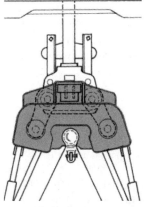

Fig. 14-5; Hensley Arrow converging linkage

There is much more to this device including a built-in weight distributing mechanism that warrants a deeper look by serious trailerists. If you annually log a multitude of miles with your conventional travel trailer, you owe it to yourself to check it out.

Tow Wiring
In order to comply with Federal Regulations (FMVSS 108) all travel trailers must utilize, at a minimum, running lamps (also called trim lights or clearance lamps), turn signals and brake lamps. Additionally, if the trailer is equipped with electric brakes or an automatic absorption refrigerator, more circuits must be interconnected between trailers and tow vehicle.

Since all travel trailers come factory-equipped with some type of electrical connector, it is usually easier to configure the tow vehicle circuitry to match the existing wiring at the plug on the trailer. Usually lumped into an installation service that includes the brake controller and the hitch receiver, most RV dealers and aftermarket service providers are poised to wire any vehicle that can safely tow a travel trailer.

Though no official color code exists, some norms are associated with RV tow wiring that many RV service facilities follow. Likewise, there is no standard type of electrical connector used to mate the trailer to the tow vehicle; that is usually dependent on the number of circuits needed. Typically, the connector will contain, four,

Fig. 14-6; Four wire, flat electrical connector

Fig. 14-7; Typical seven-pin connector

six, seven or nine different conductors. The four most common conductors and their suggested colors, associated with the four standard circuits mentioned above, include:

- Ground: White
- Running lamps: Brown
- Right turn signal: Green
- Left turn signal: Yellow

In some designs, the brake lamps use the same bulb filament as the turn signals, so there is no need for extra conductors. When you step on the brakes, both right and left turn bulbs are powered. If you activate one of the turn signals while braking, that side will flash and the other side will indicate braking. Though a permanently mounted receptacle is available, most four-wire configurations typically utilize inexpensive flat connectors like these:

Other product suppliers, such as the popular Bargman line of electrical connectors, denote different colors for the circuits in its products. A typical seven-pin Bargman or Pollack connector will include:

- Pin 1: Ground—White
- Pin 2: Electric brake circuit—Blue
- Pin 3: Running lamps—Green
- Pin 4: Battery charge circuit—Black
- Pin 5: Left turn signal—Red
- Pin 6: Right turn signal—Brown
- Pin 7: Back-up lamps (or auxiliary circuit)—Yellow

If the travel trailer is equipped with an automatic refrigerator, typically a nine-pin connector is used and includes two additional conductors for the ignition circuit and the main power to the refrigerator. Although the connector must be

disassembled to view them, thankfully the pin numbers are clearly marked on the plug and the receptacle inserts on Bargman connectors.

Hitching Up

Connecting the tow vehicle and the travel trailer involves these four basic steps:

- Inserting and securing the ball mount
- Attaching the trailer coupler to the ball mount
- Positioning the spring bar assembly
- Connecting the electrical harness, safety chains and breakaway switch

Insert the ball mount into the receiver making sure it is positioned correctly and that the pin or locking assembly is secured. Clean and lightly coat the ball with a light lubricant.

Before backing the tow vehicle under the trailer coupler, make sure there is proper clearance under the coupler. Raise the coupler with the tongue jack if necessary. Position the ball directly under the coupler. This is when having a co-pilot is the most beneficial. Before lowering the coupler onto the ball, measure the distance between the ground and the front bumper on the tow vehicle (the ground should be fairly level while taking these measurements). Next, measure the distance between the ground and the rear bumper (or any point of reference).

Lower the trailer onto the ball and lock the coupler. Then raise the tongue jack again while the two are connected. Raise both units above the level plane so that a fulcrum is manifested at the ball. This makes it much easier to attach the spring bars. Insert the spring bars into the sockets of the ball mount. Make sure they are locked in place. Attach the brackets to the A frame. To find the correct location for the brackets, hold the chain straight up, making sure there are no twists in the chain. Center the bracket on the chain and tighten the bracket screw finger tight only.

The next step will require a little experimentation to find the correct link in the chain to position in the brackets. Pick one link and position it on the hook or in the slot. Using the assist handle, lift up on the arm of the bracket until it snaps into place, putting tension on the spring bar. Move the safety wire over the top of the arm. Repeat this procedure on the other side.

Now, lower the tongue jack until all the weight is on the hitch assembly. By adjusting the number of chain links up or down, the height of both vehicles can be regulated. The correct adjustment of the spring bars is attained when the difference between the measurements you took before connecting the trailer (from the ground to the bumpers) and the measurements you take after locking the spring bars in place, is within a half inch of each other. Also, when viewed from the side, the spring bars should be parallel with the bottom of the A frame and the chains should be straight up and down. It may take a few tries to identify the correct link to use. Be sure to use the same link each time. Subsequent connecting of the trailer and tow vehicle will now be quite easy.

The final procedures when hitching up include connecting the electrical plug for the running lights and other circuits. Be sure the contacts have not corroded. Brighten them with emery cloth or a commercially available contact cleaner and preservative. Install and adjust the sway control according to the manufacturer's recommendations. Connect the breakaway switch cable to the frame of the tow vehicle or to the hitch receiver. Do not attach the cable to the ball or the ball mount. Finally, attach the safety chains. They should be crossed under the coupler so they form an X to catch the coupler should the hitch fail. Chains should be long enough to handle the sharpest of turns,

yet short enough not to drag.

After everything is connected, pull the trailer forward a few feet and check all the equipment for any adjustments that may be necessary. Adjust the mirrors for maximum visibility, and you are ready to go.

Trailer Sway

Not as bothersome as in years past, nonetheless, trailer sway still remains high on the list of concerns for RVers who tow trailers. Modern manufacturing techniques and advances in equipment, however, seem to have all but eliminated the nuisance of trailer sway. Trailer sway has usually been attributed to poor weight distribution on the trailer frame during the construction of the RV or to poor loading techniques by the end user. Sway can further be aggravated by passing tractor/trailer rigs, which many times induce the fish-tailing process. To minimize trailer sway, check the setup for:

- Proper loading
- Adequate tongue weight
- Proper equipment

Proper Loading

Proper loading and stowing of personal items and camping gear is paramount to safe towing. A balance in weight primarily between the two sides of the trailer will help minimize trailer sway. In other words, stow half of your bowling ball collection on the right side of the trailer, the remaining half on the left side of the trailer, preferably directly over the axle.

Adequate Tongue Weight

More common in years past, inadequate tongue or hitch weight has been a significant contributor to trailer sway. With today's engineering standards being more defined, this probable cause from the past has been lessened quite a bit. Still, in terms of Class IV or Class V hitches, the ideal tongue weight should be at least 12% of the total weight of the fully loaded trailer. Some of the larger trailers may have tongue weights nearing 17% of the total. Anything less could have a tendency to be the cause of sway, should it be experienced. If necessary, move heavier objects forward of the front axle of the trailer to add to the tongue weight.

Proper Loading

Proper loading and stowing of personal items and camping gear is paramount to safe towing. A balance in weight primarily between the two sides of the trailer will help minimize trailer sway. In other words, stow half of your bowling ball collection on the right side of the trailer, the remaining half on the left side of the trailer, preferably directly over the axle.

Adequate Tongue Weight

More common in years past, inadequate tongue or hitch weight has been a significant contributor to trailer sway. With today's engineering standards being more defined, this probable cause from the past has been lessened quite a bit. Still, in terms of Class IV or Class V hitches, the ideal tongue weight should be at least 12% of the total weight of the fully loaded trailer. Some of the larger trailers may have tongue weights nearing 17% of the total. Anything less could have a tendency to be the cause of sway, should it be experienced. If necessary, move heavier objects forward of the front axle of the trailer to add to the tongue weight.

Proper Equipment

To combat trailer sway, sway control devices can be added to the hitch setup. Though electronic sway control is now available, the two most common types of mechanical sway control are; friction-type and dual cam-type. Friction-type sway controls connect from the ball mount to

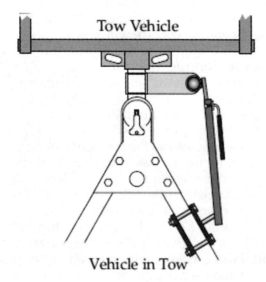

Fig. 14-8; Friction Sway Control Device

Fig. 14-9; Reese Dual Cam sway control

the side of the A-frame coupler on the trailer. A friction pad, similar to a brake lining, rubs against a steel bar as it slides in the housing. This creates a more rigid connection between tow vehicle and trailer, thereby reducing the effects and severity of trailer sway.

Although the turning radius may be slightly reduced, the use of a friction-type sway control does not necessitate removal prior to backing up. Proper installation instructions must be followed, however, and measurements must be carefully taken. After installation, slowly try to jackknife the tow vehicle and trailer. If there is no obstruction and you are not close to actually hitting the sway control, then you will have no problem backing up with the sway control in place. You should, however, reduce the tension or the adjustment on the sway control while driving under slippery road conditions.

The dual cam-type sway control, uniquely manufactured and perfected by Reese Products (www.reeseprod.com), attaches to the trailer A-frame and engages the spring bars directly through two cams with corresponding recesses. Once connected, like the friction-type, a more rigid structure exists that will resist trailer sway. When cornering, the cams disengage from the recessed position so as not to affect the turning radius of the tow vehicle and trailer combination. Sway control is not in effect when this occurs since the rigidity is lost when the cam comes out of the recess. However, this is not a concern. If you are making such a turn that causes the cam and the recess to become temporarily separated, you will be going slow enough that sway control is not needed anyway.

Accessories for Towing

What has been described above is considered the bare bones of towing a travel trailer. What follows is a list of various aftermarket products that can enhance your towing experience. As technology has progressed, so have many items of safety, efficiency and performance. The following products are simply recommended based on their ability to contribute to one or more of these three elements. Many more products are available; however, this list will give you an idea of the various areas to consider for upgrading.

- Heavy duty alternator
- High volume radiator
- Transmission cooler
- Power steering cooler
- Powered mirrors
- High performance exhaust system
- Turbocharger
- Ride-Rite air springs
- Steering stabilizer
- Fuel injection
- Gear Vendors over/underdrive auxiliary transmission

Hitch Maintenance

The construction of most hitches and related equipment is quite sturdy. After all, a lot rides on the structural integrity of the hitch. Maintenance, although important, is minimal when it comes to the towing equipment. It will not take a lot of effort to check the following items, yet it is wise to perform them regularly.

Hitch Ball

Keep the ball lubricated. Many RV stores carry grease specifically designed for hitch balls, but should you choose to use a generic grease be certain it is the high temperature variety. Lube the hitch ball each time you hook up.

Ball Mount and Receiver

If the ball mount or hitch is the bolt-on type, periodically check the bolts and nuts for tightness. Look for any signs of rust on any component. Be sure to check inside the sockets where the spring bars slide into. Also lube those sockets.

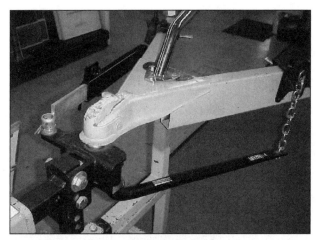
Fig. 14-10; Spring bars attached to trailer A-frame

Spring Bars

Check the chain and bar for any wear or defect. Call the manufacturer or your local dealer if a replacement is necessary. Over time, deflection of the bars may indicate a need for replacement.

Sway Controls

For friction-type sway controls, visually inspect the lining each camping season and replace it if the wear patterns expose metal. After extended trips or every 10,000 miles, remove the slide bar and clean it with emery cloth or steel wool. All that is necessary with the Reese dual-cam sway control is to inspect the bolt attachment points for tightness and to apply a thin layer of lubricating grease to the cams and their respective recesses.

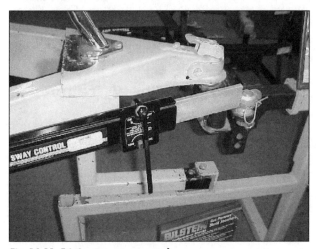
Fig. 14-11; Friction-type sway control

Trailer Coupler

Check these areas for rust. As you hitch and unhitch over a period of time, scratches may occur. Sand and touch up any scratches or nicks in the paint. Lube the locking mechanism on the coupler.

Safety Chains

Inspect each link periodically. Look closely at those links closest to the ground for wear. Do not use universal links to repair worn links. Replace the entire chain if necessary.

Electrical Connector

Look for signs of corrosion on the metal contacts. Clean them with a brush or a contact cleaner. Also, make sure the plug and the receptacle are dry. Check the length of the electrical harness for fraying or where it may have accidentally been dragged along the ground. Again, if damage is present, replace the entire harness.

Breakaway Switch

As with any electrical contact or connection, clean and dry are the operative words. Also, periodically pull the pin and check for oxidation (some pins may be plastic). Spray a shot of contact cleaner inside the switch housing and reinsert the pin fully. Check the braided cable that connects the pin. Again, replace it if any signs of damage exist.

All in all, very little maintenance is necessary for your towing equipment. However, this is one area in which you would not want to take any chances. Find a routine and get into the habit of performing these inspections as you travel. You will reap many miles of safe, trouble-free RVing.

Towing a Fifth-Wheel Trailer

Most RVers do not think of having much in common with truckers other than driving the same highways, but when it comes to fifth-wheel trailers, there is much similarity. For instance, the fifth-wheel got its name from the trucking industry. The "fifth wheel" is actually that smooth, round hitching disk that is easily identified on the big tractors when the trailer is not attached.

Fig. 14-12; Correct fifth-wheel clearance above truck rails

Also the jacks that poke out from their retracted positions on semitrailer front ends have counterparts on the RV fifth-wheel trailer, where they perform the same job of supporting the trailer when it is disconnected from the tow vehicle. And thirdly, the mechanics of joining the tandem via a pin on the trailer that locks into the jaws of a plate mounted on the truck is a direct steal from the trucking industry.

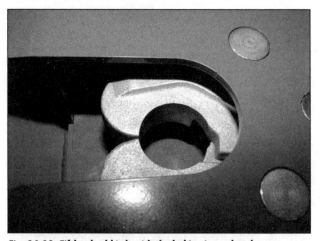

Fig. 14-13; Fifth-wheel hitch with the locking jaws closed

Ideas are liberally borrowed for a reason. In the case of the fifth-wheel, the plate pin arrangement provides a means for hitching and unhitching that is easy and almost maintenance-free. There are some demanding aspects; some muscle is needed to pull the handle that operates the jaws or to manually crank the jacks, but both chores are no more taxing than coupling a travel trailer.

This plate pin arrangement is so well accepted that many fifth-wheel owners would tow nothing else. They are a dedicated bunch bound by the much touted advantage of fifth-wheel towing - exceptional handling. It is an idea firmly rooted in reality. With the hitch weight placed directly over or just forward of the tow truck's rear axle, these trailers are quite stable in their tracking. Also, the fifth-wheel design pretty much eliminates trailer sway.

While turning and backing, a fifth wheel develops less of an angle to the tow vehicle than does a conventional travel trailer. This allows a quick recovery after a turn, but also causes increased tire wear because the two vehicles do not round corners on the same turn radius. This forces the trailer tires to "scrub" against the pavement somewhat. For the most part, fifth-wheel towing equipment is maintenance-free, and the tasks for the responsible owner are the ordinary pre-trip checks that any RVer would perform.

Hitches differentiate in design, however. The hitch installed on the tow vehicle must be compatible with the hitch that is installed on the trailer by the manufacturer. The first-time buyer has a head start on these decisions if he or she has some understanding of how fifth-wheel hitches differ and the relative advantages of each.

Choosing the Tow Vehicle

Although some fifth-wheel trailer manufacturers produce specialty trucks that are packaged with their trailer, most owners can find a suitable tow vehicle among the stock units manufactured by the auto industry. There are, however, special considerations.

In most cases, a hefty truck is required for fifth-wheel towing. There are several reasons for this. One is that whereas the hitch weight of a travel trailer is usually about 12 to 15% of its gross weight, the pin weight of a fifth-wheeler generally runs about 20 to 25% (for a 6,000-pound trailer, that is 1,200 to 1,500 pounds!). Also, the higher profile created by the second level bedroom of the trailer causes more wind resistance and consequently, more drive train power and better cooling are needed, as well as beefier brakes.

Although some small fifth-wheel trailers can get by with a properly equipped half-ton pickup truck, generally a three-quarter-ton truck is the smallest tow vehicle found for most fifth-wheel trailers. Some larger coaches require a one-ton truck or larger. The overall weight of the trailer is the primary concern since most fifth-wheel rigs weigh substantially more than conventional travel trailers.

All pickup trucks used for towing fifth-wheel trailers should always be equipped with a towing package. Stock towing packages generally include any or all of the following:

- Bigger engine
- Specially geared rear axle
- Higher capacity alternator
- Larger radiator
- Transmission oil cooler
- Trailer wiring harness
- Heavy duty suspension
- Powered mirrors

Another recommendation for trucks that pull fifth-wheel trailers is a Gear Vendors under/overdrive auxiliary transmission. This addition to the tow vehicle will provide an additional gear in between each of the stock gears in the existing transmission. This results in more power to the drive wheels, less wasted energy and better performance, including an increase in fuel efficiency.

Fifth-Wheel Hitches

TThough fifth-wheel hitches do not share classifications with the ball-type hitches for conventional travel trailers, they are however, rated by

Fig. 14-14; Fifth-wheel trailer and tow vehicle

Fig. 14-15; Crossbar/side rail hitch

Fig. 14-16; Floor mounted hitch.

weight in the form of design loads. Fifth-wheel hitches typically have design capacities of 15,000 pounds, 22,000 pounds and 25,000 pounds depending on the overall length of the unit. Similarly, the pin boxes are also rated in those terms; therefore, the fifth-wheel hitch installed in the pickup should be equal to or greater than the pin box rating on the fifth-wheel trailer.

Some pin boxes are adjustable, meaning they can be telescoped in or out of an outer sleeve to adjust the ride height of the fifth-wheel trailer for optimum towing. The recommended clearance space between the bed of the truck and the bottom edge of the fifth-wheel overhang is about 5-1/2-inches.

Four basic fifth-wheel hitch designs are in use today:

- Crossbar or side rail design
- Pedestal or floor mount
- Inverted or gooseneck concept
- Air hitches

Crossbar Hitch

The most popular designs, the crossbar/side rail and floor mount types, share many of the same type of components. Each has a circular plate or "fifth wheel" mounted in the truck bed. Each type requires a pin protruding from a box mounted on the trailer overhang (the king pin). Both have spring-loaded levers for releasing the locking jaws in the plate and both have locking pins for preventing the lever from being accidentally dislodged from the locked position.

They differ only in the way each hitch mounts to the truck bed.

Side rails create a support structure for the hitch plate. Side rails are made up of steel side pieces mounted on each side of the truck bed and a box-like crossbar that contains the plate. The bar is bolted to the side rails that are, in turn, anchored to the truck frame on either side of the wheel well.

Side rails are either mounted over the fenders or just inside of them. The over-the-fender mount has the advantage of leaving more of the truck bed open for storage items, but it does not provide as firm an anchor as the inside the fender choice.

Pedestal Hitch

The advantage of the floor-mount design is that the hitch takes up little space in the truck bed and the plate is easily removable so that the truck can be put to other uses. This is accomplished with a metal framework that is bolted to the truck bed floor and to ribs that tie in to the truck frame.

Some fifth-wheel crossbar platforms mounted to the floor area of the bed tilt fore and aft to adjust to dips in the roadway while driving. Those that tilt only fore and aft are called standard platforms. Others are designed with a full-floating platform and tilt fore and aft as well as side to side. This design offers the maximum in flexibility and handling while towing.

Inverted/Gooseneck Hitch

This hitch is a marked departure from the others since it has neither hitching plate nor pin. Instead, a larger, heavy duty coupler, similar to standard coupler found on the A frame of a conventional trailer, is welded onto a pin box which is mounted on the trailer. The term gooseneck comes from this coupler mounting which resembles the silhouette of… you guessed it, a goose's neck.

A flat steel base plate is secured to the bed of the truck and to the frame of the truck. The hitch ball, again, similar to an ordinary trailer hitch ball except larger and heavier, is attached to the base plate. Some gooseneck designs are such that the ball actually can be recessed into the bed of the pickup and either popped up or flipped over for use when towing, such as the Turnover Ball (www. turnoverball.com) and the Flip-Over Ball (www.popuphitch.com). When not towing, it disappears from sight leaving the bed completely flat and usable for other tasks.

Fig. 14-17; Popup Hitch Flip-Over Ball

PopUp Industries (www.popuphitch.com) has also developed a unique adapter that modifies the typical king pin on a fifth-wheel trailer and converts it to a gooseneck design.

Fig. 14-18; King pin adapter

This is a viable option for those fifth-wheel trailers that ride too high in the bed of a pickup using a traditional pin box and crossbar hitch.

Hitch Installation

Fifth-wheel hitches, as with all hitches, should only be installed by an experienced, qualified shop. Some manufacturers recommend mounting the hitch directly over the axle, and some say no, it should be two inches in front of the axle. While it is always prudent to follow the manufacturer's recommendations, it may not always be possible since all truck beds and fifth-wheel trailers are not the same. That's why it's important to rely on the expertise of the qualified installer.

Newer designs of fifth-wheel hitches are available for the plethora of short-bed pickup trucks. Some incorporate ingenious sliding mechanisms and are worth looking into if you favor the short-bed design in a tow vehicle. In some cases added space between the rear of the short-bed pickup and the front bulkhead of the fifth-wheel trailer can make a huge difference, especially during turns. That extra space can be obtained by the addition of a fifth-wheel adapter. The RV5 by the aforementioned, PopUp Industries, adds 10-inches of clearance.

Fig. 14-19; PopUp Industries RV5 adapter

Air Hitches

Some fifth-wheel hitches even allow the trailer to float on air such as the E-Z Floater by Hitch Crafters, (www.hitchcrafter.com).Crossbar/side

Fig. 14-20; E-Z Floater air hitch

And the TS3 Trailer Saver by Hensley Mfg., (www.trailersaver.com). The TS3 fits into most of the standard bed rails as produced by many platform hitch suppliers.

Fig. 14-21; TS3 Trailer Saver air hitch

Here's the Easy Rider Air Hitch by Reese,

Fig. 14-22; Easy Rider air hitch

Fig. 14-23; Trailair® air hitch

And the Trailair Air Ride System by Trailair® (www.trailair.com). And this is just a sampling of air products available today!

Comfort is obviously the new operative word when it comes to fifth-wheel towing. With the vast majority of long-haul trucks employing air ride suspensions, it stands to reason that many aftermarket air products are now designed for the active fifth-wheel RVer. The above brands are just a sampling of what you'll find in the marketplace.

A relatively new towing concept for fifth-wheel travel trailers has been developed by American Automation Technologies, Inc. Called the Automated Safety Hitch, (www.safetyhitch.com), this new design is centered around a heavy duty truck axle housed in its own chassis. When connected it literally becomes an integral portion of the towed fifth-wheel trailer. Hitching up is simplified by the use of a handheld controller and winch. No longer is brawn and strength necessary to make the coupling. The trailer basically connects itself.

Fig. 14-24; Automated Safety Hitch

Tow vehicles are no longer limited to pickup trucks and custom haulers. Using a Putnam frame extension, this hitch can even enable a SUV to haul a fifth-wheel travel trailer. The Automated Safety Hitch is equipped with hydraulic disc brakes, (actuated by any dash mounted brake controller), which boost the factory braking ability of the tow vehicle by 50% or more. Furthermore, the weight of the trailer is fully supported by the all-welded steel unit. At speeds below 25 mph the hitch is automatically steerable; above 25 mph the axle remains parallel to the rear axle of the tow vehicle for true tracking. During turns, the Automated Safety Hitch automatically steers proportionately in the direction of the turn.

Appropriate to both fifth-wheel and gooseneck hitch assemblies under 6,300 pounds pin weight, this new concept deserves further due diligence by the serious fifth-wheel enthusiast.

Typical Hitching and Unhitching

Crossbar/side rail and pedestal/platform mount designs allow hitching from a range of angles. The only requirement is that the truck be maneuverable beneath the trailer overhang. Hitching involves lowering or removing the truck tailgate (a costly mistake should one forget to do so), opening the "jaws" of the plate by pulling the lever, backing up the truck until the pin is caught by the plate and seated (a loud snap will be heard), and locking the jaws by releasing the spring-loaded lever, then inserting the lever lock pin.

The trailer jacks and landing pads are raised by cranking a simple hand crank. This can be done manually or, on many fifth-wheels, automatically, by simply flipping a switch. The heavy fifth-wheel trailers almost always are equipped with electric or hydraulic landing jacks. Other details for hitching up include attaching the breakaway switch cable to the truck frame and plugging in the electrical connector.

Unhitching is the opposite procedure. The first step is cranking down the landing gear jacks until they are firmly planted on the ground. All seasoned RVers carry wood planks to aid in this step, invoking a larger footprint. This is followed by disconnecting the electrical connector and breakaway cable, lowering the tailgate, pulling the release lever and driving the truck out from under the trailer. The trailer can then be leveled and stabilized normally for day-to-day living.

Special hitching and unhitching instructions will accompany all fifth-wheel hitches, especially air hitches, so be sure to carefully read the user's guide.

Tow Wiring

Wiring between the fifth-wheel trailer and the tow vehicle will follow the same logic as for conventional travel trailers. Simply refer to that section above.

Hitch Maintenance

Fifth-wheel hitch equipment requires little attention other than keeping the hitch plate and locking mechanism clean and well lubricated. Maintenance chores center on the peripheral items that all trailerists should include in pre-trip checks:

- Lubricating the plate: Any good quality high-temperature automotive grease will do this. Keep a generous amount on the plate. If it gets thin, replenish as necessary.

- Electrical connector: Electrical plugs and receptacles are generally well designed to keep grime and moisture out when they are connected. However, during period of nonuse, they may corrode. Make sure the contacts are clean and dry.

- Breakaway switch: Examine the cable on the breakaway switch and make sure that it is firmly attached to the truck. The cord must have enough slack to allow full turning in both directions.

- Tire pressure: Check all tires for proper pressure and correct if necessary.

- Trailer battery: Make sure the battery is fully charged prior to departing on an extended excursion.

Towing with a Motorhome

Today, seemingly, more than just a few motorhome owners are adopting the practice of towing a small vehicle behind the coach. Affectionately called "dinghy" towing, this facet of RVing appears to be at an all-time high. The popularity and the attraction is evident enough; a smaller second vehicle allows for local side trips and errand running without breaking camp, unhooking the motorhome and leveling it again upon your return. For many RVers it also seconds as a larger closet to stow supplies and camping gear while traveling. There is a long list of good reasons to opt for one.

There are some limitations, though. With a car in tow, it is difficult to back up. The RVer must be cognizant of steep driveways, as well as space limitations, when searching for a parking area. The extended length of the rig necessitates longer stopping distances and more time for lane changes, plus special precautions may be mandated, etc.

Yet, motorhome enthusiasts overwhelmingly are willing to overlook any negatives in favor of the obvious benefits. Take an informal survey sometime and count the number of RVs you see towing a small car behind. It can open a whole new world of side trips to destinations you may never have thought of visiting because you thought you would be limited by the length of your coach.

Choosing the Dinghy
Although the previous statement may be true, limitations on dinghy towing still exist. The limiting factor is primarily determined by the motorhome. Mainly, how much is the motorhome rated to tow? Tow capacity rating is set by the coach manufacturer and is based on many things: engine size, transmission, rear end ratio, frame structure, etc. Modifications can be made to the motorhome that will increase the towing capacity such as adding an auxiliary transmission, a high performance exhaust system and an engine turbocharger.

If your motorhome has the power and performance to tow, the limiting factor then becomes gross combined weight rating (GCWR). This is the combined weight of the RV (and everything in it) and the towed vehicle (and everything in it). Some motorhomes may be further restricted solely by their design. Many extended Class As and Class Cs have a very long overhang—a lot of coach behind the rear axle. This may diminish their capacity to tow. It only has a minimal effect if you plan to tow a vehicle with all four wheels on the ground, however. The actual tongue weight in such cases is comparatively slight.

A third limiting factor when choosing a small

vehicle is the overall length of the combined units. Some states have a limit on the total length. If your motorhome is extremely long, the car you choose may push you over the combined length limit. Measure carefully.

Consider what interests you in a second vehicle. What features do you look for in a small car or pickup truck? If you are planning to purchase a new dinghy, ask your dealer about towing it behind your motorhome. Some can be towed without any modifications; others will need special towing equipment outlined later in this chapter. Many will have speed or distance restrictions as well. Do some homework in this area and you will avoid any unpleasant surprises.

Motorhome Magazine (www.motorhomemagazine.com) annually publishes a list of those vehicles suitable for towing behind a motorhome. The annual dinghy towing guide is available to download from their website.

Keep in mind that not every vehicle that can be towed behind a coach is listed. Some automakers may shy away from publishing that information, fearing liability issues. Additionally, although the listed models can be towed, previous year models may not share that attribute. It is strongly suggested you contact the service department at the auto dealer of your interest to inquire for sure whether a certain model is authorized for dinghy towing. The auto dealer should also be able to state which aftermarket devices are needed for the vehicle you are considering.

Motorhome Hitches
Unlike standard tow vehicles, such as trucks and utility vehicles that have a known frame design for which the hitch makers already have a corresponding hitch, most motorhome frames have been modified or "stretched" to accommodate the RV section. Sometimes this is done by the chassis maker and other times by the coach manufacturer. There is no design guideline. Structural integrity is the only goal. So when it comes time to install a hitch on a motorhome, you may find it necessary to have a custom hitch fabricated to fit. Many coach manufacturers offer a hitch as an optional item, so check with your RV dealer first.

Fig. 14-25; Typical Class IV receiver.

When installing any hitch on any motorhome, keep in mind this important fact: all holding tanks and fuel tanks must be accessible and be able to be removed. There can be no permanent structure prohibiting the removal and reinstallation of either type of tank. It is permissible, however, if the custom hitch is fabricated and then bolted to the frame of the motorhome. It cannot, however, be permanently welded in place directly below a holding tank.

Methods of Towing

So how does one go about towing a dinghy? The single-most important aspect involving tow-

ing a car behind a motorhome is planning. Sound planning is a must. First of all, realize that there are different methods of towing a second vehicle.

The three basic methods are:
- Tow trailer
- Tow dolly
- Tow bar

Tow Trailer

The tow trailer is the least popular method mainly because of the bulkiness of the tow trailer itself. Also many motorhomes just do not have the towing capacity to lug a car and a full trailer behind. With the tow trailer, the entire car is positioned and secured on the trailer. A tow trailer may be fully enclosed or simply an open platform with short side rails.

Tow Dolly

The tow dolly, however, continues to be a popular method. Many models from various manufacturers are on the road today. The tow dolly's principle revolves around placing the wheels of only one axle onto a specially designed single-axle trailer. This is a preferred method by many who own front wheel drive dinghies. The rear

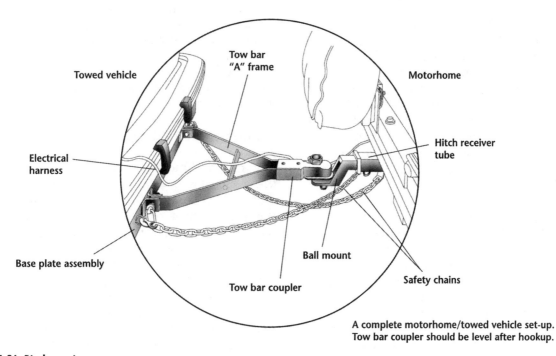

A complete motorhome/towed vehicle set-up.
Tow bar coupler should be level after hookup.

Fig. 14-26; Dinghy towing components

Ramps fold up.

Hitch folds back.

Fig. 14-27; Demco folding KarKaddy

axle of the car spins freely while the front end is on the dolly, so no other major equipment need be purchased. Plus the dinghy need not be further modified.

Demco Manufacturing (www.demco-products. com), a long-time leader in the tow dolly field, produces the KarKaddy with an interesting auto-steer feature that permits easy tracking of the towed vehicle.

Stowing the dolly while you travel and storing it at home, however, may sometimes be a nuisance. Demco has countered this challenge by producing a model of its

KarKaddy dolly with folding ramps and a unique folding hitch that reduces the overall length of the 133-inch dolly to a mere 67-inches for a more compact unit that will easily fit behind your motorhome is most campgrounds. Some campgrounds may have restrictions on where full-length dollies may be kept during your stay. It may be wise to check ahead during the planning of your trip for any stipulations concerning a tow dolly in the campgrounds you will be visiting.

Tow Bar
The most common method of towing a small car behind your motorhome is with a tow bar. This principle permits all four wheels of the dinghy to be on the ground, which results in less tongue weight on the motorhome and easier hitching and unhitching. In most cases, however, special equipment is necessary and modifications may have to be made. The good news, thanks again to the RV aftermarket, is

that almost any small car can now be towed in this manner.

When considering tow bars, realize that different types and styles exist that may need to be analyzed prior to purchase. Also understand that you must already know which vehicle you will be towing. Like hitches, tow bars are rated by weight classification. Tow bars are available in three basic styles or types:

- Removable
- Tilt-up
- Collapsible or telescopic

Although all tow bars today are removable in the truest sense of the word, there is a basic or standard tow bar available that must be removed when not in use. All tow bars today attach to the frame of the dinghy instead of the bumper. In years past, the removable bar could be attached to either the frame or the bumper. However, with today's high tech, collision-resistant plastic auto bumpers, it is a mandate that all tow bars attach solidly to the vehicle frame.

The tilt-up variety is similar in design except that it consists of a baseplate that attaches to the frame of the towed car and a pivotal A frame assembly that attaches to the baseplate. It has a mechanism that allows the A frame portion to be lifted vertically 90 degrees and locked into position to allow driving of the car. There may be some local restrictions on this. The contention is that the upright tow bar impedes the driver's view. Check local codes. Other styles allow for the tow bar to flip up and be secured against the rear of the motorhome.

The third and most popular type of tow bar is the collapsible or telescopic type. Two versions are available; one that mounts to the front of the towed vehicle and one that mounts to the rear of the motorhome. Those that mount onto the dinghy are less costly while those that attach to the motorhome allow a cleaner look to the front end of the towed vehicle. They can also be easily locked to prevent theft. This type of tow bar also eliminates the need for a deep drop ball mount that can sometimes become problematic when entering or leaving steep driveways. Both types, however, are retractable and fold into a neat, compact package when not in use.

Perhaps the most approved feature of this type is the self-aligning manner in which it is attached to the hitch. In other words, during the process of hooking up to the hitch ball on the motorhome or to the attaching point on the dinghy, all you have to do is get close. After the coupler is attached to the ball all that is necessary is to pull forward a few feet and the car and motorhome automatically become aligned and the tow bar locks into place. Attach the safety chains, plug in the electrical pigtail and go!

Regardless of which tow bar you choose, correct ball height is essential for safe and effortless towing. Some tow bars are designed with an off-set in height. Your hitch installer will be able to advise you as to which one is better suited for your setup. The correct setup will find the car and motorhome level and the coupler on the tow bar parallel to the ground when hitched up.

Dinghy Towing Accessories
In years past, in order to tow a rear wheel drive vehicle equipped with an automatic transmission behind a motorhome with all four wheels on the ground, it was necessary to remove the drive shaft completely from the car so that the rotating rear axle would not turn the transmission while traveling. All automatic transmissions and some current manual transmissions require lubrication whenever the transmission turns.

Also, due to the explosion of front-wheel drive, automatic transmission-equipped vehicles today, other considerations are in order if you wish to haul that dinghy with all four wheels on the pavement. Remco Manufacturing (www.remco-towing.com) and others have an assortment of add-on accessories that makes it possible to tow virtually any small vehicle. Here are some of the products that have made a difference with the industry's dinghy towing populace.

Drive Shaft Coupling
This drive shaft product can fully disengage the drive shaft of rear wheel drive vehicles with the pull of a cable mounted inside the towed vehicle. When you reach your destination or wish to take a side trip, simply push the cable in and the mechanical clutch once again engages the

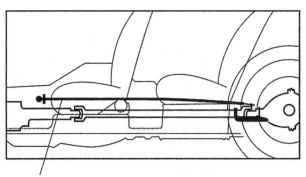

This push/pull cable engages and disengages the disconnect coupling

Fig. 14-28; The cable mounts under or near the driver seat

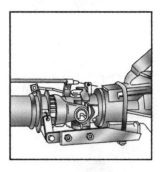

Driveshaft coupling

Fig. 14-29; Driveshaft coupling linkage

Fig. 14-30; Remco Drive Shaft Coupling

drive shaft for driving. The existing drive shaft must be shortened to accommodate the unit, or another drive shaft must be purchased with the kit. If you plan on towing your car a lot of miles, however, this is the device to consider. With the drive shaft disconnected, no mileage will be recorded by the odometer of the towed vehicle. The coupling is also a good anti-theft device. Installation is simple and requires only common hand tools.

Axle-Lock
If your towed vehicle is front wheel drive, as most are, a whole new set of rules comes into play. The drive shaft is an integral part of the front axle assembly, which also includes the transmission. For those vehicles that cannot be towed with all

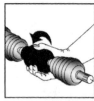

Easily reached just inside the right front tire, the axle lock device is engaged with a simple 1/3 twist.

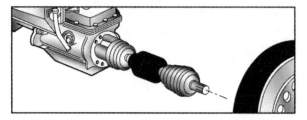

The axle-lock kit includes new replacement axle and two new boots. Permanently installed behind the right front tire, it doubles as an anti-theft device while driving solo.

Fig. 14-31; Axle Lock details

Fig. 14-32; Remco Axle-Lock

four wheels on the ground, Remco has produced a device called the Axle-Lock. This device mounts behind the right front tire and is activated or deactivated by hand with a one-third twist of the device. It, too, can second as an antitheft device.

Transmission Lube Pump

The Axle-Lock solves only one part of the problem for front wheel drive vehicles. Some automatic transmissions must still be lubricated even when one of the axles is disabled. A lube pump is also needed. This device attaches to the towed vehicle but is powered by the battery on the motorhome. When activated, it pumps transmis-

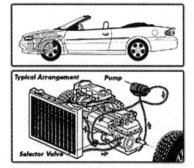

Fig. 14-33; Remco Lube Pump

sion fluid from the pan, through an in-line filter, to a selector valve that routes the fluid on a path to be cooled by the radiator and then on to the transmission and back to the pan.

Some manual transmissions must also be lubricated while turning. It may not be as simple as just putting it in neutral, hooking up and driving off. Check with the manufacturer of the towed vehicle.

Running Lights

Just as a travel trailer or fifth-wheel trailer has running lights, turn signals, stop lights, etc., so also must the towed car. Whether a tow dolly or a tow bar, it is a requirement that any towed vehicle be equipped with proper running lamps (the tow trailer will have its own lights).

There are a couple of options here. You can use the towed vehicle's existing lights by tapping into the wiring, or you can install a temporary light bar that attaches to the rear of the towed vehicle by suction cups. The light bar method does not modify the existing lamps on the towed vehicle. All power for the light circuits will come from the motorhome and terminate at an electrical connection near the hitch. An electrical umbilical (pigtail) attaches to the towed vehicle to complete the circuit.

Almost all imported small cars and trucks, as well as most domestics, have amber turn signals that cannot be used for stop lamps. Special converter boxes are necessary to transform what is termed a three-wire system to a two-wire system. Complete kits are available in RV stores that reduce such wiring conversions to a relatively easy task. If, however, you opt for the temporary light bar, then no modification to the towed vehicle is necessary. Simply attach the light bar to the rear of the towed vehicle, route the wiring harness over the car and plug it into the motorhome.

Auxiliary Braking

In some instances, the weight of the towed vehicle may demand more braking capacity than can be provided by the motorhome alone. Please see the following chapter for more details on auxiliary braking systems for dinghy towing.

Maintenance

As with any device with moving parts, tow bars require a small amount of attention and periodic maintenance. The main focus in tow bar maintenance is lubrication. Each time you hook-up the tow bar make sure the hitch ball is properly lubed. Also check the coupler on the tow bar. The locking mechanism periodically needs a lubricating spray. On telescopic tow bars, keep the machined surfaces free from road grime and dirt that can scratch the sliding parts. Apply a thin amount of household lubricating oil at least every other month while traveling.

Weekly, take a close look at the motorhome hitch, ball mount, safety chains, etc. If chain links become damaged, replace the entire chain. Avoid the use of "master" links. If painted surfaces become scratched or nicked, sand and repaint. Check the hitch mounting bolts for tightness at least once every camping season.

Check the electrical connector plug and pigtail for corrosion. As always, keep electrical equipment clean and dry. Regularly check the operation of the running lamps on the towed vehicle. Have someone verify that the turn signals, stop lamps and clearance markers are in working order.

Dinghy Towing Tips

You have chosen the dinghy, outfitted the motorhome, added all the necessary equipment to tow your front wheel drive automatic and you are ready to go. But before you do, here are some tips suggested by experts who regularly tow a small car behind the motorhome.

Carry an extra set of tow bar attaching pins:
All tow bars attach to the base plate with steel pins that are secured in place with a special clip. Periodically these pins and clips become damaged or lost. Never use a common bolt to attach the tow bar.

Be aware of state laws concerning towing:
Some states prohibit using tow dollies without a special permit or special licensing. The contention is that it is "triple towing," three distinct vehicles attached to one another. Check with the highway patrol of the states you plan to travel to avoid any unnecessary obstacles. AAA publishes a

yearly volume, the Digest of Motor Laws, which lists all traffic and towing requirements, road rules, etc. for each state and all of Canada. It is a wise investment if you plan to travel the breadth of North America. Call your local AAA office for additional information regarding availability.

Call your insurance agent:
Let the agent know you are towing a car behind your motorhome. A special insurance rider may be necessary. A discounted rate may even apply since your car will not actually be driven much at all. Better to be safe than sorry should something unfortunate happen.

Avoid backing up:
Plan ahead as you drive. Carefully consider gas stations, parking lots, etc. It is best to avoid those circumstances that require backing up when towing a second vehicle. You can, however, always unhitch in order to get out of a jam. Also, know your exact overall combined length and approximate turning radius.

Remember to unlock the steering wheel:
It may be necessary to leave the ignition key in the dinghy to keep the wheel unlocked. It is also a viable trick to attach bungee straps to the steering wheel to keep the wheel centered.

Have the front end aligned on the towed vehicle:
This will minimize adverse tire wear as the car tracks behind the motorhome.

Utilize a vehicle bra or rock guard:
Road debris, gravel, pebbles, etc. all have a detrimental effect on the front end of anything being towed behind a motorhome. Ever wonder why travel trailers always have rock guards covering the front window? Avoid mounting wide mud flaps or full width devices on the motorhome. Wide objects that block off the area between the motorhome and the road surface actually trap heat under the motorhome as it travels. High heat can cause numerous types of damage to various components on the motorhome. A front-end vehicle bra will provide the protection needed.

To get the most out of your recreational enjoyment by towing a dinghy behind your motorhome, carefully analyze your requirements based on the vehicles you choose.

Try to preview the towing devices and equipment discussed in this chapter. Most well-stocked service facilities will have a display area depicting the various tow bars and accessories available. Ask questions, take your time, then equip yourself and go!

Chapter 15

Tow Braking

Overview

Few thoughts send stronger shudders up the spine than the thought of brake failure while towing a travel trailer or a fifth-wheel trailer. Fortunately, because of brake design, the RVer usually has advance warning and is in a great position to spot the early signs of brake trouble.

Fig. 15-1; Triple axle travel trailer

Likewise, towing a small car (dinghy) behind a motorhome down a steep hill with winding S curves to navigate can add a few lighter shades of hair color to any driver. Thankfully, a proliferation of supplemental braking devices is available today to not only safely tow, but to safely stop that dinghy hanging onto the back of the motorhome.

Even though disc brakes and electric/hydraulic assemblies are becoming more commonplace, by far, the majority of trailer brakes are of the electric variety. That will be the main focus of this chapter. An understanding of how electric trailer brakes work, how to tell if they are working properly and how to recognize trouble indicators are paramount to keeping the braking system in top working condition, thus ensuring the availability of dependable braking power when needed. Taken as a whole, the braking system may seem complicated, however, when viewed as individual components, an understanding soon develops that will enable RVers to fully comprehend just how a trailer actually stops so effortlessly. The major brake system components include:

- Electric trailer brakes
- Breakaway switch
- Electrical connector
- Brake controller

Electric Brake Design and Operation

Electric brakes resemble automobile drum brakes in that two components, shoes and drums, interact to apply braking force. Shoes are curved plates with a frictional facing material affixed to the outer surfaces. There are two shoes in each brake assembly mounted on a backing plate secured to a stationary part of the axle. The drum is a circular container that fits over the brake shoes and, since it is mounted to the rotating part of the hub, spins with the wheel. The shoes rest inside the drum, with a small space between the relaxed shoes and the drum wall. Braking force is applied by the shoes being forced outward and pressing against the drum wall. The harder the shoes press, the greater the frictional drag exerted on the spinning wheel and the quicker the stopping action.

Fig. 15-2; Components of the brake assembly

Here, the similarity with auto drum brakes ceases. Automotive drum brakes are operated hydraulically, by the pressure of fluid that moves levers and forces the shoes outward. Electric trailer brakes, on the other hand, are operated by 12-volt direct current (DC) electricity originating at the tow vehicle battery.

At the heart of the electric brakes is the magnet. When the magnet is energized by the controller mounted in the tow vehicle, it is attracted to the armature, a metal disc fixed inside the drum that spins with the drum. As the magnet moves toward the armature, it is pulled in the direction of motion causing the lever to push the shoe against the drum. Both shoes are linked so that the movement of one activates the other. Braking continues as long as the magnet continues to receive the appropriate voltage from the tow vehicle.

Fig. 15-3; Example of a brake magnet

Maintenance

Maintenance on electric trailer brakes involves basically three different areas: inspection, cleaning and adjustments. The informed RVer with basic mechanical ability and a few inexpensive specialty tools should have no problem performing the needed maintenance on trailer brakes.

Inspection

Trailer brakes must be inspected and serviced at yearly intervals or more often as use and performance dictate.

Before beginning any procedure outlined here, make sure the trailer is properly raised and blocked safely with the tires completely off the ground. Remove the drum by first removing the dust cover, cotter pin and spindle nut and washer. Carefully remove the outer wheel bearing and cover it with a shop towel so dust does not settle on it during the time it is removed.

Pull the drum away from the remainder of the brake assembly (it may be easier in some instances to first remove the tire and wheel). Look for worn shoe linings. Replace shoes if the lining is 1/16-inch thick or less. Replace them also if they are saturated with grease or oil or are cracked or gouged, or if the lining has become separated from the shoes.

Inspect the magnet arm for any loose or worn parts. Check the shoe return springs, mounting springs and adjuster spring for deformation. Manually move the actuating arm or lever and check for any binding or rubbing. Replace the magnets if they show signs of uneven wear. Some magnets may have recessed screws on the side. If the wear is down to the screws, the magnets should be replaced. In some instances it will be necessary to have the armature plate resurfaced. This cannot be done without a special lathe. Call the local service facility if an armature has developed a pattern of grooves due to worn or damaged magnets.

It is wise to replace all the same items of the same axle even if only one side necessitates replacing. If, for instance the right side magnet is worn, but the left side is okay, replace them both. Keep all like components on the same axle, the same age.

Two areas of the brake drum are subject to wear and require periodic inspection: the drum surface where the brake shoes make contact during stopping and the aforementioned armature surface where the magnet contacts (see Fig. 15-3). The drum surface should be inspected for exces-

Fig. 15-4; Inspect armature surface where the magnet makes contact

sive wear or heavy scoring. If the wear marks are worn more than 0.020 inches, or the drum has worn out of round by more than 0.015 inches, then the drum surface should be turned. If scoring or other wear is greater than 0.090 inches, the drum must be replaced. Newer brake drums have an incorporated armature—all in one piece. In which case, if either the drum or the armature exhibits signs of grooving or scoring beyond 0.090 inches, the complete assembly will have to be replaced.

Fig. 15-5; New brake drum

To ensure proper contact between the armature face and the magnet face, the magnets should be replaced whenever the armature face is resurfaced.

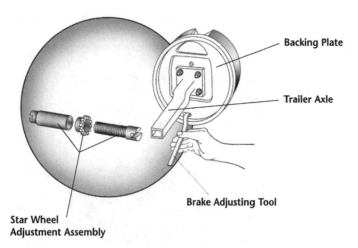

Backing Plate

Trailer Axle

Brake Adjusting Tool

Star Wheel Adjustment Assembly

Fig. 15-6; Adjusting trailer brakes

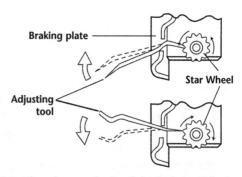

Braking plate

Star Wheel

Adjusting tool

Fig. 15-7; Adjust the star wheel until the tire has a slight drag

Cleaning

Clean each brake assembly carefully with a soft, damp rag or brush. Never use compressed air to blow out the brake assembly. Some brake shoes may contain asbestos materials that are harmful. Make sure the brush or rag that is used is indeed damp. This will eliminate the spread of dust particles that can be inhaled. It is further recommended that a face mask filter and eye protection be worn while working on electric brake assemblies.

Before reassembling any parts that may have been taken apart during the inspection, apply a small dab of white lithium grease to the areas behind the shoe where the shoe rubs on the backing plate.

Adjustment

Unlike most automotive brakes that are self-adjusting, electric brakes require periodic adjustment to keep the shoes and drums properly spaced. The main symptoms of brakes in need of adjustment are brakes that get hot while driving down the road (the shoes are dragging against the drum) or brakes that simply will not hold. Adjustment is simple but important.

For shoe adjustment, jack up and properly support the trailer so that the weight is off the wheel. Jack stands are recommended. Do not leave the weight of the trailer on the jack itself. Remove the plug from the back side of the backing plate, if so equipped, so that an adjusting tool can be inserted through the slotted hole (see photo). Slip the tool tip into a notch in the star wheel and ratchet, and rotate the star wheel to expand the shoes against the

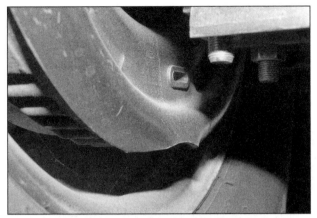

Fig. 15-8; Oval hole where the adjusting tool is inserted

Fig. 15-10; Breakaway switch on a fifth-wheel trailer

drum (rotation may be clockwise or counter-clockwise, depending on the brake manufacturer). Expand the shoes until you cannot rotate the tire any further. This centers or "seats" each shoe evenly against the inside surface of the drum. Then back the adjustment off in the opposite direction until the wheel turns freely but has a very slight drag during rotation. Replace the plug to keep dirt and moisture out. Repeat this process on all brakes.

Fig. 15-9; Close-up view of the star wheel

The adjustment tool engages the star wheel inside the brake assembly and expands or loosens the shoes.

(Note: Electric trailer brake adjustments are detailed in the RV Doctor's Do-It-Yourself RV Care DVD entitled, *RV Preventive Maintenance.* The DVD is available directly from the author at www.rvdoctor.com/dvd.html or through RVIA.org)

Breakaway Switch

The breakaway switch is designed to apply full trailer braking should the trailer and the tow vehicle separate due to hitch or coupler failure. It is extremely important to remember that the breakaway switch receives its voltage from the battery on the trailer, therefore, be certain the trailer battery remains fully charged at all times.

Mounted on a conventional trailer at or near the A frame or on the kingpin assembly of a fifth-wheel trailer, it is wise to inspect and test the breakaway switch regularly. As with any electrical contact or connection, clean and dry are the operative words. Periodically pull the pin and check for oxidation (some pins may be plastic). Spray a shot of contact cleaner inside the switch housing and reinsert the pin fully. Check the braided cable that connects the pin. Replace it if any signs of damage exist.

A combined method to test the brakes and the breakaway switch concurrently, although it takes a little longer, is to jack up each side of the trailer until the tires have been lifted off the ground. Manually spin each tire and then activate the controller. Do it again, but this time pull the pin on the breakaway switch. In both instances, each tire should slam to an immediate stop. Repeat this process on the other side of the trailer. The advantage of this test is that if you only had three out of four brakes working, you would know exactly which one was not working properly.

There is no adjustment on the breakaway switch. With the pin pulled, full braking occurs. With the pin in place, no braking is applied.

Fig. 15-11; Electrical connection on tow vehicle

Electrical Connector

Look for signs of corrosion on the metal contacts. Clean them with a brush or a contact cleaner. Also, check to make sure the plug and the receptacle are dry. Check the entire length of the electrical harness for fraying or where it may have accidentally been dragged along the ground. Again, if damage is present, replace the entire harness.

Electronic Brake Controllers

In recent years, with the advances in technology, the electronic brake controller has become the dominant design. Today's electronic trailer brake controllers consist of two basic types; inertia (modulated) and timer-based. Much simpler to install and maintain, electronic brake controllers are also more precise in delivering the modulated amount voltage necessary to apply smooth stopping of the travel trailer or fifth-wheel.

Inertia Controllers

The majority of inertia electronic controllers regulate the amount of voltage delivered to the trailer brakes by employing an internal pendulum or by bending a fiber beam, depending on the manufacturer. This type of controller will apply a proportional amount of voltage to the trailer brakes as is needed and mandated by the actual force of the tow vehicle coming to a stop. As the tow vehicle slows, more voltage is delivered to the trailer brakes. All electronic controllers have a sensitivity adjustment for varying loads in the trailer. Obviously, the heavier the trailer and the stowed gear, the more braking is needed.

Properly installed, today's smart controllers can be fine-tuned to these varying loads. Likewise, a gain adjustment is sometimes included that will help prevent the trailer brakes from locking up under normal towing circumstances. The electronic controllers of today automatically compensate for this. Additionally, when braking on hills, most controllers will allow a little more power to the trailer brakes while going downhill and slightly less when going uphill. Another useful feature includes integral diagnostics which assures the driver that the trailer and tow

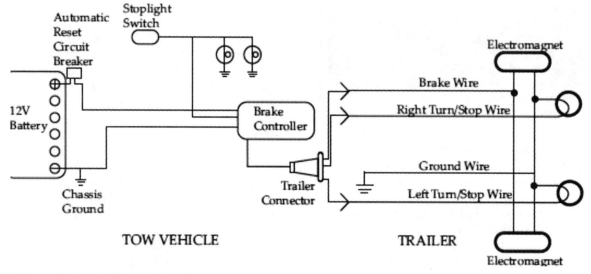

Fig. 15-12; Typical brake control and tow wiring diagram

vehicle are indeed electrically connected. Some units contain a fully modulated manual control should the operator want just a touch of trailer brakes to compensate for a change in road condition or another corrective measure. Manual operation of the controller does not activate the stop lamps as in those controllers that monitor the stop-lamp switch.

One of the newest proportional electronic brake controllers is the P3™, produced by Tekonsha (www.tekonsha.com). Equipped with a large LCD display, the P3™ has color, contrast and language options. Applicable with electric or electric-over-hydraulic trailer brakes, this advanced controller also provides easy-to-understand roadside diagnostics along with a boost feature. It contains circuitry that continually checks for proper electrical connections from controller to the magnets. It even checks for shorted magnets.

Fig. 15-13; Tekonsha P3™ brake controller

Tekonsha's popular Prodigy controller is equipped with the same boost feature found in the P3™ that enables the driver to apply more initial braking needed in certain towing circumstances. Without the boost feature enabled, while braking, the power to the electric brake magnets begins at 0.0 volts and begins to increase as the tow vehicle and trailer begin a deceleration. With the boost feature on, however, the power to the magnets starts at about 13% of the total initial power setting and further increases with deceleration. This comes in handy if the trailer brakes are not quite adjusted properly or when the towed trailer weighs 25 to 40% more than the tow vehicle. It also can be helpful in those instances where you might want the trailer brakes to become engaged slightly ahead of the tow vehicle's brakes, such as when descending a hill.

Timer-based Controllers
Also called actuator-type controllers, this type relies on pre-programmed internal electronics to determine how much voltage is sent to the trailer brakes. The longer the brakes on the tow vehicle are depressed, the more voltage is supplied. One drawback to this type is that if the brake pedal is released too soon, not enough braking voltage will be delivered. If the brake pedal is pressed again, it takes more time for the voltage to ramp up. It is crucial that timer-based controllers be adjusted carefully for the exact trailer load and the speed it will be traveling.

The RV aftermarket has many companies developing electronic brake control devices. Indeed, today's electronic controllers are quite versatile and sophisticated. It may take a little homework to determine which type and brand is best suited for your particular application. Individual product information is available on-line from most manufacturers.

Controller Maintenance
There is very little maintenance to worry about concerning electronic controllers. Simply check that all electrical connections are tight, and that wires are protected where they pass through the firewall or other areas. Route wires away from exhaust components. Periodically check the 12-volt automatic circuit breaker that is used in the circuit between the vehicle's battery and the controller. Sometimes it may be necessary to clean the terminals. Electronic brake controllers are not field-repairable. If an internal problem should arise, contact the manufacturer or your local dealer.

Controller Synchronization
Concerning inertia brake controllers only, synchronizing the controller to the electric brakes on the trailer will ensure the proper amount of voltage is being delivered to the brakes at any given time. Because of fluctuations in tow vehicle battery and alternator output levels, and the differences in trailer cargo weights, etc., it's important to synchronize the brakes often. The first step is to make certain the brakes on the trailer are properly adjusted as explained earlier in this chapter.

Next, be sure to read the operating instructions for your specific inertia controller. There are accelerometer and decelerometer styles of inertia-type brake controllers and slight differences in the synchronizing procedures may be necessary.

The travel trailer and tow vehicle must also be loaded as they would for normal travelling. Full water tank, full LP containers and empty holding tanks, plus all the canned goods and adult beverages in the cupboards, etc. If you happen to collect bowling balls, (and travel with them), be sure they are stowed properly also! Both vehicles should be at or near their regular travelling weight.

Begin by setting the gain level on the controller to the mid-point or slightly higher. While driving on a fairly level surface at 25 mph, apply the tow vehicle brakes. The goal is to get the gain set to a position just before the trailer brakes lock up. If the brakes lock up at 25 mph at the current setting, reduce the power setting until the trailer tires do not skid at that speed. It's probably wise to actually get the brakes to lock up first and then keep reducing the gain a little at a time until they no longer lock up or skid.

Optimum braking and the least amount of stopping distance are both achieved just before the trailer brakes lock-up. It may take a few attempts to obtain the perfect synchronization, but take your time. Proper setup will result when there is no sense of the trailer pulling or pushing the tow vehicle during the braking process.

Some controllers also have a modulating or sensitivity adjustment that also must be addressed. The purpose of this adjustment is to vary the threshold voltage to the brakes depending on the amount of pressure on the tow vehicle brake pedal and how fast the towing configuration actually comes to a stop. It's the amount of voltage first applied once the brake pedal is depressed. Think in terms of a panic stop vs. a slow gradual stop. If the brakes are grabby or "harsh" during braking, it may be necessary to reduce the threshold voltage or lower the sensitivity. Again, brake lock-up should be avoided. Refer to your specific brake controller literature for the correct method of adjusting the threshold voltage.

Troubleshooting

Most braking problems that cannot be corrected by either adjusting the trailer brakes and the brake controller can generally be traced to electrical system failures. Obviously, mechanical issues with the electric brakes will be evident during your periodic inspections. Worn magnets, bent arms, gouged drums, worn linings, etc. are pretty conspicuous. In order to troubleshoot the brake system electrically, you will need a voltmeter and an ammeter.

Voltage

Brake system voltage is best measured at the magnets in order to check the entire system. All voltage starts at the tow vehicle battery, passes through the controller, through the electrical connection between trailer and tow vehicle, and ultimately is applied at the brake magnets. Electrical integrity is crucial for safe stopping. The engine of the tow vehicle should be running when checking the voltage, so that a low battery will not adversely affect the measurements.

Attach the voltmeter in parallel with any of the brake magnets. The voltage should be zero volts at the beginning of the test. As the controller is activated, or the brake pedal depressed, the voltage should gradually increase to about 12-volts DC. This slow climb in voltage is termed modulation. No modulation means that when the controller begins to apply voltage to the brakes, the controller immediately applies a high voltage, which causes the brakes to apply instantaneous maximum power. The brakes will lock up.

The threshold voltage of a controller, remember, is the voltage applied to the brakes when the controller is first becoming activated. The lower the threshold voltage, the smoother the brakes will operate. Too high a threshold voltage causes grabby or harsh brakes.

Amperage

System amperage is the current being drawn by all brakes on the trailer. The engine of the tow vehicle should again be running. One location to measure the current is at the brake output wire right at the controller. Sometimes, however, this is easier to accomplish at the electrical connector plug at the rear of the tow vehicle. The brake wire must be disconnected and the ammeter put in-line or "in series" with the brake wire. Make sure the ammeter has sufficient capacity and note the polarity to prevent damaging the ammeter (a range of 0 to 15 amps is sufficient for single or tandem axle trailers; 0 to 25 amps is needed for triple axle trailers with six brakes).

Individual magnet current draw can be measured by inserting the ammeter in the line at the specific magnet you want to check. Disconnect one of the magnet wires (or simply slip an inductive-type ammeter over one of the wires) and attach the ammeter. By far, the most common electrical problem is low or no voltage at the brake magnets. Common causes for this condition can usually be attributed to one or more of the following:

- Poor connections
- Open circuit
- Insufficient wire size
- Broken wires hanging below the axle
- Improperly set up controller

Another common electrical problem is shorted or partially shorted circuits usually indicated by extremely high amperage readings. Possible causes for this symptom are:

- Internally shorted magnets
- Defective controllers
- Brake wire shorted to ground somewhere in the system
- Corrosion between the ground wire and the brake wire in the electrical connector plug

All electrical troubleshooting procedures should start at the controller. Try to eliminate the brake controller as the problem first. Make sure the controller is set up according to the manufacturer's recommendations. If the voltage and amperage are not satisfactory, proceed to the connector and then to the individual magnets to isolate the problem source. Twelve volts output at the controller on the brake wire should equate to a minimum 10.5 volts at each magnet. The voltage will be higher if the tests are made with the engine running as suggested. Nominal system amperage at a basic 12.0 volts with cold magnets and the controller gain adjustment at maximum, the current at each magnet should be as follows:

Brake Size	Amps Per Magnet
7 x 1-1/4 inches	2.5
10 x 1-1/2 inches	2.5
10 x 2-1/4 inches	3.0
12 x 2 inches	3.0

Some of today's electronic brake controllers are equipped with a built-in continuity tester, voltmeter or ammeter. When the trailer is properly connected to the tow vehicle, an indicator lamp is lit on the controller. This informs the driver that there is a good connection and current and voltage can flow from the controller, through the electrical connector to the brake magnets and to ground.

Properly adjusted electric brakes, a sound electrical path and a correctly installed and synchronized brake controller all contribute to not only your safety, but to an overall positive towing experience as well.

Supplemental Braking for Towed Vehicle

When towing a dinghy, the braking capacity of the motorhome must be considered. Brake capacity rating is determined by the chassis manufacturer so be sure to check with the dealer or the manufacturer to determine if any limitations pertain to the braking capacity of your particular motorhome.

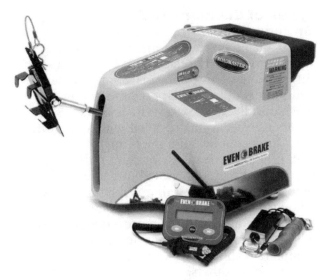

Fig. 15-14; Roadmaster Even Brake portable braking system

Various supplemental braking devices, including the Brake Buddy, (www.brakebuddy.com) and the Even Brake by Roadmaster, (www.roadmasterinc.com), are currently available (among a plethora of others) to aid in stopping the motorhome/dinghy combination. All supplemental braking devices allow independent control of the towed vehicle's brakes. Almost a dozen suppliers now provide such add-on units, most of which can be installed by the do-it-yourselfer.

Braking Systems and the Law

Although no federal law exists as of yet, many states have individual laws requiring additional braking if the towed vehicle exceeds a certain weight. For instance in Michigan, the law states that an independent braking system is required if the gross weight of the dinghy exceeds 3,000 pounds. In Delaware, supplemental braking is required if the dinghy weighs 4,000 pounds. In Texas, it is 4,500 pounds.

It is often emphasized that while state or local laws may be obscure or variable, the law of physics is nonnegotiable. If the vehicle you are towing weighs 1,500 to 2,000 pounds or more, seriously consider the addition of supplemental braking. Tow trailers and tow dollies usually have electric or surge brakes, but towing with a tow bar and all four wheels down provides no additional braking. It becomes a safety issue. Best to err on the side of safety!

Types of Supplemental Braking Systems

The available types of supplemental braking systems include those activated by hydraulic surge and mechanical means. Some utilize a pendulum controlled air pressure system that mechanically applies the vehicle brakes. Still others use electronics coupled with an air cylinder. Other suppliers use the principle of hydraulics to activate the brakes on the dinghy. Others are vacuum-activated. Regardless of the type of system employed, it is the prudent RVer who also includes a breakaway system in the event the dinghy and the motorhome unexpectedly part company. Some systems are shipped complete with the breakaway feature, while it is an option on others.

Keep in mind not all supplemental braking systems are compatible with diesel-powered motorhomes, although many are. Price range varies substantially, so do your homework on which applications fit the needs based on your motorhome and dinghy. Once installed, most supplemental braking systems can be hooked up and disconnected in a matter of minutes, so ease of use rates a ten. In any case, safety should always trump economic concerns. You can never be too safe! The wise motorhomer who tows a small vehicle behind will have a supplemental braking system employed.

Overview

The words tires and safety—words congruent to bacon and eggs or salt and pepper—go hand in hand. Understanding that safety includes having the correct tire at the proper inflation pressure is crucial to reliable RVing. The vitality of tires on any motorhome, tow vehicle or trailer cannot be understated. Thousands of safe RVing miles can be realized when the RVer is cognizant of the role of tires and knows what to look for while RVing. Diligence in use and periodic inspections can lengthen the life of RV tires and help guarantee a safe ride.

Fig. 16-Typical motorhome tire

Advances in design and technology have also markedly increased tire life. Tires are becoming a more valuable asset to RVers than merely a means for rolling the vehicle along the pavement. Evolving tread designs and overall construction improvements contribute to better fuel economy and safer handling of the RV. However, as dependable as they may be, tires sometimes do wear out, and an improperly loaded tire can even fail.

A basic understanding of tire construction, load capacity, inflation pressures and differing applications can help the RV owner select the best tire replacement when the original tires become worn or rendered unusable because of the age of the tire. Rarely do RV tires wear out from normal tread loss over time. Typically the tires "age" out before they wear out. The exceptions being abnormal wear patterns due to improper tire pressure or equipment failure or maladjustment.

Dating a Tire

No, it doesn't involve a dinner and a movie, but to determine the age of an RV tire, look on the sidewall for the DOT code. It will appear as a string of numbers and letters that denote the manufacturer, the plant where it was made, the size, any other optional identifying marks plus the date of manufacture. The last four digits of the DOT code indicate the week and year it was made. For example, a DOT code that ends in 0504 means that tire was made in the fifth week of 2004. Keep in mind, your tires may be older than the year of your RV! Go by the DOT code when dating the tires, not the year of manufacture of the RV.

Prior to the year 2000, the DOT code contained only 3 digits to determine the week and year of manufacture. If your DOT code only has 3 digits at the end of the code, you should immediately have the tires replaced; they're too old right now!

Tires approaching five or six years old should be inspected closer than a newer tire. Sidewall cracking is an indication of deterioration due to ozone and UV exposure as discussed later in this chapter. The sidewall is the weakest section of the tire and, regardless of the condition of the remaining tread, should be the determining factor when considering the time to replace. Sidewall cracks that measure 2 mm or deeper (deeper than 2/32") should mandate replacement even if the tread is barely worn.

Tire Construction

If a typical tire were to be dissected, it would reveal various layers, or plies, beneath a thick outer layer, which also bears the tread. The entire tire may be made of various combinations of:

• Rubber, reclaimed rubber or synthetic rubber
• Polyester, nylon or steel cord plies
• Rayon, fiberglass or steel belts

Regardless of which materials go into the construction, tires are classified into one of the following categories based on how the belts and/or cords are applied during the manufacturing process.

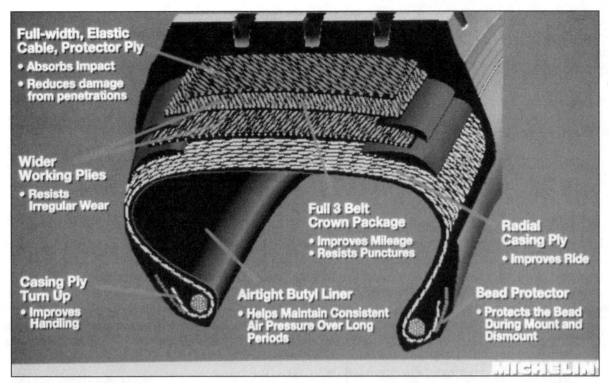

Fig. 16-2; Anatomy of an RV tire

- Diagonal or bias
- Belted bias
- Steel Belted radial
- All steel radial

Although applications may vary according to manufacturer's recommendations, all four types can be found on trailers, motorhomes and tow vehicles.

Diagonal or bias-ply tires may have two or four or more body plies that cross the center line of the tread at nearly a 35-degree angle. Both the sidewall and tread are strengthened by this design involving alternating plies.

Belted bias-ply tires are similar to diagonal-ply tires in construction, except that belted bias-ply tires have two or more belts under the tread to provide greater stability. Additionally, the belts reduce tread movement during contact with the road. This, too, improves tread life and traction.

Steel belted radial tires differ from either bias-type tire in that the body cords run perpendicularly across the center line of the tread from bead to bead (the bead is that point where the tire meets the wheel rim). They will have a radial fabric casing.

All steel radials will have a steel radial casing along with two or more steel belts under the tread.

Tire Sizes
Although tires have many different sets of measurements available, the tire size designation can

Fig. 16-3; Sidewall data

provide the most practical information to RVers, especially when related to other information embossed on the tire sidewall. Generally expressed as a grouping of letters and numbers or as two linked sets of numbers, the tire size designation gives information about cross-sectional size, load range capacity, construction and the diameter and contour of the wheel rim. Because of the degree of detail embedded into the information on the sidewall, obtaining a matching or replacement tire is a fairly simple task in most cases.

Diagonal-ply tires have designations such as 7.75-15, where 7.75 indicates bias construction as well as a cross-section approximately 7.75 inches wide at the widest point. The number 15 indicates a rim diameter of 15 inches with a five-degree tapered bead ledge.

There are typically just two rim taper angles: the aforementioned 5-degree taper and a 15-degree taper. The 15-degree taper can be recognized by the designation as a half-size increment such as 15.5 for a light truck tire or 19.5 on a larger motorhome. The 0.5 indicates the rim has a 15-degree taper. Even though it is possible to stretch a 15-inch tire over a 15.5 rim or a 19-inch motorhome tire over a 19.5 rim, it is not recommended. The bead will not quite properly fit the taper of the rim. This could easily result in tire failure. It is important that the types of rims are not mixed on the same vehicle. Any professional tire shop will know the difference, but some RV dealers may not. Tire and rim combinations must be matched for diameter and taper angle.

Although diagonal-ply tires also use an alpha-numeric designation, it is more commonly found on belted bias tires. The belted bias equivalent of the 7.75-15 diagonal-ply tire used in the example above would be either an F78-15 or an F70-15. The term equivalent is used in the sense of load carrying ability rather than size.

These tires use a series size number, such as 78, 70 or 60, to indicate the tire's profile: a height-to-width ratio. For instance, a 70 series tire is approximately 70% high as it is wide. The letter in front of the series number ranges from A to N and marks the relative size and load capacity of

the tire at its designed load pressure. Simply stated, an A78-14 tire is smaller and is rated for lighter loads than a B78-14 tire at the same air pressure.

Radial tires use the same designation system as that for belted bias tires, but an R is added to the number such as, FR78-15. Some radials are marked with metric sizes, such as 195/75R-15, with 195 being the cross-sectional width in millimeters.

Although corresponding sizes of different types of tires may have the same load limits, they are not interchangeable because of differences in dimensions, load ratings, fender clearances, rim sizes, ride characteristics and other factory recommendations. These differences may seriously affect vehicle handling characteristics. Never mix different sizes or constructions (bias or radial) on the same axle except for temporary use, perhaps when used as a spare tire.

Load Range

In the past, RV tires were formerly rated by the number of plies in their construction, but now are designated by the load range they are designed to carry. Load ranges are closely linked to inflation pressures and the load limits within a given range are determined by the pressure. The higher the load, the more air pressure is required, up to the maximum inflation for the load range of the specific tire and rim. This emphasizes the importance of knowing how

Fig. 16-4; Load range information

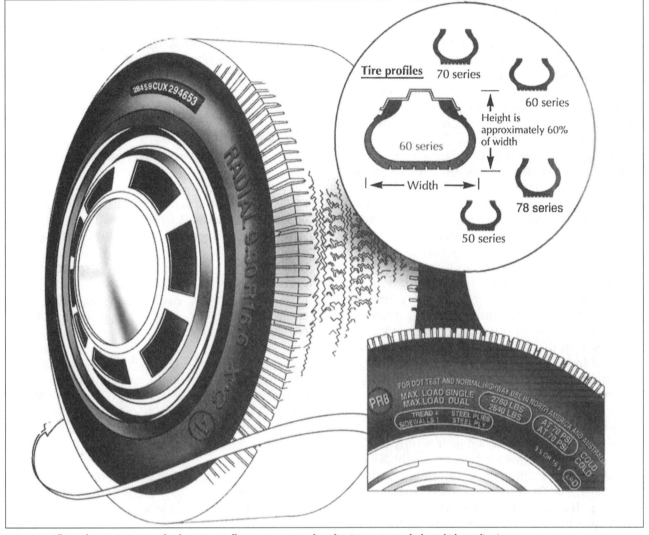

Fig. 16-5; All tire data: construction, load capacity, inflation pressure and application must match the vehicle application

much the RV actually weighs. Knowing the load range required by the RV is crucial when choosing replacement tires.

Inflation

Proper inflation is paramount for maximizing tire safety, vehicle handling characteristics and improving mileage. It is also one area over which the RVer has direct control on a daily basis. Correct tire inflation provides proper sidewall deflection and safe operating temperatures for the tires. Under-inflation causes excessive tire deflection and heat buildup; excessive wear on the outer tread ribs and can lead to premature tire failure. Over-inflation causes tires to ride

hard and makes them more vulnerable to impact damage and an overall weakening of the tire body. Proper inflation is one aspect of tire care in which the seasoned RVer excels. See the Sample Inflation Chart at the end of this chapter.

Air pressure should be checked when the tires are cold. A cold tire has been defined as 68°F or cooler, or before being driven less than one mile. Heat generated by friction temporarily increases air pressure anywhere from 10 to 20%, so never release pressure from a presumably over-inflated, hot tire. Check for correct inflation at the beginning of a trip and recheck periodically when the tires are cold. Just before pulling out of the campsite after breaking camp is the ideal time to do it. It should become an automatic function of the RVer's daily routine.

As stated earlier, incorrect inflation pressures can lead to tire failure, handling problems, overheated brakes, shortened tire life and premature breakdown of other related components on the chassis; any of which may contribute to a disabling delay or even worse, an accident. Most RVers know that the maximum inflation rate is molded into the sidewall of all tires. It is a federal law. Also, many know that this number represents the maximum amount of air for that size tire at that load range. It is the astute RVer, though, who is aware that perhaps not all tires will require the maximum amount.

So how much air pressure should the tires actually hold? Since all RVs are loaded and used differently, and each tire location may carry varying weights, no definitive textbook answer can generically fit all situations. Like many things within the RV realm, the amount of air required in each tire is subjective and unique to that tire, or at the very least, unique to that axle, as it carries a specific load.

To know exactly how much air to put in each tire, the RV must be weighed as it is fully loaded for travel—the complete traveling weight. This includes all the canned goods, camping gear, personal effects, fishing poles, etc. Prior to weighing, have the fuel tanks and fresh water tank—as well as the liquid propane (LP) container—completely filled, but leave the holding tanks empty. Don't forget to include all passengers or at least remember to approximate the weight of each person traveling in the RV. The more accurate the weight measurement, the more precise the inflation pressure can be determined.

Once the weight each tire is carrying is known, then refer to the manufacturer's recommended inflation chart for the exact amount of air for each tire. See a sample inflation chart at the end of this chapter.

Public scales that can accommodate RVs are available in many areas. Some truck stops and auto recycling yards may have platform-type scales available to the public. Moving companies are another good source to call when look-

ing for a set of scales. Quarries, gravel pits or concrete plants are also usually equipped with scales. The facility may charge a fee for each weight recorded, but knowing the individual weight measurements is too important to be concerned about a minimal cost.

RV Weights, Definitions and Facts

How is an RV accurately weighed on a platform scale? Before the specifics are offered, here are some definitions and facts that will provide a better understanding of weights and measurements.

Gross vehicle weight rating (GVWR): Maximum permissible weight of the RV. It should be equal to or greater than the sum of the unloaded vehicle weight (UVW) plus the cargo carrying capacity (CCC), defined below.

Unloaded vehicle weight (UVW): Weight of the coach as built at the factory. If a motorhome, it includes full fuel tanks, engine oil and coolants. The UVW does not include cargo, fresh water, LP, passengers or any of the various dealer/aftermarket-installed accessories.

Cargo carrying capacity (CCC): Formerly called the net carrying capacity (NCC), the CCC is that weight equal to the GVWR minus the:
- UVM
- weight of the filled fresh water storage tank
- weight of the filled water heater
- weight of all filled LP containers
- sleeping capacity weight rating (SCWR)

Fig. 16-6; Many public scales can accommodate RVs

The total weight of installed options and accessories plus the weight of generator fluids will further reduce the CCC.

Gross combination weight rating (GCWR): If a motorhome, the value specified by the manufacturer as the maximum allowable loaded weight of the motorhome along with its towed vehicle. If a travel trailer or fifth-wheel trailer, it is the value specified by the tow vehicle manufacturer as the maximum allowable loaded weight of the tow vehicle and the towed trailer combined. GCWR minus the GVWR is the maximum allowable weight for the towed vehicle.

Gross axle weight rating (GAWR): Maximum total weight for which that particular single axle is designed.

Gross axle weight (GAW): The GAW is the actual weight of a fully loaded RV carried by that particular axle. Because of the variances of how the RV is loaded, the GAW can be misleading. In other words, even thought the weight on the total axle may be within its rating, it may be overloaded to one side of that axle.

Gross vehicle weight (GVW): The actual weight of the fully loaded RV include cargo, passengers, liquids, any towed vehicle, hitch weight, etc. The GVW must never exceed the GVWR.

Sleeping capacity weight rating (SCWR): This rating is designated by the coach manufacturer as the number of sleeping berths multiplied by an arbitrary 154 pounds for each position. Travel trailers do not have an SCWR since no one rides in the trailer while it's being towed.

Additional tire facts:
- An RV in a 10% overloaded condition reduces tire life by 15%.
- An RV in a 50% overloaded condition reduces tire life by 60%.
- To be accurate, the platform scales must allow positioning of the RV for weighing a single side and yet remain level.
- Cargo includes all contents of storage pods, roof racks, bicycles or motorcycles on carriers, food, canned goods, galley equipment, clothing, refrigerator contents, personal effects, etc. Virtually everything on board while traveling.
- Liquid weights include:
  - » Water: 8.33 pounds per gallon
  - » LP: 4.25 pounds per gallon
  - » Gasoline: 6.00 pounds per gallon
  - » Diesel Fuel: 7.00 pounds per gallon

When weighing the RV using a full-platform scale, the following instructions are general in design and intent. Not all of the measurements will apply to every RV. For example, for a typical Class A motorhome with just two axles, only measurements 1, 2, 3, 8, 9 and 10 respectively are required. Only record the measurements that directly apply to your particular RVing configuration.

Measurements 1 through 7 are taken with the RV laterally centered on the scales. Measurements 8 through 13 pertain to only one side of the RV and are taken while an imaginary center line is aligned with one edge of the scale platform.

Measurement	Instructions
1	Pull straight onto the scales until only the front axle is on the platform. Record this weight: GAW (front).
2	Pull further onto the scales until all the axles on the RV (or tow vehicle) are on the platform. Record this weight: GVW.
3	Pull forward until only the rear axle (or rear axle and tag axle, if so equipped) is on the platform. Front axle is off the scales. Record this weight: GAW (rear or rear and tag).
4	If a motorhome with a tag axle, pull forward until only the tag axle is on the platform. Record this weight: GAW (tag).
5	If towing another vehicle, pull forward until only the towed vehicle is completely on the platform. Stay connected to the

tow vehicle. Record this weight: GVW (towed vehicle).

6   If the towed vehicle has three axles, pull forward until only the middle and rear axles are on the scales. Record this weight: GAW (axles 2 and 3).

7   Pull forward until only the rear axle of the towed vehicle is on the platform. Record this weight: GAW (rear).

8   Keeping the imaginary center line at one edge of the scale, pull forward as in measurement 1. The vehicle must be level from side to side. Record this weight: Single Side (front axle).

9   Pull forward as in measurement 2. Record this weight: Single Side (all axles).

10   Pull forward as in measurement 3. Record this weight: Single Side (rear axle[s]).

11   If a motorhome with a tag axle, pull forward as in measurement 4. Record this weight: Single Side (tag axle).

12   If the towed vehicle has three axles, pull forward as in measurement 6. Record this weight: Single Side (axles 2 and 3).

13   Pull forward as in measurement 7. Record this weight: Single Side (rear axle).

Once all the pertinent measurements are recorded, actual loads can be calculated for each tire position by simply doing the math. The actual weight each tire position is carrying can now be compared to the manufacturer's published inflation pressure guides (see Sample Inflation chart at the end of the chapter).

Each tire manufacturer compiles tire inflation guides; they are available at all retail tire shops or directly from the manufacturer and on-line. It is advisable to contact a professional tire shop rather than to rely on the advice administered by a typical RV dealer, unless, or course, that dealer is well-versed in tires.

Fig. 16-7; Properly ramped leveling blocks

Fig. 16-8; Correctly placed and leveled blocks

Fig. 16-9; Improperly blocked tire

While inflation pressure is considered the single-most important area to consider with RV tires, there remains other important facets to also contemplate.

Proper Blocking Techniques

RVers are aware that for the refrigerator to operate properly while standing still, the coach must be leveled. Oftentimes the tires are run up on homemade or aftermarket leveling blocks. Harm is caused to the tires when the blocks are not sized correctly. Over time, uneven distribution of weight while using leveling blocks can damage the steel cables, the casing and especially the sidewall of a tire. Maximum support is mandated in order to avoid warranty discrepancies and premature tire failure.

All leveling blocks should be wider and longer than the individual tire footprint it supports. In rear dual-tire applications, both tires must be fully supported by the blocking material. If multiple blocks are used to gain additional height, the uppermost block, the one in direct contact with the tire, must still be wider and longer than the footprint (see Fig. 16-7, 16-8 and 16-9).

Tire Inspection and General Care

Inspect tires regularly for signs of excessive or uneven tread wear. Bulges, fabric breaks, cuts, weather checking (dry rot) and any other damage should be addressed immediately. Anything embedded in the tread, such as stones or other road debris, should be removed. Tires should be replaced when the tread is worn to 1/16 of an inch in two or more adjacent grooves, or when the tread wear indicators, which are molded into the bottom of the tread grooves on some tires, are flush with the tread ribs. Again, if in doubt, have a questionable tire checked by a reputable tire dealer.

How often should tires be inspected? A thorough inspection should be made at least once a year at a bare minimum. When stored for lengthy periods, try to inspect them at least once a month. While camped, inspect the tires once a

Fig. 16-10; Inspect the tires for abnormalities

week and, as previously mentioned, every day as you travel.

Alignment
Tire misalignment symptoms usually appear as uneven tread wear, although a small amount of misalignment can be detected by careful measurements. Potholes, extremely rough roads, bumps and curbs are all detrimental to wheel alignment that, if not corrected by a qualified service shop, will shorten tire life and may lead to a dangerous driving or towing situation. Have the alignment checked annually or every 10,000 miles of normal highway driving but more frequently if much rough road driving is done.

Wheel Balance
No tire or wheel assembly is absolutely round, nor is every tire in balance as it comes off the assembly line. Once mounted on a rim and inflated, a tire must be balanced by adding lead wheel weights to the rim as indicated by sophisticated balancing equipment. If the tire assembly is not balanced, stresses from centrifugal force will lead to uneven tread wear and premature tire failure will result.

All new tires should be balanced immediately after mounting. Tires should also be balanced again when remounting after repairs or after rotating. Once balanced by a service station or tire dealer, tires should not need additional balancing unless they become damaged or a wheel weight is dislodged or lost. Be sure to note the placement of the balance weights on each tire.

Storage
For seasonal storage, it is best if the RV can be

raised so the majority of the vehicle's weight is removed from the tires. Hydraulic levelers make this task relatively easy on so-equipped motorhomes. If it is not possible to raise the RV during long storage periods, an alternative plan would be to periodically move the coach forward or backward a few feet so the contact point between the tire and the ground is varied. It is also wise to cover the tires during the storage period to help block the ultraviolet rays from the sun.

Ultraviolet and Ozone Damage

According to a major tire manufacturer, ozone and ultraviolet (UV) radiation are the principal enemies of uncovered tires. UV radiation travels freely in the air and is harmful to all plastics, rubber and fiberglass. Tire makers add a level of prevention by using carbon black during the manufacturing process. Carbon black is a UV stabilizer that actually absorbs the damaging rays and converts them to a simple byproduct of heat. That is the good news. The bad news is that all UV stabilizers are eventually used up during the protection process and must be replenished periodically. As a competitive absorber, carbon black eventually loses its ability to protect against the never-ending assault of the UV rays. The other bad news is that there is no such thing as a permanent UV blocker.

Ozone is an atmospheric gas, found in the free air that attaches to other oxygen-related chemicals. The combined chemicals in ozone have an extra oxygen molecule that attacks tires and causes damage that cannot be restored or reversed. During the making of tires, manufacturers blend ozone-resistant rubber compounds into the mix to help combat ozone. These ozone-resistant protective waxes form a barrier of sorts. To be effective, these waxes must constantly be brought to the surface of the tire. This is usually accomplished by the normal flexing and movement of a tire during travel. A fresh layer of combative waxes is always kept at the surface.

When RVs are stored for lengthy periods, the tires do not receive enough "exercise" to allow the waxes to migrate to the surface; therefore, ozone has a virtual picnic on any exposed areas, especially on the vulnerable sidewalls. Ozone

and UV damage can be reduced with the proper application of a treatment such as 303 Protectant (www.303products.com).

Proper sizing, loading, maintenance, usage and periodic inspections of the RV tires can all contribute to safe, trouble-free traveling. Do not underestimate the importance of each. RV tires seldom wear out, so diligence in these areas will reap thousands of safe RVing miles. For additional information, contact one of the tire manufacturers listed:

Bridgestone	www.bridgestonetire.com
Firestone	www.bridgestone-firestone.com
Goodyear	www.goodyeartires.com
Goodrich	www.bfgoodrichtires.com
Michelin	www.michelin-us.com
Uniroyal	www.uniroyal.com

You can also write to: Tire Industry Safety Council, P.O. Box 3147, Medina, OH 44258.

Sample Inflation Chart

Not all sizes and load ranges are listed in this sample inflation chart[1]. Check with the dealer for your brand of tires for the exact chart for your vehicle.

1-Sample inflation chart courtesy of Goodyear.

Sample Load/Inflation Information Regarding RV Tires

305/70R22.5 LRL

PSI		75	80	85	90	95	100	105	110	115	120		MAXIMUM LOAD AND PRESSURE ON SIDEWALL			
kPa		520	550	590	620	660	690	720	760	790	830					
LBS	SINGLE	5375	5660	5940	6220	6495	6770	7040	7300	7570	7830	S	7830	LBS at	120	PSI
	DUAL	9530	10030	10530	11030	11510	12000	12470	12950	13420	13880	D	6940	LBS at	120	PSI
kPa	SINGLE	2440	2550	2700	2810	2960	3060	3170	3310	3410	3550	S	3550	KG at	830	kPa
	DUAL	4340	4540	4800	4980	5240	5440	5620	5880	6060	6300	D	3150	KG at	830	kPa

315/80R22.5 LRL

PSI		85	90	95	100	105	110	115	120	125	130		MAXIMUM LOAD AND PRESSURE ON SIDEWALL			
kPa		590	620	660	690	720	760	790	830	860	900					
LBS	SINGLE	6415	6670	6940	7190	7440	7610	7920	8270	8810	9090	S	9090	LBS at	130	PSI
	DUAL	11680	12140	12790	13090	13540	13880	14420	15220	16020	16540	D	8270	LBS at	130	PSI
kPa	SINGLE	2910	3030	3150	3260	3370	3450	3590	3750	3980	4125	S	4125	KG at	900	kPa
	DUAL	5300	5500	5800	5940	6140	6300	6540	6900	7240	7500	D	3750	KG at	900	kPa

365/70R22.5 LRL

PSI		80	85	90	95	100	105	110	115	120	125		MAXIMUM LOAD AND PRESSURE ON SIDEWALL			
kPa		550	590	620	660	690	720	760	790	830	860					
LBS	SINGLE	7350	7710	8070	8430	8780	9130	9480	9820	10200	10500	S	10500	LBS at	125	PSI
	DUAL											D		LBS at		PSI
kPa	SINGLE	3320	3510	3660	3840	3980	4120	4300	4440	4620	4750	S	4750	KG at	860	kPa
	DUAL											D		KG at		kPa

445/50R22.5 LRL

PSI		75	80	85	90	95	100	105	110	115	120		MAXIMUM LOAD AND PRESSURE ON SIDEWALL			
kPa		520	550	590	620	660	690	720	760	790	830					
LBS	SINGLE	6940	7310	7680	8030	8390	8740	9090	9370	9780	10200	S	10200	LBS at	120	PSI
	DUAL											D		LBS at		PSI
kPa	SINGLE	3150	3320	3480	3640	3810	3970	4120	4250	4430	4625	S	4625	KG at	830	kPa
	DUAL											D		KG at		kPa

WHEEL DIAMETER - 24.5"

11R24.5 LRG

PSI		70	75	80	85	90	95	100	105		MAXIMUM LOAD AND PRESSURE ON SIDEWALL			
kPa		480	520	550	590	620	660	690	720					
LBS	SINGLE	4820	5070	5310	5550	5840	6095	6350	6610	S	6610	LBS at	105	PSI
	DUAL	9320	9740	10140	10520	11020	11350	11680	12010	D	6005	LBS at	105	PSI
kPa	SINGLE	2190	2300	2410	2520	2650	2770	2890	3000	S	3000	KG at	720	kPa
	DUAL	4220	4420	4600	4780	5000	5160	5320	5450	D	2725	KG at	720	kPa

275/80R24.5 LRG

PSI		70	75	80	85	90	95	100	105	110		MAXIMUM LOAD AND PRESSURE ON SIDEWALL			
kPa		480	520	550	590	620	660	690	720	760					
LBS	SINGLE	4545	4770	4940	5210	5420	5675	5835	6040	6175	S	6175	LBS at	110	PSI
	DUAL	8270	8680	9080	9480	9860	10410	10620	10990	11350	D	5675	LBS at	110	PSI
kPa	SINGLE	2060	2160	2240	2360	2460	2575	2650	2740	2800	S	2800	KG at	760	kPa
	DUAL	3740	3940	4120	4300	4480	4720	4820	4980	5150	D	2575	KG at	760	kPa

Synthetic Roofing Materials

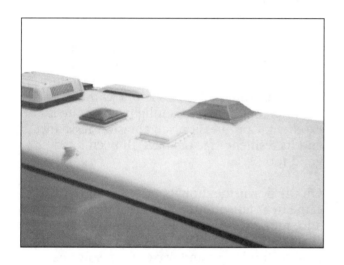

Overview

Few innovations in the RV industry can boast of continued interest over an extended period of time. Along with other leading-edge design concepts such as the basement model motorhome and slide-out rooms, the advent of synthetic roof coverings such as EPDM rubber and TPO has generated a lot of awareness along with some misconceptions as well. Equipped on RVs since the 1980s, ethylene propylene diene monomer rubber (EPDM) and thermoplastic polyolefin (TPO) have now enjoyed industry-wide acceptance on many RVs, plus many decades of successful use in other industries.

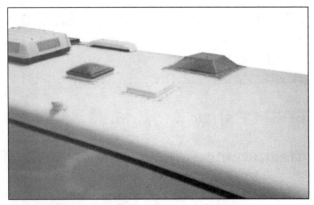

Fig. 17-1; RV with a synthetic roof

TPO

Considered a next-generation synthetic, TPO was first introduced to the RV market in 1994 by Alpha Systems (www.alphasystemsinc.com). Though TPO is similar to EPDM in some characteristics, it does have a few unique qualities all its own. For one thing, organic additives are added to the mix for ultraviolet (UV) protection; the effectiveness of these additives is not lost over time. Many UV protectants, such as those used in tires, however, are self-sacrificing and lose their ability to fight the UV bombardment over the course of its existence.

Since there is no degradation of the polymer, there is no chalking associated with TPO membrane. And since the polymer is actually a plastic, some damage can be repaired through a plastic heat welding process, though this is typically beyond the scope of the RV owner.

EPDM

Why is rubber roofing on RVs so popular? According to a published polymer selection guide spec sheet, EPDM membrane is ideal for outdoor applications, such as the roofs of RVs, because it has an excellent resistance to UV light, ozone and oxidants, and can withstand severe weather conditions. Such characteristics allow many EPDM manufacturers to guarantee their membrane for long periods; ten to twelve years in some cases.

EPDM has excellent resistance to heat which makes it extremely well-suited for RVs in any climate. It is capable of enduring temperature variations from –50°F to +240°F without cracking or deteriorating. Its sunlight aging rate is excellent. Compression set, abrasion resistance and its resilience factors have all been rated good too.

On the downside though, tear resistance only came in at fair, and the solvent and oil resistance rating is poor. Other inherent negative characteristics of EPDM include a susceptibility to absorb oils, fats and waxes from solvents having a low polarity. An example would be the resultant bubbling or wrinkling that would occur if an oil-based roof coating, commonly used on aluminum RV roofs, is mistakenly applied to EPDM membrane.

Contrary to what is often read and heard, EPDM rubber requires no protection from UV rays or ozone bombardment, though it is prone to oxidize. Normal oxidation is a condition caused by the disintegration of surface binders or elastomers by weathering. Other destructive environmental conditions can also add to the degree of chalking. The result is that surface chalking actually removes a portion of the rubber. This is a normal occurrence and the RVer should not be concerned about the direct effect on the rubber.

Oxidation will, however, usually manifest itself as long, unsightly streaks running down the sides of the RV. We have all seen it. The streaks are usually caused by dirt, road grime and airborne pollutants that settle and adhere to the roof and are washed over the side along with the loosened powdery surface elastomer. Some white streaking may also contain remnants of titanium dioxide, which is used as a whitening agent, along with calcium carbonate, used as a filler compound.

The simple solution is to keep the roof clean. The degree of chalking associated with EPDM may vary from coach to coach, but tighter controls during the co-polymerizing procedure leads to a slower rate of oxidation, though most will surrender up to 10% of the overall thickness during the life of the roof.

Roof Installation Techniques

All synthetic roof installations require a solid decking under the surface membrane. Called the substrate, the decking typically consists of 1/4-inch or 3/8-inch plywood. Thinner substrates can be utilized, but the thickness usually depends upon the amount of load and the number of accessories that will be installed on the roof.

The synthetic roofing material is cemented to the prepared substrate. If a bonding-type cement is used, such as a contact cement, it must be applied to the bottom surface of the membrane as well as to the plywood substrate. When a water-based adhesive or a pressure sensitive cement is used, it is only applied to the plywood surface.

EPDM rubber is rolled out to the entire length

Fig. 17-3; New EPDM rubber roofing installation

of the RV resulting in a simple, one-piece layer of rubber as the finished roof material. During installation, the rubber extends the length of the coach, with excess rubber also extending over the sides of the RV, enough to fold down behind the drip molding or awning rail. The same is true for TPO.

The membrane is folded back, front to rear, about halfway and cement is applied by brush, roller or spray gun. Solvent-based contact cement is applied to the substrate and the membrane and allowed to dry. Once dry, the material is laid out and adhered to the substrate decking. If a water-based, pressure-sensitive adhesive is used, the membrane is laid in place while the cement is still wet. This appears to be the most common application.

Air pockets are rolled out from the center line of the coach to the sides with a lightweight roller or a push broom. At the front and rear of the RV where the covering terminates, an insert molding bar is installed across the entire width of the RV. This termination bar should overlap the exposed edge of the membrane. Be sure to use a compatible butyl caulk underneath the molding bar before it is secured to the roof. This same technique is used on those RVs with front and rear fiberglass caps as well, though the caps may overlap the edge of the synthetic material.

At the RV sides, the material is folded over the edge of the roof and stapled to the sidewall on top of the siding material. Butyl tape or caulk is applied to the back of a drip channel or awning

Fig. 17-2; Synthetic roofing during factory installation

rail, which is then secured to the sides of the RV. Excess material hanging below the molding or rail is simply trimmed off with a razor knife or scissors.

After the roof is completely cemented in place, all the openings for the sewer vents, the refrigerator vent, the 14-inch vents, the roof air conditioner opening etc. must be cut into the material. Once all the openings have been cut, butyl tape is applied to the vents installed as usual. Additionally, all screws, flanges and edges are sealed with an appropriate lap sealant.

The relative ease in which EPDM and TPO membranes can be installed has resulted in many older coaches going through an upgrade process by removing the old, soft aluminum roof, for example, and adding new insulation, a substrate decking and the new synthetic material. When RVs have experienced water leaks that simply cannot be resolved, oftentimes the best cure is a new roof topped with a synthetic material.

EPDM Repair

As hard as we try to avoid them, sometimes accidents just happen. As stated earlier, one of the pitfalls of EPDM rubber membrane is its propensity to easily tear. Not so with TPO. In fact, TPO can have anywhere between 20 to 50% higher resistance to rips and tears than EPDM. Such damage can occur while backing into a campsite with low, overhanging tree limbs or by a careless repair person or RV owner walking on the roof. Flying projectiles launched during a severe rain or wind storm can also result in damaged EPDM rubber membrane.

Additionally, if the EPDM roof was not properly prepped at the factory during the original installation some surfaces may develop small bubbles that indicate a bonding problem between the cement and the substrate. In some instances perhaps all of the moisture was not removed correctly. What is to be done if such damage is incurred?

Repairs can easily be accomplished by adding a layer of EPDM membrane over the damaged area. Here's how.

1. Cut a piece of rubber roofing material two to three inches larger than the damaged area. Be sure to cut the patch using rounded corners.

2. Center the patch over the tear or hole and trace a line around the entire patch.

3. Lift the patch and clean the damaged area under the patch with an aftermarket splice cleaner or a clean cloth lightly dampened with mineral spirits or hexane. The section to be repaired must be very clean. Also clean the entire bottom area of the patch itself.

4. Apply adhesive to the patch and the damaged section of the roof. Spread the sealant evenly to extend beyond the perimeter of the mark by about 1/4-inch. When the adhesive has dried, align the patch and press it into place. After the patch is secured, apply a bead of lap sealant around the entire patch.

In instances of minor bubbling, the bubble itself can be carefully slit with a razor knife and then a patch overlay installed as outlined above.

Fig. 17-4; Patchit EPDM repair kit

The RV aftermarket also offers many ready-made patch kits, which are available at RV parts stores. One that has proven to be successful is produced by Carlisle SynTec (www.carlisle-syntec.com), one of the leading EPDM producers, and distributed by Dicor (www.dicor.com). Called Patchit, this handy repair kit comes complete with a peel-and-stick EPDM patch coated with an appropriate butyl adhesive sealant and a standard tube of industrial lap sealant. Simply following the detailed instructions on the kit will easily result in a successful repair.

Fig. 17-5; Pro Guard Coating's Liquid Roof

Another effective method of repairing EPDM membrane damage is by using a product called Liquid Roof, produced by Pro Guard Coatings (www.proguardcoatings.com). Liquid Roof is simply a liquefied version of EPDM rubber. It is self-adhering and self-leveling. According to the manufacturer, Liquid Roof does not chalk and can actually be employed to eliminate chalking of existing membranes. It has proven to be extremely effective at sealing around roof appurtenances. Simply brushed on, it creates a thin, single layer of EPDM rubber that acts like a shield to protect exiting caulks and sealants around vents, etc.

Though some aftermarket repair products exist that are compatible to both EPDM and TPO, if a doubt exists, check to be certain that product will work with your particular membrane before attempting any repair or maintenance process.

Maintenance

As mentioned earlier in the chapter, the best preventive maintenance is a clean roof. Cleaning the synthetic roof should be a regularly scheduled maintenance task performed often enough to keep the surface white. Usually four or five times per year will suffice depending on the local climate and the propensity of your RV to gather dirt, plus how pure the co-polymerizing process was performed during manufacture.

Cleaning practices differ for EPDM and TPO, so it's vital you truly understand which synthetic is up there on the roof.

For EPDM roofs, cleaning can be accomplished by washing the roof with a mild laundry detergent or one of the many RV aftermarket products now being offered. Alpha Systems (makers

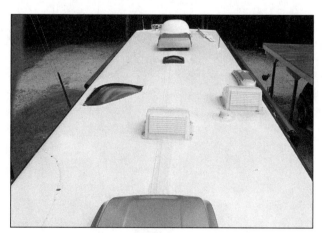
Fig. 17-6; The best PM is a clean roof

of the EPDM membrane) recommends Protect All Rubber Roof Cleaner and their Rubber Roof Treatment; both specifically formulated for use on EPDM rubber. Though stains are nigh impossible to avoid forever, proper cleaning and treating will certainly minimize any unsightly stains.

Other contributory factors that determine how easy it is to clean EPDM membrane include the time of year, the type of stains incurred and how well the roof had been previously maintained. In short, the best prevention is frequent inspections, immediate repair procedures and regular cleaning. For extremely tough stains or grease, some manufacturers recommend a product called hexaprene, a hexane-based solvent for rubber cements and adhesives. Hexane and all of its derivatives should be treated with extreme care as they are highly flammable.

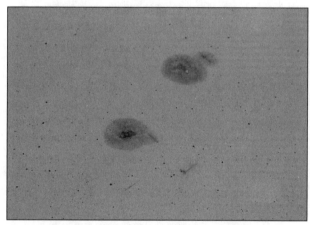
Fig. 17-7; Mold and mildew spores are difficult to eliminate

One of the biggest complaints regarding rubber roofing is its propensity to attract mold and mildew spots. There's a simple explanation why; most EPDM rubber roofing is white in color. The white reflects heat and keeps the RV cooler during the hot summer months, plus a white roof is more aesthetically pleasing to the eye. The downside is that because not much heat is absorbed into the roof of the RV, mold and mildew, both a form of living fungi, cannot be killed at the lower temperatures. The roof of any rubber roofed RV is the perfect environment for these living organisms. Plenty of sunlight, lots of moisture and enough carbon and nutrients found in the air and on the roof to thrive.

At best, their proliferation can only be minimized.

The best defense is a strong offense; aggressive and proactive cleaning of the roof. Suppliers recommend a minimum of four washings and treatments per season. Additionally, it's a good idea to periodically sweep the roof clear of gathering dust, leaves and dirt in between the scheduled washings. Keeping the roof clean goes a long way.

For existing spots, a rag daubed in mineral spirits will help minimize or eliminate the stains. Do not pour mineral spirits directly onto the roofing or allow it to saturate the rubber membrane. Doing so will cause it to swell and disengage from the substrate and further troubles will follow.

Fig. 17-8; Inspect sealant around attached roof components closely

During roof inspections, pay particular attention to the sealant around the various components attached to the roof. Be sure to only use lap sealants and caulking that are compatible with the membrane. Also, be extremely cautious when washing or cleaning the membrane. EPDM rubber becomes dangerously slippery when wet, especially if a soap solution is utilized. TPO, on the other hand, is often used for boat decking, so walking on that membrane is not as tenuous. Still, care should be taken any time you are on the roof of the RV Cleaning TPO is also vital, but avoid using granulated cleansers on TPO surfaces. They could damage the surface of the membrane. Murphy's Oil Soap

applied with a soft nylon brush is approved for cleaning TPO. When using any roofing care product be sure to follow the directions explicitly.

All RV manufacturers and product suppliers do agree on one thing: a regularly maintained synthetic roof will last longer and develop fewer problems than one left unattended.

Chapter 18

Water Damage

Overview

Scenario: It first appears as an unobtrusive small speck and you pay no attention to it; maybe it's just a bit of dirt on the wall. Later you notice an innocent spot and you make a mental note to check it out; tomorrow would be ideal to see to it because you'll be doing some maintenance on the water heater anyway. A few weeks later you think you see a stain and wonder who spilled the coffee, and this time you make a written note to yourself to clean it next month when you winterize the coach.

The next time you think about the situation is when you begin the spring shakedown and notice that half a sheet of interior paneling has delaminated and peeled away; the musty smell almost knocked you over when you opened the door. Later, while fumbling through the kitchen junk drawer looking for the outside storage compartment keys, you come upon the note you wrote last summer. Then your mind takes you back even further and you suddenly remember that morning when you made that mental note to check out that spot. Hmmmm…

An over-dramatization? Perhaps. Realistic? It happens every camping season! Unfortunately, many RVers ignore the early warning signs of water leaks and consequently end up paying the price for a more costly repair later. Spotted early, water damage can be minimized and repair costs limited to simply the purchase of the supplies needed. Virtually all water leaks can be addressed by the RV owner and rectified, if action is taken as soon as the evidence appears.

Preventive Maintenance

An assertive preventive maintenance program can often eliminate unnecessary repairs caused by seeping water. The antithesis is the very real fact that left unabated, water damage can be one of the most costly repairs an RVer may face if the damage spreads to wooden frame members or the floor, and destroys the structural integrity of the coach.

How can RVers prevent such unwelcome damage? Keep alert to any telltale signs of moisture.

Regularly inspect various key points in and around the roof area. Check and even periodically test the sealants around the windows and doors by spraying them with a garden hose. Order a spare roof air conditioner gasket. Ideas abound, but the pivotal, proactive decision must be regular inspection.

Roof Precautions

If the RV is equipped with a ladder, it probably has a solid, laminated roof that will support an individual during the roof inspection. If, however, the coach has hollow wall construction and a soft roof, take the necessary precautions to protect the roof while on it.

It will be necessary to place boards or plywood across two or more rafters to protect a soft roof while moving about. More damage and leaks can result if pressure is administered between the rafters. Never try to walk on the rafters without the boards. Do not take chances while on the roof of the RV. Remember, never compromise the safety factor.

Support boards can be made from a single sheet of 3/8-inch plywood. Cutting a four-foot by eight-foot sheet of shop grade 3/8-inch plywood in half, the long way, will yield two, two-foot wide pieces to work on while on the roof. There will always be one on which to work and one to move to the next area on the roof. These boards are also helpful when crawling around under

Fig. 18-1; RV ladder

the coach for inspections or repairs as well. Wear athletic shoes or another type of soft-soled shoes.

Roof Inspection Areas

Closely inspect all areas of the roof. Look for low areas that may collect or pool water. This is one reason to avoid stepping between the rafters on a soft or hollow roof.

Seams
If the rolled roofing has locking seams spaced every so many feet, inspect the entire length of each cleat and seam. Gently push down on each side of the seam to see if it may open up slightly. Any crack is a potential leak waiting to materialize.

Edges
Visually inspect that portion of the roof that is folded over the sidewalls and behind the molding. Many times the aluminum roof material cracks at this 90-degree bend. Apply an appropriate sealant to any openings or cracks that are discovered. Additionally, ethylene propylene diene monomer (EPDM) rubber roofing may sometimes tear at this bend. Rubber roofing requires a specific lap sealant for repairs in this area. Silicone sealants will not work on rubber roofing.

Trim Moldings
While at the edges, closely inspect the drip railing or corner molding depending on how the coach is constructed. An awning rail may be on the passenger side of the RV. Look especially for open areas behind the flange of the rail or trim pieces. If there is a vinyl or rubber insert molding that covers the screw heads, remove it and look at each screw head. Is there any evidence of rust? Replace the insert molding if it is cracked and weathered or if it simply will not stay put.

If many screws show evidence of rust like the one in the photo, remove that entire piece of trim and probe into the framework with an ice pick or small knife. If moisture is evident or the wood is soft, further investigation is in order.

If the framework is steel or aluminum, simply

Fig. 18-2; Rust damage around body screws

scrape off the old sealant and apply fresh putty tape and reinstall the molding. Be sure some of the putty tape squeezes out whenever tightening a screw. Check to make sure there are no voids behind the molding where water may seep. Seal any voids or gaps carefully with clear or white silicone sealant. If any screws in the molding appear stripped and will not tighten properly, it is imperative that another larger screw be installed. This simple step can prevent a leak from developing in the future.

Sewer Vents
Many owners tend to overlook sewer vents when considering water entry into the coach. Most owners do seal around the base of the vent, which is good, but many forget to seal around the actual vent pipe that extends up through the roof. All sewer vents must have removable covers, so remove and inspect inside the vent base around the vent pipe.

RV manufacturers are prone to use a 2-inch or 2-1/2-inch hole saw to cut the opening in the

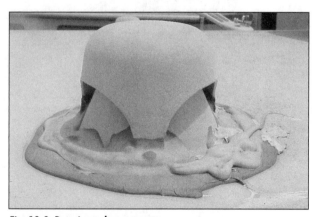

Fig. 18-3; Deteriorated sewer vent

roof for the vent pipe. Then they install a 1-1/2-inch vent pipe through this 2-1/2-inch hole, leaving a huge gap between the pipe and the perimeter of the hole; plenty of room for water and holding tank odors to gain entry into the ceiling area.

Plug this gap with putty tape or, if necessary, a piece of aluminum with an opening the exact size as the outside diameter of the vent pipe. This aluminum piece can be sealed and secured in place, all under the protection of the sewer vent base assembly. Then use an appropriate sealant around the vent pipe before reinstalling the vent cap.

Roof Vents and Escape Hatches

Roof vents are regularly opened and closed many times during a camping season. This movement, coupled with normal expansion and contraction, can loosen the mounting screws or crack the sealant. Closely inspect around the flange area for such conditions. Again, plug any gaps or crevices with silicone sealant or an equivalent. Also, keep in mind many vent flanges are molded plastic that may deteriorate with constant exposure to the ultraviolet (UV) rays of the sun. If flaking or cracking of the plastic is evident, it may be time to replace the entire vent assembly. Additionally, check the 14-inch vent lid itself. Some are prone to cracks at the corners caused by the sun. Replace the lid if any cracks have developed. The crack can be sealed temporarily with silicone; however, replace it as soon as possible.

Fig. 18-4; Inspect all roof vents closely

Fig. 18-5; Rear cap problem area

Front and Rear Caps

Most RVs, especially Class A motorhomes, have large molded fiberglass or plastic front and rear end caps that extend from the bumper to the roof. Typically, the cap is secured to the roof and sidewalls with screws, and this seam or joint is covered with a molding. As the cap goes through normal expansion and contraction, gaps or cracks may develop in this area. Especially with the wracking and twisting a moving vehicle causes.

Fig. 18-6; Eternabond OneStep tape application

One invaluable product for sealing seams, edges, caps and components on the roof is Eternabond OneStep Miracle Tape (www.eternabond.com). This 4-inch wide tape is designed for a multitude of sealing and weather-proofing tasks on any recreation vehicle. OneStep is aptly named; simply roll out enough tape to cover the entire seam, remove the backing a press it over the seam. One caveat; be sure you place it where you want it!

Fig. 18-7; After applying, press into place

It will not move, especially once pressed into place. Eternabond products will not adhere to silicone, however, so if any prior attempts at repairing a leak involved silicone, be sure to completely remove all remnants prior to installing the OneStep tape. It can also be used around roof vents, sewer vents, etc., virtually anything attached to any RV roof regardless of the surface material. Other Eternabond products can be used for installing windows, patching tanks and other tasks.

Roof Air Conditioner

Though not technically attached to the roof, the air conditioner (it actually "sandwiches" the roof between the inside plenum and main unit on top) can still be a moisture entry point. All roof air conditioners have condensation drain holes strategically located in the bottom pan situated on the roof. If leaves, twigs, dirt and debris are allowed to collect in the pan, effectively blocking the drain holes, water can enter the roof area. Usually it will drip into the air distribution box inside the coach and be quite evident from inside. Other times it may simply seep into the roof area around the 14-inch square opening over which the air conditioner is installed.

Periodically remove the inside discharge duct of the air conditioner and visually check the gasket situated around the opening. If it appears crushed, cut or mis-positioned, replace it. Typically, this gasket is only visible from inside the RV and only after removing the discharge ducting and/or the plenum.

Synthetic Roofing

Most new RVs are manufactured with a one-piece synthetic roofing material such as EPDM (rubber roofing) or thermoplastic polyolefin (TPO) (See Chapter 17). Having one-piece synthetic roofing remains one of the best ways to minimize the chances of developing water leaks. In fact, it is recommended that a synthetic roof be installed as an upgrade on older RVs as well. This will add trade-in value to the coach.

Should tears or cuts develop in the EPDM roofing, they are easily repaired with a patch kit such as Dicor's Patchit or Eternabond tape. Only use repair materials recommended by the manufacturer of the rubber roof.

Synthetic roofs can be retrofitted on virtually any of the older RVs, even those with soft, hollow beam construction. It will be necessary, however, to completely remove every item from the roof and cover the entire roof area with plywood decking before cementing on the synthetic membrane material. Check with a reputable and knowledgeable RV body shop for estimates.

Miscellaneous Areas

Skylights, solar panels, refrigerator roof vents, TV and satellite antennae, and any number of other aftermarket widgets may also be attached to the roof. Whenever any item is secured to the roof, there exists a potential for water leaks. Check the mounting techniques used to install any of

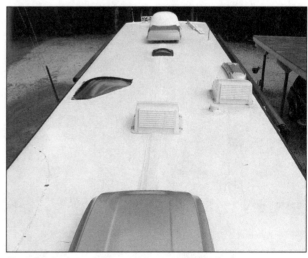

Fig. 18-8; Every roof component is a potential leak source

these items. Look for cracked or deteriorated sealants, caulking, etc. Also check for loose or rusted mounting hardware. Be sure to seal any problem areas immediately. Be sure to scrape and remove any old caulking prior to applying the new sealant.

It is further recommended that all non-synthetic roof seams, vent flanges and other miscellaneous mounting hardware be covered with a roof coating. Even after applying the sealant, brush on a protective coating such as Liquid Roof. Though designed specifically for rubber roofs, Liquid Roof has proven effective over virtually any roof surface. Additionally, many coatings and sealants are available in reflective colors that help keep the interior of the RV cooler. In some areas with extremely high temperatures, it may be advisable to coat the entire roof with a reflective coating.

Exterior Sidewall Inspection Areas

After verifying the roof is sealed against any possible water entry, inspect the sides of the RV. Here are the important areas to investigate.

Windows and Entry Door
If neglected, all windows and the entry door can become areas where water can easily enter the RV. Check the putty tape closely all around them. If any portion shows signs of deterioration, it is recommended that the entire window or door be

Fig. 18-9; Seal around windows and doors

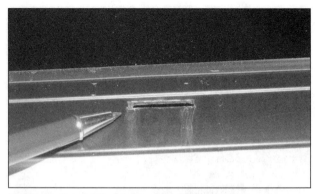
Fig. 18-10; Examine the window drain slot for obstructions

Fig. 18-11; Remove the drain slot caps to check

removed and resealed with new putty tape. Over time, all putty tape will harden and crack. Resealing only with silicone will help, but eventually new butyl caulk will have to be applied.

Be sure to remove all of the old sealant before applying the new. Keep in mind, different sidewall "skin" patterns have deeper recesses and may require more than one layer of putty tape. It is recommended that a liberal amount be applied and allowed to squeeze out when the screws are reinstalled. Remember, if the screws do not tighten properly, replace them with the next larger size.

After the door or window is secured to the sidewall, trim the excess putty with a sharp razor knife for a nice, crisp finished seal. Be careful not to cut through the siding. The exposed edge of the putty tape can be smoothed easily by moistening a shop towel with a spray of Protect All Protectant. This helps close any pores that may be evident in the putty.

Remember that most sliding windows for RVs have drain slots or weep holes cut into the bottom edge of the extruded frame. Sometimes these drain holes become plugged and water may gather in the slide track and run down the interior walls. Check to make sure these holes are clear and free from debris. Some drain holes may have small plastic caps covering the slots (see Fig. 18-10 and 18-11). You will need to remove these in order to check the drain.

Storage Compartments
Treat storage compartments the same as the entry door and windows. All are secured to the sidewall in much the same manner. The common point being that wherever a screw or rivet penetrates the sidewall, a leak can potentially develop.

Take special note if there is moisture noticed inside the storage compartment. Investigate its source without delay. It could be simple condensation, common with some metal enclosures, or it could be a leak. Do not make any assumptions. Treat any moisture as a possible leak from somewhere and then try to disprove it.

Appliance Exhaust Vents
All liquid propane (LP) appliances are vented to the exterior with the exception of the range and cooktop. The exhaust fan above the stove exits through the sidewall also. Inspect these components closely, especially the furnace exhaust. The high heat factor associated with the furnace exhaust vent rapidly dries out the sealants placed behind it. Sealants and putty tape at this location will require replacement sooner than at other locations.

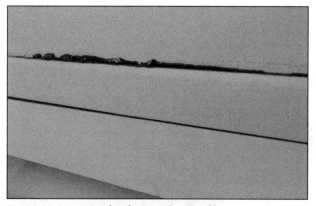

Fig. 18-13; Deteriorated sealant at sidewall molding

Miscellaneous Areas
Much like everything attached to the roof, any item connected to the sidewalls should also be closely scrutinized. Check all items such as wheel skirts, city water inlet, window awnings, fresh water storage tank fill and drain, shoreline cord door, fuel tank fill doors, moldings at the floor line or any vertical seams in the siding. Seal any discrepancies using a thin bead of clear or white silicone. A little more attention to aesthetic detail should be taken when applying silicone on the sidewalls, since most areas are readily visible. Often overlooked as potential points of entry for moisture are the mounting lag screws that attach the upper arms and brackets for the RV patio awning. They usually are drilled and mounted through the awning rail and into wood blocking at or near the roof line. Many installers forget to seal these lag screws. If your awning bracket lag screws are not sealed, here's the procedure:

- Extend the awning in order to gain full access to the lag heads.
- Carefully remove one lag screw at a time.
- Squeeze silicone sealant directly into the vacated hole, then reinstall that lag screw.
- Repeat this process with each of the mounting lag screws, one at a time.
- As a final precaution, squeeze some silicone inside the awning rail next to each lag.

Rain water can enter the rail at any location and run inside the rail itself to any point of entry such as the lag screws. Water can then seep into the sidewall by following the threads of the lag screw.

Fig. 18-12; Check appliance vents often for signs of water entry

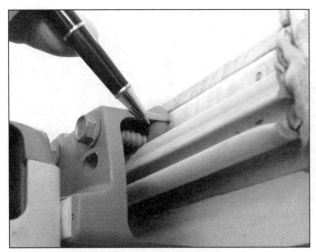

Fig. 18-14; Sealing the awning lag screws can prevent leaks

Do not overlook the bottom bracket mounting screws either. Typically they are secured to the sidewall at the floor line. A leak here could damage the flooring or a support structure over a period of time.

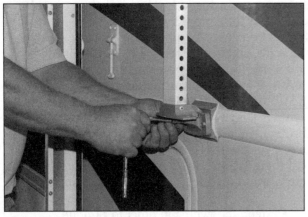

Fig. 18-15; Lower awning mounts can be a source of leaks

Another often overlooked situation involves the add-on screen rooms that accompany many RV awnings today. Some end panels to such rooms attach to the sidewall of the RV with snaps or twist latches that are permanently installed on the RV. It is important that these are also carefully waterproofed as well.

Cracks in the fiberglass or plastic front or rear end caps that penetrate the entire thickness may be patched with Insta-Glas, (www.rvtrailersupply.com), a premixed, multipurpose material.

Interior Water Damage

Usually any type of moisture absorbed by interior walls and the ceiling, especially if the damage has deteriorated to an advanced stage, precipitates replacement of the panels. By and large, saturation of plywood or veneered paneling results in permanent stains, splitting or separation of the layers. Many types of glue simply cannot hold up after constant exposure to even small amounts of moisture. Repairs, therefore, are limited to minor cosmetic cover-ups. Some cleaners and stain removers are worth a try on those areas that may be stained, but are still basically intact. Most RV supply stores carry a variety of plywood and wood panel care products. Many also carry colored putty and patching materials that may be helpful in some cases.

Determine the composite of the damaged panels and choose an appropriate cleaner, patch or polish. Carefully read the directions on the container to verify it will apply. Chances are, however, replacement will be the only cure.

Unfortunately, because of the construction of the RV, interior wall and ceiling panel replacement is extensive and better left to the professional, unless there is a covered work area available, plenty of time, and some expertise in the construction trade.

Most panels are assembled and attached during the building of the coach. For instance, the completed ceiling and roof, as one piece, is set on top of the sidewalls and secured. In other words, the ceiling panels extend over the top of the sidewalls and cannot simply be removed and replaced without first removing the roof section. Many times the trim molding located in the corner at the intersection of the upper sidewall and ceiling, is stapled to the top of the sidewalls before the entire roof section is even lowered in place.

Additionally, interior cabinets are usually attached to the walls from the outside before the exterior siding is in place. Therefore, in order to completely remove the interior paneling, the exterior "skin" needs to be removed along with the wall insulation. Then the cabinets can be removed so the damaged panels can be taken

Fig. 18-16; Removing installed cabinets and paneling can be difficult

down and replaced. It is quite extensive and usually requires specialty tools and heavy equipment.

Water damage detected early can be rectified easily. Left unchecked, it may become a major repair. Assertive, competent inspections may avoid these issues altogether. The key is to find the leak and repair it immediately. Don't wait for that spring shakedown.

Remember, water will seek its own level; therefore, just because water stains appear in the galley, don't assume that's the entry point. The rear 14-inch vent may have deteriorated sealant allowing the water to gain entry into the void between the ceiling and the roof. Water, powered by gravity, will travel until it is absorbed by the ceiling and/or the insulation, or it may continue until it finds a low spot to pool and then begin its negative action. Investigate carefully. The key, therefore, is early detection and immediate action. Inspect regularly; those who do, avoid costly repairs.

Interior Repairs

Overview

Critical water damage notwithstanding (see Chapter 18), even the most casual RVer can become proficient at completing quite a few interior repairs and adjustments successfully.

Due to the constant wracking and twisting most RVs endure while bouncing down the highway, it's not uncommon to find interior doors, drawers and cabinet accessories that need tweaking from time to time. This chapter will cover two major areas: cabinet doors and flooring. The key to making these types of repairs yourself is patience. Be sure to read through the entire section before attempting the repairs listed here.

Fig. 19-1; Mis-adjusted latches can cause drawers to extend during travel

Repairing Cabinet Doors

Interior RV doors such as cupboards, wardrobes and storage cabinets most often attract attention in transit when they bounce open. Many latches installed on RV doors simply give way to the constant jiggling of relentless vibration while in motion. The unhappy RVer usually solves this nuisance by installing positive or magnetic latches. Other complaints about RV doors include warping, poor alignment and sagging entry doors. Since these problems are more difficult to repair than loose latches, it is fortunate that they occur less frequently.

Realigning and replacing doors can be tackled by the RV owner, provided the hurdle of obtain-

ing the correct materials and parts is cleared. Specific entry doors and panels with particular finishes are readily available for RVs of fairly recent vintage, but materials are difficult to locate for older models or RVs built by manufacturers who are no longer in business. Here, the owner can take the coach to a local RV cabinet shop or body shop or improvise the repair.

The drawback of doing it yourself, however, is that what started out to be a simple cupboard door replacement may blossom into the need to replace all the cabinet doors.

Hardware Headaches

The most common annoyances with cabinet and interior storage compartment doors are usually caused by hardware problems. Poorly designed latches and improperly mounted hinges make a door open and close in jerky movements, or even bounce open while driving. Both can be easily corrected by the owner.

Loose Latches

The long-term solution for latches that pop open in transit is complete replacement with ones better suited for road vibration. Select replacements carefully. Examine the many designs stocked by RV accessory stores to find ones that require forceful turning or pulling to disengage the latching mechanism. These are the most secure.

Temporary repairs are possible with certain types of latches. For instance, one of the com-

Fig. 19-2; A variety of replacement latches

mon designs is a barrel catch made up of plastic rollers that mount to the cabinet and a metal clip that is affixed to the door that grasps the rollers when the door is closed. If the clip becomes distorted and no longer gaps, simply squeeze the ends of the clip and bend it back to its original shape but a little tighter.

Improperly Mounted Hinges

Straighten and plumb the movement of crooked doors by repositioning the hinges. To do this, remove the entire door leaving the hinges attached to the door. Position the door and hinges on the cabinet and mark the new mounting location. Seal the old screw holes in the cabinet with wood putty, pressing the soft putty into the holes and waiting for it to dry into a hard filler before drilling the new pilot holes. Stuffing toothpicks or wooden match sticks in the abandoned holes is another method of filling the holes. This method works quite well for repairing holes that become stripped out, but not necessarily needing repositioning.

Repairing Scratches

Tiny chips or scratches can mar prefinished surfaces. Repair these with a colored putty stick as sold in the big box stores. Obviously, select a color as close to the grain of the cabinet as possible. Natural stain cabinetry will require a correct color match. Carefully follow the directions of the stain manufacturer.

Working with Warped Doors

Doors most prone to warping are usually the taller ones used for the bathroom and wardrobe closets. These can absorb moisture from repeated exposure to the humidity of cooking and hot showers.

Straightening Warped Doors

Many doors are reinforced with a steel brace that can be removed, bent in the direction opposite the warp and reinstalled to correct the problem. Some doors can be so distorted, however, replacement is the only cure.

Repairing the Entry Door

Road vibration is the major cause of problems with sagging entry doors. Over time, aluminum hinges yield under the stress of bouncing down the highway. This occurs more in coaches with the entry door located to the rear of the rear axle. Here, gravity compounds the problem and accentuates the sag.

Another entry door malady is difficulty opening and closing the entry door. Usually, the striker plate is often at fault. This plate is mounted on the doorjamb and must align with the lock bolt. Periodic adjustment may be necessary.

Fixing a Sagging Entry Door

With some RV doors, the hinges alone can be replaced, but the more common design is one in which the hinges are integral to the door assembly and the entire assembly must be replaced. If the RV is only a few years old, order a new door from the RV manufacturer or from a well-stocked supplier.

Professional technicians have the tools and expertise to install a new door quickly so that labor costs are small. The do-it-yourselfer can install a new door, but the job may be complicated by a floor that slopes or a doorway that has one or more sides out of plumb.

If the choice has been made to install the door yourself, a door assembly, putty tape, possibly new inside trim and a power screwdriver will be needed. This is where an investment in a quality cordless, reversible drill is truly appreciated. A door installation may involve as many as 70 screws.

Before installing the door, test for a proper fit by holding the door assembly in place in the opening. If the floor sags, examine it carefully. It may be necessary to shim the entire assembly to compensate for frame sag or for an irregular rough opening. Liberally apply putty tape around the edge of the door frame before inserting the assembly into the opening. Be generous with the putty tape and carefully check the installation for complete sealing. Plumb and screw the hinge side of the door first. Shim the opposite side until the door frame opening is square. A large framing square is ideal for this task. Carefully trim away the squeezed out putty tape with a razor knife after securing all the mounting screws.

Repositioning the Striker Plate

The striker plate is usually mounted in slotted holes on the door frame and does not have to be completely removed for repositioning. Some have corresponding aligning screws that protrude from the edge of the door. It may be necessary to reposition these aligning screws to fit the plate on the door frame. Study the installation to determine in what direction the plate or screws should be moved. Experiment until the door closes easily, then secure the striker plate.

Additionally, it may be necessary to paint stripes or apply striping decals to finish the exterior of the door to match the original. Perhaps a local RV collision repair shop can perform this task for a reasonable price.

Fig. 19-3; Removal of the striker plate may not be entirely necessary

Fig. 19-4; Alignment bolts on the door are adjustable

Repairing Flooring

Undetected plumbing leaks, a leaky air conditioner gasket, cracks around roof vents, faulty window sealants and a few other moisture-producing ills can all lead to damaged floors within any RV. Left unchecked, moisture damage can eventually ruin an otherwise viable RV. Unfortunately, most damage may be hard to detect unless the RVer performs conscientious yearly inspections. Occasionally, damaged areas may be inadvertently exposed while performing other tasks, such as recarpeting the RV or replacing the toilet.

If moisture happens to seep into the floor from any source, over time it will be necessary to replace the damaged sections. There is no quick fix for water induced damage—replacement is the only true solution.

The good news is that in most cases replacing damaged flooring can be performed by anyone with access to some power tools, some common sense, a little construction aptitude, a block of time and a generous amount of patience. Many RV owners can easily handle this chore. If, however, the affected area extends beneath slideouts, wall partitions or cabinets, it is best to have a professional do the job.

In severe cases, all cabinets and partition walls must be removed. The repair process can then become quite complex. More often than not, though, damage is contained to a small area and repairs can be accomplished with relative ease.

In most instances, floor damage will be quite evident by pulling back the carpeting or by removing the toilet, or by simply investigating a suspicious spot or stain. If the carpeting is still usable, carefully remove the entire section and safely store it until the flooring has been replaced. But if floor repairs are necessary, chances are the carpet will need to be replaced anyway. The appearance of wood rot is so unmistakable; it is not easily confused with any other malady. Dark stains, softer wood, flakes of particles, mildew and the presence of moisture are all signs of an affected area.

Floor Construction

RV floor construction details vary from manufacturer to manufacturer, but the typical floor is usually bolted to a steel chassis after assembly. The floor framework may consist of a sandwich design with a pressed wood composite, fabric, plastic or metal underbelly with wood or metal floor joists, topped with a covering of plywood or pressed wood. Inside the framework, insulation fills the voids between the joists. The top floor is usually applied in four-foot by eight-foot sheets. The joists are typically 16 or 24 inches on center, but this dimension may vary between floorplans and categories of coaches. The size and positioning of the supports, cross beams and joists also vary depending on the weight and overall length of the RV. The floor section of the RV is usually one of the first components constructed. The rest of the RV is then built on top of this foundation.

Main support members are spaced about four feet apart from front to rear. Other braces run crosswise to form a grid configuration. Quite often, the top flooring is attached to the beams with screws, nails or staples, so a visible line of fasteners will indicate where most supports are located. When replacing damaged flooring, the replacement piece should extend a minimum of four inches into the existing good wood—that wood immediately around the damaged section.

Replacing Flooring

Many times flooring cannot be repaired and simply has to be replaced. The steps below outline the procedure to replace damaged flooring.

Determining the Thickness

To replace the flooring without damaging the support members (or the saw itself if the floor joists are made of steel), determine the exact floor thickness of the flooring material. The easiest way to determine this is to drill a hole in the damaged area, away from cross supports or floor joists. Use any size hole saw attached to an electric drill motor to accomplish this. The larger the hole saw the better. Not only will a sample plug of the floor thickness be obtained, but a large hole saw will allow for an easy inspection of the inner floor area by using a flashlight and mirror. The drilled out sample plug can be retrieved from the hole saw to determine the

top flooring thickness.

Marking the Cut-Out Area

After determining the location of cross supports, joists or other blocking that may be in the subfloor, lay out and mark the damaged piece to be removed. It is always best to replace enough of the flooring to extend from one joist or support to another. If the damaged area extends further, go to the next one.

The cut lines should be directly over the center of a floor joist so that when the new piece is inserted, it will be supported by an existing joist or beam on at least two sides. Additional supports running the opposite direction may have to be added in order to accomplish this. Be sure the cut-out area is straight and true.

Making the Cuts

Set the depth of the circular saw cut to a depth a little less than the measured floor thickness if the joists and supports are made of steel. If they are all wood, the saw blade depth should be set a little deeper than the thickness of the flooring. In most cases, you should be able to make at least two of the cuts with the circular saw.

If the damaged area extends to the base of a cabinet or dinette, it may be necessary to obtain a reciprocating saw that will enable a cut to be made closer to the obstructing cabinet. A worst-case scenario may find one using a hammer and a chisel to make those cuts that adjoin cabinets or other obstacles. (Remember the patience factor.)

Once all the perimeter cuts have been made, remove any and all screws, staples or nails that may have been used to secure the original flooring to the supports. After all fasteners have been removed, lift or pry the damaged section out.

Installing the New Section

After removing the damaged piece, examine the beams and subfloor supports for rot or damage. If unaffected, proceed with the replacement. If there has been extended damage to wooden joists or supports, those rotted pieces must, likewise, be removed and replaced.

Measure the lengths needed and cut new

supports out of appropriately sized lumber. Secure these to the available good wood inside the floor. (Note: In some cases it may be necessary to remove a larger section of plywood than was originally intended in order to secure subfloor components to the existing, structurally sound framework. The goal is to have a solid support below the entire perimeter of the replacement piece prior to inserting it in place.)

After the subfloor components are in place, measure the entire cut out area and transfer the dimensions to the new piece of plywood of the same thickness as the existing flooring. Be sure to replace all wet, rotted or deteriorated insulation found inside the floor. This step is doubly important in the colder climates.

Test the new piece for a proper fit, then apply wood glue to the new section at the supports and secure it with the appropriate type of flathead screws. Be sure the screw heads are countersunk slightly into the plywood so as not to interfere with the finished floor covering. Use a readily available, pre-mixed floor patch to fill in any voids or gaps around the perimeter of the replacement section. Then sand smooth any rough areas or joints; commercial grade floor patch is available at most hardware stores or home centers.

Sealing the Leak

Water damage does not occur from one night of rainfall seeping through a leaky window seal. It happens gradually over a period of time and continued saturation. It is imperative that the source of the invading moisture be located and repaired accordingly. It would do little good to invest the time and materials needed to complete a large floor repair and then not to repair the source of the water leak. When considering RV floor damage, key locations where moisture may enter include:

- Directly under sink P traps
- Behind or near the toilet
- At or near the shower stall or tub enclosure
- Below a 14-inch roof vent or air conditioner
- Anywhere near the water pump, fresh water tank or city water inlet
- At the rear of the water heater

According to industry-mandated construction codes for RVs, all water fittings must be accessible. It may be necessary to remove a panel or gain access by removing an appliance, but it should be possible to observe every connection in the coach. Periodic inspection of these areas can minimize major damage to the floor caused by water. A good time to inspect these areas is during the spring shakedown each year.

Do not let moisture-induced damage take you by surprise. Repair all water leaks as soon as they are detected.

Repairing Carpeting

Simply through normal use over the passage of time or from blatant abuse, the carpeting in the RV can become an embarrassing eyesore. Stains and wear patterns are a natural result of any of these occurrences. Since RVs are meant to be used and enjoyed, carpet wear may reach a point where replacement is a valid and warranted expense. Cleaners and stain removers can only go so far. Throw rugs can only mask the problem for a while. Carpets do take a beating in the RV since the foot traffic is in such a concentrated area.

Fig. 19-5; Wear patterns may develop quickly in high traffic areas

For the typical RV handyman, the recarpeting task can be handled with relative ease using common hand tools. Allow plenty of time. The key to re-carpeting the RV involves proper planning and careful execution of a few simple tasks.

Fig. 19-6; Carpeting under a slideout

Obviously, if the flooring underneath the existing carpet is in need of repairs, those items must be completed before new carpeting can be installed.

In the case of slideouts, it can be nigh impossible to replace the carpeting that disappears under the leading edge of the slideout. In some cases the slideout can be overextended manually or tilted from its fully extended position in order to accommodate new carpet installation. It is best, however, to contact the manufacturer of the slide mechanism and the customer relations department of the RV manufacturer prior to attempting to replace carpeting directly under the slideouts.

Choosing Carpet
Personal tastes will obviously reflect the choice of colors and style of carpet, but consider this: it is best to avoid the deep pile varieties. Most crush easily under heavy foot traffic and will not recover completely. Better choices are commercial grade, close-loop piles that can be luxurious, easy to clean and reasonably simple to install. Always invest in a quality carpet pad. Padding saves wear and tear and is well worth the added expense and labor.

Removing Old Carpet
During manufacture, some RV floors are fully carpeted before the partition walls, cabinets and furnishings are installed. Many RVs with slideouts have the carpeting fully installed before the slide unit is even installed. This method creates

a handsome appearance and makes sense at the time of manufacture, but it presents a time-consuming job for anyone wanting to replace the entire carpet.

Complete removal is not always necessary since the old carpet can serve as padding or be selectively retained in closets and under storage areas. Of course, if water has damaged the entire carpet, it is crucial to remove the entire carpet, repair the source of the leak, and if necessary, repair the wood flooring prior to installing the replacement carpet. Additionally, if the original carpet contains odors as well as stains, it might be a good idea to remove the complete carpet anyway.

If the existing carpet was installed before the cabinets and partition walls, carefully cut along the walls and cabinets with a sharp razor knife to cut out the old carpet. Save these pieces. They may be used as a pattern for the new carpet. Try not to destroy or rip the old carpet.

Be sure to check the floor area carefully after removing the old carpet. Staples or tacks may still be present. If there are any rough joints or splinters in the wood flooring, now is the time to sand and smooth them. Completely sweep the wood flooring clean.

Laying New Carpet
As a preliminary step, remove any item secured at or near the floor. Cabinet doors that are low to the floor should also be removed for easier handling of the new carpet. It may be necessary to remove the liquid propane (LP) leak detector since it, too, is mounted close to the floor. Be sure to mark the wires before cutting or removing the detector.

If a thicker carpet and pad are going to be installed, some cabinet doors may have to be repositioned to accommodate the added thickness of the carpeting. In most cases, this is not a major concern. There is usually enough room for such an adjustment without having to modify the doors.

If it is decided to use a carpet pad, install it first. It can usually be cut with sharp scissors or a razor knife. The pad can be attached by stapling

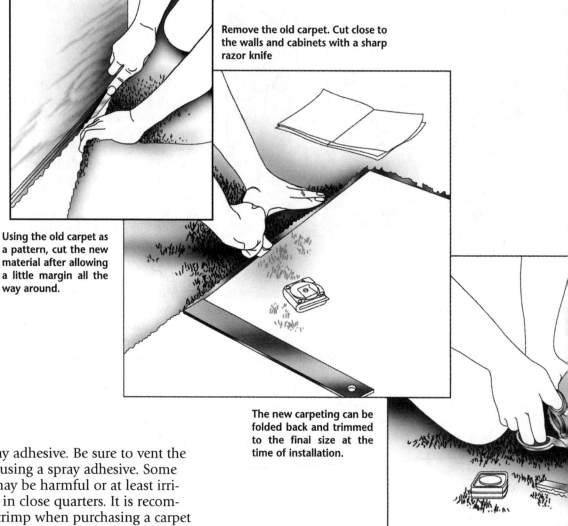

Using the old carpet as a pattern, cut the new material after allowing a little margin all the way around.

Remove the old carpet. Cut close to the walls and cabinets with a sharp razor knife

The new carpeting can be folded back and trimmed to the final size at the time of installation.

or by using a spray adhesive. Be sure to vent the coach well while using a spray adhesive. Some adhesive fumes may be harmful or at least irritating when used in close quarters. It is recommended to not scrimp when purchasing a carpet pad. Get a good one.

Cutting

As mentioned, any removed sections of the old carpet can be used as a pattern for cutting the new one but it is wise to leave a little extra material all the way around the perimeter and trim the pieces to fit exactly at the time of placement. A razor knife with a new blade works best for cutting virtually all carpet materials. Stock up on razor blades and change them often during the installation process. Carpet cutting quickly dulls the blades. Use a metal straight edge with the razor whenever possible to produce a nice, crisp edge.

After cutting the carpet to fit, lay it out flat inside the coach and work from one end of the RV to the other. Force the new carpet into the edges at the cabinets and carefully trim the remainder of the excess with a sharp razor knife. Remember to change blades often. Since the area in the RV is relatively small, a carpet knee-kicker is usually not needed.

Attaching

Today, the carpet tack has given way to the staple Other means can be used for securing carpet, but the stapler reigns supreme because it is fast and easy to use, and the pile of the carpet easily conceals staples. It is recommended that an electric or air-powered stapler be rented or otherwise obtained for the task of securing the carpeting. Manual staplers are impractical for this size of job, and staple choice is somewhat limited.

The staple design is dependent upon the choice of pile and style of carpeting. Overall thickness of the pad and carpet also needs to be factored in to determine the length of the staple needed. Ask the carpet salesperson what he or she recommends when choosing the carpet and pad.

Double-faced carpet tape is also quite handy for attaching the carpet in close quarters and under

cabinets where a stapler may not fit. Such carpet tape is also used when joining two separate pieces of carpet. This, too, can be obtained at the time the replacement carpet is purchased.

Abutting Two Pieces
In larger RVs, it is not probable that the carpeting can be installed in one complete piece. Generally, the carpet has to be pieced together. If possible, choose a convenient location to make the butt joint, such as in a doorway leading to another section of the coach, for instance.

To make the butt joint, overlap the two pieces and using the straight edge, make one straight cut at the exact point of the joint. Cut deeply and firmly since two layers of carpet are being cut. Use the carpet tape to affix both sections of carpet to the floor at the joint. Avoid using too many staples in the area of the joint; it may accentuate it. The goal is to have the joint sim-

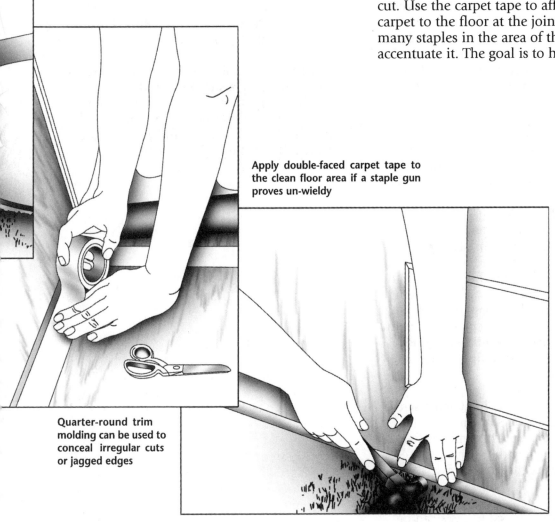

Apply double-faced carpet tape to the clean floor area if a staple gun proves un-wieldy

Quarter-round trim molding can be used to conceal irregular cuts or jagged edges

Fig. 19-7; Illustrations and tips for removing carpet

ply blend in with the rest of the carpet. Also, avoid making a joint in the carpet pad at the same point as the joint in the carpet itself. A few feet either side of the finished joint is recommended.

Meeting Other Flooring

In most RVs, there is a point where the carpet meets linoleum, tile or a wooden section in the galley or lavatory. Usually a metal or wood threshold is used to mate the carpet to other floor coverings. Another method is to simply fold the carpet under and staple it to the floor. If there is an existing threshold, remove it. If not, purchase one of sufficient length and cut it to fit.

When folding the carpet under, try to remove any backing from the carpeting first, then cut the padding back the width of the fold (about two inches or so), so that the folded carpet lays as flat as possible. This method works well when staples cannot be used, such as when meeting ceramic tile.

After the carpet has been secured to the floor, reinstall all ancillary components such as table bases, furnace ducts, LP leak detectors or cabinet doors that may have been removed prior to the installation.

Miscellaneous Carpet Tips

When carpeting in the bathroom, it is best to remove the toilet completely and to allow the carpeting to cover the floor all the way up to the perimeter of the floor flange. It can be difficult to accurately trim around the base of the toilet. Also, if the toilet were to need replacing at some point in time, the carpet cuts will usually not match the new one. After installing the carpet, reinstall the toilet.

If it is necessary to drill a hole or attach a screw through the carpeting, always cut an X in the new carpet before doing so. This will eliminate the probability of snagging the weave and permanently damaging the carpet.

Should recarpeting the cab area of a Class C motorhome be desired, the same steps can be followed, except that a carpet pad is rarely used in this instance. Also, since most floor assem-

Fig. 19-8; Carpet edges can be folded under or a threshold can be used

blies in Class C's are made of steel, a spray adhesive or contact cement in lieu of staples to secure the carpet will have to be used. Always try to use the old carpet as a pattern.

Taking your time, double checking measurements and using a sharp razor knife will make the job of carpet replacement a fairly easy task. A new carpet will reflect a personal touch that can be enjoyed for many, many miles. And it always adds to the trade-in value.

Chapter 20

Exterior Repairs

Overview

The many exterior body repair techniques on RVs are almost as varied as the different brands of RVs available. Construction methods are many; therefore, repair procedures will also vary depending on how the RV was originally constructed. It is imperative that prior to undertaking any exterior repair on any RV to fully explore the manner in which the coach was put together. If in doubt, or there is a question concerning construction, be sure to contact the dealer or the manufacturer for the details before beginning.

Always allow plenty of time for exterior repairs. This is especially true if working on the roof area. Also, the larger the repair, the more it may be exposed if major portions of the RV are uncovered. If possible, perform the exterior repairs inside a garage or under a covering of some type. Weather, especially moisture-laden air, makes some repair procedures more difficult. As with any repair, proper preparation is crucial to a successful job, so begin right by keeping the area clean and dry.

That said, be aware that not all exterior body damage repairs can be performed by even the most astute RVer. Here's an example of body damage better left to the work of professionals!

Fig. 20-1; Major damage should be repaired by a professional

Coach Construction Methods

Before delving into the actual repair practices, consider the different types of coach construction. Though variations of each exist, basically three major types of sidewall and roof construction techniques are used today:

- Solid laminated construction
- Soft, or hollow, wall construction
- Aircraft design

Laminated

Laminated or "sandwiched" sidewalls and roofs are multi-layered, rigid and extremely strong. It is probably the most popular method used today. The process entails gluing and sandwiching the interior finished paneling, the framework, the insulation and the exterior "skin" in one operation.

One typical method of construction allows each wall to be laid out on a large assembly table one layer at a time. The laminations are glued, pressed and clamped together and subjected to a vacuum that literally sucks the moisture and air out of the "sandwich." The result is a strong, dry, bonded one-piece section that can now be affixed to the chassis portion and assembled with other RV sections that have also gone through this process. Cut-outs and openings for the windows, doors, vents and storage compartments are also made while the section is on the assembly table.

Fig. 20-2; Laminated sections awaiting assembly

This type of sidewall and roof construction is the favored method by many of today's RV builders. The main advantage of having a laminated roof is the strength factor. Solid roofs are durable enough on which to walk, to attach storage pods or to stow other related camping gear. Most Class A motorhomes are equipped with a roof rack and a ladder for just this reason.

Hollow Wall

Another method of construction, popular especially with the travel trailer and slide-in camper makers, is the soft, or hollow, wall construction. This method is most similar to house-type wood construction in which a finished interior panel is affixed to a stud wall, then insulation is installed and finally the exterior siding, or skin, is applied in a separate procedure. The interior paneling is usually applied to the framework before the sidewalls are placed onto the chassis.

The advantage to this type of construction is reduced cost. It is much less expensive to build an RV with soft sidewalls and roof. The obvious disadvantage is lack of support or strength, especially on the roof. Thankfully this type of construction is quickly vanishing in favor of the stronger and more durable laminated types.

When climbing onto or working on a soft roof, first place lengths of walking boards or supports that will span a minimum of two or three roof rafters. If anyone accidentally steps in between two rafters, damage or leaks may result. Soft roofs are not designed to be walked on. This is one reason they are popular with certain lines of travel trailers. Rarely do you see roof racks, ladders or stowed gear on top of such vehicles.

Aircraft

The third major type of construction is the aircraft type (think Airstream, Avion, etc.). Those sleek coaches with the non-painted, buffed aluminum exteriors have a construction all their own. These RVs characteristically have individually performed sectional pieces of aluminum riveted onto a framework of aluminum steel. Sprayed in foam-type insulation is then filled into the cavities from inside the coach, and finally, the interior sectional pieces, also preformed, are then riveted or screwed in place.

Construction Materials

Since lamination is today's preferred construction method, it is probably only fair that this method also has the largest variety of building materials available. The interior wall paneling and ceiling panels are typically prefinished sheets of plywood or veneer, approximately 1/8-inch to 3/16-inch thick plywood or veneer is used. Some top of the line makers may use real wood paneling instead of veneered plywood.

The framework of the laminated wall can be constructed from wood, aluminum tubing or steel tubing. Each has its advantages and disadvantages ranging from cost to weight. Also, many coach builders run electrical conductors inside these laminated sections. Most sidewalls will have wiring run inside and some roof sections will also have the 120-volts alternating current (AC), 12-volts direct current (DC) wires or both, encased inside the bonded section.

Insulation is usually sheet or block polystyrene foam or the equivalent, approximately 3/4-inch to 1-inch thick, which is cut and inserted into the voids between the framework studs and supports. Routing channels are sometimes cut into the insulation when positioning the wires into the laminate prior to pressing and final assembly.

Next, a thin piece of plywood, usually 1/8-inch thick, is placed just to the outside of the framework. This paneling, commonly luan plywood, proves a smooth gluing surface for the final exterior finish. It also adds to the profound strength of the total laminated section.

The final layer in the laminated construction wall is the outside skin. This siding is made from a number of materials. Fiberglass, acrylonitrile-butadiene-styrene (ABS) plastic, fiberglass reinforced plastic (FRP), such as Filon and aluminum siding are the most popular materials for the exterior skin on the laminated wall. Fiberglass and FRPs are also used to form the large front and rear caps and radius molding or corners on most coaches.

Laminated roofs are constructed much the same as the sidewalls are with the exception of the final outside layer of skin. Roof materials may

Fig. 20-3; Roof section during factory installation

be one-piece aluminum sheeting, rolled aluminum roofing containing seams or the popular one-piece synthetic roof covering. All bonded roof assemblies are also built on a special laminating table, and the whole assembly is set upon the upright vertical sidewalls during the construction phase of the RV.

In the photo above, the completed roof section is rolled into position and then lifted into place on top of the already-installed sidewalls. Note how the wiring is already installed and coiled at various points for further routing in the body of the RV.

The soft or hollow wall construction consists of an interior panel stapled, riveted or screwed to a framework consisting of wood, steel or aluminum studs or supports. Either woven fiberglass insulation or blown-in foam insulation is applied to the back of the interior paneling, and an outer skin of aluminum is stapled or riveted to the framework.

The aircraft-type of construction is much the same as the soft or hollow wall construction except typically no wood is used at all. The framework is aluminum or steel square tube welded together. The exterior preformed pieces are riveted into place. Then the insulation is installed. Lastly, the interior panels, also preformed and made from aluminum, are riveted into place.

Wherever electrical wiring passes through a wooden frame member, a protective plate should be situated to protect the conductor from screws or staples that may be accidentally driven through it. One of the most difficult electrical repairs is finding and repairing a "short" or an "open" in a wire hidden somewhere in the sidewall or ceiling of the coach. If the RV framework is metal-framed instead of having wooden studs, be sure a grommet is used to protect the wiring where it passes through. Some manufacturers protect the wiring using silicone caulking.

Aside from the easily recognized design of the aircraft-type construction, RV aluminum siding is available in a variety of designs, corrugations and patterns with strange names and with various dimensions. Names like mesa, mesa 1, mesa with reverse, yoder, mini-yoder, old and new aristocrat and greyhound are just a sampling of the various patterns that have been used over the years.

Additionally, acrylic panels of FRP may adorn some sidewalls as well. This material is usually available in a flat, smooth finish or a pebble-like, rough finish. Typically, all are cemented to the thin sheet of luan paneling as part of the bonded, laminated wall sections.

To find out which design is used on your RV, take the coach to a reputable and knowledgeable RV collision repair shop and have the estimator examine and measure the siding to determine the exact size and pattern.

Types of Exterior Damage

In order to choose the correct repair procedure for damage to the exterior of the RV, first determine the type of damage that has occurred to the RV. Here are six different types of damage and a definition of each.

Dent: A depression (ding) or indentation in the exterior of the RV that has not punctured the skin (see Fig. 20-4).

Crack: There are two distinct types of cracks. One, which resembles a spider web and is usually located near the corners of doors or windows,

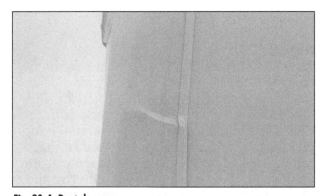
Fig. 20-4; Dent damage

is called a stress crack. It is considered a surface crack in the outermost layer of gelcoat on the fiberglass siding. The other type of crack is more severe. A through-crack is deeper than a surface crack. It will be cracked all the way through the thickness of the panel.

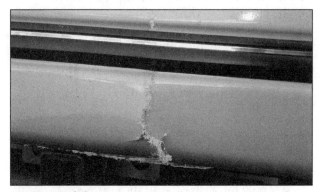
Fig. 20-5; Crack damage

Hole: A hole penetrates all the way through the siding. It could be a cut, a slice or a puncture. The damage, however, is usually confined to a very small location.

Fig. 20-6; Puncture damage

Impact: An impact usually causes major sidewall damage, typically the result of a collision. Frame members may be bent or broken, and interior walls may show evidence of damage. Some pieces may even be missing.

Delamination: Delamination is when the exterior siding has separated from the cemented and bonded sandwich. The glue simply did not hold or was applied incorrectly and the siding appears to be rippling away from the side of the RV. Moisture intrusion is another main cause of sidewall delamination.

Water damage: Water damage is caused by a water leak that was ignored. It's usually confined to the interior paneling, the insulation and/or wooden structural members inside the wall cavity. It usually does not affect the exterior skin or siding except in cases where the luan paneling has deteriorated as a result.

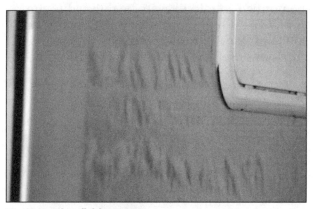
Fig. 20-7; Sidewall delamination

Repair Techniques

The type of damage, sidewall construction and the siding used should all be considered to properly determine the correct repair procedure. In many cases, the scope of the repair may be beyond the means of the RV owner. In those cases, the repair is better left to the professional body shop.

Damage so extensive the entire side sections need to be rebuilt should probably not be attempted by the owner—likewise with massive

Fig. 20-8; A trip to a professional body shop may be the best option

sidewall delamination damage. This usually requires complete stripping off of the siding and special prepping and gluing (remember, improper gluing probably contributed to the original cause of the delamination in the first place).

Additionally, it is recommended that any damage so severe that an insurance company must be notified should likewise be directed to the professional body shop. Collision repair shops are familiar with insurance claims and estimating forms and paperwork. This will also expedite the repair.

Once the entire scope of the damage has been assessed and the decision is made to address the repair yourself, choose the repair option. They are:

- Quick Fix
- Patch
- Replacement

Quick Fix
The quick-fix approach is nothing more than a cosmetic cover-up of a small, diminutive dent or puncture or tear. This is where it is common (and very inexpensive) to simply install a louvered vent over the opening to hide the blemish. If the skin is punctured, fill the hole with silicone sealant prior to installing the vent. Choose the smallest, least obtrusive vent available, and simply screw it or pop-rivet it to the side of the coach over the hole. Be sure to seal the edges with putty tape. Decorate decals or other trim items can also be used to conceal small dents or holes. Literally hundreds of dollars of sidewall damage repair can be avoided with the simple

purchase of an inexpensive vent.

Patch
The patch method is a common cure for both types of sidewall cracks discussed earlier. Minor cracks are easily repaired with a patch kit. The best product for patching stress cracks is Insta-Glas. Distributed by Bri-Rus, (www.rvtrailersupply.com), Insta-Glas is a ready-to-use kit that can be applied to fiberglass, plastics, metal and even wood, if necessary. It is very effective and easy to carry, unlike a two-part epoxy resin and catalyst that must be carefully mixed and hurriedly applied.

Insta-Glas is premixed and contains a photo-curing acrylic resin and strands of fiberglass. The curing process is generated by an ultraviolet (UV) lamp or sunlight. Once the compound has been applied, simply position the coach in direct sunlight for faster curing. This is the patch repair procedure:

1. Remove any moldings or trim that might conceal any portion of the crack.

2. Remove the door or window if the crack is in that area.

3. Rough-sand the area at the crack and at about one inch of the surrounding area.

4. Apply the Insta-Glas to the entire cracked area.

5. Smooth out the compound and place a piece of clear plastic over the repair area.

6. Starting at the center, slowly work any air bubbles to the sides of the plastic with a flexible putty knife or other flat object. Try to obtain a smoothness as close to the finished form as possible to avoid excessive sanding after it cures.

7. Allow the patch to naturally cure in the sunlight or direct a UV lamp onto the repaired area.

8. After curing, remove the plastic and sand the patched area.

9. For fine surface blemishes that may exist after sanding, apply a thin layer of finishing resin and allow that to cure.

10. Finish sanding the area, then mask, prime and paint.

11. Reinstall all windows or doors, trim and moldings, etc. Be sure to use the proper sealants, such as putty tape or Eternabond.

To patch deeper gouges, punctures, holes or through-cracks, it may be necessary to administer two applications of Insta-Glas. Or, if the damage is in an area with immediate access behind the hole or crack, such as in a wheel skirt, front or rear cap or lower skirt area, repeated layering of fiberglass resin and glass mats can be applied to build up a reinforced segment to help strengthen the repair. The thickness of the damaged material will ultimately determine how many fiberglass layers will be needed.

After reinforcing the area behind the damage, simply apply the outer Insta-Glas repair patch as outlined above. Take your time. Most people have a tendency to rush body repairs. Careful sanding, inspection, filling and more sanding are the keys to a quality body repair.

Replacement

The best method is replacement, especially regarding hollow wall construction damage.

Aluminum siding is originally installed from the roof line down. It may be in many sections, top to bottom. The lowermost section typically slips into a locking seam on the piece immediately above it to ensure a leak-proof seam. The next piece fits into the one directly above it and so on. RV manufacturers may choose different colors and widths of siding for an aesthetically pleasing appearance. First determine which piece of the siding is damaged. It is possible that more than one piece is damaged. Inspect the area closely.

Replacement panels can be ordered through various suppliers, but keep in mind a local RV dealer may have to place the order. Many suppliers sell only to a dealer network. If you have any questions concerning ordering any aluminum

siding, a source of information is All-Rite (www.all-rite.com). The company can provide the name and location of the closest dealer.

Replacement Procedure

Be sure to carefully evaluate any other materials that may be needed; check for damaged moldings, vent, lights, drip rails, awning rail, etc. It is recommended that all replacement materials be on hand prior to beginning the replacement procedures.

1. Prepare a clean, dry work area, preferably under a protective cover.

2. Remove all compartment doors, appliance vents, windows, wheel skirts, entry doors, moldings, trim, city water inlet, etc., virtually any item that is at or below the damaged area. If the water heater will have to be removed, be sure to turn off the source of liquid propane (LP) at the container prior to continuing. To be safe, plug the LP line at the water heater, using a 3/8-inch flare plug, to keep contaminants out.

3. Starting at the bottom, remove all pieces of aluminum siding up to and including the damaged area. Each piece, including the uppermost damaged piece, will have to be removed from the bottom up. If some lower pieces are unaffected by the damage, they must carefully be removed anyway and set aside for reinstallation later. Remove each piece by carefully pulling the staples located at the sides and along the bottom of the locking Pittsburgh or S seam. It is advisable to wear protective gloves when handling aluminum siding. Some edges are extremely sharp. Long, thin pieces of siding have a tendency to kink; therefore, additional help may be needed when handling these long, cumbersome sections.

4. If the damaged area does not include the uppermost piece, and there is no frame or stud damage, begin installing the new panels by sliding the top edge of the new piece into the locking seam of the upper piece on the coach. Have someone hold the panel firmly and then check to make sure it is inserted fully into the seam.

5. Staple along the lower edge below the locking seam into the wooden framework. It is recommended that an electric or pneumatic stapler be used for any siding replacement jobs. They are available at most equipment rental facilities. Use a wide crown staple horizontally along the bottom of the locking seam and a narrow crown staple when stapling vertically up the sides of the siding and around openings. Do not cut the siding for openings or for length at this point. Just allow the piece to extend beyond the edge of the sidewall.

6. Install the next lowest piece in this same manner taking care not to kink or dimple the new siding. Some thin sheets are very delicate to handle.

7. After all new pieces and any undamaged original pieces have been installed, carefully trim the edges using aviation snips or aluminum shears. Now, cut out the openings for all the peripheral components removed earlier. Take your time and trim carefully being sure to stay at the edge of the cut-out and not to wander into the middle of the newly installed panels.

8. After trimming all cut-outs, staple the siding along the ends and around the edges of the larger openings such as doors, windows, etc. It is not crucial to staple around the smaller openings such as the city water inlet. The mounting screws for the inlet itself will suffice to secure the siding.

9. Be sure to seal along the exposed vertical edges at the corners of the RV with a thin bead of silicone sealant. Apply putty tape to the backside of the molding, J rail and/or awning rail before securing with screws. Use a liberal amount of putty tape and trim the excess that squeezes out with a sharp razor knife.

10. Reinstall all doors, windows, etc., taking care to properly seal against leaks. As always, apply putty tape behind the mounting flange. If necessary, a thin layer of clear silicone sealant can be applied after trimming the putty tape. Note: Some siding patterns, like yoder, for instance, may require more than one layer of putty tape to adequately fill in the voids behind the

mounting flange of doors and windows. It is vital that every portion of the void be filled with putty tape to ensure no water leaks will develop.

Inside the Wall
With the siding removed, inspect the insulation and framework. If water damage has rotted a stud or frame support, now is the time to replace it. Cut a new piece to fit and secure it to existing good wood with nails, screws or staples.

Likewise, replace any insulation that has deteriorated. Seldom are the inside of the walls exposed like this, so carefully evaluate all that you can see at this time. Is the wiring secure? Are there any visible openings leading to inside the coach? Are mounting bolts secured? Check everything while it's exposed.

Roof Repairs
Bonded, laminated roofs with seams should be sealed with a sealant tape such as Eternabond (See Chapter 18). Seal around every item attached to the roof, 14-inch roof vents, plumbing vents, the refrigerator vent, roof racks, antennae, skylights, etc.—any place a screw penetrates the roof should be checked. Eternabond is very effective at sealing all types of roof seams or patching ethylene propylene diene monomer (EPDM) rubber or thermoplastic polyolefin (TPO) roofing material.

If damage from low-hanging branches has punctured a laminated roof, the repair is identical to that for sidewalls as explained earlier in the chapter. If, however, a soft roof has a hole, the roof can be patched by installing a flat aluminum panel that spans two rafters (if the hole is large) or simply a small piece for small holes. First fill the hole with putty tape or silicone sealant, then cover with the patch. Screw or pop-rivet the patch in place and carefully seal the entire area with Liquid Roof or Eternabond tape.

If major damage to the roof area has occurred to a soft, hollow roof, it will be necessary to replace the entire roof section. All roofing aluminum, with or without seams, comes rolled and in one piece. Roof replacement is not a quick job and is best left to the professional

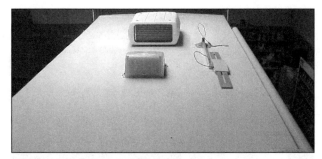

Fig. 20-9; A well-maintained RV roof

Fig. 20-10; A blemished roof

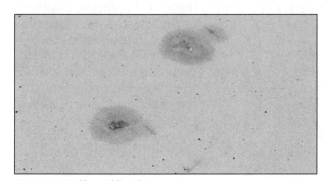

Fig. 20-11; Mold or mildew damage

body shop. It is further recommended that a soft roof be replaced with one that is covered with a thin layer of plywood and a synthetic roofing material. This will add strength and stability to the roof area, and the synthetic roof needs little or no maintenance other than a few washings each year.

Patch kits are available for synthetic roof repairs. Simply follow the directions on the kit for an effective repair should the roof membrane develop a tear.

Finishing Touches

After any type of exterior repair, the most important follow-up is to make sure there is no chance for water to enter again. Leaks are the biggest concern.

Other final touches to exterior repair include painting and adding decals, decorative striping or logos that were ruined by the damage and subsequent repair. It is probably best that a body shop prime and paint the damaged area, unless of course, it was a fairly small area that was patched.

Decals, striping and other manufacturer-produced graphics can perhaps be ordered by the RV dealer. If the manufacturer no longer exists, perhaps a brand-specific owner's club or association can be of assistance.

Remember, only tackle those repairs with which you feel comfortable. If you think it is beyond your capabilities, call an RV collision repair shop. Never compromise the safety factor. With proper study though, RVers should be able to easily handle almost any small exterior body repair.

Repairing Running Lamps

When one ponders just how far technology has progressed with RVs, it is hard to imagine any item more aggravating than having intermittent running lights. They sometimes burn out, flicker off and on or can just be plain temperamental. However, it seems we must all go through this dilemma from time to time; label it another RV fact of life. The two predominant causes of problems with running lights containing incandescent bulbs can be categorized as corrosion and road vibration.

Running lights, turn signals, backup lamps and brake lamps are all subject to dirt, dust and corrosion that erode electrical contacts, along with vibration, which loosens connections. Most exterior lighting problems can be remedied easily and quickly by keeping spare bulbs and fuses on hand and by using a systematic, detective-style approach when making repairs.

If all of the lamps do not work, for example, one cause could be a blown fuse for that circuit.

Fig. 20-12; Running lamps can become a source of aggravation

Fig. 20-14; Clean and preserve electrical connections

If only the turn signals do not work, the first step is to locate the fuse block that contains that circuit. Take the suspect fuse out of its holder and inspect it visually. Is the filament broken? To be doubly sure, try substituting a new fuse of the same rating, or check to see if there is continuity through that fuse by using a volt-ohm meter (VOM) on the ohm scale.

Sometimes a fuse that appears to be good really is not. Always keep spare fuses on hand. If a short exists and the next fuse also blows, substitute a resettable circuit breaker with test leads for the fuse while searching for the short. Never substitute a fuse with one of a higher amperage rating.

One common reason why an entire circuit fails in a travel trailer, for example, can be attributed to a poor electrical contact in the wiring connector between the tow vehicle and trailer. Water can invade the tow vehicle socket or the trailer plug and corrode the contacts. A spray can of DeoxIT can clean and preserve all electrical contacts.

If only one lamp is not working, remove the lens and inspect the bulb to see if the filament is broken. Although a burned out bulb is not the most frequent cause of light malfunction, it is the easiest to spot.

If the bulb is good, the lamp may be suffering from corrosion inside the fixture. Check the wiring connections inside. They should be clean and firmly attached. Take the bulb out and brighten the

An often overlooked entry point for water is through the hole where clearance and tail light wires exit the exterior.

A thin bead of silicone sealant around the top edge of clearance lights will minimize the possibility of moisture entering the walls

Seal around the top of the lamp

The sealant should extend to a point below the mounting screws

Plug these holes with silicone sealant

Corrosion on the bulb contacts are an indication of possible water entry

Fig. 20-13; Running lamp maintenance

base with fine sandpaper or emery cloth. Also burnish the inside of the clip and the contact strip that touches the bulb tip. Examine the strip to make sure it indeed contacts the bulb. If it does not, bend the strip to make sure it pushes against the bulb tip. If the corrosion is rampant, replace the entire fixture.

Corrosion inside the fixture can be caused by moisture seeping in and around the lens. To prevent this from recurring, put a small amount of silicone sealant on the edge of the lens before it is reinstalled. If the light still does not work, very likely a faulty ground exists. Another indication of a poor ground is a lamp that flickers on and off or works only when tapped or bumped.

To check for a defective ground, remove the lens and activate that circuit. Attach a length of wire or a test lead to the side of the bulb's base. Touch the other end of the wire to one of the lamp's mounting screws or to another bare metal part on the RV (such as an aluminum window flange). If the bulb now lights, invariably the cause is a faulty ground.

Most RV lamps have a ground wire running from the light fixture to somewhere on the chassis, or the ground path may simply be the aluminum skin on the RV. If when removing the lens cover you only see one wire, then the ground path is to the skin through one of the mounting screws. If, however, there are two separate wires, then the ground path is usually through the second wire to a point somewhere on the chassis. This two-wire setup is mandatory with coaches with nonmetallic mounting surfaces such as fiberglass. Trace the ground wire to make sure that it is unbroken and firmly attached to either the chassis or the connector. In some instances it is actually easier to simply run a new ground wire rather than spend an inordinate amount of time looking for an electrical open in one section.

Other RVs, as mentioned, are grounded through one of the screws that hold the light fixture to the RV's aluminum skin. To cure a poor ground with this type of fixture, tighten the screw. If that does not work, remove the screw and replace it with one a size larger.

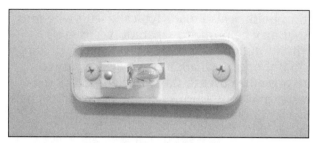

Fig. 20-15; Running lamp with a separate ground wire

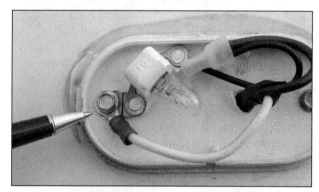

Fig. 20-16; Ground connection must be clean, dry and tight

If the lamps on a particular circuit are dim, it may be because the positive, or hot, lead to the lights is leaking or shorting current into the chassis. Follow this hot wire from the light and check for worn insulation. Damaged insulation can be repaired with electrical tape or solderless connectors. While tracing the hot wire, check any wire connector the manufacturer may have used to splice wires together. Sometimes water can get into these connectors and corrode the contacts. When replacing butt splices, it is always wise to use heat shrink tubing around the wire and the connector to protect and weatherproof the connection.

Many clearance lamp circuits for RVs begin at one of the rear tail lamp assemblies. If none of the clearance markers are working, remove one or both of the tail lamp assemblies and check the wire nuts or attaching points behind it. Chances are vibration has caused one or more of the wires to become disconnected.

Some electrical harnesses on travel trailers and fifth-wheels terminate in a void or cavity inside the subfloor just under the front of the trailer behind the A frame. Here, the harness links up with the wiring inside the trailer. This connection point is also made typically with wire nuts that may be prone to separation caused by vibration. If one or more outside lamp circuits do not operate at all, it may be necessary to remove the cover to this space and check the wires and connections within. If the turn signals flash rapidly and not very brightly, install a heavy duty flasher in the tow vehicle.

Another key to troubleshooting running lamp problems is to isolate the problem area, using the process of elimination. Check individual lamps and connectors with a 12-volt test light. Try to obtain a set of electrical prints for that particular model. Many manufacturers can supply the construction prints that were used for that RV. One good habit is to always wrap electrical tape around wire nuts to make sure simple vibration will not loosen them. This one step alone could save considerable frustration while traveling.

As frustrating as these running lamps may sometimes be, the persistent RVer can rectify many problems associated with intermittent or non-working running lamps.

Chapter 21

Winterizing and Storing the RV

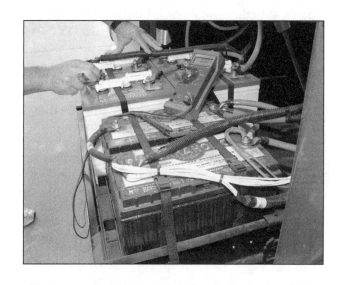

Overview

Although many individuals and families enjoy the RVing lifestyle as full-timers, many others appreciate the benefits on a more limited basis, such as during vacations, holidays, weekend getaways or maybe combination trips of business mixed with pleasure. For those who utilize the RV of their choice only part-time, there comes a time when the RV must be stored for a period of non-use. If located in one of the colder regions of the country, it will also be necessary to protect the RV against the cold by winterizing the coach. Whether the RV will be stored in cold or temperate climates, certain precautions need to be taken.

Specific tasks and procedures for each of the major systems and components of the RV must be performed in order to store or winterize the coach effectively. One of the most damaging effects that can happen to an RV, short of abuse, is ill-prepared non-use. To get the most from the RV, following the procedures in this chapter will ensure the RVer of extended coach life and many more joyful RVing miles. For optimum efficiency, the following strategic and sequential steps are designed to be implemented in the order written so that nothing falls through the cracks.

Fig. 21-1; Begin with a clean RV

As a preliminary step to winterizing or storing the coach, completely wash the exterior. Doing so will get the storing preparation off to a good start. A clean coach will reveal items that need to be addressed prior to the spring shakedown.

Fresh Water System

The primary reason why winterizing techniques are so important is basically because of the fresh water system. If left unaddressed, water in the lines and components will freeze, expand and cause damage during a cold winter. Replacing damaged water lines can be an expensive repair. Do not underestimate the importance of following the correct winterizing procedures! Begin by removing the water source (city water or on-board water pump) and opening all the hot and cold water faucets in the RV.

Water Lines

Most coaches are equipped today with low-point drain valves for both the hot and the cold lines. Usually located at the lowest point in the RV, low point valves aid in gravity draining as much water as possible from the lines.

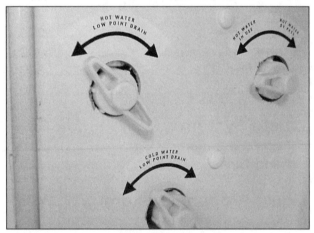

Fig. 21-2; Low point valves inside a compartment

Valves may be located at or below the floor level. Some are found underneath the coach. Others may not be valves at all, but rather

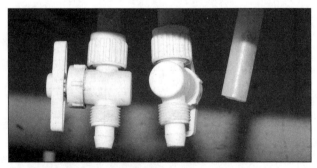

Fig. 21-3; Low point drain valves

Fig. 21-4; Low point drain tubes may be simply pipe plugs

simple pipe plugs. Still others may have the valves located inside a dedicated water bay.

Water Heater

Drain the water heater completely. It is easy to forget that this appliance is an extension of the fresh water system. All water heaters have a drain plug or drain valve accessible from the outside of the coach, located near the bottom of the front panel. Set the bypass valves to the bypass function.

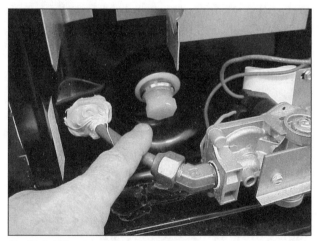

Fig. 21-5; Water heater drain plug location

If your water heater is not equipped with a bypass kit, it's best to install one now. The bypass kit consists of a series of individual water valves that enables the water heater to be totally isolated from the remainder of the plumbing system. The kit is permanently installed at the rear of the water heater and will pay for itself quickly. More on the water heater to follow in the appliance section (Also see Chapter 10).

Fresh Water Storage Tank

Drain the water from the storage tank in the usual manner. Drain valves may be located on the outside of the coach, inside a compartment or underneath the chassis. All storage tanks will have a drain valve somewhere.

Fig. 21-6; Fresh water tank drain

Toilet

Regardless of which type of toilet is found in the RV, it will be necessary to remove any water from it. Usually, it is just a simple matter of operating the flushing mechanism while the water pressure is turned off.

Fig. 21-7; Drain the toilet simply by flushing

Shower Hose

An area that seems to often get overlooked is the shower hose. Even though it is equipped with an anti-siphon backflow preventer, many times water stays trapped in the shower hose. Simply unscrew the handheld showerhead and lower the hose to a point below the faucet attachment point.

Fig. 21-8; Water heater bypass kit

Other Items

Additionally, many RVs are equipped with ice-makers; either as a stand-alone appliance or incorporated into the refrigerator. Be sure to remove the tubing leading into the icemaker and drain any residual water remaining.

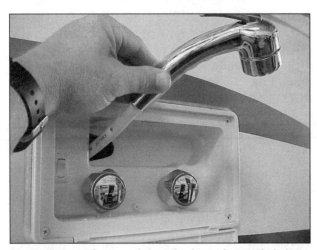

Fig. 21-9; Exterior faucets and showerheads are often overlooked

Also, don't forget exterior faucets or shower-heads. All fresh water components must be protected.

Likewise for those RVs equipped with a washer/dryer combination. Drain the water hoses by disconnecting them at the rear of the washer section.

Depending on the climate in which the RV is located, next choose between using the dry method of winterizing or the wet method.

Dry Method

The dry method requires blowing out all the plumbing lines with compressed air. Accessories are available such as a blowout plug that attaches to the city water inlet to force all the water from the lines. Leave all the faucets and drain valves open and screw the blowout plug into the city inlet and apply no more than 60-psi of compressed air. Do not use gas station-supplied air as many filling station air tanks are contaminated.

Fig. 21-10; Blowout plug air attachment

Once all remnants of water have been eliminated, turn off all the hot and cold faucets. This may be all that is necessary to safely prepare the fresh water system for storage. However, if the RV will be stored in below-freezing climates, the use of the wet method is the recommended choice.

Wet Method

The wet method mandates the use of RV anti-freeze. Caution: Be sure it is RV anti-freeze! Standard automotive anti-freeze contains poisons that will contaminate the fresh water system. There are two basic techniques of adding the anti-freeze to the system:

- Via the water pump
- By backfilling

The water pump method involves filling the fresh water storage tank with the appropriate amount of anti-freeze (approximately two gallons or more depending on the size of the RV), and then simply pumping it through the entire fresh water plumbing system via the demand water pump.

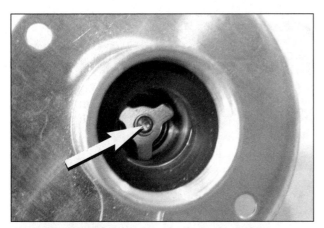

Fig. 21-11; Depress the city water inlet check valve until RV anti-freeze is expelled

Fig. 21-12; Backfill method

After pouring the anti-freeze into the tank, turn on the water pump and open all the hot and cold faucets. Make sure the water heater bypass kit is in the bypass mode.

At the city water inlet, manually depress the spring on the check valve (see arrow above) allowing anti-freeze to be expelled out through the city water inlet, thereby protecting that branch of the cold water piping.

When the colored anti-freeze appears at each faucet, the showerhead(s), the toilet and the city water entry point, close the faucets and turn off the pump. This method ensures anti-freeze is protecting not only the fresh system piping, but the water pump itself.

Kits are available that are comprised of a permanently mounted auxiliary tank just for the anti-freeze and may include a separate pump to distribute the liquid throughout the piping system. Some larger motorhomes may be equipped in this manner from the factory. Other coaches have a tee fitting, a valve and a short section of hose installed between the fresh water tank and the water pump. In this case, the hose can be inserted into an open bottle of RV anti-freeze and pumped through the system.

The backfill method invokes the use of a hand-operated pump that attaches to each individual faucet. Anti-freeze is hand-pumped directly from the container into the system. This method takes longer, but can be just as effective, especially on smaller campers and travel trailers.

By either manner, the goal is to protect the water lines from freezing by having them filled with RV anti-freeze.

Waste System

P Traps

The P traps probably have anti-freeze in them already, but to be sure, pour another 1/4-cup down the drain at the kitchen and lavatory sink and also in the shower/tub drain.

Holding Tanks

Flush and clean all holding tanks. Many after-market products make this undesirable task a little easier. Water hose attachments, like the one pictured, can be inserted into the holding tank through the toilet. This one employs a swivel head that revolves as water pressure is delivered through the hose. The spray action reaches all areas of the holding tank. Others are permanently installed into the sides of the holding tanks.

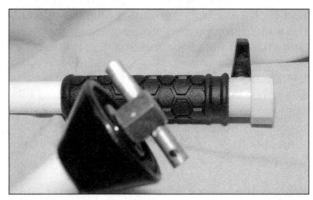

Fig. 21-13; Holding tank water hose attachment

For the best in holding tank cleanliness, contact All Pro Water-Flow (www.allprowaterflow.com) to find its closest dealer. The All Pro process is quite effective and thoroughly cleans the insides of both the black and gray holding tanks by injecting clean water at about 6,000 pounds per square inch (psi).

After cleaning, drain each tank and close the termination valves completely. If the valves are sticking or are hard to slide, disassemble them and apply a light coating of Dow 111 grease to both sides of the blade to ensure smooth operation come spring.

Fig. 21-14; Termination valve disassembled

Be sure a mixture of water and RV anti-freeze covers the entire bottom area of each holding tank.

Liquid Propane System

Most of the emphasis will be placed on the four liquid propane (LP) burning appliances during the winterizing process, but there are a few tasks that relate to the LP system in a general sense.

LP Storage Container
The coach may have a permanently mounted LP tank located under the coach, or it may have twin upright cylinders, such as those found on the tongue of most travel trailers. In either case, make sure the service valve is turned off completely.

Remove the POL or ACME Type I fitting(s) and cover them with tape to prevent dust, dirt or

Fig. 21-15; Remove DOT cylinders and store separately if possible

critters from inhabiting the lines. If the RV is equipped with removable DOT cylinders, it is best to completely remove and store them in a clean and dry location — never inside the RV.

Next, clean and cover the LP regulator. This prevents moisture from freezing inside the body of the regulator and keeps dirt out. Finally, if an electronic LP leak detector is in the system, be sure to disconnect it at this time. Now, focus on the individual appliances.

Appliances

Water Heater
Aside from adding the bypass kit, make sure that the water heater is turned off completely. Now is the time to totally flush out any mineral deposits that may have accumulated at the bottom of the water heater tank. Follow the procedures outlined in Chapter 10 – Water Heaters.

In harsh dusty/windy climates it may be advisable to cut out a cardboard insert to fit inside the fold-down door of the water heater. It can simply be taped in place and the cover latched. This will help minimize the gathering of dirt, dust and debris at the burner area. Before taping in place, place a couple of moth balls on the shelf near the burner assembly just behind the fold-down door.

Furnace
Turn the thermostat completely off. If the furnace is equipped with a manual LP valve located outside the furnace enclosure, turn it off also. Use tape or aluminum foil to cover the intake

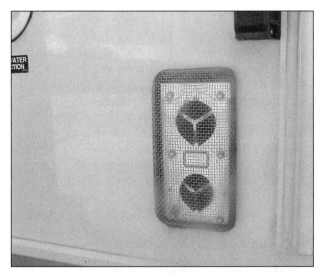

Fig. 21-16; A protective screen should only be used during storage

and exhaust vents to prevent wasps or other critters from entering. Blue painter's tape works well for this task.

An alternative is to install a protective screen over the intake/exhaust assembly such as the one pictured above. However, it is recommended to remove this screen prior to placing the furnace back into operation. Though it looks unobtrusive enough, it may restrict the fresh air flow needed by the furnace during operation. Be safe and remove the screen before lighting the furnace.

Refrigerator

Clean and dry the inside of the refrigerator after turning it off completely. Prop open the doors slightly. Most units have pre-existing latches that permit this. Outside, at the rear of the refrigerator, cut a cardboard insert for the access door, as was done for the water heater. Tape this inside the access panel to keep excess dust and debris out.

Up on the roof, check the condition of the screening material underneath the refrigerator roof vent. If not already present or damaged, it is a good idea to install wire mesh under the roof vent cover of the refrigerator. Birds and wasps love to build their nests on top of the condenser coils located at the back of the refrigerator and this presents a fire hazard.

Range

Not much effort needed here. Just make sure the cooktop and oven are turned off completely and that they are clean and dry. The range is the only appliance that is not vented directly to the exterior, therefore, there are no vents to cover or tape.

Electrical System

The focus here will be at the power source since most electrical devices seldom require individual preparation for storing or winterizing.

12-Volt DC System

Disconnect all batteries in the direct current (DC) system. If possible, remove each battery and store them in a cool, clean and dry place for the winter. Take the time to fully charge each battery. This is especially true if the batteries will be left in the RV. If the batteries are wet cell flooded batteries, check the level of the electrolyte and fill accordingly. It is imperative that they be fully charged after adding water. Charging the batteries will mix the electrolyte solution, thereby decreasing the chance of freezing. If the coach is stored for an extended length of time, it will be necessary to periodically recharge the batteries. All lead acid batteries will self-discharge over time.

If the batteries must remain in the RV, disconnect the negative cables for all batteries, thereby isolating them completely from the DC circuits. Do not overlook the many dry cell batteries common to most RVs. It is best to remove them

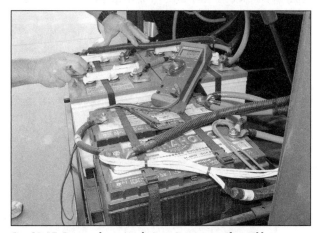

Fig. 21-17; Remove batteries during winterization if possible

also. Dry cell batteries are commonly found in:

- Digital clocks
- Smoke alarms
- Carbon monoxide alarms
- Flashlights
- Refrigerator interior lamps
- Auxiliary fans

120-Volt AC System

Minimal effort at the alternating current (AC) system will ensure a safe storage period. First, turn off all the breakers at the panelboard distribution box.

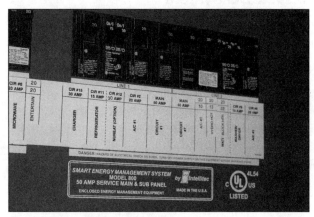

Fig. 21-18; Turn off all circuit breakers

Some boxes are located in overhead compartments, while others may be combined with the DC power converter and located at the floor level or inside a cabinet.

As a safeguard against rogue lightning strikes and transient electrical maladies, unplug any 120-volt

Fig. 21-19; Unplugged RV refrigerator

device that is plugged into a receptacle such as the microwave, refrigerator, televisions and entertainment centers, etc. This way a lightning strike cannot damage the components via the neutral wire in the circuit. The neutral wire, remember, is not interrupted by a circuit breaker.

Finally, cover the plug end of the shoreline cord with a plastic baggie and secure it with a rubber band to minimize water intrusion and to help keep the contacts from excessive oxidation.

If the coach is equipped with a generator, thoroughly clean the exterior prior to storage. As done with the vents to the appliances, cover the exhaust pipe of the generator with foil or tape to keep wasps from building nests in there.

Miscellaneous Areas

Roof Area

Prior to winterizing make sure the roof is clean and free from debris. Now is the perfect time to check the sealant around each roof vent, air conditioner, roof seam, etc. Pay special attention along the edges and across the front and rear caps. Reseal if necessary before winter sets in.

A cover for the roof air conditioner is also recommended. This is the best way to keep dirt and critters from entering, as well as to protect the condenser fins from flying debris. Be sure it is made from a breathable fabric. Solid vinyl covers can trap moisture.

If you are expecting a lot of snow, periodically have the accumulation removed from the roof of the RV during the storage time.

Windows/Doors

Check the sealant around each and reseal if necessary. From the inside, cover glass sections with foil or a protective layering of thin plastic. Even in the winter, it is possible that the sun's rays may fade upholstery and fabrics.

Slide-Outs

Fully extend each slideout room and inspect the rubber seals around the opening in the side of the RV as well as the seals positioned on the slide unit itself. If cuts, gaps or other damage is

Fig. 21-20; Must-have slideout products

Fig. 21-21; A clean slide mechanism

Fig. 21-22; Inspect all slideout cables and hoses

Fig. 21-23; Carefully check LP hoses attached to slideouts

found, be sure to rectify them now before storing the RV.

Clean and treat all rubber seals on the slideouts with Protect All's Slideout Rubber Seal Treatment. This protective foam will preserve the rubber gaskets and seals through the harshest of winters, wet or dry.

Carefully inspect any exposed slideout mechanism components. Be sure they are clean and free from dirt, grit and road grime. Lightly lube all metallic portions with Protect All's Slideout Dry Lube Treatment. Avoid using WD-40 or other products that have a predisposition to attract dirt and dust particles.

Check other ancillary components attached underneath the slideouts such as electrical

harnesses, LP hoses or cable raceways as pictured (Fig. 21-22, 21-23). Secure any loose items found.

Finally, retract all the slideouts and disarm the system. It is not recommend store the RV with the slideouts extended. Keeping them in the travel position over the winter will keep dirt, dust and debris from entering the RV. If the slideout system is hydraulically operated, be sure the reservoir is filled to the proper level.

Tires
Inspect each tire and thoroughly clean it with an approved product. Take the weight off the tires by placing the RV on jack stands when possible. If a motorhome is equipped with HWH (www. hwh.com) hydraulic levelers, it is permissible to extend the levelers to relieve the weight from the tires.

If it is not possible to remove the weight from the tires, periodically move the coach during its storage time to eliminate any flat spots that

Fig. 21-24; Move the RV periodically to avoid flat spots on the tires

Fig. 21-25; Verify the protection level of the engine anti-freeze solution

may develop from being in the same position for an extended period. Cover the tires to protect them from the damaging ultraviolet (UV) rays of the sun.

Always store the RV fairly level with perhaps a slight lean to one side to help drain any water that may gather during rainstorms.

Awnings

Be sure they are clean and dry before retracting each awning on the RV. Eliminating moisture is a key element to minimizing mold and mildew growth.

Undercarriage

Inspect under the RV for any openings around drain pipes, LP lines or electrical wiring harnesses. Rodent-proof the underside of the RV by plugging even the smallest of cracks or space. Rats and mice can squeeze through unbelievably small holes. Use Eternabond or aluminum plates to eliminate such openings.

Motorhome Considerations

Although most of the aforementioned procedures apply to virtually all types of RVs, the motorhome has a few additional areas that need to be addressed.

First and foremost, check the strength of the coolant in the radiator. It may be necessary to flush the radiator and add a stronger solution of anti-freeze for the expected climate. Do not take

any chances in this area. It is much better being protected for a far lower temperature than to short change the solution strength.

Also, be sure all the liquid levels in the motorhome are at the correct operating levels. Besides the radiator coolant, check the following:

- Engine oil
- Transmission fluid
- Differential gear oil
- Brake fluid
- Power steering fluid
- Slideout/levelers reservoir
- Windshield washer
- Fuel tanks

Topping off the fuel tanks will reduce the space for moisture to accumulate. Add a fuel stabilizer if recommended by that engine maker. Drain or replace all fuel filters in the system. Filters trap moisture, which subsequently may freeze if old filters are left in place over a harsh winter.

Diesel owners, please refer to the specific chassis owner's manual for the necessary precautions.

One additional thought for any RV is to invest in a total coach cover. Custom covers are available that will completely cover the RV from top to bottom, front to rear. Special measurements are taken to allow for mirrors, air conditioners, TV antennae, satellite receiver, etc. This method is very effective for protecting the exterior finish from even the harshest of winters or the ravages of the hottest desert climates during temporary

Winterizing and Storage Checklist

(Check off each item as completed)

Fresh Water System	Waste Water Systems	LP System
❏ Drain hot/cold low point drain lines	❏ Flush & clean holding tanks	❏ All appliances turned off
❏ Flush & drain water heater	❏ Inspect termination valves	❏ Service valve(s) off
❏ Bypass water heater	❏ Clean/lube termination valves	❏ Plug/cap service outlet
❏ Drain fresh water tank	❏ Anti-freeze in P traps	❏ Cover LP regulator
❏ Empty toilet valve	❏ Anti-freeze in holding tanks	❏ Other:
❏ Drain shower hose	❏ Other:	**Furnace**
❏ Drain exterior faucets/showerhead	**Water Heater**	❏ Thermostat turned off
❏ Drain washer connection	❏ Verify in bypass mode	❏ Furnace completely off
❏ Drain icemaker tubing	❏ Water heater completely off	❏ Cover intake/exhaust vents
❏ Blow out with compressed air (or)	❏ Cover opening with cardboard	❏ Other:
❏ Add RV anti-freeze to fresh tank	❏ Electric element off	**Batteries**
❏ Pump anti-freeze throughout system	❏ Other:	❏ Disconnect all batteries
❏ Other:	**Range**	❏ Check electrolyte level
Refrigerator	❏ Range completely off	❏ Fully charge all batteries
❏ Refrigerator completely off	❏ Clean & dry	❏ Remove & store separately
❏ Clean & dry inside	❏ Other:	❏ Remove dry cell batteries
❏ Block doors open	**120-volt AC System**	❏ Other:
❏ Baking soda placed inside	❏ Circuit breakers switched off	**Roof Area**
❏ Cover opening with cardboard	❏ Unplug appliances & devices	❏ Inspect all components
❏ Check screening on roof vent	❏ Cover shoreline plug	❏ Check all sealants
❏ Other:	❏ Other:	❏ Reseal as necessary
Generator	**Tires**	❏ Roof vents closed
❏ Clean & dry	❏ Remove weight if possible	❏ Other:
❏ Drain fuel filter	❏ Apply UV/ozone protectant	**Doors/Windows/Compartments**
❏ Block tail pipe opening	❏ Cover tires	❏ Check all sealants
❏ Other:	❏ Other:	❏ Reseal as necessary
Roof Air Conditioner(s)	**Motorhome Specifics**	❏ Other:
❏ Air conditioners completely off	❏ Test engine coolant strength	**Slideouts**
❏ Inspect condenser for damage	❏ Top off fuel tanks	❏ Inspect all rubber seals
❏ Install cover(s)	❏ Verify all liquid levels	❏ Clean and treat all rubber seals
❏ Other:	❏ Other:	❏ Lube slideout mechanisms
Miscellaneous		❏ Inspect harnesses/cables
Awnings	**Undercarriage**	❏ Retract and disarm rooms
❏ Clean & dry	❏ Inspect completely	❏ Top off reservoir (if hydraulic)
❏ Lube mechanical components	❏ Plug holes & gaps	❏ Other:
Date:	Performed by:	Notes:

periods of non-use. The cover must be breathable and have precautions to guard against abrasion with the RV's exterior surfaces.

Finally, be sure to read the fine print in the owner's manual for your specific RV! Always follow the manufacturer's instructions, even if they contradict sections in this chapter. After all, it's their coach!

Be sure to repair any discrepancies found during this preparation. Doing so now will eliminate those conditions that can only worsen over a long period of downtime. Plus it will make for an easier Spring Shakedown at the start of the next RVing season.

A detailed DVD showing many of the winterizing procedures is available directly from the author or through RVIA:

http://www.rvdoctor.com/dvd.html

Chapter 22

Spring Shakedown

Overview

After each period of non-use, regardless if the RV was winterized, stored in the backyard or kept in a closed garage, each coach must be given a thorough once-over to get it ready for that next trip or for the upcoming camping season. Differing circumstances abound for different RVers and RVs, but by and large, every owner must at some point in time go through the yearly ritual of what is termed the spring shakedown.

Keep in mind these procedures can be performed at any time. It is not necessarily tied to spring. Simply stated, it is that time of year we clear out the cobwebs, dust off the road maps, pack some groceries, fill up with fuel and hit the road.

When the spring shakedown is viewed from a systematic approach; inspecting each major component, system by system, there is assurance that nothing will fall through the cracks. The goal is to be back on the road safely enjoying the finer points of RVing. Ready to go?

Just as it was done prior to storage, the first step in preparing for each new camping season is to thoroughly wash the RV. A clean coach puts everything in a fresh light.

Remove any window or windshield covering that may have been installed during the winterizing process and open all the windows fully.

Fig. 22-1; Remove all window coverings and air out the RV

This will help air out the coach as you go through the process of checking the rest of the systems and components. An air freshener may help get rid of that stale air that has accumulated during the closed-up period.

Exterior Inspection

If discrepancies are found during the exterior inspection, be sure to take care of them immediately. Items put off are likely to be forgotten. The last thing you want to encounter is a crisis repair on your first trip of the season!

Roof

Everything should be in fairly good order on the roof if the advice was followed in the preceding chapter. However, now is the time to double-check all the roof seams and the sealant around all roof components. Take your time and look closely.

Fig. 22-2; Questionable roof seam

Windows, Doors and Compartment Bays

Next, check the operation of all windows, doors and storage compartments, including locking doors for the fuel fill and generator if so equipped. Lubricate all moving parts and locking mechanisms.

Fig. 22-3; Faulty window sealant

Fig. 22-5; Battery electrolyte level check

Check the sealant around all windows and doors. During storage, it's not uncommon to find that some sealants have dried out or become distorted. This is especially true in warmer climates. Notice anything wrong with this window?

Awnings

Now is the time to fully extend each awning and lubricate all the moving parts. While each awning is extended, search for any pinholes that may have developed. You'll want to repair them now, before you take off on that first excursion. Awning repair kits are available at any well-stocked RV accessory store or on-line. You'll need to know exactly what type of material the canopy is made of, however.

Fig. 22-4; Inspect all awnings

12-Volt DC System

Reinstall the batteries if they were removed for the winter. Make sure all the contacts and terminals are tight, clean and dry.

After the batteries are in place and secured, check the electrolyte level. It is quite possible the fluid has diminished during the storage period. Add water if necessary and charge the batteries fully. (See Chapter 4)

Go through the entire RV and turn on the various 12-volt components to ensure the batteries are indeed powering the RV and that everything works so far.

Don't forget to reinstall the dry cell batteries in the smoke alarm, carbon monoxide alarm, etc. Now is the perfect time to verify that all the safety items in the RV are operating properly. Check the charge level of all fire extinguishers.

120-Volt AC System

Remove the shoreline cord from the plastic baggie and inspect the prongs for oxidation. Brighten the prongs with fine sandpaper or steel wool.

Before plugging in, it's a good idea to measure the voltage and check the polarity at the receptacle you'll be using. Plug the shoreline cord into an appropriate service receptacle only if the volt-

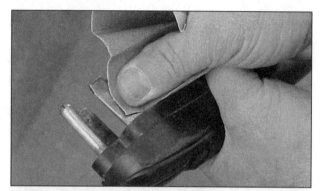

Fig. 22-6; Brighten the shoreline cord contacts

Fig. 22-7; Check all the 120-volt receptacles

Fig. 22-8; Make sure the GFCI is working properly

age and polarity check correctly. The same holds true as you begin your travels; always verify the campground voltage and polarity at all sites before plugging in.

Now go through the RV and plug in all the components and appliances that were unplugged last fall. Turn on all the circuit breakers. An audible click may be heard as the relay in the converter closes. If you have a charging converter, (most are), measure the DC voltage at the battery bank to verify the voltage increases when the converter is powered up.

Test the ground fault circuit interrupter (GFCI) located at or near the lavatory sink or at the panelboard distribution box. Make sure it trips and fully resets. Even though it may click, snap or make some audible noise, that in itself, is no guarantee the GFCI is making and breaking the electrical contact. To be absolutely sure, plug the polarity tester into the bathroom receptacle and the exterior receptacle while performing the

GFCI tests. The exterior and bathroom receptacles are two that must be protected by the GFCI. If the circuit is not broken when the GFCI test button is pushed, there is no GFCI protection and a replacement or at least further troubleshooting is necessary. Next, move over to the fresh water system.

Fresh Water System

If you employed the dry method of winterizing, begin by adding a few gallons of fresh water to the water tank. If you used the wet method, start by draining the anti-freeze in the tank and throughout the system. RV anti-freeze can be captured and used again, so it may be prudent to collect it at the tank drain as well as at the hot and cold low point drains.

Add fresh water to the tank then drain and refill it until all remnants of RV anti-freeze are gone.

Fig. 22-9; Strainer attached at water pump

Fill and flush with fresh water until you are satisfied with the smell and taste of the fresh water.

Next, clean or replace any filter or strainer installed in the fresh water system. Some may be connected to the water pump (see arrow in Fig. 22-9) or installed anywhere in-line between the tank and the pump.

After the water tank has been filled, remove the water heater from by-pass so that fresh water can be pumped through all the hot and cold faucets. Then turn on the water pump, open all the faucets and begin pumping fresh water throughout the system.

At the water heater, open the P&T relief valve (see arrow below) to aid in filling. Once water begins gushing from the relief valve, close the lever. When water is flowing swiftly from every faucet, close them all. It may take a few minutes of running the water to rid the entire piping system of the anti-freeze and to fill the water heater. Be sure to flush the toilet a couple of times as well.

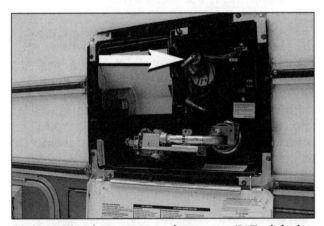

Fig. 22-10; Water heater pressure and temperature (P&T) relief valve

If the RV is equipped with exterior faucets or a showerhead, don't forget to run fresh water through them as well. The same for icemakers and the washer/dryer combination. Every component in the fresh water system should be checked for proper operation.

Now, connect the fresh water hose to the city water connection and turn off the water pump. With city pressure applied, inspect in, under and

around all water piping in the RV. Look for any leaks that may have developed during the off-season. If no leaks are evident, disconnect the city water pressure.

Open the water heater P&T relief valve one last time and leave it open until water stops dripping, then close it. This ensures there is expansion space on top of the water inside the tank. The final step is to chlorinate the fresh water system. Refer to Chapter 6, Page 94 for those detailed procedures.

Waste Water System

Drain the fresh water from each holding tank that has accumulated during the preliminary check of the fresh system. Now is the time to check the operation of the termination or dump valves. Most can be removed, disassembled and lubed if necessary. If lubed during the winterizing procedures, they will probably be just fine now.

Plug each sink and fill with water, then remove the drain plugs to ensure the vent piping is in good order. If either sink drains slowly, further troubleshooting of the venting system may be needed. Verify the toilet operates properly.

Next, treat the holding tanks for odor control and waste degradation. In the past, formaldehyde-based chemicals used as a deodorant seemed to work best. However, as technology has progressed and the environmental dangers of formaldehyde came to be understood, other

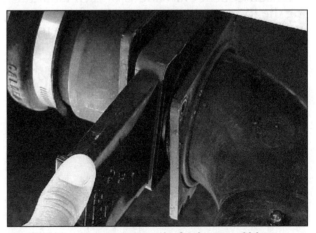

Fig. 22-11; Removing termination valve for cleaning and lubing

Fig. 22-12; RM Tank Care holding tank treatment

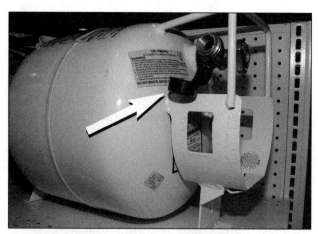

Fig. 22-13; Acme valve cap on a horizontal DOT cylinder

options became a reality. In fact, formaldehyde and other alcohol-based chemicals are no longer recommended for use in either holding tank. Most RV campgrounds and state parks now prohibit the dumping of formaldehyde-laced holding tanks into their waste systems.

The safest way to treat the holding tanks and to eliminate odors is to use a non-chemical, enzyme-based product that contains live bacteria. The live bacteria actually digest the odor-causing molecules, which helps to eliminate the odor and break down the solid waste. Add four or five ounces of a product called RM Tank Care, produced by Tri Synergy (www.trisyn.com), along with enough fresh water to cover just the bottom of each tank. After subsequent evacuations of each tank during the RVing season, add another four or five ounces. This will ensure the tanks will remain fresh and free of odors, and that you are doing your part to protect the environment.

Inspect the sewer hose and check for pinhole leaks. Also, check all the seals on the hose adapters and sewer cap. Start the season right by not having messy sewer leaks.

Liquid Propane System

Carefully inspect the DOT cylinders or the permanently mounted horizontal ASME tank. If

any scratches or nicks are noticed that have developed into rust, use a wire brush and some touch-up paint now to eliminate potential problems. If a cap or plug was previously installed, remove it from the service valve now (see arrow above). If one was not used, quickly open and close the service valve allowing the burst of LP pressure to blow away any contaminates that may have accumulated in the throat of the unprotected service valve.

Now connect the regulator to the system, open the service valve and leak test the POL or ACME fitting. Many RV accessory stores carry a leak detector solution that can be brushed onto any LP fitting. However, a solution can be mixed using common liquid soap detergent and water and stored in a spray bottle for those hard-to-get-to fittings in and under the coach (avoid using detergents containing ammonia or

Fig. 22-14; Examine the LP containers and connections

chlorine products). A child's bubble blowing solution works well also.

Before moving on to the individual appliances, remove the tape or foil previously applied to the furnace intake and exhaust vents as well as the cardboard pieces at the water heater and refrigerator access doors/vent.

Inspect and clean each of the four LP burning appliances as needed. Please refer to the individual chapters for specific instructions on the water heater, refrigerator, range and furnace. Those chapters detail the step-by-step procedures for performing the yearly cleaning and maintenance tasks necessary for safe, trouble-free operation. Eventually though, it will be necessary to operate each appliance during the spring shakedown, before taking off on that first trip.

An important step prior to lighting the appliances is to rid the system of air. Light a stove burner and simply let it burn while the other appliances are lit. Prior to lighting the other three appliances, however, three things to verify are:

- Foil or tape is removed from the furnace vents
- Cardboard is removed from refrigerator and the refrigerator is comfortably level
- Cardboard is removed from water heater, and water heater is filled with water

Now light the remaining three appliances. After cycling each appliance through its sequence of

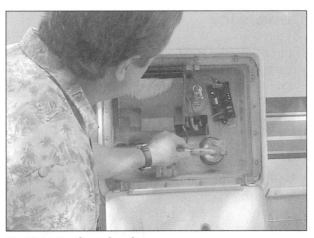

Fig. 22-16; Test fire each appliance

operation, turn them all off and verify that the LP pressure is set correctly. Refer to the details for properly setting the LP regulator operating line pressure in Chapter 8. The RV must be taken to a service facility at least once a camping system to have this step performed if a manometer is not in your tool kit. Finally, activate the LP leak detection device.

Roof Air Conditioner

Remove the cover and inspect the condenser fins for any damage that may have incurred during storage. Clean or replace the return air filters. Refer to the owner's manual for your particular brand and model of air conditioner. Most filters are accessible from inside the RV. Cycle each air conditioner through a cooling cycle. Check for unusual noises or vibrations.

Fig. 22-15; Inspect all burner assemblies before lighting

Fig. 22-17; Clean or replace the A/C filter

Generator

If the RV is equipped with a generator, change the oil according to the manufacturer's recommendation. Replace all appropriate filters such as:

- Oil filter
- Air filter element
- Fuel filter

Clean and lube the throttle linkage at all the pivot points. Manually move the governor arm to ensure there is no binding. Log the hours on the hour meter. Check it against the maintenance chart for other periodic maintenance that may be due.

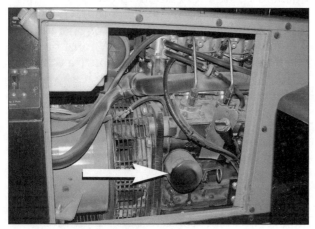

Fig. 22-18; Generator oil filter

Clean and reinstall the spark plugs. Remove the tape from the exhaust pipe. Wipe the entire unit down with a damp rag. Make sure the generator compartment is clean.

Test fire the unit. Remember, it may be a little rusty from sitting so long. Once the generator has started and is running smoothly, allow it to power the coach. This happens normally in one of three ways:

- Manually plug the shoreline into a 30-amp receptacle inside the RV
- Manually throw a switch or manipulate a breaker
- An automatic switching device makes the connection

Once connected, turn on a roof air conditioner

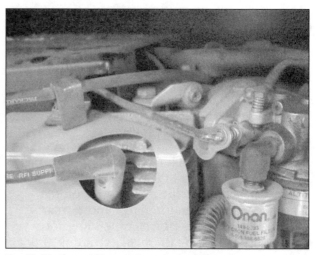

Fig. 22-19; Clean and inspect the generator linkages

(or both if so equipped) to put a larger load on the generator. Let it run for a minimum of 30 minutes. Turn off the air conditioners before shutting down the generator. Always remove all loads before starting and stopping any RV generator.

Slideouts

Enable all the individual slideout rooms; extend and carefully inspect each one. Look for damaged seals or weather-stripping. Run each room in and out and observe the full travel of movement. Be sure each room operates properly. If hydraulically powered, verify the proper fluid level in the reservoir after all rooms have been retracted. If equipped with a topper awning, be

Fig. 22-20; Verify all slideouts operate properly

sure it is operating correctly and the canopy is clean and dry.

Finally, lubricate each slide mechanism; be sure to use a dry lube.

Undercarriage

Hopefully the vehicle is in a location that is suitable for crawling underneath and inspecting the undercarriage. If the coach was stored in a grassy or wooded area, be on the lookout for insects or other choice critters that love to hide and maybe hibernate under the cozy confines of a dormant RV.

While under the coach, look for any obvious signs of damage or discrepancy. Loose wires, twigs, rocks, etc. are items that may need to be addressed prior to moving the RV. Take a close look.

Fig. 22-21; Inspect the undercarriage for damage or abnormalities

Motorhome Considerations

Check all the fluid levels on the motorhome chassis. Those that are typical to most gasoline powered chassis include:

- Engine oil
- Transmission fluid
- Rear axle differential oil
- Power steering fluid
- Brake fluid
- Radiator coolant
- Battery electrolyte
- Windshield washer fluid
- Fuel tanks
- Leveling system reservoir

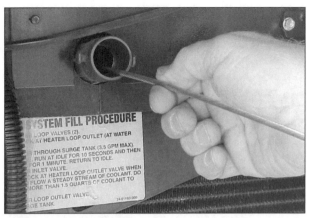

Fig. 22-22; Check all fluid levels

Fig. 22-23; Check all fluid levels

(Diesel coach owners, follow the manufacturer's recommendations in the owner's manual for your particular chassis.)

Check the air cleaner element and test-fire the engine. Check the mileage to see if it is time for a tune-up or a brake inspection. Next, check the operation of all running lamps, turn signals, headlamps, etc., as well as antennas, entry steps and all other accessories. Inspect and test the automatic levelers if so equipped. Be sure the automatic setting for the leveling system conforms to the needs of the refrigerator.

Finally, take the motorhome on a short road test; be aware of strange noises, vibrations and issues with steering and handling. Be sure the chassis is ready to go in every aspect.

Travel Trailer Considerations

Inspect the electric brakes. It is recommended that one side of an axle and the opposite side of

Fig. 22-24; Inspect/adjust electric brakes

another axle be inspected at least annually. The spring shakedown is just as good a time as any for this inspection. In the case of a triple axle trailer (as pictured above), inspect at least one brake assembly on each axle.

Refer to Chapter 15 for all the details regarding inspecting, cleaning, adjusting and maintaining electric brake components. Be sure to perform the break-away switch test also.

Verify all running lamps are operable as well as all mechanical accessories like TV antennas, entry steps, roof vents, stabilizers, etc.

If all the above checks out, next clean and inspect all hitch components. Lubricate the hitch ball and connect the RV to the tow vehicle. Test and adjust the brake controller per the manufacturer's specification. Note: it will be necessary to re-adjust the controller once the trailer is fully loaded for travel.

Hitch up and take the trailer on a short test run and be alert to any noises, vibrations or sway issues that need to be addressed. Now's the time to take care of them!

Miscellaneous Considerations

If a small car is towed behind a motorhome, be sure to check the electrical wiring between those two units and that the auxiliary braking system is set up correctly.

Check the air pressure in all the tires. Do not overlook the spare if there is one. Keep in mind the only way to know exactly how much air to squirt into each tire is by having the RV weighed. Please review Chapter 16 for all the details.

Note: a detailed DVD showing many of the spring shakedown procedures is available directly from the author or through RVIA. Please visit:

http://www.rvdoctor.com/dvd.html

One final step is to review the owner's manual to verify nothing was left out of the spring shakedown process. Only when you are thoroughly satisfied nothing is amiss, load up and head out on that much needed vacation or weekend getaway.

Spring Shakedown Checklist

(Check off each item as completed)

Windows & Vents	Roof Area	Batteries
❑ Remove coverings or shades	❑ Inspect all sealants	❑ Reinstall or reconnect all batteries
❑ Check operation	❑ Reseal as necessary	❑ Clean & tighten all terminals
❑ Open all windows & vents	❑ Other:	❑ Check electrolyte level
❑ Lubricate as necessary	**Fresh Water System**	❑ Fully charge each battery
❑ Other:	❑ Drain & capture anti-freeze	❑ Operate all 12-volt components
Awnings	❑ Clean/replace pump strainer	❑ Other:
❑ Operate all awnings	❑ Flush & fill fresh water tank	**Doors/Compartments**
❑ Lube mechanical components	❑ Remove water heater from bypass	❑ Check all sealants
❑ Inspect for damage or pinholes	❑ Pump water throughout system	❑ Lube mechanical components
❑ Other:	❑ Check all faucets & connections	❑ Lube locks
120-volt AC System	❑ Connect city water hose	❑ Other:
❑ Brighten shoreline cord contacts	❑ Check system for leaks	**Waste Water Systems**
❑ Plug in appliances & devices	❑ Chlorinate fresh water system	❑ Drain holding tanks
❑ Verify voltage & polarity	❑ Other:	❑ Inspect termination valves
❑ Plug RV into shore power	**Water Heater**	❑ Lube valves if necessary
❑ Switch circuit breakers on	❑ Remove cardboard covering	❑ Check vent operation
❑ Verify converter output	❑ Blow out burner area	❑ Verify toilet operation
❑ Test GFCI	❑ Verify filled with water	❑ Treat holding tanks
❑ Check all receptacles	❑ Replenish expansion space	❑ Inspect sewer hose
❑ Other:	❑ Test fire - have serviced if necessary	❑ Inspect sewer cap seal
LP System	❑ Other:	❑ Other
❑ Inspect LP container(s)	**Range**	**Refrigerator**
❑ Clean & install LP regulator	❑ Clean & test fire cooktop & oven	❑ Remove cardboard covering
❑ Open service valve	❑ Other:	❑ Blow out burner area
❑ Bubble test fitting	**Roof Air Conditioner(s)**	❑ Verify levelness
❑ Burn air from system	❑ Remove covers	❑ Test fire - have serviced if necessary
❑ Set LP delivery pressure	❑ Inspect/straighten condenser fins	❑ Other:
❑ Leak test entire system	❑ Clean/replace filters	**Furnace**
❑ Activate LP leak detector	❑ Cycle each air conditioner	❑ Remove cover from intake/exhaust
❑ Other:	❑ Other:	❑ Clean thermostat contacts if possible
Generator	**Slideouts**	❑ Test fire - have serviced if necessary
❑ Remove tail pipe blockage	❑ Enable & extend each room	❑ Other:
❑ Change oil	❑ Check operation in & out	**Undercarriage Inspection**
❑ Replace all filters	❑ Inspect all rubber seals	❑ Check for plumbing leaks
❑ Lube pivot linkages	❑ Lube slideout mechanisms	❑ Check for damage
❑ Clean spark plugs	❑ Verify fluid level (if hydraulic)	❑ Tie up loose wires
❑ Test fire	❑ Inspect & clean roof section	❑ Plug any holes or cracks
❑ Other:	❑ Other:	❑ Other:

Continue on next page

Spring Shakedown Checklist (continued)

(Check off each item as completed)

Motorhome Specifics	Travel Trailer Specifics	Miscellaneous
❏ Check all fluid levels	❏ Inspect/adjust electric brakes	❏ Verify operation of all running lamps
❏ Check air cleaner element	❏ Pack wheel bearings if necessary	❏ Check all accessories & running gear
❏ Test fire engine	❏ Clean/inspect/lube hitch components	❏ Check all safety devices
❏ Notate mileage	❏ Check pressure in all tires	❏ Fire extinguisher
❏ Check pressure in all tires	❏ Adjust brake controller	❏ CO monitor
❏ Check owner's manual	❏ Check owner's manual	❏ Smoke detector
❏ Test drive	❏ Test drive	❏ LP leak detector
❏ Other:	❏ Other:	❏ Other:

Date: Performed by:

Discrepancies

Plumbing Systems	Electrical Systems	LP System/Appliances
Date rectified:	**Date rectified:**	**Date rectified:**
Performed by:	**Performed by:**	**Performed by:**

Notes:

Spare Parts Kit

Overview

Throughout this handbook, there have been mentions of various spare parts recommended to carry aboard the RV during travel. Obviously, space limitations and common sense should prevail when considering the extent of the spare parts kit. The optimum, of course, would be to have one of everything on hand, just in case it is rendered faulty, but that is far from the intended purpose of a viable spare parts kit.

The purpose for carrying a few spare components is two-fold. First, it is intended to minimize, or totally eliminate any downtime encountered while traveling. Second, repair dollars can be decreased simply by having some key parts on hand, regardless if you install them or a service technician installs them.

By performing the preventive maintenance tasks described in the RV Owner's Handbook, it is hoped the spare parts kit will never even need to be unpacked. But just knowing the required part is on hand is reassuring, especially when traveling off the beaten path. Who knows, it may even be possible to help out a stranded fellow RVer with a crucial part from the kit. It is just simply a cost-effective investment, an insurance policy, if you will.

No attempt will be made to list spare components for the chassis portion of motorhomes or the automotive portion of any tow vehicle. Obviously, items like spare belts or a lower radiator hose would be beneficial, but it would transcend the scope of this chapter to list chassis components here.

This chapter will list, system by system, those components that will be helpful in the event of a fault within that system. They may or may not apply to all exact situations. The utility of such a spare parts kit is that it can be customized for any RV; you may even think of other items you should carry along. Here, then, are some recommendations to ponder.

Electrical System

Generator Tune-Up Kit

If the RV is equipped with an on-board generator, it is advisable to carry a generator tune-up kit. This kit should contain spare spark plugs, fuel filter, air filter element, oil filter, ignition circuit fuses and a schematic or wiring diagram of the generator. A few feet of flexible rubber fuel hose and assorted hose clamps may also come in handy.

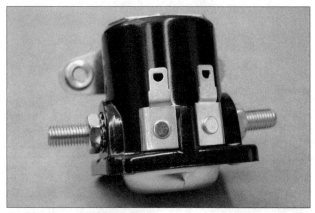

Fig. 23-1; Generator start solenoid

An extended version of the generator tune-up kit would include perhaps a spare start solenoid and a start relay.

12-Volt Fuses

Inspect the 12-volt direct current (DC) fuse box and determine which fuse sizes will be needed. Be sure to check all in-line fuses common to either battery system. Be aware that the automo-

Fig. 23-2; Assorted fuses

tive fuse block may have a different type of fuse altogether. Check the chassis manual if a doubt exists.

12-Volt Circuit Breakers

Some low voltage applications call for a 12-volt automatic resettable circuit breaker instead of a fuse. The electric brake controller circuit is an example. Carry spare 12-volt breakers for the sizes needed.

Fig. 23-3; 12-volt circuit breaker

In-Line Fuse Holders

In case of the necessity for an emergency wiring repair, an in-line fuse holder can be spliced in at any point in the circuit. Carry spares in the kit.

12-Volt Lightbulbs

Though the age of the electronic LED lamp is upon us, many RVs still use the tried and true light bulb for clearance markers, stop lamps, turn signals and assorted interior incandescent lamps. Go through the rig and list each bulb number used in your coach. The bulb number is located on the brass colored base portion of each bulb. This addition to the kit could prevent a moving violation in some states!

Battery Terminals

Carry at least two spare battery terminals. Terminals may become corroded beyond cleaning and will need to be replaced.

Dual Battery Solenoid

Similar looking to the generator start solenoid, yet entirely different, a heavy-duty dual battery

solenoid, (Chapter 4, Fig. 4-21), is commonly used to separate the RV battery bank from the automotive or chassis battery system. Even if your motorhome is equipped with a dual battery isolator, (Chapter 4, Fig. 4-19), a battery solenoid switch can be used in an emergency to keep you on the road.

Dry Cell Batteries

Clocks, smoke alarms, carbon monoxide monitors and flashlights all use dry cell batteries. Keep a couple spares of the needed sizes in the RV refrigerator.

Waste System

Sewer Drain Cap

A sewer drain cap is not a life-threatening component to be without. It certainly will not leave an RVer stranded somewhere should it be lost, but the fact is, some campgrounds are sticklers and rightly so. Some may not allow check-in without a leak-free drain cap in place.

Flange Gasket

Some toilets may be installed with a wax gasket at the flange seal, but the rubber gasket is preferred. The rubber one is easier to store and will not soften or melt during hot summer days. Always replace this seal whenever the toilet is removed for repairs or maintenance.

Fig. 23-4; Toilet flange gasket

Spare Toilet Parts

Toilet parts to consider carrying as spares include a vacuum breaker assembly, spare nuts for the closet bolts or even a spare water inlet

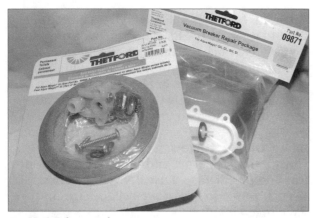

Fig. 23-5; Toilet repair kits

valve. Flush mechanism seals and gaskets are also recommended as an addition to the spare parts kit. Check the parts listing in the owner's manual for specific parts for your toilet.

Holding Tank Patch Kit

If the holding tank is constructed of acrylonitrile-butadiene-styrene (ABS) plastic, it is recommended to carry at least one of these patch kits. They are also useful for patching a leak in any ABS fitting or pipe joint as well; a must when traveling off the beaten path. They are only truly effective on ABS tanks. They may work as a temporary fix on polyethylene or polypropylene tanks, however.

Termination Valves

Nothing is worse than having a holding tank dump valve fail while traveling. Disagreeable as it may be, having a spare valve for each size in the waste system will eliminate unnecessary downtime when traveling. Spares are available for all the common sizes and come complete with new mounting bolts and seals.

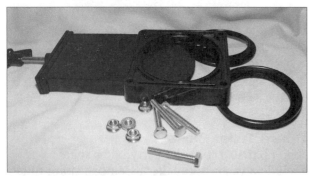

Fig. 23-6; Termination valve kit

Well Nuts

These simple fittings are used in holding tanks and fresh water tanks at the liquid levels that correspond with the monitor panel wiring. As any seasoned RVer will tell you, oftentimes the level probes become fouled which can render a tank inaccurate on the monitor panel. This is especially troublesome with the black water holding tank when moist tissue or waste stick to the probes on the inside of the tank.

Fig. 23-7; Well nuts

Well nuts are installed by simply drilling a clean 3/8-inch hole through the sidewall of the tank an inch or two away from the offending level probe.

Fig. 23-8; Well nuts installed through tank wall

Tightening the well nut facilitates a leak-free installation when pipe sealant is applied to the mounting screw. Attaching the monitor panel wire to the new well nut will quickly bring that level indicator back to accuracy.

Well nuts can be purchased at any well-stocked RV accessory store.

Fresh Water System

Water Pump Strainer

Located between the fresh water tank and the inlet to the pump, (Chapter 22, Fig. 22-9), this strainer protects the pump; it does not purify the water. Oftentimes during manufacture, sawdust, plastic shavings, insulation fragments, wood chips and other debris can fall into any opening in the tank. When this "tank trash" migrates to the water pump, it can damage it. Keeping a spare strainer on hand will keep any

Fig. 23-9; Tank trash

offending particles in the water tank from entering the water pump.

In-Line Check Valve
This simple fitting is available in any number of pipe thread sizes. Most city water inlets, however, will come equipped with 1/2-inch pipe threads. Having a spare check valve in the tool kit will enable you to stay on the road should the one in the city water inlet fail at any time. Be sure to follow the flow designation when installing check valves.

Pressure Regulator
Why bother to carry a spare regulator? Sad to say, some have been known to disappear overnight or when the campsite is vacated for a day trip. Plus, it is always nice to have a loaner on hand to help out a novice RVer who forgot his or hers.

Fig. 23-10; Water pressure regulator

Hose Repair Kit
Male and female ends can be easily repaired without tools with this kit. Every RVer at some time

has flattened an end on the fresh water hose. Having one each of these on hand will insure the water hose will be ready to supply the RV.

Shower Vacuum Breaker
Some vacuum breakers are made of plastic and are therefore prone to breakage. Having a spare vacuum breaker fitting will guarantee no loss of shower facilities if it breaks off at the threads.

Assorted Spare Water Line Fittings
This broad category of assorted fittings is determined by the type and size of the fresh water lines in the RV. Spare nipples, couplings, as well as plugs and caps, should be in the kit. If the toilet needs to be removed, for instance, by plugging the incoming line, other portions of the fresh water system can still be utilized without interruption. Look through the RV and choose those fittings which will be needed the most. PEX repair kits are available at well-stocked RV stores or on-line.

Liquid Propane System

LP Regulator
A liquid propane (LP) regulator is by far the most important spare item to carry during travel. A defective LP regulator can render the RV dead in the water without an alternative plan. Having a spare two-stage regulator has saved many vacations from becoming disasters and has kept many full-timers from becoming temporary motel dwellers. All regulators are preset at the factory, so they can be installed safely

Fig. 23-11; LP pressure regulator

without having to pinpoint the exact pressure. They cannot be installed incorrectly as each end houses a different size pipe thread. Be sure to use an appropriate pipe thread sealant and test the system for leaks whenever any device or component has been replaced in the LP system.

Thermocouples

Having spare thermocouples can be a very inexpensive insurance policy if any of the appliances are pilot models. Universal thermocouples are available that will work on either the water heater or the furnace. The thermocouple used on the refrigerator is a different size thread on the button end. Still, it is recommended to include a spare thermocouple for each of those three appliances. There is no thermocouple associated with the oven or cooktop.

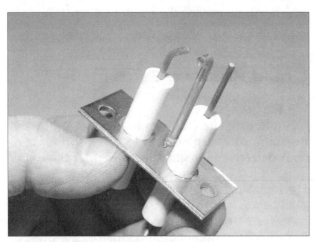

Fig. 23-12; Appliance electrode assembly

Electrode Assemblies

The most common operational component associated with water heater and furnace troubles is the electrode assembly. Oftentimes they become carboned, pitted and corroded beyond the resolve of a simple cleaning. Others become useless if the ceramic insulators are cracked or broken. By carrying an electrode assembly for both the water heater and the furnace, downtimes can be minimized or eliminated in the direct spark ignition (DSI) models of those appliances.

3/8-Inch Flare Plugs/Caps

Easily installed since they require no sealant on the threads, flare plugs and caps are needed whenever an appliance is removed for mainte-

Fig. 23-13; Flare plugs and caps

nance or repair for two main reasons. First of all, a plug or a cap keeps dirt and dust from entering the LP system while the appliance is out of the coach, and second, they are a safeguard in case someone inadvertently turns the LP gas back on. Sometimes an appliance may have to be transported to a service facility for repairs. The flare plug or cap will enable the remaining appliances to be operated while the other one is out being repaired. Some LP systems may be plumbed with 1/2-inch flare fittings, so check first.

There are many other items to consider for inclusion in the spare parts kit such as cabinet latches, a spare sewer hose, LP appliance orifices, etc. Mull over those items that you would not enjoy living without should they become broken or otherwise useless. Add to your spare parts kit accordingly.

Miscellaneous Supplies

Aside from specific components, an assortment of supplies should be carried by the RVer. In order to accommodate the replacement or installation of many items, some supplies are also mandatory. Though certainly not all encompassing, the following list may be considered a recommended list of RV supplies:

- Electrical tape
- Duct tape
- Masking tape
- Putty tape
- Silicone sealant

- Teflon lubricating spray
- Dry graphite lube
- Dow 111 grease
- Bri-Rus Insta-Glas – quickly repairs fiberglass damage
- Pipe thread sealant – for LP and fresh water
- RM Tank Care
- Loc-Tite® thread sealant
- Nylon wire ties – various lengths
- Solderless wire terminals and wire nuts – assorted variety
- ABS patch kit
- ABS cement
- Liquid Roof Sealant
- Rubber Roof patch kit
- Eternabond tape
- Protect All Spray
- Protect All Rubber Seal Treatment
- Protect All Dry Lube Protectant
- Caig DeoxIT – contact cleaner and preservative

By having these supplies on hand, you will be equipped to handle almost any maintenance chore around the RV along with a few simple repairs if necessary.

Master Maintenance Schedules

Overview

Throughout this book, generous detail has been given to specific maintenance procedures for every system and major component found on today's RVs. An attempt has been made to relate to all types of RVs as generically as possible when listing and explaining the various procedures.

As a general guide to help remember the many aspects of owning and operating an RV, this chapter will, in chart form, list many maintenance tasks along with the time intervals at which to perform them. They are presented system-by-system or by broad category. These charts are designed as a memory aide only. Use these reminders and then refer to the specific chapter if more details are needed. Also, refer to the owner's manual that came with the RV for other pertinent information.

Keep in mind not every element may be listed here. Your coach may contain additional equipment or aftermarket products that also need maintenance but are not featured in this handbook. Examples would be a satellite TV system or hydraulic levelers. This master schedule is tailored to the typical RV containing the usual accoutrements.

Please notice that there may be more than one interval noted for any given item on the chart. Some components may need attention at varying times throughout the year. If more than one mark appears, the longest interval should be considered the minimum requirement, while the shorter duration interval marks may be considered the recommended time frames.

To illustrate this point, on the LP system chart, for the item Leak Test Entire RV, it is recommended that this maintenance procedure be performed as part of a pre-trip check-out or as necessary (in case the odorant in the LP is detected, for instance). But at the very least, check for leaks twice a year.

As mentioned, use these charts as a guide only and refer to the main text for the specific details. For instance, on the Fresh Water System chart, for the item Chlorinate System, turn to the General Fresh System Maintenance section of Chapter 6,

Page 94, for the details on how to properly chlorinate the fresh water system. These charts are to be considered time interval reminders.

Factors such as extremely dusty conditions, RVing full-time or when traveling in extreme heat or cold may demonstrate a need for a certain amount of flexibility within these guidelines. Be prepared to modify the maintenance schedule based on the particular set of circumstances and traveling habits as they relate to your RV.

It is hoped that by following the procedures within this book, many miles of trouble-free operation will be attained, and you will glean an abundance of leisure memories and traveling enjoyment from your RVing experiences. At least that is my goal for you. And remember, RVing is more than a hobby, it is a lifestyle!

Motorhome Chassis and Running Gear

Task	Pre-Trip	As Necessary	Weekly	Monthly	Quarterly	Bi-Annually	Annually
Inspect brakes components		●					●
Inspect exhaust system						●	
Torque lug nuts	●					●	
Inspect & clean tires	●			●			
Check air pressure in all tires	●	●	●				
Check all running lamps	●			●			
Check all fluid levels	●	●		●			
Inspect engine belts & hoses	●				●		
Check battery electrolyte	●		●				
Check shocks & stabilizers						●	
Engine tune-up		●					
Check dash A/C operation	●	●					
Inspect suspension components							●
Inspect & lube leveling jacks	●					●	
Pack wheel bearings		●					
Measure alternator output						●	
Check all accessories	●	●					
Review owner's manual	●	●					
Test drive	●						

Notes:

Towing and Tow Equipment

Task	Pre-Trip	As Necessary	Weekly	Monthly	Quarterly	Bi-Annually	Annually
Lube hitch ball or platform	●		●				
Inspect ball mount	●				●		
Inspect receiver or platform	●				●		
Inspect spring bars	●						●
Lube sway control device	●						●
Inspect & lube hitch coupler	●					●	
Check tongue jack/landing gear	●						●
Test break-away switch	●					●	
Inspect electric brakes	●						●
Adjust electric brakes	●	●					●
Pack wheel bearings		●					
Inspect electrical connectors	●					●	
Adjust brake controller	●	●					
Inspect tow bar components	●						●
Test auxiliary braking device	●	●					
Inspect dinghy vehicle	●						●
Check air pressure in all tires	●	●	●				
Torque lug nuts	●			●			
Inspect & lube trailer stabilizers	●						●
Check all running lamps	●			●			
Measure alternator output	●					●	
Review owner's manual	●	●					
Test drive	●						

12-Volt DC Electrical Systems

Task	Pre-Trip	As Necessary	Weekly	Monthly	Quarterly	Bi-Annually	Annually
Check battery electrolyte levels	●		●				
Clean battery and terminals	●				●		
Check cables and conductors	●				●		
Tighten all connections	●					●	
Check & clean chassis ground	●					●	
Fully charge all batteries	●	●				●	
Measure converter output	●					●	
Measure alternator output	●					●	
Operate all 12-volt DC devices	●	●					●
Spare fuses onboard	●						

120-Volt AC Electrical Systems

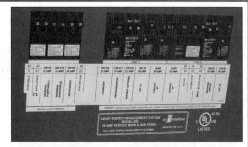

Task	Pre-Trip	As Necessary	Weekly	Monthly	Quarterly	Bi-Annually	Annually
Inspect shoreline cord for cuts	●						●
Clean shoreline cord contacts	●						●
Check circuit breaker operation							●
Test GFCI	●			●			
Check polarity at all receptacles	●	●[1]					
Measure incoming voltage		●[2]					
Measure converter output	●					●	
Measure inverter output	●					●	
Generator	Maintenance schedule based on hours of operation – See Chapter 5						
Operate all 120-volt appliances	●	●					

[1] Always check the polarity of the incoming power at every campground pedestal PRIOR to plugging in the RV.
Do not connect if the polarity is reversed or an open ground or open neutral exists.

[2] Always measure the incoming voltage at every campground pedestal PRIOR to plugging in the RV.
Do not connect if the incoming voltage is below 103 volts or above 130 volts AC.

LP System

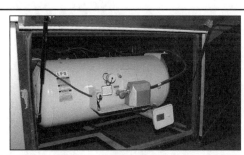

Task	Pre-Trip	As Necessary	Weekly	Monthly	Quarterly	Bi-Annually	Annually
Inspect LP container(s)	●					●	
Have DOT cylinders recertified		●					
Clean & inspect LP regulator	●					●	
Set LP pressure[3]	●						●
Test entire system for leaks	●	●				●	
Inspect/tighten hoses & fittings	●	●					
Clean & service all appliances		●					●
Test fire all appliances	●	●					
Test LP leak detector	●		●				
Test CO monitor	●			●			

[3] Requires a manometer. Refer to Chapter 8 for the detailed procedures or contact a professional RV service facility.

Fresh Water System

Task	Pre-Trip	As Necessary	Weekly	Monthly	Quarterly	Bi-Annually	Annually
Inspect all components	●						●
Flush & fill fresh water tank	●	●					
Clean or replace pump strainer	●	●					●
Test entire system for leaks	●						●
Inspect/tighten hoses & fittings							●
Flush water heater	●	●					●
Clean faucet aerators		●					●
Chlorinate entire system	●	●					●
Clean/replace purifier element	●	●					●

Waste Systems

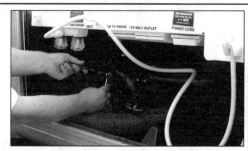

Task	Pre-Trip	As Necessary	Weekly	Monthly	Quarterly	Bi-Annually	Annually
Inspect all components	●						●
Rinse & flush all holding tanks	●	●				●	
Clean & lube termination valves	●	●					●
Test entire system for leaks	●						●
Clean P traps	●	●					●
Check holding tank vents	●						●
Check & lube ASTVDs		●					
Inspect sewer roof vent caps	●						●
Inspect sewer hose	●						●
Check seal on sewer cap	●	●					●
Check seal on hose adapter	●						●
Add holding tank additive	●	●					
Test toilet bowl seal	●	●					●
Lube toilet flushing mechanism	●	●					●
Check toilet mounting bolts							●

RV Exterior

Task	Pre-Trip	As Necessary	Weekly	Monthly	Quarterly	Bi-Annually	Annually
Wash & wax	●	●					●
Lube door & compartment locks	●						●
Inspect roof seams & moldings	●				●		●
Seal roof seams		●					
Inspect roof components	●				●		●
Clean & treat synthetic roofing	●	●			●		
Check doors, windows & vents	●						●
Lube window sliders	●						●
Reseal doors & windows		●					●
Inspect undercarriage	●						●
Seal holes/gaps in undercarriage		●					
Lube entry step	●					●	
Check operation of all slideouts	●	●					
Lube slideout mechanisms	●					●	
Clean & treat slideout seals	●						●

RV Interior

Task	Pre-Trip	As Necessary	Weekly	Monthly	Quarterly	Bi-Annually	Annually
Clean & vacuum interior	●	●					
Inspect for water damage	●						●
Check cabinet latches & hinges		●					●
Check drawer glides & stops		●					●
Check pocket door alignment	●						●
Check operation of roof vents	●	●			●		
Operate all doors & windows	●						●
Lube window sliders	●						●
Check all seat belts		●					
Check & test all accessories	●	●					
Check shower door latch	●						●
Check all window shades	●	●					

Index

About the Author

Gary Bunzer

Since the late 1960s, Gary Bunzer has been active in the recreation vehicle industry in a variety of roles. From RV service technician to service manager to RV training specialist; from technical writer to columnist to author, Gary has spent the last 25 years educating professional service technicians and RV owners by presenting informative technical training seminars at various venues around the country.

He has written and produced technical training video tapes for RV owners and professional service technicians, as well as service manuals and product installation instructions for many RV supplier manufacturers. The year 2009 will mark the 33rd anniversary of his popular question and answer column, "The RV Doctor," with continuous publication of that column somewhere every month for 33 consecutive years.

Gary is currently an Adjunct Professor at Northampton Community College in Bethlehem, Pennsylvania, where he develops and administers an Internet-based distance learning program for anyone interested in RV repair and maintenance. The RV training program's purpose is to develop professional service technicians and ready them for Industry Certification, but anyone can enroll and learn more about the technicalities of RV service.

For more information visit:

http://www.northampton.edu/distancelearn/ programs/rv_default.htm

He continues to write feature articles for RVers, product reviews and the ongoing "The RV Doctor" column from his home base in Seattle, WA. You can send inquiries to:

Gary Bunzer
Bunzer Consulting
PO Box 19562
Seattle, WA 98109

Or visit Gary on the Web at www.rvdoctor.com